The Invention of Rum

EARLY AMERICAN STUDIES

Series editors: Kathleen M. Brown, Roquinaldo Ferreira, Emma Hart, and Daniel K. Richter

Exploring neglected aspects of our colonial, revolutionary, and early national history and culture, Early American Studies reinterprets familiar themes and events in fresh ways. Interdisciplinary in character, and with a special emphasis on the period from about 1600 to 1850, the series is published in partnership with the McNeil Center for Early American Studies.

A complete list of books in the series is available from the publisher.

The Invention of Rum

Creating the Quintessential Atlantic Commodity

Jordan B. Smith

PENN

UNIVERSITY OF PENNSYLVANIA PRESS

PHILADELPHIA

Publication of this volume was aided by the
C. Dallett Hemphill Publication Fund

Published by
University of Pennsylvania Press
Philadelphia, Pennsylvania 19104-4112
www.pennpress.org

Printed in the United States of America on acid-free paper
10 9 8 7 6 5 4 3 2 1

A Cataloging-in-Publication record for this book is available from the Library of Congress.

Hardcover ISBN 978-1-5128-2818-4
Ebook ISBN 978-1-5128-2819-1

For Erika and Zora,
With Love

CONTENTS

NOTE ON THE TEXT

For ease of reading, I have standardized spelling and capitalization in primary sources throughout the text where doing so does not alter the meaning of quotations. Any emphasis in the quotations is reproduced from the source. I have adjusted dates to account for January 1 as the beginning of the new year for years prior to 1752. Unless otherwise noted, translations are my own.

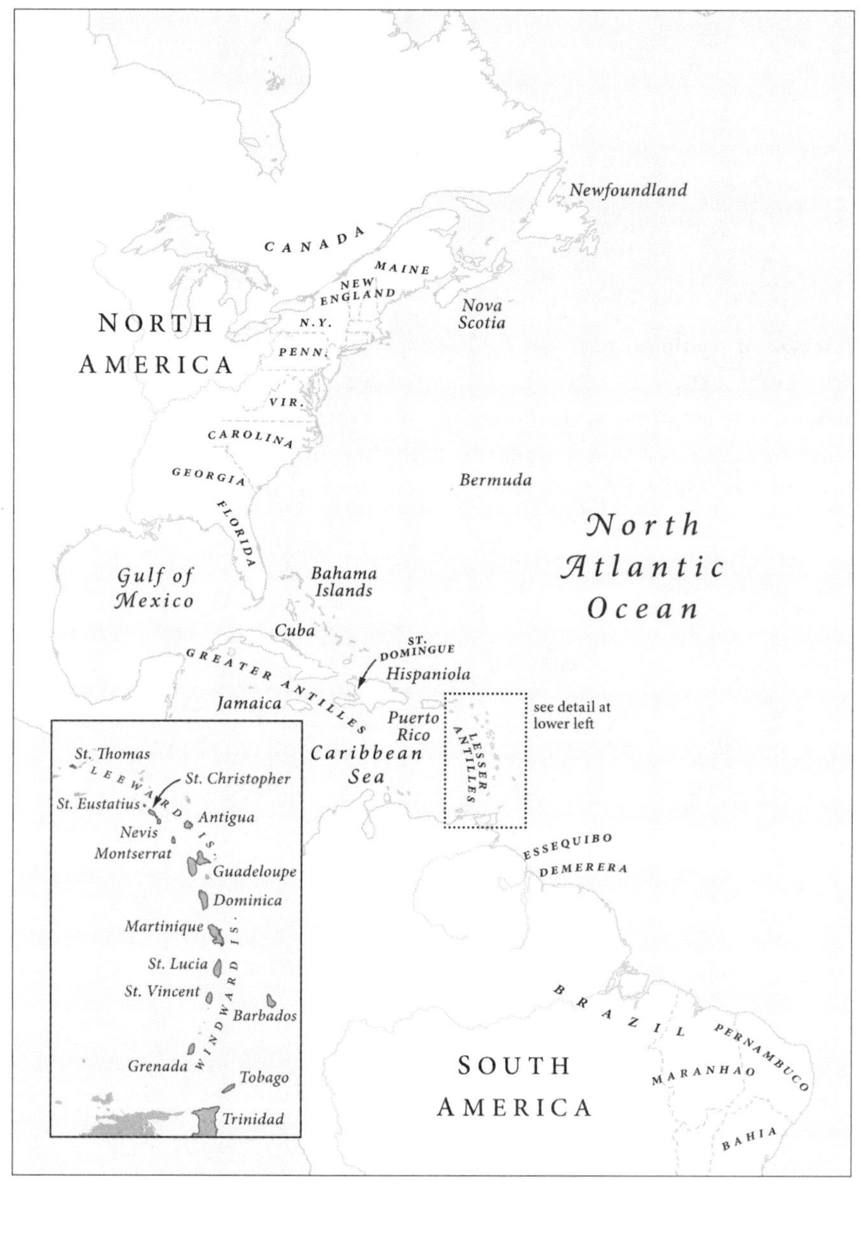
Newfoundland
CANADA
MAINE
NEW ENGLAND
N.Y.
PENN.
VIR.
CAROLINA
GEORGIA
FLORIDA
NORTH AMERICA
Nova Scotia
Bermuda
North Atlantic Ocean
Gulf of Mexico
Bahama Islands
Cuba
ST. DOMINGUE
Hispaniola
GREATER ANTILLES
Jamaica
Puerto Rico
Caribbean Sea
LESSER ANTILLES
see detail at lower left
ESSEQUIBO
DEMERERA
St. Thomas
LEEWARD IS.
St. Christopher
St. Eustatius
Antigua
Nevis
Montserrat
Guadeloupe
Dominica
Martinique
St. Lucia
St. Vincent
WINDWARD IS.
Barbados
Grenada
Tobago
Trinidad
BRAZIL
PERNAMBUCO
MARANHAO
BAHIA
SOUTH AMERICA

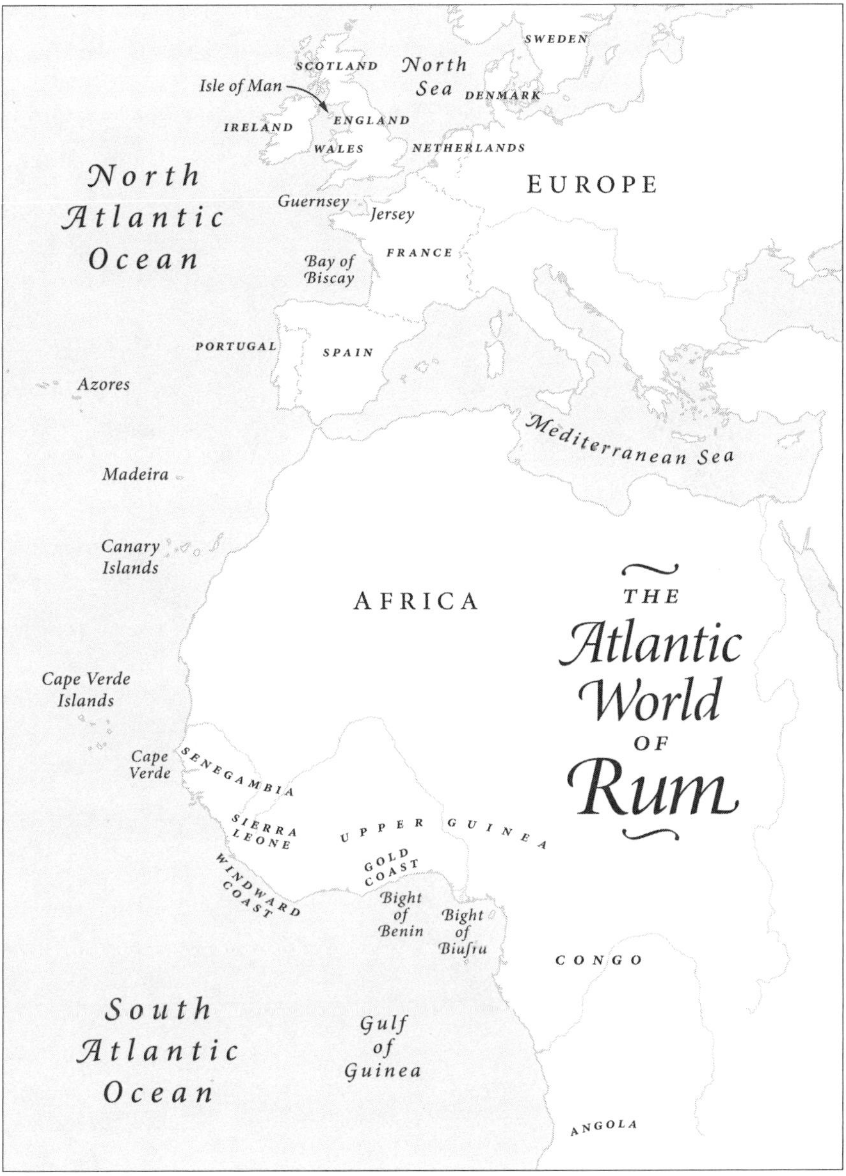

The Atlantic World of Rum

SWEDEN
SCOTLAND
North Sea
Isle of Man
DENMARK
IRELAND
ENGLAND
WALES
NETHERLANDS
North Atlantic Ocean
EUROPE
Guernsey
Jersey
FRANCE
Bay of Biscay
PORTUGAL
SPAIN
Azores
Mediterranean Sea
Madeira
Canary Islands
AFRICA
Cape Verde Islands
Cape Verde
SENEGAMBIA
SIERRA LEONE
UPPER GUINEA
GOLD COAST
WINDWARD COAST
Bight of Benin
Bight of Biafra
CONGO
South Atlantic Ocean
Gulf of Guinea
ANGOLA

Introduction

A World of Rum

The rum would have been transported in puncheons from Barbados to Harewood House, north of Leeds, first by ship and then by wagon. Some of it had rested on the bent staves that contained it for a relatively short period, picking up only a slight hue from the tannins and char of the wood. This rum remained stronger—nearly 70 percent alcohol by volume. Other rum sat in the barrels—either in Barbados or England—for longer, darkening with time, picking up a velvety texture and losing some of its alcoholic content as the wood breathed. Aging allowed the flavor to mellow and caused lead particles to settle, delivering a safer, better-tasting experience to consumers willing to pay a little bit more. Once in Britain, household workers decanted both qualities of rum into hand-blown bottles, corked and waxed them, and stored them in two bins in the basement of the country estate. Cellar records aver that the bottles were slowly consumed in the eighteenth and nineteenth centuries, before the Lascelles family largely forgot about them until their rediscovery in 2011.[1]

All indications suggest that this rum followed a well-worn path before it reached England. In the midst of another grueling sugarcane harvest, enslaved workers on one of the Lascelles family's sugar plantations in Barbados encountered sweet substances that could not be easily converted into a salable form of the commodity. They collected the damaged pieces of cane, tainted juice, froth that rose to the top of boiling pans of sugar, and molasses that oozed out of curing pots of sugar in the plantation distillery. Enslaved distillers carefully mixed the ingredients, supervised the conversion of sucrose into ethyl alcohol through fermentation, and used copper stills to vaporize and recondense most of the alcohol into rum. Their mental and physical labor was crucial for ensuring that expectations for taste and alcoholic content were met. Workers packed the liquor that trickled out of the stills into hand-hewn puncheons that carried the rum to nearby markets and along turbulent crossings to North America, England, and

West Africa. The work that went into making this particular batch of rum was simply too commonplace to leave an impression at Harewood House.[2]

Something had changed by the twenty-first century, though. After the 2011 rediscovery, the Lascelles family worked with wine sellers to test the contents, stabilize the bottles, document their provenance, and bring the world's "oldest" rum to auction at Christie's, with proceeds of the sale benefiting a local charity with ties to the Caribbean. An allotment of twelve bottles of "light" and "dark" rum blew by preauction estimates in 2014 and fetched over £78,000 ($130,000). Rum that could have been acquired for mere pennies in 1780 now summoned bids from individual and corporate collectors and companies. The auction made international news.

Some of the bottles have since been resold for a profit or decanted into specialty products including luxury watches.[3] At least one bottle has been consumed. In 2018, two dozen collectors, spirits dealers, and journalists gathered in London to taste the lightly aged rum, offering this room of participants an unparalleled opportunity to sip one of the most commonly produced, exchanged, and consumed goods of the early modern world. Writing of the gravity of the experience, one invitee exclaimed, "No way could any rum live up to the hype of the bare stats—1780; found by accident; oldest from Barbados; most expensive ever; ancient; pure; a window into Ago."[4]

But what did it taste like? According to one taster, "The rum was golden, much lighter than I figured, but to the nose, it was big, funky, and full of heat."[5] Another suggested that his glassful "took a huge, fiery swing at my nasal passages."[6] Yet another—the most complimentary of the bunch—described the rum as "fantastic." He went on to note that "for all the changes that have occurred in the industry and the technology between 1780 and 2018, the truth is that the current inheritors of the tradition of quality rum-making aren't that far away from what was once being made."[7] The reviews all offered respect for the experience but were varied in their overall impressions of the centuries-old rum when compared to modern alternatives.

Nearly 250-year-old rum may still be recognizable as rum, but the odyssey of the Harewood rum evocatively shows how much the production, sale, and consumption of the spirit has changed in the intervening years. Nowhere is this distinction clearer than in the tasting event itself. A 1.5-ounce serving of aged Caribbean rum would have been worth a little over a penny in London in 1780. Even after adjusting for inflation, the Harewood rum had appreciated in value approximately a thousand times by the 2014 auction.[8] Quotidian, unaged rum—which had been available to just about every denizen of the Atlantic world in the seventeenth and eighteenth centuries and whose twenty-first-century value was enhanced by the fact that nobody else had bothered to save some—was now being poured and tasted as the signature experience of a "posh affair."[9]

This stunning reinvention of an eighteenth-century commodity obscures what made rum desirable and valuable for producers, merchants, consumers, and imperial administrators around the early modern Atlantic world. Far from a luxury good or marker of status, early modern rum was an everyday alcohol that could be conjured from sugary wastes that had previously been relegated to trash pits or feed troughs. Enslaved and free laborers combined their own knowledge and the cutting-edge technologies available on Caribbean sugar plantations to transform those products into a potent and palatable spirit. As these innovations took hold in Caribbean, North American, and British distilleries, rum appealed to an expansive market because of its availability and affordability. From the mid-seventeenth to early nineteenth century, the makers and drinkers of rum remade the Atlantic world in the commodity's image: a highly replaceable product that treated almost everyone and everything in its path as equally fungible. Rum made the Atlantic world anew.

To date, narratives of economic change in the Atlantic world have most often been told through sugar. As the story goes, early colonists—and the European empires that they represented—responded to growing tastes for sweetness and supply problems in the Middle East and Europe by experimenting with the manufacture of sugar in Atlantic islands like Madeira and ultimately in early Caribbean and American colonies. Cutting-edge sugar manufactories dependent on newfangled mill designs, an emphasis on enslaved labor, and mercantile networks spanning the Atlantic Ocean took hold in Brazil in the late sixteenth century. Sugar transformed English and French outposts in the Caribbean by the 1650s, where each plantation tended to include its own mill and boiling house. While existing sugar colonies continued to thrive and new ones formed, historians generally posit that the sugar industry in the tropical Americas entered a period of stagnation in the mid-seventeenth century that lasted for over a century. By the late eighteenth century, innovators suddenly awakened to Enlightenment ideas about economic progress, challenges to the logic of slavery, and the advent of steam technology to revolutionize the industry again. Through two periods of sudden change and a long intermission in between, modernity arrived in hogsheads of sugar.[10]

Over the past fifteen years, however, a bevy of commodity histories have offered new interpretations of economic and cultural changes afoot in the early modern Atlantic world.[11] In a world—and a historiography—often dominated by sugar, these scholars have shown that goods as varied as rice, mahogany, pearls, and chocolate thrived on the long-distance circulation of materials, people, and ideas around the Atlantic world. Consumers in the Atlantic world confronted exponentially more choices in what they could purchase as a result of emergent commodities emanating from distant places, new sources of long-valued goods, and greater access to the marketplaces that supplied them. In almost all cases, these commodity cultures of the Atlantic world were underwritten by Indigenous and African slavery.

While the histories of sugar and other commodities often align in their narration of wholesale changes afoot in the Atlantic world, two significant points of divergence stand out. First, studies of commodities other than sugar challenge any interpretation of the eighteenth century as a period of stasis. Madeira wine, for instance, underwent a stunning refinement over the century as producers and, especially, merchants experimented with mixing grape varieties; fortifying with brandy; aging, agitating, and heating the wine to manipulate its taste; and determining the optimal ways to package and transport it.[12] And in British islands dominated by sugar, planters helped to create a demand for luxury mahogany as a means to hedge their bets against the unpredictability of sugar.[13] Histories of Madeira and mahogany demonstrate the ways in which the eighteenth-century Atlantic world remained a space of innovation.

Second, recent commodity histories have largely disrupted interpretations of commodity production or consumption simply being imposed by metropolitan elites in Europe. For instance, Europeans smoking tobacco observed rituals of consumption learned from Native people, while the allure of pearls resided, in part, in the fact that their value could be held and transferred by a range of historical actors, including enslaved women.[14] Whether focused on how consumption patterns were pioneered or values set, these histories of the Atlantic world demonstrate that the function of emerging commodities was negotiated by a panoply of historical actors.

The power of intellectual traditions and labor originating outside of Europe to remake Atlantic economies and societies has been most evident, however, in research on commodity production. Scholars have joined in questioning the level of European ingenuity and control in colonial settings by emphasizing European adaptation of non-European ideas and technologies. For example, some scholars of eighteenth-century South Carolina argue that enslaved West Africans introduced a system of rice cultivation and processing to the Americas.[15] Although other historians question the transplantation of a fully formed system from West Africa to South Carolina, these skeptics nonetheless agree that

African-descended people performed the vast majority of work in Carolina rice fields, transported certain ideas pertaining to rice production with them from West Africa, and likely contributed new ideas to adjust to local conditions.[16]

Discrepancies over the pace of change in the eighteenth century, as well as the drivers of that change, suggest the limitations of understanding the emergence of modern forms of production solely through the history of sugar. Some of these incongruities are interpretive, as evidenced by recent interventions that emphasize the skill of enslaved people supporting sugar production or innovations in sugar production extending into the late seventeenth century or beginning by the mid-eighteenth century.[17] However, certain essential qualities of sugar, such as its familiarity to Europeans prior to colonization of the Americas, the ideal of it being a "pure" sweetener, the capital- and labor-intensive nature of its production, and its market dominance, distinguish the history of sugar from the history of the Atlantic world—and the birth of modernity—more broadly. Understanding the history of sugar on its own terms—which was responsible for more than 3 percent of the British gross domestic product late in the eighteenth century—is crucial, but it is an imperfect exemplar for larger processes afoot.[18] Notably, it gives the wrong impression of how innovation unfolded, which scholars have convincingly shown tended to progress incrementally and in ways dependent on the input of a multiracial group of individuals often coerced to perform everyday acts of production.[19]

The history of rum in the Atlantic world both expands what we know about familiar processes and offers a new way of making sense of the immense changes wrought by an era defined by Atlantic trade, colonization, and plantation slavery. The production and sale of rum was integral to the economic success of sugar plantations in and beyond British Caribbean colonies. By the eighteenth century, rum accounted for 27 percent to 43 percent of the revenues from sugar plantations in Barbados. In Jamaica, rum constituted a slightly smaller—but still significant—20 percent to 30 percent of sugar plantation profits.[20] These local rum sales normally covered the operating costs for one of the most lucrative economic endeavors that the world had ever seen. Sugary wastes generated by these British plantations, joined with those exported from non-British islands or extracted from sugar during additional rounds of processing in American or British refineries, supplied distilleries elsewhere. Flowing out of a constellation of distilleries throughout the Caribbean, North America, and Britain, rum expanded the reach of the sugar industry into markets engaging metropolitan consumers (like those imbibing at Harewood House), colonists, Native North Americans, and African slave traders.[21]

Scholars of rum have documented how this offshoot of sugar fed industrialization, created markets, and drove alcohol consumption in different corners of the Atlantic world, but the significance of rum to our deeper understanding of the sugar industry has been slower to develop. Histories of the sugar industry emphasize the heavy human costs of converting the finicky sugarcane grown in Caribbean colonies into the most colorless and tasteless form of sucrose that technology would allow. As scholars have shown, this was a technical process that plantation operators transplanted to new colonies in a largely recognizable form from the sixteenth through the nineteenth centuries. Accounting for the most common use of molasses and sugary wastes adds a new dimension to this narrative by centering the dregs that could not be whitened and crystallized and whose questionable utility and comparatively limited value allowed it to seep through hardening imperial boundaries. Studying how myriad people on sugar plantations, on the docks, in cargo holds sustaining Atlantic trade, and throughout a scattered patchwork of distilleries responded to the inefficiencies and ungovernable qualities of sugar by-products like rum restores the focus to the Atlantic world as it was experienced rather than how plantation owners, merchants, or politicians hoped that it would operate. It supports a reframing of the history of sugar that emphasizes near-constant tinkering over a long eighteenth century that drew in plantation owners and operators, enslaved workers, imperial officials, merchants, and the many people who consumed rum.

But understanding the history of rum is about more than amending how we make sense of the history of sugar (as important as that is). It also exposes something substantively new about the Atlantic world. The invention of rum rested on a fledgling idea that a combination of labor, ingenuity, and technology could shape-shift trash into treasure. Specifically, the detritus generated by early modern sugar production was no longer simply disposed of but was collected, mixed, fermented, distilled, packaged, shipped, sold, and consumed. Making, marketing, and drinking rum constituted a new kind of alchemy, almost magically transmuting the physical characteristics of matter—and equally firm attitudes—to conjure a highly desired comestible.

The same qualities of disposability and innovation on which the invention of rum depended extended to people and environments in the Atlantic world through the decisions of its makers and drinkers. The consistently low price of rum signaled its easy replaceability, while the processes necessary to maintain that price treated nearly everything that rum touched as equally fungible. The plantation economy offered scant protection to the health of its enslaved producers, treating them as both consumable and replaceable, while also devouring local sources of fuel and soil nutrients at breathtaking rates. Moreover, the physiological effects of consuming too much rum—as well as rum tainted with lead—imperiled some of its most eager customers, treating them as disposable too. And the fact that rum could easily transform into other drinks such as gin and punch and was eminently replaceable carried a crucial trade advantage for British and colonial merchants in North America and West Africa who exchanged it for comparatively durable items including furs, land, and even people. Through private transactions, government contracts, and taxes, profits from rum created new pools of disposable income for individuals and colonial and metropolitan governments. Chasing profit, merchants sought wealth in rum distilleries and the transatlantic slave trade, often in brief and fleeting endeavors. The Atlantic world in which a transatlantic constellation of rum makers and drinkers prospered was a world coming to terms with the profitability of thinking and acting in immediate terms that saw objects and people as impermanent and replaceable.

Rum could be addictive, though its makers and drinkers rarely understood it as such. In 1712, the Puritan clergyman Increase Mather wrote that "not one of a thousand of those unhappy souls who have been enslaved to it have been delivered from their bondage."[22] More than sixty years later, a Quaker abolitionist and temperance advocate named Anthony Benezet used eerily similar language when he described "unhappy dram-drinkers [who] are so absolutely bound in slavery to these infernal spirits."[23] He went on to share a doctor's advice on weaning oneself from what later scientists would consider a chemical dependence on alcohol.[24] Yet historians have shown that reformers in the eighteenth century rarely understood drunkenness to be a compulsion and usually suggested that individuals could stop drinking if they tried.[25] Although consumers chose to drink rum in part because it could unleash physiological effects that some individuals habitually sought out, it is imperative not to overstate the explanatory power of a chemical dependence that the makers and drinkers of rum did not comprehend.[26] To do so risks losing sight of how the context of commodity production and consumption has changed over time, shifting the cultural meanings attached to it.

There was another way in which some inhabitants of the Atlantic world understood rum to be addictive, though. In a 1725 pamphlet, Francis Rawle claimed that colonists in Delaware were "strongly addicted to rum" because they chose to consume cheap rum originating in the Caribbean rather than more expensive, locally produced, grain-based alcohols.[27] The compulsion to make and drink rum functioned, then, on several levels. Rum delivered the effects of inebriation in a more intense manner and at a lower cost. In turn, it pulled in millions of willing distillery operators, merchants, and consumers who overlooked its unsavory origins, as well as the human, social, economic, and environmental harms unleashed by it. Coalitions linking individuals making and drinking rum—within a world marked by profound inequality—were able to overcome distance and political division in the Atlantic world and, in the process, thrive by treating ingredients, ideas, and even people as disposable. A pathway initially forged because of the unique qualities of rum became easier to retrace with other ingestible commodities of the nineteenth and twentieth centuries that were harvested and manufactured from detritus.[28]

Considering how and why the many people who encountered rum devised, capitalized on, and often suffered from a culture of disposability and innovation depends on engaging an expansive archive and method. *The Invention of Rum* tracks how ideas and materials from West Africa, the Indigenous Caribbean, and early modern Europe contributed to the emergence of rum and how the new beverage then remade the Atlantic world. To trace these everyday exchanges that regularly connected distant places, *The Invention of Rum* incorporates evidence from forty-five libraries and archives in Barbados, Jamaica, England, Wales, Scotland, and ten US states. It also draws from digitized versions of newspapers and rare books, published document collections, and rapidly expanding digital archives.

Much can also be learned from trawling sources that are not always imagined as the province of historians, including visual and material artifacts. Each chapter of *The Invention of Rum* begins with one of these items. This coterie of paintings, prints, maps, song lyrics, and a bowl provide additional vantage points from which to observe the emergence of this quintessential Atlantic commodity. These particular sources were created exclusively by people of European descent, which introduces interpretive challenges in light of the questions asked by this book. But by alternatively searching for clues in the margins of written evidence and questioning incongruities exposed by material culture, new narratives emerge.

Engagement with an expansive set of archives is imperative because of the difficulty of reading account books, private letters, prescriptive literature, government records, and visual and material objects for histories of innovation. As historian Pamela Smith has recently explained, artisans and readers in the early modern world understood that some knowledge of productive processes could not be written down. This body of knowledge was instead embodied by makers and learned and passed on through practice. For historians to understand these artisans' critical role in histories of innovation, careful attention must be paid to "processes of making" rather than just texts or objects.[29] A detailed understanding of how distillation worked is crucial for this sort of project, as is wide-ranging archival work that is most likely to identify details shared sparingly that unite to provide a fuller picture of everyday production and innovation.

Accounting for the relationship between making, consuming, and knowing is doubly important because so much of the production process was carried out by enslaved workers. African and Indigenous drinkers also consumed considerable volumes of rum. Keepers of business, personal, and government records generally held little interest in recording the acts of creation, tastes, and habits of consumption designed by non-Europeans. How the archive was created—and for what purposes—is a vital consideration for historians of the seventeenth- and eighteenth-century Atlantic world.[30] Once again, an expansive archive yields considerable insights. Sometimes research can uncover extended journeys. As later chapters will detail, a man named Quacqo was enslaved in distilleries in Barbados and then Boston. And Sibell—despite surviving the Middle Passage and being enslaved in Barbados for decades—recollected how palm wine was made in West Africa. Far more often, though, the experiences of Indigenous and African-descended distillers and drinkers were reduced by others into single paragraphs, sentences, or even words that can nonetheless combine to enhance what historians know about the early modern Atlantic world of rum. Pirates kidnapped a "head stiller" named Jeffrey. Francois absconded from a New York distillery, and John York fled one in London. A Munsee sachem named Rathquack mourned sixty kinsmen whose lives tragically ended while "in their drink" over the previous three years.[31] Such evidence must be read exceedingly carefully, but it nonetheless contributes to a remarkable body of evidence that can illuminate the complex and often brutally coercive human relationships at the core of the invention of rum.

This sort of archival work supports a narrative that diverges from many other studies that narrate economic, social, and cultural change in the early modern Atlantic world through the history of either commodities or capitalism. Scholars have long shown that great explanatory potential lies in demonstrating the power of salable goods to establish and transfer meanings through multiple stages of a commodity's life cycle.[32] These commodity studies offer crucial insights into historical processes underpinning globalization, mercantilism, and capitalism. But in many cases, one entity's ability to dictate the social meaning of a commodity tends to dominate each narrative.[33] In turn, such approaches can mute the give-and-take between a commodity's producers, traders, consumers, and regulators.

The Invention of Rum takes another tack. The book is organized to understand different stages of a commodity's life cycle unfolding in different parts of the

Atlantic in tandem. Though unconventional for a commodity history, this organizational structure is necessary to demonstrate that neither producer nor merchant nor consumer—nor one geographical region—could dictate rum's negotiated, and shifting, qualities. Nonetheless, readers who find themselves disoriented by the lack of a traditional technical explanation of how rum was made early in the book may find value in consulting the glossary included at the end of the book.

Moreover, this study centers the choices that individuals made that transformed rum from an experimental, highly localized brew to a commodity of global significance over the course of the seventeenth and eighteenth centuries. It does so by tracing the stories of people—coerced and free, American, African, and European—who made rum, traded it, and drank it. By focusing on personal experiences, we can question the "mythos of modernity" that lends far too much explanatory power to technologies, institutions, or commodities themselves or reinforces notions of advanced industries copied and pasted from Europe to distant colonies.[34] In the individual experiences and choices of many people whose lives intersected with rum in the seventeenth and eighteenth centuries, it is possible to appreciate how rum production became a cutting-edge process, linking the extractive and agricultural enterprises that dominated the first 150 years of European colonization in the Americas to the highly regimented and globalized forms of production usually attributed to the nineteenth century.[35]

Of course, colonialism, slavery, and economic inequality sharply limited the choices of many individuals whose lives intersected with rum. *The Invention of Rum* considers how choice was often constrained, how compulsion affected the lives of rum's makers and drinkers, and how extreme power differentials factored into the history of the commodity. Unlike a mahogany table, pearl necklace, or elegant dress, however, rum was designed to be consumed by just about anybody. Beyond rare moments when they were forced to consume rum, a full gamut of consumers could choose to drink or forgo rum. Individuals could also express personal choices, desires, and tastes amid everyday experiences where suffering reigned. Rum could, as historian Stephanie Camp observed for enslaved people in the nineteenth-century US South, be used to access "the intoxication of pleasurable amusement" as an assertion of bodily control and an act of resistance.[36] Regardless of whether they saw drinking rum as a resistant act, however, many individuals could be simultaneously desirous of drinking it and harmed by being compelled to make or transport rum or to accept it in lieu of other foodstuffs or trade goods. The contested possibilities of rum provide further opportunity to reflect on the role that subjugated people had in shaping the production, trade, and consumption of commodities.

People in Britain, its colonies, and the spaces where British traders operated embraced rum because it met individual tastes while simultaneously serving many goals of empire. Starting in the mid-seventeenth century, English colonizers grasped the incredible potential of repurposing the waste products of colonial sugar plantations as a distilled spirit that could lessen their dependence on continental European brandies and wines. Intent on protecting domestic viniculture, Spanish and French officials found the possibility of colonial rum industries threatening for precisely the same reasons, and they actively discouraged alcohol production as a result.[37] Geography circumscribed rum's potential within other empires. Dutch colonies centered on exceedingly small islands unfit for widespread sugar cultivation.[38] And while Brazil exported tremendous volumes of sugar-derived spirits to Angola, its production took place in centralized mills and distilleries in the South Atlantic with few connections to the North Atlantic.

Non-British sugar plantations sometimes produced rum or a close analogue, but published treatises on distilling and private correspondences of distillers alike rarely reveal distilling practices or even preferred qualities for rum being consistently shared between metropoles. These empires were far from hermetically sealed, however. Colonists in Brazil and the French Caribbean experimented with making alcohol from sugar in the seventeenth century, and Indigenous people transported from South America to Barbados introduced new alcohols to English settlers on the island. North American distillers transformed molasses smuggled through Dutch and French entrepôts into rum despite British mercantilist policies designed to outlaw this activity. In West Africa and the American interior alike, French and Danish traders sometimes found little recourse other than to acquire and resell rum produced in Britain and its colonies. While each of these transimperial contexts is described in this book, whether the patterns observed in British Atlantic contexts can be traced in the archives generated by these localities and other empires awaits further study.

The Invention of Rum examines how many groups of people in the Atlantic world arrived at a commodity—and the set of human relationships necessary to sustain it—built on reimagining the boundary between what should be disposed of and what could be valuable. It examines rum's place in the Atlantic world from the moment of its creation around 1640 until its meaning and utility became harder to change by 1810. In the intervening 170 years—roughly coinciding with an era where methods of sugar production are understood to have largely remained stable—the many people who touched and tasted rum continued to tinker with how and where it was made, what it should look like, its taste and cost, and who should drink it. A profound reimagining of the nature of what could be potable and profitable was made possible by rum's emergence as a commodity without a clear antecedent and its makers' ready embrace of near-constant innovation. By remaking waste into a sellable good through a series of hyperextractive processes, the invention of rum offered a blueprint for new types of commodity production and consumption that transformed the Atlantic world and its component parts. What follows is a book about rum that also reveals a story about how the very nature of things changed with the development of Britain's Atlantic world.

Chapters in this book are loosely chronological but also overlapping. The first two chapters uncover the seventeenth- and early eighteenth-century emergence of a new commodity. The final chapter considers the standardization of what rum was, which was occasioned by late eighteenth-century challenges to slavery and slave-produced commodities. The intervening five chapters, however, largely cover the middle decades of the eighteenth century when the rum industry flourished. To fully account for the world that at once made—and was reshaped by—rum, these chapters attend thematically to the exchange of ideas, goods, and people, as well as the processes by which opportunities and costs were inequitably distributed.

Before rum could remake the Atlantic world, it first had to be created, a process around which Part I of the book coalesces. Historians used to apply a straightforward formula to the Atlantic plantations creating vast quantities of goods like sugar, rice, and cotton: European ideas plus African bodies plus American land equaled something new.[39] The invention of rum was never so simple. Native, African, and European people possessed—and created anew—their own ideas about both alcohol and the best ways to make it. Parallel negotiations took place in several places during the first half of the seventeenth century, but the actions of a multiracial cast of producers and innovators living in Barbados offer the clearest example of how an array of individuals thrust into a new place reimagined and transformed sugary wastes into a merchantable good. Invention entailed more than just creating a beverage, though. On diverse landscapes around the Atlantic basin, makers, traders, and drinkers worked out a name for rum, what its preferred qualities should be, who could drink it, and what its consumption conveyed. As the demand for rum grew, distilleries opened in almost every British American colony and in England and Scotland, quenching the thirst of many and engendering disputes about the real and imagined chaos that abounded throughout an intoxicated Atlantic. For the industry to continue adapting to changing circumstances, rum producers in different places worked out a system of communicating best practices and innovations through forced labor, travel, conversation, published writings, and objects themselves. This quintessentially Atlantic process of creation involved both cooperation among scattered producers and unrelenting forms of control.

Part II of the book, centered on extraction, demonstrates how the emerging rum industry rested on highly extractive systems that centered profits in the hands of elite Englishmen and colonials and ill effects on many others who were often of Indigenous American or African origin. None of these processes were foreordained. Instead they were devised—and contested—by various parties. From the start, plantation operators and owners of stand-alone distilleries alike depended on the intellectual and physical work of enslaved people predominantly of African descent. Enslavers relied on instances and threats of outright violence to control the labor of the enslaved. Moreover, the labor demanded of enslaved rum producers reshaped myriad environments. In the Caribbean and North America, decisions made to sustain or increase the efficiency of rum production uniquely contributed to deforested landscapes prone to flooding, subject to disease outbreaks, and generally less hospitable to human life. Distillery operators forced laborers to live and work in those environments, exposing them to the ill effects of ecologies in crisis. Relationships centered on profitably extracting labor, ingredients, and value at high individual cost shaped how rum was traded as well as consumed. Merchants carried rum processed in pewter equipment that could cause lead poisoning to many markets. They routed particularly large quantities of North American rum to regions of West Africa, including Upper Guinea and the Gold Coast, and traded it for captured Africans who they transported to repeople the sugar-growing regions of the Americas. The decision—and growing ability—of American rum distillers to meet local West African demands for rum delivered an ever-growing number of people into Atlantic slavery to replace those succumbing to overwork and the effects of disease and disaster.

As Part III, titled "Connection and Conflict," details, the power of those individuals operating rum distilleries did not go unchallenged. Several groups questioned the actions that distillery owners and operators took to maximize profits at high economic and human costs as the eighteenth century progressed. On the one hand, various levels of government officials sought to regulate to whom rum could be sold, the tax burden placed on merchants and distillers, and occasionally the conditions of enslavement that many distillery workers labored under. For the most part, distillery operators resisted these regulatory efforts to great effect. They prioritized profit over their allegiance to other people or their government. Alternatively, opponents of slavery, sometimes responding to the actions of the enslaved themselves, found fleeting success in challenging the labor regimes synonymous with rum production. On occasion, enslaved people physically attacked distilleries. Because of the visibility of African-descended slaves in making rum—and resisting their enslavement—throughout the Atlantic world, rum began to appear to some as a compromised commodity. Attempts to transition toward free labor as a result of protest floundered, however, in part because formerly enslaved people with experience making rum generally opted to avoid the industry. Efforts to define rum and delineate the ethical issues surrounding its production calcified definitions of what made rum rum. New circuits defined by disposability first connected by the invention of rum survived and thrived.

PART I

Creation

CHAPTER 1

The "Invention" of Rum

Sometime around 1600, a Bruges-born artist living in Florence and calling himself Stradanus completed a set of nineteen prints cataloging the modern inventions that distinguished contemporary Europe from both antiquity and the New World. The frontispiece of his *Nova Reperta*, reproduced in Figure 1, highlighted the greatest discoveries of the era. A man representing "old knowledge" departs to the right as an Amazon points to a map of the Americas. The silk tree epitomizes commodities to be transplanted to these new environs. A stack of American guaiacum—used to treat syphilis, an introduction from the Americas to Europe—alludes to novel goods originating in discovered lands. Stradanus also represented cutting-edge European technologies including the printing press and clockmaking. Distillation equipment highlights the continent's newfound ability to make chemicals, medicines, and drinks that do not occur naturally.[1]

Nova Reperta confirms that Stradanus's Europe had recently acquired all that was necessary to make rum. A print depicting sugar production showed that Europeans could cultivate sugar and use wind and water power to harvest its sweetness. American colonization opened up vast swaths of tropical landscapes to grow these and other crops. New distillation technology, as depicted in the hands of European men in Figure 2, made it easier than ever before to concentrate the alcoholic qualities of fermented beverages. Perhaps if Stradanus had been working a century later, rum would have figured prominently in the *Nova Reperta*. But in 1600, despite many recent discoveries, rum was nowhere to be seen.

Simply possessing the base ingredients that could be turned into rum did not, in and of itself, lead to the invention of rum. Instead, people had to organize these discoveries in new ways. Some of those individuals instituting changes were, no doubt, the European technicians celebrated in Stradanus's engravings who constructed larger stills, designed windmills and water mills for sugar

Figure 1. *Nova Reperta* by Jan Collaert after Stradanus (c. 1600). The Metropolitan Museum of Art, Harris Brisbane Dick Fund, 1934.

production, and introduced cultivars to new places. But new discoveries also depended on the ideas and innovations of Native American and African people coerced to work by European colonizers—individuals almost entirely absent from Stradanus's renderings.

The European technicians Stradanus celebrated, who adapted to new knowledge gleaned from European colonization, rarely explained what they learned from Indigenous American and African alcohol producers. Yet a variety of observers commented on the various beverages that people drank in the first half of the seventeenth century. These commentaries show that several distinct cultures of making and drinking coexisted in the colonies that would eventually convert the wastes left over from sugar production into a new distillate. Piecing together the creative collisions between distinct cultures of alcohol production in three places purported to be cradles of rum production—Brazil, the French West Indies, and, especially, Barbados—reveals processes of experimentation that drew in people and ideas originating in Europe, Africa, and the Americas and ultimately created something new. In each place, sugar cultivation, alcohol

Figure 2. Plate 7 in *Nova Reperta* by Jan Collaert after Stradanus (c. 1600). The Metropolitan Museum of Art, Harris Brisbane Dick Fund, 1934.

production, and racialized slavery followed separate trajectories. These distinct, though parallel, processes dispel notions of the invention of rum as straightforward, foreordained, or inevitable. Instead, it appears as a collective process unfolding over many years and in many different places. Even after rum emerged in Barbados, it took further experimentation and negotiation to embrace its transformative potential.

Sugar Without Rum

In the same years that Stradanus completed his designs, sugar production expanded rapidly in Brazil. And, as *Nova Reperta* continued to be consulted during the first decades of the seventeenth century, the French and English made early forays into the Lesser Antilles. Scholars have alternatively proposed that the Portuguese in Brazil, the French in Martinique and Guadeloupe, or the English in Barbados first made rum.[2] Such arguments generally rest on a series of assumptions: that waste products extracted from curing sugar were immediately deemed safe and desirable to consume; that these sweets could be reliably and efficiently converted into alcohol; and that the individuals interacting with these waste products had access to stills. Assumptions such as these tend to place processes of invention entirely within transplanted, European ways of knowing. Strikingly, the fermentation and distillation of sugary wastes did not happen immediately in Brazil, the French Caribbean, or Barbados. Instead, individuals seeking sustenance, entertainment, or spiritual fulfillment through alcoholic beverages created other concoctions. They distilled sugar syrups but not its waste. They experimented with other alcohols made from roots, fruits, grains, and honey.[3] Others drank fermented sugar wastes but did not possess the tools or expertise necessary to distill them. Arriving at a solution that in hindsight appears so straightforward took considerable time and intellectual work.

Although sugarcane was transported to earlier sites of colonization in the Atlantic and Caribbean islands, plantation production in the Americas first prospered in Brazil, and a strain of accompanying experiments regarding its alcoholic potential began there too. These processes developed slowly. Starting around 1550, settlers from Portugal coerced labor from the Tupinambá and other Indigenous groups, and eventually from enslaved Africans, in order to grow and refine sugar.[4] It was only in the early seventeenth century, however, that both the consumption of sugar by-products and the practice of distillation became commonplace. One occurred in the shadows of Brazilian *ingenios*—or centralized sugar works—while the other was carefully controlled by the mill owners and operators.

In the early seventeenth century, sugar workers in Brazil began to ferment cane syrup—and especially wastes generated though its production—into an alcoholic beverage. In 1610, the French navigator François Pyrard de Laval visited Salvador de Bahia and wrote about a beverage called *aguardiente*. He explained that his hosts made "wine from sugarcane, which is cheap, but only to serve to the slaves and to the Indigenous."[5] By the end of the decade, sugar boilers collected the froth from the top of boiling cane syrup, added water to it, and fermented it into a beverage that they called *cachaça*. In 1618, a mill owner named Ambrósio Fernandes Brandão suggested that Native populations believed it to be a "'marvelous' drink."[6] The historian João Azevedo Fernandes argues that fermented cachaça—which crucially had not been refined and concentrated through distillation—"was traded by sugar mill slaves to other slaves and free men who did not have direct access to the production of sugar."[7] In the early seventeenth century, making and drinking undistilled "wine" from sweets unfit to be converted into sugar happened largely among coerced laborers.

These Native and African workers initially lacked access to the tools necessary to distill alcoholic beverages even if they wished to. The first still in Brazil was not recorded until 1611.[8] Early stills enriched sugar planters and mill operators at the expense of coerced workers. In 1636, the governor-general of Brazil, Pedro da Silva, temporarily outlawed the production of aguardiente. He noted "many stills" engaged in this business while observing that the alcohol was "very harmful to the people" and especially to the enslaved. Tellingly, Da Silva also differentiated between aguardiente and cachaça, suggesting a careful distinction between the former—fermented and distilled from high-quality sugar—and the latter—dregs that could be fermented and consumed straightaway.[9] In regions that grew inferior sugarcane, fermenting and distilling aguardiente emerged as a prudent use of the cane being grown. But producers made no mention of distilling any by-products.

In the latter half of the seventeenth century, the Portuguese crown consistently opposed converting syrups that could be made into sugar into aguardiente. Some of this resistance aimed to protect Portugal's wine and brandy makers from the competition of upstart alcohols. However, the crown expressed far more concern about the effect of aguardiente production on the viability of Brazil's sugar industry. Late in the seventeenth century, Maranhão's governor, Gomes Freire de Andrade, recalled to the Overseas Council repeated decrees by the king that "ordered the prohibition and the dismantling of alembics, because of the losses they cause to the sugar mills, consuming their sugarcane."[10] Spirits made from waste products, of course, would have added value to the sugar production process, yet producers and policymakers rarely mentioned them. The silence suggests that such spirits may not have been widely produced in Brazil until late in the seventeenth century. However, when the crown once again tried to prohibit aguardiente production in 1684, the king allowed for a limited number of stills to process distillates from the "foam" generated during sugar refining.[11] This alteration to regulations in the Amazon region of Brazil generally coincides with the date when slave traders increased the volume of distilled spirits—including those produced from waste products and delineated as *gerebita*—that they sold in Angola.[12] Distilling sugary wastes altered Brazil's economy by the late seventeenth century but probably not much earlier.

Impressed by the economic potential of Brazil, but initially shut out of colonizing the Americas, northern Europeans began looking for a foothold in the Caribbean in the early 1600s. The French landed on Martinique and Guadeloupe in 1635, promptly introducing the cultivation and production of tropical commodities. By introducing both sugarcane and stills, the supplies were in place to ferment and distill sugary wastes, but the product itself took longer to discover. In April 1639, the Compagnie des Îles d'Amérique offered a Flemish man named Daniel Trézel a six-year monopoly to produce sugar in Martinique.[13] In August of that same year, Jean Faguet received the sole right to produce brandy "of wine or of any other fruits or vegetables that he is able to make or collect" in Martinique and St. Christopher. Even with a sugar monopoly in place, the contract continued to assume that any brandy would most often be made from grapes.[14] In the case of St. Christopher, a small island jointly occupied by the English and French since the mid-1620s, tobacco remained the dominant crop until at least midcentury, likely limiting the availability of sugar syrups there.[15] Furthermore, the challenges faced by the Trézel family and others who sought to grow and market sugar for export in Martinique or Guadeloupe in the 1640s and 1650s, suggests that Faguet also would have struggled to procure cane syrups on those islands.

Into the 1650s, French settlers yearned for a local source of alcohol. Describing what he witnessed during a 1646–1647 voyage to the West Indies, Maurile de Saint-Michel noted that the Dutch brought beer and the Normans cider, "but it does not keep long." According to Saint-Michel, "all of the world struggles to supply eau-de-vie." On St. Christopher, distillates were made of "wine of sugarcane," *oüicou*, and *mobbie*. The latter two products were brews favored by the Indigenous Kalinago of the Lesser Antilles—oüicou from cassava and mobbie from sweet potatoes—which were then sometimes run through a still of European construction to concentrate the alcohol.[16] The world of alcohol production and consumption that Saint-Michel described was one of various knowledge cultures coexisting and colliding as inhabitants sought a new kind of alcohol to consume, although nobody mentioned fermenting or distilling molasses or other sugary wastes.

Other émigrés arrived on the French islands in the mid-1650s, bringing additional knowledge of sugar and alcohol production to the region. Following their failed colonization of and expulsion from Brazil in 1654, hundreds of Dutch settlers resettled in Guadeloupe and Martinique. Some of these refugees brought with them slaves experienced in the sugar industry. Among the new inhabitants of Guadeloupe were two individuals who, according to the French priest Jean-Baptiste Du Tertre, "knew how to make the shapes" and "prepare the boiling houses to whiten the sugar." Before this forced migration, French planters had depended on Dutch refiners to complete these tasks.[17] Aided by enslaved experts transported against their will, many sugar producers with Dutch surnames operated in the French Caribbean.[18]

By the 1650s, some constellation of Flemish planters, French distillers, Dutch émigrés, Native inhabitants, and enslaved West Africans began fermenting and distilling sugary wastes. Speaking to the centrality of enslaved makers to this system, Du Tertre noted in 1654 that "Blacks make intoxicating drinks" from damaged canes, skimmings from the boilers, and any spilled sugar "that sells well."[19] The fact that Du Tertre located the production of the spirit largely in the hands of enslaved peoples suggests the possibility that, as had been the case in Brazil, sugar-based alcohols were made, exchanged, and consumed by enslaved workers before Europeans took notice and joined in.

Fewer than 150 miles from Martinique, in Barbados, similar inventive processes unfolded, largely separated from what happened in Brazil or the French Atlantic. One clear indication of innovation occurring in Barbados is that publications of the era likely to be read by early colonists and their financiers did not yet describe waste-based distillates. In 1648, *Historia naturalis Brasiliae* was released by a prestigious Dutch publisher. The book detailed the on-the-ground explorations of the Dutch naturalist Willem Piso and a Leibstadt-born scientist named Georg Marcgrave while in Dutch Brazil from 1638 to 1643. The authors' northern European roots appealed to readers distrustful of Iberian Catholic naturalists, and the book was widely read and cited in northern Europe.[20] Readers accessing the duo's observations on sugar plantations in hopes of applying their lessons to other colonies would have been left with a distinct impression that different by-products of sugar had clearly delineated purposes. A first round of skimmings removed from pans of boiling sugar—called "cagassa"—provided "food and drink only for farm animals." Dregs collected during a subsequent round of boiling were "sufficient for slaves to eat, who, satisfied by them, complete such hard and constant labors." The enslaved also added water and waited for the slurry to ferment into a wine called *garapa* that "the Natives seek very eagerly." Finally, from a more refined syrup, an array of substances including sugar and "burnt wine"—possibly made on stills used to prepare medical treatments—could be produced.[21] Piso and Marcgrave offered little indication that a waste-based distillate held the potential that Barbados sugar producers would soon attach to it.

The slow adoption of stills in Barbados further suggests experimentation during the first decades of colonization. A still is a closed pot that feeds into a bulbous top chamber and then a coiled cooling system. By applying heat to the bottom of the pot, alcoholic vapors of the liquid inside of the still gather in its head, enter the coil (which is submerged in cool water), and reconstitute as a liquid with a significantly higher proportion of alcohol. The earliest European stills date back to twelfth-century Italy. It is unlikely that this technology existed in West Africa or the Americas before Europeans established trade centers in those places in the early modern period.[22] Starting in the late sixteenth century, manufacturers in the Netherlands, and soon elsewhere in northern Europe, began to construct larger stills crafted from copper rather than glass or clay. These European-manufactured stills were indispensable for making rum.

The English—and not Dutch or French interlopers—probably introduced the first stills to Barbados. The lack of economic development in the first decades of England's occupation of Barbados disincentivized foreign merchants from stopping on the island.[23] The earliest stills instead likely arrived with apothecaries and metallurgists who participated in early English expeditions.[24] In a 1631 letter to his son George, Henry Colt described Barbadian settlers as "good distillers."[25] Colt did not remark on what was being distilled, and his letter makes no mention of sugarcane on the island, though it is possible that the English fermented and distilled some of the low-grade sugar that they grew in those early years of settlement. Indeed, at the end of the seventeenth century, the merchant Dalby Thomas suggested that the first settlers on Barbados only used sugarcane "to make refreshing drink for that hot climate."[26] But there were other uses for stills as well. Sometime in the late 1630s, Archibald Hay resolved to send an English still to Barbados to produce an orange liqueur before ultimately reversing course.[27] His plan to send a "distillator" nonetheless demonstrates that some planters considered a use for this piece of equipment other than—and likely before—distilling rum.

Many of the first stills on the island occupied separate properties than plantations or sugar works, offering additional evidence that the earliest stills were not necessarily imported to make rum. A 1642 inventory of the Three Houses Plantation listed "one engine for sugar" but no stills or other alcohol-producing equipment.[28] Conversely, a 1643 inventory passing a forty-six-acre farm to William Williamson listed various livestock and "1 copper still" but no sugarcane, sugar mill, or coppers.[29] Into the 1650s, estates with stills did not always process sugarcane, and plantations with a sugar works sometimes lacked the requisite equipment to make rum.[30] Sugar and stills appear to have arrived on the island separately, and plantation owners (and the people they forced to work for them) initially came to disparate conclusions about the promise of distillation. Conversely, plantations that were settled a generation later commonly paired sugar and rum production from the start, and observers described rum as a distinctly Barbadian concoction.[31]

Global Ideas of Production on a Small Island

The distinct experiments in alcohol production ongoing in seventeenth-century Brazil, the French West Indies, and Barbados suggest that inhabitants of each place were working things out locally, but with input from people originating—and often taken against their will—from many corners of the Atlantic world. Migration, enslavement, and colonialism forced groups with their own distinct cultures of knowing and making into close contact with each other. The attendant experiences of dearth in remote colonies furthermore rewarded experimentation that could yield more nutrients, numb the exhaustion of overwork, or fend off boredom. Early inhabitants of Barbados encountered novel ideas, combined them with their existing knowledge, and organized this information in unique ways. The origins of rum serve as a critical reminder that the collision of cultures in the early modern world did not simply move ideas, things, or people from place to place but forced the creation of new forms.

Native, European, and African people converged on Barbados, bringing with them distinct ideas of how and why to make and drink alcohol. In February 1627, a ship captained by John Powell landed on the island. Powell's nephew described Barbados as "then vacant, without house or inhabitant," though Richard Ligon noted in 1657 that Native people had intermittently visited the island prior to English arrival.[32] Within two weeks of landing, Powell's brother, Henry, proceeded to the Essequibo River in South America to trade with Native people "for all things that was to be gotten for the planting of this island."[33] The bounty included "roots, plants, fowl, tobacco seeds, sugar canes and other materials" and collectively "were the first that were ever planted" in Barbados.[34] When he readied to return to Barbados, Henry claimed that three canoes of Native people chased him down. They explained that their ancestors had previously visited the island and that they wanted to go with him "as free people to manure those fruits" and to develop "a constant trade between the island and the main."[35] Henry carried thirty-two Indigenous men, women, and children back to Barbados, possibly freely or perhaps under duress. Many were ultimately enslaved.[36]

The presence of these Native experts attests to the centrality of Indigenous labor to early colonization efforts. Two decades after the journey from South America to Barbados, Henry Powell expressed his shock that Indigenous people, including a woman named Yon and a man named Barbadoes, had been reduced from "free people" to enslaved.[37] Yet as early as August 1627, Henry Winthrop noted that the only non-European residents were "forty slaves of Negroes and Indians."[38] In the years that followed, the English forcibly moved additional Kalinago and Arawak people to Barbados. Few observers commented on the number of Native people on the island. However, in 1652 a German mercenary recollected laboring on a plantation where the owner kept "100 Indians as slaves," which comprised one-third of the coerced workers.[39]

Colonizers sought out Indigenous laborers because of their acumen in growing crops and processing them into comestibles. Henry Powell explicitly stated that he brought these thirty-two individuals to Barbados in order to plant the island with foodstuffs. Although Europeans beginning with Columbus had introduced sugarcane to the Americas, Powell's recruits first introduced the grass to Barbados. They may have determined when the cane should be planted and cut in this particular climate. Indigenous laborers also transported and planted cassava and sweet potatoes, two tubers often converted into alcohols.[40] Before being consumed, cassava root must be processed to remove cyanide. Because the root originated in the Americas, Indigenous cultures had the longest-running familiarity with this crucial process. Even at mid-century, Ligon remarked that enslaved Native women remained instrumental for this work.[41]

Indigenous agricultural practice was closely tied to alcohol production. Native people fermented masticated cassava into an alcoholic beverage in the tropical Americas. In the late sixteenth century, Jean de Léry described this practice among members of the Tupi language group, a South American people with significant biological and cultural ties to the Kalinago and Arawak who inhabit the greater Caribbean and who were two key populations enslaved by the English in Barbados.[42] Women cut and boiled cassava, and then "chew[ed] them and twist[ed] them around in their mouths, without swallowing them," as seen in Figure 3. After once again boiling the cassava, Native women allowed the slurry to rest. The *caouin* fermented in as little as twenty-four hours. De Léry further noted that the Tupi believed that women must perform this labor and that European attempts to make the alcohol without "spitting" did not work.[43]

Indigenous women continued to deploy their expertise to produce cassava brews after they became enslaved in Caribbean colonies. During a 1635 trip to Martinique, Jacques Bouton identified a cassava-based "drink of the country" that Native people called "Hoücou." He observed that when the beverage was well made, it "is of relatively good taste, nourishes, and taken to excess could intoxicate."[44] "Excellent" cassava beer could be procured on Barbados as well, according to a letter penned by Thomas Verney.[45] Ligon described the same beverage—which he termed *perino*—as a "drink which the Indians make for their

Figure 3. Indigenous women masticating cassava. From Joseph François Lafitau, *Moeurs des sauvages ameriquains, comparées aux moeurs des premiers temps* (Paris, 1724), 2:80, detail. Courtesy of the John Carter Brown Library.

own drinking." As was the case elsewhere, its production depended on "their old wives, who have a small remainder of teeth, to chew and spit out into water."[46]

Oüicou featured prominently in the social and spiritual lives of the Kalinago. At the end of the seventeenth century, Jean-Baptiste Labat observed multiday Kalinago festivals—called *vins*—that preceded military or trade expeditions. The organizers spent days gathering provisions, hunting and barbecuing meat, and fermenting oüicou. After the guests ate heartily and drank to the point of intoxication, the host proposed a military raid. A female elder reminded the inebriated men of the "wrongs they suffered at the hands of their enemies."[47] In 1627, shortly after the initial settlement of St. Christopher, a Native ally of the English witnessed this ritual and warned the colonists to sail away before an impending attack. The English massacred the Kalinago instead.[48]

The Kalinago also used cassava brews in rituals designed to mark the connections between past, present, and future. After the birth of a Kalinago man's first child, he would spend four or five days lying in his hammock without food or drink. For the next four days, his only sustenance came from oüicou.[49] An oral history shared by the Carib-speaking Makiritare described another way in which a ceremony involving the production and consumption of cassava-based alcohols connected generations to each other: "It's always the same, now as before. The way we ate once, we do over and over again. We obey. We remember. The old ones sing beautifully. We just repeat."[50] The Kalinago also offered allotments of food and drink to spirit helpers, but the ceremonial uses of oüicou generally aimed to nourish those still living. They believed that they "would grow old sooner, be unsure of foot, and unable to see fish in the water" if these practices were not followed.[51]

English and French observers also noted the presence of a beverage that the Kalinago—and eventually Barbadian colonists—called mobbie.[52] In the early years of colonization, Native people taught settlers in Barbados how to boil sweet potatoes, crush them, add liquid and sometimes ginger, and ferment the concoction for a couple of days.[53] By mixing ginger—a tuber originating in Asia—into the mobbie, Indigenous people showed a predilection for adapting new ingredients to their traditional ways of making alcohol. The beverage became a staple for the English, too. Thomas Verney wrote to his father from Barbados in 1639 that "we brew in the morning to drink at noon, and at noon to drink at night, and [do] so every day in the year."[54] Charles de Rochefort likewise found it to be the "best and most common" beverage in the French islands, noteworthy for its ability to "refresh and quench thirst wonderfully."[55] European accounts of mobbie reveal the survival—and even reworking with a new spice blend—of Indigenous brews, as well as colonists' adoption of them.

According to John Powell's boatswain, John Cleere, Africans also arrived in Barbados with the English in 1627. He noted how "ten negroes taken in a prize" during the English fleet's journey to Barbados built shelters, cleared land, and assisted in planting the earliest crops once the ships reached the island.[56] English colonizers probably captured these people from a Spanish slaver prior to arriving in Barbados. Ninety percent of Africans captured by privateers between 1624 and 1636 originated in Angola.[57] Angolans, like many other people in western Africa, produced palm wine, or *malavu*. Men climbed trees and attached a dried gourd, waiting for the sap to collect and eventually ferment.[58] Because it was a common—and important—drink in much of western Africa, many of the one thousand Africans forcibly transported to Barbados in the 1630s, and the twenty-five thousand people who arrived in the ensuing decade, probably knew how to ferment palm wine.[59]

West Central Africans consumed alcohol to perform many social and ritual functions. In non-Muslim regions of Africa, men and women most often drank either beer brewed from sorghum or palm wine.[60] Palm wine was most likely to feature in ceremonies such as marriages and funerals among the Kongolese and their enemies. Marriage negotiations and contracts were conducted over it throughout the region.[61] The Imbangala, an Angolan warrior group who sold their captives to the Portuguese in the early seventeenth century, sought to connect with the deceased through palm wine consumption. They poured the wine over the graves of their ancestors and drank palm wine in such quantities that they could enter trances or have their spirits possessed.[62] It is unclear whether using alcohol to cement oaths, as part of treaty-making, and for use in funerary practices crossed the Atlantic at a specific moment or if such practices in the West Indies emerged independently.[63]

From the earliest decades of colonization, African crops and foodways captured the attention of planters on the island. White Barbadians readily provisioned their estates with plants of African provenance. Reflecting on his time in Barbados from 1647 to 1650, Richard Ligon identified the presence of African cultivars including watermelons, plantains, bananas, and yams. Ligon advised would-be planters how to cultivate majestic plantain trees, whose fruits the enslaved harvested green, then boiled, and subsisted on.[64] By the 1640s, some colonists set land aside for plantain cultivation.[65] Bananas were sometimes processed into a drink in parts of Africa and the Caribbean.[66] Englishmen paid close attention to African botanical transplants that could serve their needs.

The arrival of palm trees in Barbados by the 1640s provided another opportunity for the adaptation of African plants—including using them for making traditional alcoholic beverages. Ligon described the "very delicious kind of liquor" being produced in Barbados in the 1640s, but he did not comment on who was making it.[67] He even suggested that the tree originated in the East Indies, which further muddied its provenance. Other observers traced a clearer connection between African and Caribbean palm wine production. Rochefort described how, following African precedent, "some Negroes draw wine by making incisions under its branches."[68] In the eighteenth century, an elderly African woman enslaved in Barbados named Sibell recalled memories of palm wine from her childhood. She briefly recollected that "when we want good drink in my country we go and cut the tree and the juice will run, and kept some time will make good strong drink."[69] Such memories of life in Africa may have fueled the production and consumption of palm wine in Barbados.

Large numbers of English and Scottish voyagers resettled in Barbados by the mid-seventeenth century, importing their own understandings of alcohol's place in society. European migrants of varied classes drank heavily. In 1631, Henry Colt referred to the settlers as "devourers up of hot waters and such good distillers thereof."[70] Little seems to have changed by the time of Father Biet's visit to the island in 1654 when he described afternoon bacchanalias at the house of planters where "quite often one is so drunk that he cannot return home." They indulged in brandy, cordials, wines, and "sweetened mobbie."[71] Not one libation available to Father Biet was traditionally made by the English or Scottish.

Britons, like Natives and Africans, knew how to ferment alcohols and attached social and spiritual meanings to the resulting beverages. The low alcoholic content and chemical instability of ale rendered it prone to spoilage. The English transitioned to brewing beer with hops over the late medieval period in order to mitigate this issue, but these alcohols remained volatile and bulky. Because of their low alcoholic content, one also needed to consume large quantities of English brews to achieve inebriation.[72] Employers provided allotments of ale and beer to workers, while alehouses offered a commercial space to buy additional alcohol and socialize while consuming it.[73] Furthermore, Europeans joined other contemporary civilizations in believing that consuming certain alcohols carried special powers. Most Christians believed that taking communion transformed wine into the blood of Christ. Transubstantiation emerged as one of the key theological ruptures between Catholics and Protestants during the Reformation, but Communion remained an important, albeit less common, ritual even in protestant England.[74] Europeans paid increased attention to distilled spirits around 1600, as evidenced by Stradanus including a distillery in his celebration of new discoveries.

Despite prodigious experience as drinkers, the English men and women most likely to relocate to Barbados possessed limited knowledge about how to make alcohol. While alcohol production in West Central Africa and the Caribbean remained diffuse, it had been centralized in England. By the late sixteenth century, twenty-six common brewers plied their trade in London.[75] Commercial breweries were operated by technically skilled, male workers and largely replaced the home production of ales by female brewers by 1600.[76] Because most Britons purchased their alcohol, the landless poor who sailed from English port cities in the early seventeenth century were less likely to have had experience in the industry.[77] While some English women continued to produce ales and ciders at home, their expertise was unlikely to transfer to the Caribbean because of the gender breakdown of migrants. For instance, a 1640 inventory of a Barbados plantation with equipment on hand to make mobbie listed the names of twelve servants, all of whom were male.[78] On many Barbadian estates reliant on migrant European labor, alcohol production must have fallen to men with limited previous experience making alcohol.

Expertise in distilling was even less likely to transfer from Britain to Barbados. Distillates only supplanted beer in popularity in England around 1700.[79] There simply were not very many experienced distilled spirits producers in England in the mid-seventeenth century. Those who had become experts in this fledgling industry probably had little incentive to migrate. And Caribbean-based distillers do not appear to have sought training in London.[80] Scottish servants may have had some experience with *aqua vitae* production, as the fermentation and distillation of grains began in Scotland as early as the thirteenth century. However, industrial whiskey distillation did not take hold until the eighteenth century. Instead, its production remained a minor enterprise, usually practiced on a small scale and on family farms.[81] Commercial distillers from England and Scotland probably would not have had the financial means or incentive to purchase a Caribbean plantation outright but would have been financially secure enough to avoid indentured servitude.

Relying on European manufactories to make up for a shortage of on-the-ground expertise pertaining to alcohol production and quench Barbadian thirst posed problems due to the difficulty and expense of ocean transport. Rough sea crossings and the Caribbean climate spoiled imported beers and wines. Although brandy resisted spoliation, the English could not source this distillate domestically. Instead, English merchants had to give limited specie to European traders in exchange for wine-based brandies.[82] These factors drove up the price of imported alcohols in a cash-strapped colony.[83] In the middle of the seventeenth century, Barbados residents searched for local alternatives.

Creative Collisions

The quest for local substitutions for European alcohols encouraged European settlers and visitors to observe Native and African beverages and compare them to familiar drinks. Ligon preferred perino, which he contended "tastes the likest to English beer."[84] Rochefort likened palm wine to "white wine."[85] Breton equated mobbie to a "*petit*" white wine.[86] Other observers made their comparisons based on alcoholic content more than flavor. A Swiss doctor named Felix Spoeri visited Barbados in 1661 and described mobbie as "an excellent drink" that "satisfies like beer or wine."[87] Whether judging based on familiar tastes or physiological effects, Europeans considered how new alcohols met preexisting desires.

Britons in Barbados experimented with new ways to make or store beverages as their palates for American and African alcohols developed. Inventories

Figure 4. Enslaved man grating cassava. From Charles de Rochefort, *Histoire naturelle et morale des iles Antilles de l'Amerique* (Rotterdam, 1665), 105. Courtesy of the John Carter Brown Library.

from several Barbadian plantations in the 1640s and 1650s include references to "presses" and "mobbie tubbs," suggesting that some early planters invested in improved production techniques for Indigenous beverages.[88] Metal graters, like one wielded by an African-descended man in Figure 4 eased grating cassava to make perino.[89] Spoeri noted that after fermentation, mobbie could be barreled and stored in a cellar.[90] By adapting European storage techniques, the shelf life for Indigenous beverages lengthened considerably. In the mid-seventeenth century, colonists consumed—and sometimes adapted—alcohols introduced by the people they enslaved.[91]

As they initially discovered new types of alcohol introduced by Europeans, men and women around the Atlantic basin tried to make sense of the new things that they were tasting. They often sought to adapt new products to existing patterns of consumption. Kalinago people began to call their "oüicou" festivals "vins" instead. The adaptation of the French word suggests a general willingness to incorporate European-made alcohols into these political gatherings. For their part, French colonizers disagreed over whether cassava-based alcohols could replace wine in Communion. Maurile de Saint-Michel noted in 1652 that the ready supply of oüicou and scarcity of wine sparked theological debates. The

Catholic missionary derided local Calvinists who substituted "*cahoum des sauvages*" for the blood of Christ and reiterated the Catholic Church's position that such a substitution was improper for Communion.[92] The viability of commodity substitution across cultures depended on whom you asked.

Despite frequently commenting on the alcoholic beverages that they had not previously encountered, visitors to Barbados generally overlooked the intellectual and physical work that non-European people expended in their production. Only Ligon described Native women's work making perino. Contemporary descriptions of mobbie offered even less insight into its creation or production. Other visitors might acknowledge the ubiquity of novel alcohols but offered little indication about who made them.[93] Heinrich von Uchteritz went a step further than these visitors, suggesting that the "gentry make a drink from the potato root."[94] In his retelling, an alcohol bearing a Kalinago name was made by Barbados's social elites from a tuber native to South America. This obfuscation of where new forms of alcohol came from and who produced them achieved several goals. It downplayed the presence of enslaved Native alcohol producers in the English Caribbean in an era when their enslavement continued.[95] Like adapting English troughs, barrels, or cellars to store and preserve Indigenous beverages, eliding Indigenous production techniques also helped repackage Indigenous ideas as English ones.

Experimentation was by no means only—or even—the province of the "gentry." In fact, creative uses for molasses and sugar skimmings originated among those tasked with working in the cane fields and sugar works of the Caribbean. Ligon noted that a "common" beverage came from "the skimming of sugar, which is infinitely strong, but not very pleasant in taste." He furthermore worried that "the people drink much of it, indeed too much." Ligon also described a "punch" of "water and sugar put together, which in ten days standing will be very strong, and fit for laborers."[96] Ligon connected working people often with insecure access to nourishment to experimental brews.

Observers in the French islands, who were generally more likely to attribute new technologies to non-Europeans, suggested other uses for sugar and its by-products. Rochefort observed that those who crossed the fields "suck with pleasure the excellent juice" of the sugarcane.[97] In addition to connecting people of African descent to the production of alcohol from sugary wastes, Du Tertre observed at midcentury that people had also begun to add molasses to their oüicou. The added sweetness caused the ferment to "bubble and makes it as strong as the best beer in Flanders."[98] Laborers of Indigenous and African descent found new uses for sugar's by-products as they tweaked familiar recipes and explored new ones.

Distilling drinks that had previously only been fermented constituted another adaptation that drew from several cultures of alcohol production. Indigenous-introduced alcohols were being distilled in European stills by 1652.[99] A spirit distilled using European technology from a fermented beverage of Indigenous provenance would have been legible to multiple groups. In early Barbados, experimentation entailed mixing newly encountered ideas—some of which involved rethinking what was considered potable—with existing technologies to concoct new things.

As they continued to try out alcohols derived from cassava, sweet potatoes, palm sap, and sugar, an island population thrust together by colonization and enslavement began to collect sugary wastes, manage their fermentation, and distill them into a liquor that they alternatively called kill devil, rumbullion, and, eventually, rum. Such a concoction drew from sugarcane originating from the "Old World" but transplanted to Barbados from South America, fermentation techniques and consumption habits honed on several different continents, and stills carried from England in order to create something new. Rum emerged in Barbados on the heels of decades of transcultural exchange. It was, and would continue to be, an invention of the Atlantic world.

By 1644, sugar, a still, and knowledge of fermentation and distillation converged on a single Barbadian plantation. A lease from that year stipulated that Christopher Thompson held the right to any "sugar, ginger, or strong water" produced by the plantation's fields, sugar works, and distillery. The spatial layout of the estate embraced the logic of maximizing sugar production and converting any damaged canes, skimmings, and molasses into rum.[100] Archival records do not detail who was responsible for this new setup.

The limits of what early colonizers of the Caribbean chose to record and, alternatively, overlook creates boundaries of what can be known. In a 1789 commencement speech at the University of Pennsylvania, George Baynton lamented, "It is no small mortification to me that I am not able to trace the invention of this noble liquor to its author. . . . Gratitude must here, therefore, be silent."[101] Baynton spoke sarcastically, but he identified an issue that historians continue to grapple with. Nobody recorded when somebody in Barbados—or Brazil or Martinique—first collected sugary wastes, fermented them, loaded them into a still, and decided to consume the resulting product. Nobody asked how early makers knew what they did.

All of this uncertainty highlights a different, less recognized attribute of invention in the early modern Atlantic world. Europeans sought out wealth in overseas colonies but often lacked the creativity or manpower to succeed on their own. Instead, they coupled the coerced labor and ideas of African and Indigenous American people with their own tools and experiences, in this case tied to making and drinking alcohol. Makers brought together on seventeenth-century Barbados applied their experiences with palm trees, potatoes, and cassava to new ingredients, including sugar brought to the region by Europeans. In so doing, plantation workers transformed substances previously discarded or reserved for use as a cheap sweetener or animal fodder into something potable and desirable. Exploration, colonialism, and enslavement reorganized people, ideas, and processes and created new worlds—full of previously undiscovered things to make and consume. The way in which contemporaries wrote about these exploits can make it easy to misunderstand invention as rapid, monocultural, and European-driven. The extended process by which a local curiosity became an economic driver of colonial expansion and racialized slavery tells a different story.

Devising a System of Production

When Christopher Thompson signed his contract to distill "strong water" on a sugar plantation in 1644, a well-developed blueprint for making rum had not yet emerged. Various landholders made individual decisions about the place of rum on their fledgling plantations. Over the decades that followed, however, Barbadians turned a novelty—a locally produced and consumed alcohol—into a highly prized commodity. In the process, plantation operators, enslaved workers coerced through violence, merchants, and sailors redesigned sugar production to prioritize making as much rum as possible. This process of commodification once again depended on various groups of people lending their ideas, labor, and desires to the creation of a new product.

Rum was present in Barbados starting in the 1640s, but visitors to the island may not have immediately encountered it. Beauchamp Plantagenet's 1648 description of Barbados noted the presence of sugar mills on the island, but when it came to alcoholic beverages, he only described mobbie.[102] Individuals briefly on the island, and possibly confined to Bridgetown or Speightstown, may not have encountered rum. Ligon noted that a significant portion of rum was consumed on the estates that made it. Any excess was often sold "to such planters, as have no sugar-works of their own, yet drink excessively of it."[103] At first, the spirit largely remained a product made and consumed on plantations.

Some plantations still lacked the means to produce rum on their own. The plantation that Heinrich von Uchteritz labored on in western Barbados in 1652 still fed damaged sugarcane "to the pigs as fodder" instead of making rum out of it.[104] Other plantations lacking stills may have sold molasses and skimmings to neighbors who were making rum. Some planters invested only cautiously in rum making. Rather than building single-use distilleries, they might purchase a small still and place it in the kitchen. Such estates tended also to employ fewer enslaved people, which means that the landowners or their families may have been responsible for early rum production.[105] Some planters responded to the invention of rum cautiously.

Lingering uncertainty over whether sugar plantations should also distill rum may have been connected to questions of who would drink it. Ligon praised the economic, social, and even medicinal value of rum. He believed it would "cure and refresh the poor Negroes . . . by the labor of whose hands, our profit is brought in."[106] Enslaved people working on rum-producing plantations likely chose to consume the beverage because it was readily available, it had a pleasant taste, and the physiological effects of consuming alcohol provided a brief respite from the drudgery of their daily lives.[107] African and Indigenous people also incorporated rum—and the effects that they accessed through intoxication—into existing spiritual celebrations such as funerary practices and festivals that predated European encounters.

The ways that enslaved, indentured, and poor people used rum worried other observers. The Barbados Assembly sought to limit alcohol consumption among sailors in a 1652 act. Sixteen years later, they introduced legislation aimed to prevent the enslaved and indentured from trading stolen plantation goods for rum.[108] By 1671, the governor of South Carolina, Joseph West, complained that "one English servant is worth two Barbadians, for they are so much addicted to rum that they will do little but while the bottle is at their nose."[109] Some planters may have resisted making rum on their own plantations in order to limit access to it among the individuals from whom they extracted labor. Such questions about who should drink and for what purposes took many decades to settle.

Despite rum being made out of sugary wastes, nothing dictated that one must join the two production processes. Sugar and rum production each required distinct equipment. The goods sold in different markets. And both commodities demanded the most intensive labor at the same times of year. Each of these factors could have led to the emergence of separate sugar refineries and rum distilleries, as became the case in Brazil, North America, Britain, and India. Yet planters in Barbados—and eventually the rest of the English Caribbean—paired these two commodities in the same complex of outbuildings in order to maximize the economic potential of their investments. While they are often referred to as *sugar* works and *sugar* plantations, they are equally notable for the rum that was manufactured within them and helped to determine the cadence of the work.

Richard Ligon and Henry Drax invested in state-of-the-art rum distilleries that they incorporated into their sugar works in the mid-seventeenth century. Upon arriving on the island in 1647, Ligon and his business partners purchased half of William Hilliard's plantation consisting of five hundred acres, with cane already planted on two hundred of them. The works included a sugar mill, boiling house, curing house, and distillery. Ligon likened the intermeshed work of each part of the sizable plantation to "wheels in a clock," praising European experts for their ingenious management of the complex system. He worried that, as with a clock, breakdowns on one part of his plantation would halt the entire enterprise. For instance, if a cog in the mill could not be replaced, the mill would stop running, "Or if the stills be at fault, the kill devil cannot be made."[110] By the late 1640s, Ligon and his partners esteemed rum production to be a crucial part of their sugar plantations. When Henry Drax penned his instructions to a plantation overseer named Richard Harwood three decades later, he also noted the centrality of rum production.

In order to produce as much sugar and rum as possible, plantation operators sought to harness the energy of humans, animals, and natural forces. As an enslaved plantation worker in Barbados purportedly detailed to a seventeenth-century visitor, "The devil was in the English-man, that he makes everything work; he makes the Negro work, the horse work, the ass work, the wood work, the water work, and the wind work."[111] By describing the plantation as a machine or equating natural power with animal and even human labor, these accounts presented the work of individuals as unthinking and interchangeable. However, as Ligon's and Drax's instructions demonstrate, successful production of sugar and rum required humans to work in very particular ways. This largely coerced work of rum-making was crucial both for the emergence of the spirit as a global commodity and for helping to define the expectations of plantation production throughout the English Caribbean.

The economic logic of pairing sugar and rum production shaped the experiences of laborers in the boiling houses used to purify sugar. There, enslaved refiners ladled the cane juice into a large boiling pan, and then a series of progressively smaller ones, as they removed imperfections and concentrated the sugar into a dark, thick syrup. Those refiners used their judgment to remove the right amount of frothy imperfections that rose to the surface of the pans, which they spooned into a trough draining down to the still house. Henry Drax recognized the skill and attention to detail that these boilers must possess. He instructed his plantation manager, "If there be a mistake in the clarifier it's hard to be rectified in the rest of the coppers therefore your head boilers in each watch must have particular charge of clarifying and upon their neglect to be soberly punished."[112] If the skimmings were still treated as plantation refuse, then this level of care would not have been so crucial. But now highly technical work supporting the distillery was exacted through the threat of punishment because it impacted a plantation's bottom line.

Likewise, the rum distilleries connected to Barbados sugar works shaped the work undertaken elsewhere on the plantation. In early Barbados, planters expected that most of the syrups that drained out of curing sugar—molasses—should be reboiled into a lower quality of *paneles* sugar. However, as rum production took hold, this molasses was instead sent to the distillery.[113] Along with any spoiled cane juice sent straight from the mill and sugar skimmings from the boiling house, these ingredients made up the fermentable matter that would ultimately become rum. Lead chutes connected each of these workspaces to the distillery, demonstrating how integrated the entire process had become. Drax reminded his overseer that the piping required regular maintenance. To prevent loss, he instructed that the "wood stockers" should complete this task and be "punished if not careful."[114] Again, correction awaited people who did not properly contribute their work to the rum production process. Drax's 1679 instructions show that the distillery had become more than a waste receptacle for a plantation's scraps: it now turned trash into something merchantable.

This highly regimented work continued inside plantation distilleries. Enslaved and indentured workers mixed the lees left over from earlier rum batches with the sweet syrups and waited several days or even weeks until the liquid turned properly sour and sugars transformed into alcohol. When an expert deemed the wash ready to distill, workers filled their stills, the largest of which likely held around seventy to a hundred gallons at this point. The firemen then fed the fires with wood to heat the liquid and vaporize the alcohol (which had a lower boiling point than water). An hour or so later, concentrated distillate began to pass into the condenser, allowing the spirit to flow from the still. Workers needed to empty spent wash from the still and redistill the low wines once or twice more before the rum reached the desired strength.[115]

Plantation owners relied on the mental and physical abilities of an array of workers in order to make rum. Both Ligon and Drax singled out the importance of the work of hired overseers for the production of rum. Many of these supervisory roles were filled by former indentured servants who possessed the same training and work experiences as the enslaved people they now supervised.[116]

Drax noted that the plantation distillery "brings in very considerable profit with little charge" and therefore should "be minded with great care and diligence." For the time being, he trusted the management of his distillery to a "servant whom I take to be as good as most are here to be hired." Drax planned to eventually send a skilled distiller from London to take over, but in the meantime he incentivized good management on the part of the untrained attendant: if the distillery produced over 20,000 gallons of rum in a year, the distiller would receive 2,025 pounds of muscovado sugar as payment. If the distillery only yielded 14,000 gallons, then the distiller only deserved 1,000 pounds of sugar. However, if the distillery yielded less than that amount, "he must be very negligent and therefore will deserve nothing." Drax threatened even his hired workers.

Drax enumerated what he expected from his distiller. He had to properly monitor the fermenting liquors, decide when to distill them, and ensure that workers stopped collecting product when its flavor and alcoholic content declined. These calculations required familiarity with the intricacies of fermentation and distillation. But Drax's instructions suggest that he hired distillers at least as much for their supervisory abilities. He stressed that the distillery should work quickly, with "great expedition." And the distiller needed to be watchful and lock the door every time he left in order to prevent the distillery's enslaved workforce from appropriating the product of their labor.[117] Plantation operators in mid-seventeenth-century Barbados hired distillers and overseers as managers of the enslaved people who performed most of the work.

The work of making rum increasingly depended on enslaved people of African descent as well. Ligon's plantation relied on a workforce consisting of "96 Negroes, and three Indian women, with their children; [and] 28 Christians."[118] The fact that as much as 75 percent of the inhabitants of the plantation were of African descent means that they must have carried out a wide array of tasks. This included work in the distillery, as evidenced by the tragic death of one enslaved man who caught on fire when decanting rum into a barrel by candlelight.[119] When Drax wrote his instructions, he expected that it would mostly be enslaved people of African descent who cut and milled the sugarcane, boiled the sugar, set up the curing pots, kept the piping clear, mixed the several ingredients for rum, built and stoked the still fires, regulated water levels to keep the worms cool, collected and evaluated the distillate from the stills, and constructed, loaded, and measured the rum puncheons. This assemblage of duties required a set of skills never before exercised by a single workforce.

Operators of sugar and rum plantations in seventeenth-century Barbados devised a system of labor management designed to cheaply control the intellectual and physical labor of coerced sugar refiners and distillers for as long as possible. After a failed attempt to overthrow King James II, a group of "Monmouth rebels" were sentenced to transport to Barbados for a period of ten years in 1685. The lengthy term of service made these men especially desirable among planters. Five years into their servitude, Governor James Kendall explained, "The planters accordingly bought them, and thinking themselves secure of them during that time taught them to be their boilers, distillers and refiners, and neglected to teach any others as they would otherwise have done."[120] Planters who had invested in these servants feared that a change to the terms of the Monmouth rebels' indenture threatened the profitability of their enterprise.

More commonly, to rely on people whose term of service was longest meant to depend on enslaved people to perform specialized jobs. As an unnamed observer wrote in the 1660s, "The planters, grown now full of Negroes, design to have all other tradesmen, sugar boilers, refiners (or at least many of them) of their Blacks." He lamented a situation where those enslaved for life "work at their respective trades in a good condition," while "Christians" indentured for a finite period performed less-skilled duties.[121] Enslavers recognized the potential for enslaved people to occupy specialized roles precisely because of the economic value attached to controlling their labor for life. Rum incentivized a unique form of plantation agriculture that extracted expertise from the enslaved in order to create a new commodity.

Rum on the Move

Just as they helped to determine how rum would be made on individual properties, enslaved people of African descent also played a crucial role in transforming rum from a plantation product to a commodity with recognized attributes and value beyond the estate. As planters began producing more rum than was being consumed locally, they created new markets for the commodity. To place rum in the hands of merchants who could sell it locally or abroad, however, it first had to be sent to Speightstown or Bridgetown. Bondspeople hitched carts carrying a hogshead of rum or sugar to teams of horses or oxen and slowly moved the goods toward Barbados's leading ports. Their forced labor connected local production to broader exchange networks.

Other market activities undertaken by these enslaved carters took place beyond the control of those enslaving them. Drax noted how the act of carrying rum to market opened up the possibility of informal commodity exchanges.

Once they left the plantation, enslaved carters moved beyond the gaze of their enslavers and overseers. Drax worried that carters pilfered the sugar, molasses, and rum for their own consumption or to sell illicitly. In order to prevent those he enslaved from encountering the sorts of rogues who were "apt to spoil by their bad example," Drax instructed his plantation manager to dispatch the carters from Drax Hall to Bridgetown early in the morning, preferably with "a spy" among them.[122] Unsanctioned exchanges became so common that the Barbados Assembly passed repeated laws barring the enslaved from buying or selling rum or molasses.[123] In opposition to slaveholders' expectations and economic interests, bondspeople used this "secret trade" to create their own supply and demand for rum in early Barbados.

Merchants continued the process of building a market for rum once it reached port. Many plantation owners—including Henry Drax—owned stores in Bridgetown and employed local merchants to handle the sales of their rum. While sugar was destined for metropolitan markets, rum tended to sell in country. Planters hoped that their storekeepers could recoup enough value from these local sales to purchase anything that needed to be bought locally. Some of the rum sold in town was consumed by residents of the town or the island who did not grow sugarcane or produce rum themselves. The government also supplied some spirits to the island's militia.[124] Nonetheless, as early as May 1653, the grand inquest in Bermuda noted with concern "the great quantity of strong drinks which are brought into these islands from the Barbados." This trade had become significant enough that some Bermudians worried that limiting the trade could lead to diminished commerce with Barbados.[125]

The many hands that rum passed through from plantation to market exacerbated the need for a standard name for the commodity. Early observers used different names for the spirit before beginning to settle on the modern name for their invention in the 1650s. Befitting a commodity whose invention was shrouded in mystery but depended on the presence of Indigenous, African, and European knowledge of alcohol production, the origins of the name remain opaque.[126] In 1651, a Barbados resident named Giles Silvester reported on the preeminent alcohol made on the island: "a hot hellish and terrible liquor" called "rumbullion, also kill devil." The name may have referred to contemporary Devonshire slang for "a great tumult." The following year, a correspondent in Leiden made mention of "the spirits of rombustion, which our men there make."[127] Sometime thereafter, inhabitants of Barbados began shortening one of these names to "rum."[128] By the mid-1650s, the term was in use in both Barbados and North America.[129] The increasingly common usage of the word *rum* signifies a movement toward creating a shorthand for what producers were making. A common name became increasingly important starting in the 1660s as larger quantities of rum—and even suggestions to produce it—began to depart Barbados for places including Jamaica, North America, and England and Scotland.

From the mid-1660s until the 1680s, sailors carried ever-growing volumes of rum to markets throughout the Atlantic world. At the beginning of this period, Barbados exported 11,529 metric tons of muscovado sugar; 529,943 liters of molasses; and 567,827 liters of rum per year. Rum comprised less than 6 percent of the value of these exports. But its economic significance increased over the following two decades. By the late 1680s, annual muscovado sugar exports from the island declined to 7,386 metric tons, while molasses and rum exports rose to 3 million liters and 1.4 million liters, respectively. At this point, the value of rum surpassed one-quarter of the value of Barbados's exports.[130] Forty-eight percent of the value of the exports traveled to London compared to 21 percent to New England, 11 percent to the Chesapeake, and 11 percent to the rest of the Americas.[131] Merchants likely shipped the vast majority of the sugar to London for further processing, while an equally high proportion of the molasses and rum went to North America.[132] By the 1660s, and more so by the 1680s, sales of rum produced in Barbados and sent to distant markets added considerably to the island's economy.

* * *

What unfolded on Barbados in the seventeenth century transpired rather rapidly. At the dawn of the seventeenth century, Europeans had not begun fermenting and distilling sugar or its by-products, and Barbados was usually uninhabited. By midcentury, highly capitalized and technologically advanced sugar and rum plantations produced hundreds of thousands of liters of rum per year. European observers struggled to keep up with these sudden changes, producing incomplete accounts of how a new commodity—and way of organizing overseas ventures—took hold. Yet a careful reading of the sources that they did produce tells a story of Native Americans, enslaved Africans, and Europeans bringing distinct ways of making alcohol to the Caribbean and experimenting with ingredients and ideas that they newly encountered in Barbados. Rum emerged from that maelstrom sometime around midcentury. Then, English landowners in Barbados appropriated the ideas and labor of their multiracial labor force to create a highly efficient system combining agriculture and industry to churn out sugar and rum, even as they elided the intellectual contributions of the people forced to do the work.

Rum transformed from something local and variable to a standard item that held value for different people in distant parts of the Atlantic world.

However, this was only one stage in the invention of rum. It was preceded by a complex cast of characters squeezing alcohol out of trees, roots, fruits, and grass in different corners of the Atlantic world. Then, after midcentury, both rum and knowledge of how to make it fanned out to newly conquered Caribbean islands, North American colonies, England, and Scotland. In these fledgling workshops—and the taverns, stores, and homes that they supplied—denizens of an integrating Atlantic world continued to work out questions related to making, selling, and drinking rum. It may be tempting to understand the invention of rum as rapid and geographically confined, but it is far more instructive to trace how the preferred qualities, ideal means of production, value, and meanings tied to its consumption remained in flux, and under negotiation, for several generations.

CHAPTER 2

Promise and Perils of a New Commodity

William Hogarth's *Gin Lane* presents an exaggerated view of eighteenth-century London in crisis. In Figure 5, a lady fences kettles and other tools at a pawnshop. Man and dog gnaw on bones already stripped bare. One mother pours liquor down her infant's gullet, while another—with a breast exposed—drops a toddler over a railing. In the background, a crumbling tower reveals a man hanging from a noose. And a rowdy crowd gathers outside of the Kilman distillery, making clear that the producers of the spirits deserve their share of blame for the crisis gripping the mid-eighteenth-century city.

The crowded streets, well-appointed buildings, and emphasis on gin place this scene in England, but the details reflect contemporary realities in other parts of the Atlantic world as well. This was, after all, an era when rum flooded the Caribbean and eastern North America, frequently factoring into outbursts of violence between and among Native people, enslaved Africans, and Europeans. Even Scotland and England experienced an influx of alcohols distilled from sugary by-products. In the Caribbean, North America, and Britain, drunkenness was on the rise from the 1670s to the 1750s, fueled by novel distillation technologies and new, colonial products to distill. Cheap and unassuming rum infiltrated new spaces throughout Britain's Atlantic world, including "Gin Lane."

New drinking patterns provoked conflict. Observers recording early experiences with a swelling supply of rum often attempted to set standards of who should drink and in what contexts and quantities they should imbibe. They suggested that inebriation was more suitable for elites than for commoners.[1] Elite Englishmen wrote especially derisively of the enslaved Africans, Indigenous polities, and women and laboring whites they sought to control and extract labor from. They dwelt on sensational details of mayhem and often wrote of

Figure 5. *Gin Lane* by William Hogarth (1751). The Metropolitan Museum of Art, Harris Brisbane Dick Fund, 1932.

the subjects in vague and impersonal ways. Descriptions of enslaved imbibers evinced a fear that unsanctioned drinking undermined slaveholder authority. Accounts focused on the ways in which alcohol was consumed by Native Americans instead harped on the cultural superiority of the colonizer compared to the colonized.[2] These latter descriptions have fed into unproven—and harmful—claims that Indigenous nations have declined or even disappeared because of a genetic predisposition to compulsive drinking.[3] In this case, over-emphasizing local particularities at the expense of a broader Atlantic history decontextualizes the rum-infused crisis of the late seventeenth and early eighteenth centuries in misleading ways.

Careful attention to the first generations of Europeans, Africans, and Indigenous Americans to make and consume rum instead shows the complicated reactions that many individuals and societies had to the new intoxicant. Rum was rarely seen as either unquestionably good or irredeemably bad in the first century after its emergence. Instead, makers, traders, and drinkers weighed the promise and perils of the new commodity. Rum offered its drinkers caloric value and access to intoxication, as well as enhanced variety in what one could choose to consume. Sometimes it served familiar goals among drinkers, and at other times it allowed for the creation of something new. Widespread desires for these benefits created opportunities for trade and diplomacy. But rum was dangerous. Intoxication could lead to violence, poverty, and challenges to legal and spiritual authority. Everybody living through the profusion of new distilled spirits had to contend with how the possibilities and pitfalls of a new commodity would play out within local contexts.

A comparison of how people in three regions that quickly followed Barbados's lead by adopting rum production and consumption for their own purposes—Jamaica, North American colonies from Pennsylvania to Massachusetts, and Britain—responded to the initial invention of rum exposes an important reality: rum pooled when and where authority was being actively negotiated in the seventeenth and early eighteenth-century Atlantic world. In these contexts, it functioned concurrently as an economic engine, source of social anxiety, and intoxicant that could alter human behavior in troubling ways. The new commodity held appeal in all three regions because colonial and metropolitan entrepreneurs hoped to profit off of changing economic realities shaped by larger processes of slavery and colonialism. Emerging social and economic relationships within this Atlantic world also provoked intense anxieties around how supplies of cheap, potent, and inebriating rum threatened the racial, class-based, and gendered order on which colonists and metropolitan elites built their authority. Probing rum's role in creating an intoxicated Atlantic highlights both the ways in which distinct groups of people living and laboring in Britain and its colonies experienced the invention of rum and the insecurity of elites' control over sovereign Native nations, enslaved Africans, women, and common workers.

The Sodom of the West Indies

Twelve hundred miles northwest of Barbados, landholders in Jamaica began to experiment with rum production—and to adjust to the increasing availability of cheap spirits—in the 1660s. Equally well situated for sugar production and settled in part by migrants from Barbados, Jamaica came the closest to directly transplanting the system of rum production pioneered in the Lesser Antilles. Sometimes rum even flowed out of stills before the infrastructure to refine sugar had been built. Enslaved people worked out their own uses for rum, as did other island dwellers. Awash in the rum produced in-country, the city of Port Royal soon gained a reputation for drunkenness and debauchery. Critics suggested that cheap and plentiful rum consumed by pirates, prostitutes, politicians, and other Port Royal residents signaled the debased nature of island society.

The English expelled the last Spanish soldiers from Jamaica in 1660, acquiring a permanent foothold in the heart of the Spanish Caribbean. By 1664, Barbadians, the servants and slaves who were compelled to migrate with them, and equipment to make sugar and its by-product commodities began flooding into Jamaica.[4] That same year, Charles Lyttleton insisted that "coppers, stills, and all utensils [necessary] for a mill and sugar works" were crucial for settling plantations there.[5] He was emphatic that stills to make rum were nonnegotiable components of economic development in the new colony.

Cary Helyar was one of a growing number of Englishmen who joined this project.[6] He initially operated as a merchant, supplying the island's struggling plantations with the human chattel they coveted for clearing and cultivating their fields. Five years later, in 1669, he had become friendly with Jamaica's governor, Sir Thomas Modyford, and his son, General Thomas Modyford—two early émigrés from Barbados. Helyar purchased land next to the governor's cacao walk in St. Mary's Parish.[7] A year later, Helyar, his overseer, and the people he enslaved had planted six acres of cacao trees, which quickly succumbed to a blight that devastated the island's plantations. Helyar searched for a new commodity.

Helyar decided to shift to sugar and rum. Both he and his visitors raved about the soil quality and the potential for a water-powered sugar mill. Helyar next asked the younger Thomas Modyford, whose nearly two decades of experience in Barbados qualified him as one of the foremost experts in plantership, to design him a small sugar works.[8] He deployed his thirty-seven enslaved workers to plant twenty or thirty acres of sugarcane. While the crop matured, he planned to supervise those same people in the construction of a mill, boiling and curing houses, and a distillery.[9] The Helyars expected to be harvesting cane by October

1672. These first canes, however, would be replanted to cultivate another forty acres in cane. If all went as planned, Cary hoped to mill and distill three acres of cane into rum to cover mounting costs.[10]

The option to produce rum before sugar at Bybrook Plantation only existed because of the experimentation that had previously taken place in Barbados. While the earliest Barbadian planters imported the workers, cane, and stills necessary for rum production separately, Helyar established his plantation with all three essential ingredients in hand. Rather than creating a new system of commodity production, he was able to rely on the Modyfords and other planters who had honed their expertise in Barbados. Some of the individuals he enslaved were previously carried through other parts of the Caribbean, likely including Barbados.[11] Beyond the material and intellectual ingredients necessary for rum production to commence so quickly in Jamaica, the business model that planters followed was also Barbadian in origin. Again and again, Cary Helyar explained how he planned to begin making rum and eventually sugar on a small scale and with relatively few enslaved workers. As he harvested sugarcane, processed it into rum, and sold it to cover expenses, he would reinvest his profits in buying more land and people. Noting the provenance of this idea, Helyar referred to this deliberate way of building and expanding a plantation as the "Barbados custom."[12]

However, local realities ensured that rum production on the island developed a character distinct from the Barbados industry. Most immediately, Helyar's decision to produce rum before sugarcane required him to amend his definition of rum. Explaining the novel beverage to his brother, he stipulated that "rum is a spirit distilled out of juice of canes, also out of the skimmings of coppers."[13] On Barbados plantations that possessed the infrastructure to boil sugar, distilling the cane juice would have shrunk the economic potential of sugar production, but in early Jamaica it was sometimes the most profitable option. By the late 1680s, Jamaican planters probably refrained from mixing cane syrup and waste products in their distilleries, but they nonetheless fermented and distilled materials including parts of the cane and molasses that their Barbadian counterparts did not. Jonathan Taylor noted in 1687 that Jamaican plantations "cut off about four foot of the lower part of the cane for sugar," while they reserved the rest of the plant for rum. Molasses, too, could be collected and "put in the steep cistern amongst the skimmings in order to be distilled for rum."[14] Saving these other waste products allowed Jamaican planters to eventually realize a higher rum yield per hogshead of sugar produced. By the end of the 1680s, Jamaica exported 24,605 liters of rum per year.[15]

Jamaica's still houses also relied less on European distillers or overseers than their Barbadian tutors. Helyar depended on enslaved people to carry out this work. Enslaved distillery workers appropriated some of the rum that they had made for their own uses. A hired overseer wrote to Helyar's heirs in July 1702 that he needed to fire an employee who "has ill-counseled your Negroes and other people from my obedience and allows the Negroes rum and [to] trade with it contrary to my order or knowledge."[16] This rum could be consumed as a form of escapism or a means to resist the subjugation on which slavery was built, used for rituals carried from West Africa or devised in the West Indies, or exchanged for other desirable goods or services.[17]

Some of these uses for rum may have originated on the Gold Coast, transported and given new life by enslaved people from the region who formed the largest fraction of Jamaica's population.[18] Fante oral histories of the introduction of palm wine suggest the deep-seated importance of the naturally fermented sap of the palm tree. One such account explains that a Fante hunter named Ansā found a palm tree knocked over by an elephant and gave some of the sap to his dog. Convinced that it was not poisonous, Ansā tried it himself and "got fairly intoxicated." He brought a pot of the palm wine to the king, who drank the entire batch himself and passed out. Convinced that he had killed the king, Ansā committed suicide. In the aftermath of the tragedy, palm wine became known among Akan speakers as *Ansā* or *Nsā*.[19] This tradition's emphasis on solitary drinking as an antisocial behavior and alcohol's ability to transport one to a liminal state between life and death offer some insight into beliefs along this part of the Gold Coast surrounding palm wine. Such priorities shaped mourning rituals where the family of the deceased would fast for days except for drinking palm wine as they sought to ease the journey from life to death. They would then renew their ties to ancestors during subsequent festivals by sprinkling alcohol on the ground. Alcohol also factored into rituals surrounding life milestones including birth, naming, puberty, and marriage.[20]

After rum became available in West Africa in the late seventeenth century, the Fante incorporated the spirit into similar practices. According to tradition, Mmoro, the "principal fisherman of Mowure," facilitated the sale of the first cargo of rum in that town. The Fante began to call the rum *mmoro-nsā*, attaching the fisherman's name to the word traditionally used to describe palm wine.[21] The adaptation of a familiar word suggests that many of the cultural uses for palm wine were adapted for rum. Indeed, the two alcohols were often used interchangeably. While men conducting business with slave traders in coastal cities received rum in exchange for their labor, most rum remained in the hands of elite merchants and political leaders and continued to be consumed for ceremonial purposes.[22]

Individuals forced from the Gold Coast to Jamaica transported and gave new life to certain understandings of rum worked out in Africa. In Kromanti—the language spoken by Jamaican Maroons—rum assumed a Fante name: *insa*.[23] Furthermore, mourners along the Gold Coast and in Jamaica both incorporated rum into their funerary practices. When Jean Barbot witnessed burials around the Brandenburg Fort in the early eighteenth century, he noted that "as soon as the corpse is let down into the grave," Fante mourners "drank palm-wine, or rum, plentifully."[24] When he visited Jamaica in 1687, Hans Sloane observed that after the death of an enslaved African "their country people make great lamentations, mournings, and howlings about them expiring, and at their funeral throw in rum and victuals into their graves, to serve them in the other world. Sometimes they bury it in gourds, at other times spill it on graves."[25] The emphasis on rum consumption as part of mourning ceremonies and spilt rum easing the transition of the deceased bears some resemblance to funerary practices observed among the Akan, though Sloane's descriptions are too vague to support any definitive conclusions.

It is also possible that enslaved Africans and the communities that they were ripped from fostered connections with departed kin through the consumption of rum. In the early twentieth century, the anthropologist Melville Herskovitz observed a Dahomey ceremony to honor one of the dead kings of the Aladahonu dynasty. A part of the prayer asked that "the Americans must bring the cloths and the rum made by our kinsmen who are there, for these will permit us to smell their presence."[26] At least 263 slaving voyages carried over 80,000 people from the Bight of Benin to Jamaica. Perhaps rum's common path from West Indian plantations to West African slave castles increased its power to facilitate reunions with dislocated ancestors.[27]

Seventeenth-century plantation operators in Jamaica pioneered new techniques of control to make it harder for the enslaved to seize rum of their own manufacture. Overseers dumped their chamber pots into the fermenting cisterns in order "to keep the Negroes from drinking it."[28] Making the undistilled rum wash unappetizing to those producing it attempted to discourage theft and minimize the need for constant surveillance. That such a practice was necessary once again shows how Jamaica's enslaved rum producers pursued their own uses for the commodity that they were forced to make. The rum that the enslaved claimed for themselves could be a source of profit, but individually consuming it in spaces and ways that they themselves decided also, as Stephanie Camp has described for a later period, "undermined slaveholders' claims to their bodies and their time."[29]

Plantation operators also dispensed limited quantities of rum as a form of control. Enslaved Native Americans—some of whom were Pocasset and Wampanoag prisoners captured and sentenced to transportation during King Philip's War—received rum from their enslavers "now and then." Families of enslaved Africans collected a standard ration of a quart of rum each Saturday afternoon.[30] Cary Helyar also dispensed additional rum to the enslaved in celebration of Christmas.[31] These rum rations offered much-needed calories to their recipients, as well as limited access to the physiological and spiritual effects of its consumption.

The Jamaica Council, through several laws in the 1680s, reinforced the power of enslavers—and enslavers alone—to patrol what their slaves drank. Following "some little disturbance" that occurred at a Saturday evening market organized by enslaved Jamaicans in Passage Fort in May 1685, Jamaica's leaders sought to shut down these sorts of gatherings. They suppressed future markets, commissioned English colonists to patrol their likely sites, and issued reminders of the impropriety of selling "rum or any other strong liquors" to Black Jamaicans.[32] Five years later, when several residents complained that illicit rum sales continued, the council ordered the night guard in Spanish Town to punish "hucksters and others who sell rum, sugar, or other commodities to Negroes on the Sabbath day."[33]

Laws meant to limit the purchase of rum by enslaved people in Jamaica were passed at a time when the Jamaica Council fretted over the presence and power of a self-emancipated, African-descended population on the island.[34] In the late seventeenth century, groups of recently arrived Fante people escaped from slavery and fled to Jamaica's forested interior. Once they established homes in the island's interior, the Maroons acquired goods—including rum—by stealing from plantations and trading with individuals who remained enslaved on them.[35] Their success in resisting slavery, along with the threat that a nearby free Black population posed to the social and economic order of island sugar plantations, scared sugar planters and their allies in the colonial government.[36] After a bloody and costly war that aimed to extirpate the Maroons, colonial officials and Maroon leaders signed a peace treaty in 1739. According to several accounts, the parties sealed the treaty by drinking a mixture of their blood and rum. Just as rum cemented business dealings and marital unions along the Gold Coast, Maroons in twentieth-century Jamaica remembered solidifying a crucial colonial-era treaty with it.[37]

Jamaica's elites also fretted over how the island's white population consumed rum. In the years that Cary Helyar engineered a switch from cacao cultivation to the manufacture of sugar and rum, observers began to comment on the saturation of Port Royal with foreign and domestic liquors. In 1663, Jamaica's governor complained that the city's merchants prioritized alcohol over necessities, and by 1668 the Jamaica Council sought to address "impertinent disputes of lawyers and readers, not seldom coming drunk into the court."[38] Port Royal's role as a haven for privateers meant that illicit profits funded alcoholic binges in the fledgling city.[39] One eighteenth-century raconteur recalled privateers staving pipes of wine, forcing passersby to drink, and spraying women down with the alcohol.[40] By 1670, Jamaica's domestic rum industry contributed to the vast quantities of alcohol being bought and sold in the city. In addition to more than a hundred licensed houses selling spirits, John Style reported to Whitehall that sugar and rum manufactories on the island sold rum license-free. He estimated that "there is not now resident upon this place ten men to every house that selleth strong liquors."[41] Unregulated alcohol sales stoked fears that unscrupulous sellers would exchange in stolen goods trafficked by enslaved and coerced workers.

The surge in available spirits precipitated by the arrival of rum production to Jamaica sparked frequent complaints about the depravity of island society. The most common gripe was that Jamaicans would drink at inopportune times and in excessive amounts. Style worried that the profligacy of European-descended Jamaicans led to financial ruin for many living in Port Royal. Impoverished from their drinking, Jamaicans resorted to privateering, sex work, or debt peonage.[42] Taylor wrote of a former priest famous for "preaching o'er a lusty bowl of rum punch." He also complained of merchants leaving their workplaces for Port Royal's taverns each day at noon, and island-born men of European descent stalking the streets, ready to "booze a cup of punch rumby with anyone."[43]

Commentators frequently suggested that overconsumption of rum in Jamaica bred sexual deviance. Taylor decried plantation owners with "brains surfeited with the steam of rum punch" passing their time with "creolian ladies."[44] Taylor's reference to "creolian ladies"—implying the women were of mixed race—suggested that the consumption of alcohol led colonial elites to transgress racial boundaries, openly consorting with women with whom sexual relationships usually took place in private. Port Royal's taverns also mixed alcohol and prostitution. Mary Carleton, a con artist transported to Port Royal where she engaged in prostitution in the early 1670s, wrote that Jamaicans had "almost deluged this place in liquor."[45] Pointing to the licentiousness of Port Royal's maritime community, Governor Hender Molesworth reported on the marriage of a pirate named Captain Bear to "a strumpet" who was the daughter of a "nobleman" and "a rum-punch-woman of Port Royal."[46] Observers linked the unbridled consumption of rum in Port Royal to behaviors that transgressed sexual mores.

Drunkenness also led to threats and outright violence. As he sought to oust privateer–turned–deputy governor Henry Morgan from his government position, Thomas Lynch complained of "his debauches, (which is every day and night) with 5 or 6 little sycophants." According to Lynch, Morgan and his brother Charles had "set up a peculiar club" that passed its time in drink.[47] They found themselves in hot water on the evening of October 3, 1683, as Jamaicans celebrated the defeat of the Rye House Plot. Morgan's cronies clashed with a group of celebrants at Charles and Mary Barre's tavern. An enslaved man threw a lit fuse onto the balcony of the tavern. Enraged by the episode, and further affected by generous toasts to the king's health, Charles Morgan descended the stairs with a pistol in each hand. Morgan angrily inquired about which "whiggish son of a whore" had launched the projectile. The ensuing brawl left a number of Port Royal residents severely injured.[48] To those looking for it, this episode offered further evidence of a leader and a city that had lost their way.

The drunkenness, privateering, promiscuity, and violence exacerbated by an ever-growing supply of rum led many observers to allude to the biblical story of Sodom. As early as 1670, Style noted that the people of Sodom would find themselves "matched, if not outdone, in all evil and wickedness" by Port Royal's Christian inhabitants.[49] To many, the metaphor seemed all the more apt after a devastating June 1692 earthquake sent much of the city crumbling into the nearby harbor. Shortly after the earthquake, a minister in the city worried that "yet for all these great disasters, great numbers of people are not at all reformed of their wickedness, which brought this upon us, but there is the same whoring and drinking, the same cursing and swearing, if not worse than formerly." If this behavior continued unchecked, he concluded, "The judgment of *Sodom* will be the next punishment you will hear of."[50]

These criticisms of the destruction unleashed by rum on Port Royal may have been place-specific, but the similarities to conversations around drunkenness unfolding elsewhere are unmistakable.[51] Observers blamed the people they thought were especially prone to drunkenness. They altered how they made rum in an effort to restrict unregulated consumption among enslaved people. They pointed out working-class people resorting to lives of crime when they could not otherwise pay for their rum. They feared for the breakdown of families and traditional gender roles. And they decried moments where social order and decency decayed. Some individuals believed these circumstances provoked an angry response from God. Others, like Charles Leslie, pointed toward the Antichrist.

As he wrote in the early eighteenth century, Leslie noted the aptness of rum previously being called *kill devil* because "thousands lose their lives by its means."[52] Of course, the profusion of rum affected Jamaica's leading port city in unique ways. But the most audible complaints concerning economic damage, breakdowns in order, and death point to a wider process of communities around the Atlantic responding to the invention of rum with fear and often unsuccessful attempts to limit its reach.

A "Noisome" Commodity in North America

As colonial elites in Jamaica warned that the overconsumption of rum posed an existential threat to the hierarchies on which they built their society, their compatriots in North America coordinated to bring Caribbean molasses—and industrial processes of converting it into rum—to colonies from Pennsylvania to Massachusetts. Rum purchased from the West Indies combined with rum that distillers began to produce themselves to sate the thirst of American colonists, as well as the Native nations with whom they negotiated and traded and on whom they depended. Desires to profit off of and enjoy the upstart commodity led colonial and Indigenous Americans alike to embrace rum even as they reckoned with how destabilizing it could be.

Alcohol production seemed almost purpose-built for the temperate parts of seventeenth-century North America. The lands that colonists initially settled on held plentiful fuel but unclear prospects for cash crops. Some early settlers therefore purchased copper stills from England beginning early in the seventeenth century. The first generation of distillers focused on converting plentiful local grain and fruit harvests into spirits. By the 1640s, several individuals, including Walter Edmands (who apprenticed with a London distiller) and Emmanuel Downing, had opened grain distilleries in Massachusetts. Short growing seasons in New England and the size of the stills in use ensured that these early distilleries remained small endeavors, and the distillery owners split their time between alcohol production and other economic activities including haberdashery and cobbling.[53]

Similar patterns held farther south in the Dutch colony of New Netherland. The founder of Rensselaerswyck Manor, Kiliaen van Rensselaer, wrote in the summer of 1632 that he planned to facilitate the construction of a brandy distillery as soon as grain had been planted. Two years later, Rensselaer shipped a new "brandy kettle for distilling brandy from my surplus grain" to New Netherland

and contracted with Jacob Albertsz Planck to handle the technical work. Rensselaer expected that his agents would sell the liquor to company men, local Mohicans, and, once a sloop was procured, "adjacent settlements."[54]

By 1660, Massachusetts distillers began to focus their efforts on distilling Caribbean molasses into a local variant of rum. Because the Massachusetts distilleries were located more than two thousand miles from the Lesser Antilles, they imported molasses rather than the fresh juice of damaged canes or skimmings. Molasses lacked some of the natural flavors and sucrose content of skimmings, which caused New England rum to lag behind its Caribbean counterparts in terms of quality.[55] But given limited alternative uses for the cheap sweetener, New England merchants appreciated the ready supply and low prices. Thomas Ruck, who traded with the Drax family and outfitted ships to trade foodstuffs for sugar in Barbados by 1648, began retailing spirits from Boston in 1653 and became a licensed distiller in 1658. Likewise, a London merchant named Simon Lynde settled in Boston by 1650 and bought a brewery (which he then converted to a distillery), a warehouse, and a wharf in the city in 1653. While Lynde continued to focus on trade to the West Indies, he hired a distiller to turn his imports into New England rum.[56] Distillery owners and operators attracted the disdain of Massachusetts' governing bodies by 1661 when the general court complained of abuses by retailers of rum and "by the distillers thereof" and outlawed liquor sales smaller than a quarter cask.[57] Legislating against small liquor transactions was one popular way to price laboring people out of the alcohol trade.

Early returns were encouraging. In 1674, a merchant in Barbados admitted to John Winthrop, governor of the Massachusetts Bay Colony, that molasses was "vendible in no part of the world but New England and Virginia" and assured him that he would encourage its shipment to Massachusetts.[58] Driven by the ready supply of West Indies molasses that could be readily acquired in exchange for local foodstuffs and lumber, North American distillers expanded their enterprises. They moved their businesses from family homes into dedicated, single-purpose distilleries. Furthermore, rather than continue to depend on family labor—and often the expertise of white women—these distillers began to acquire enslaved men to produce rum. For instance, Philip Squire's 1693 probate inventory listed "2 Negroes" among the contents of his distillery. Another Boston distiller named Michael Shaller rented an enslaved man from a Portsmouth physician.[59] In distilling the refuse of West Indian sugars (in the form of molasses), building dedicated distilleries, and relying on enslaved labor, these distilleries followed the lead of the Barbadian inventors of rum and their Jamaican acolytes.

Although these distillers' use of sugar by-products and embrace of progressively larger scales of production staffed by enslaved people resembled their Caribbean forerunners, North Americans made other adjustments to respond to local realities. Because the bulkiest ingredients were shipped to, rather than grown in, North America, these producers stuck to navigable waterways and built their distilleries in port cities. While planters in the West Indies had to balance rum production with the other needs of their plantations, urban producers focused on making their stand-alone rum distilleries as profitable and efficient as possible.

Around the time that these distilleries took hold, Puritan clergyman Increase Mather and his son Cotton Mather warned against a "flood of rum."[60] They noted how drunkenness transgressed several of the Ten Commandments and other biblical teachings. Cotton Mather suggested that even those who avoided overconsumption could still become "enslaved unto the bottle of drink."[61] Soldiers became ineffective, and otherwise healthy colonists grew sick. He went so far as to suggest that wanton consumption of rum might explain "why our fields are so meanly cultivated and are not able to feed us."[62] In a 1712 reprint of two 1673 sermons on drinking, Increase Mather furthermore suggested that the "*English men* who call themselves *Christians* have debauched the miserable Indians with it; of which there have been some tragical effects."[63] Father and son prayed for "this branch of the *Dead Sea*" to recede and implored wealthier parishioners—and certainly ministers—to abstain from rum, but both men understood that public houses selling rum would remain.[64]

For the most part, then, burgeoning supplies of both local and Caribbean rum provided would-be consumers with large quantities of alcohol and new choices regarding what they would drink. Most drinkers in the Atlantic world had limited experience with the bitterness and burning sensation—as well as the inebriation—imparted by distillates since they only became widely available and affordable in the seventeenth century. When Haudenosaunee, Lenape, and Wampanoag consumers initially encountered rum, they may have been tasting alcohol for the first time as their nations had not produced or traded for alcohol prior to European contact.[65] The fact that Europeans, Africans, and Native Americans alike had limited experience making and consuming beverages of the strength and low cost of rum opened the door for an enhanced period of experimentation regarding who should consume alcohol, in what quantities, and at what cost. In short, an array of producers, traders, and consumers continued the work of inventing and defining rum.

For some drinkers, rum replaced other traditional alcohols. For instance, laborers in parts of West Africa and England traditionally received grain-based ferments from the property owners whose lands they cleared, planted, and harvested.[66] This mutually understood practice continued with rum in North America throughout the seventeenth and eighteenth centuries. As late as 1793, George Washington noted to his farm manager that "although others are getting out of the practice of using spirits at harvest, yet, as my people have always been accustomed to it, a hogshead of rum must be purchased."[67] The recognition among enslaved and enslaver alike that agricultural work demanded a ration of alcohol had both African and European antecedents older than rum itself.

Sometimes a drinking practice from one part of the Atlantic world gained new adherents elsewhere. Wherever they colonized, the English brought taverns with them. Africans, Indigenous Americans, and Europeans frequented these spaces as they provided access to affordable rum, companionship, and accommodations. Taverns popping up in the Americas and in coastal African cities to serve new distillates such as rum introduced what one historian has termed "a veritable Atlantic creole drinking culture" to a web of far-flung places.[68]

There was also considerable cultural creation surrounding rum consumption in this era. In northeastern North America, Indigenous Americans and colonists negotiated the roles that alcohol would fulfill within their intersecting societies. Together they determined rum's value as a trade good, its place in diplomacy, where it could be traded and consumed, and how its ill effects should be understood and mitigated. Sometimes they borrowed heavily from other contexts, while on other occasions they looked for wholly original solutions. Indigenous Americans, in particular, navigated their relationship with rum by exploring the shifting world around them and creating new cultural forms in response.[69] Native people simultaneously approached contests over rum as a means to protect economic vitality, self-determination, and sovereignty and as a profound threat to individual and collective survival.[70]

One of the first questions that colonial and Indigenous leaders confronted was whether Native people should be provided access to rum. In the same decades that rum distilleries set up shop in North America, many colonial governments experimented with bans specifically targeting Indigenous consumers. By 1671, the Dutch patroonship of Rensselaerswyck had updated their ban of transmitting alcohol to Native people to include rum.[71] The founding of Pennsylvania included stipulations outlawing the sale of alcohol, even though a treaty signed with the Lenape in the summer of 1682 included gifts of rum and accoutrements with which to drink it. Repetitions and adjustments to the law followed in 1684, 1687, and 1701, suggesting that the matter remained unsettled.[72]

Colonial governments could pass laws veiled in the language of protection—and sometimes in response to specific complaints lodged by Indigenous diplomats—that sought to limit the sale of rum to Native communities, but Native leaders made their own political and economic determinations as potential allies rather than as subjects whose reduction of status required them to abide by colonial laws. Their varied decisions were powerful assertions of sovereignty. In 1653, the Narragansett sachem Ninnigrett brokered an alliance that included the Dutch, as well as the recently reconciled sachems, Pomham and Succanoco, predicated in part on commodities sold "at half the price the English sell them," ready access to gunpowder and ammunition, and "strong liquors without limits."[73] And in 1678, Thomas Mayhew fretted over drunkenness among the Wampanoag on Martha's Vineyard, singling out Rhode Island traders who supplied them with rum.[74] Native people continued to assert their agency to make decisions about what they would consume for themselves by choosing to receive gifts of or trade for a substance whose taste, physiological effects, and economic potential they appreciated.

The profusion of rum produced in North America by English colonists offered added incentive for this branch of trade and diplomacy to prevail. Cheap, locally produced distillates derived from refuse molasses could substantially undercut prices for the wine-derived brandy touted by French mercantilists. A colonist in New York explained in 1724, however, that the brandy held "no more value with the Indians" than rum.[75] New York's commission for Indian Affairs reported three years later that French officials had begun lobbying Native polities "to prevent the selling of rum," likely as a result of these differing conceptions of value.[76] A decade later, still without a consistent rum supply, French agents switched course. New York's Indian commissioners learned in the spring of 1736 that a French translator named Jean Coeur was purchasing rum from the trading post at Oswego and giving it to the Seneca "in order to promote his influence and the French designs amongst them."[77] New York's commissioners responded swiftly, introducing a law that prohibited the sale of rum to the French as a means to protect the Haudenosaunee from the scourge of alcohol.[78]

Native sachems began to associate the English with plentiful stores of rum and used it to wring more out of their counterparts in diplomacy. At a 1744 treaty negotiation in the Lancaster courthouse between representatives of the Haudenosaunee and Maryland, Virginia, and Pennsylvania colonial officials, the Onondaga sachem Conassatego took center stage. He noted, "You tell us you beat the French; if so, you must have taken a great deal of rum from them, and can the better spare us some of that liquor to make us rejoice with you in the victory." The colonists acquiesced, serving the delegation small drams of rum in "French" glasses. The following day, Conassatego acknowledged the previous day's gift of rum but prodded, "It turned out unfortunately that you gave us it in French glasses, we now desire you will give us some in English glasses." Despite running low on their supply, the colonial negotiators again served their guests rum, this time in bigger glasses meant to show "the difference between the narrowness of the French, and the generosity of your brethren the English."[79] Colonists and Haudenosaunee alike increasingly defined rum as a highly desirable English commodity.

European and Indigenous negotiators sought to construct a longer tradition of rum consumption in an effort to define its presence in their communities. As they worked to define where rum could be sold in the fall of 1728, a delegation of two sachems from each of the Haudenosaunee nations noted how their "ancestors" had acquired rum from the English settlement at Albany.[80] And as the negotiation continued into 1730, New York authorities took a similar tack when the commissioners noted that this trade had gone on since "time out of mind."[81] Inventing a history of rum and its consumption allowed representatives to advocate their preferred policies as a continuation of tradition.

Invoking a long history of rum trade and consumption evinced a belief among many that alcohol would remain part of Indigenous-colonial trade and diplomacy for the foreseeable future. Negotiators who positioned themselves as inheritors of this tradition suggested that through shared experience they had arrived at an understanding of the physical and psychoactive effects of rum consumption. They likewise knew what it should taste and look like and the quantities that they could expect in trade. Such knowledge prepared Native consumers to detect—and speak out against—deviations from what they anticipated. Indicating their fluency regarding the standard qualities of rum—especially regarding taste and strength—Native envoys often complained about watered-down alcohol.[82] Sachems representing the Haudenosaunee protested in 1726 that the adulteration of rum around Oswego created a concoction that "stinks and is noisome."[83] Such complaints rested on a shared understanding between all parties of what rum should taste like and what its alcoholic content should be.

An acknowledgment of rum's utility in trade and diplomacy does not detract from the negative qualities that Native people attributed to rum, as can be seen in the causes and course of King Philip's War. In a nuanced description of the causes of the conflict between the United Colonies and Native nations in the Northeast, Rhode Island lieutenant governor John Easton shared Metacom's explanation of two interlocking ways in which colonists' deployment of rum in trade contributed to a deteriorating relationship. First, colonists overserved Wampanoag neighbors and cheated them out of land. As two petitioners named Deogenes and Madoasquarbet wrote to the "governor of Boston" in 1677, "We love you but when we are drunk you will take away our cots and throw us out of door."[84] Easton also noted that when Native men drank to the point of inebriation, they preyed on "sober Indians" and "hurt the English cattle" in ways that their leaders struggled to prevent.[85] As the outbreak of the war brought into focus, the rum trade contributed to the expropriation of Indigenous property, tensions over land use, and the erosion of Indigenous authority.

Over the course of King Philip's War, rum's paired role as both an accessory in acts of wanton violence and a tool of fellowship and diplomacy played out. In 1676, Major Richard Waldron sentenced to either execution or enslavement a group of Native people who had gathered in Cocheco believing that they would be pardoned for past actions. Deogenes and Madoasquarbet succinctly explained Waldron's method in betraying and defeating a numerically superior group of Natives: "He gave us drink and when we were drunk killed us."[86] Yet colonists and Natives also continued to rely on rum in diplomacy. Before a tense negotiation securing her alliance, Benjamin Church offered a Sakonnet sachem named Awashonks rum. Awashonks initially refused, but after Church invited her to drink repeatedly and demonstrated that the rum was not poisoned, she took "a good hearty dram, and passed it among her attendants."[87] Leaders like Awashonks could recall plentiful examples of colonists deploying rum toward destructive ends, but also saw its utility as a substance that was capable of facilitating cross-cultural negotiations or was simply enjoyable.

Colonists also fretted over the loss of social order occasioned by Native people drinking to what settlers deemed to be excess. Along the Delaware River in 1680, they complained about a local tavern keeper who regularly sold rum to the Lenape. They would quickly consume the alcohol and then "revel and fight together and then they come furiously and break our fences and steal our corn and break our windows and doors and carry away our goods."[88] Colonists expressed even greater concern when the victims of such violent outbursts were other people of European descent. After an Onondaga man murdered Jacob Brower in 1730, New York authorities expressed their frustration over the unfortunate turn of events. They took particular aim at Natives' social response of blaming the rum rather than the person for any transgressions while in drink. The commissioners leaned on Haudenosaunee leaders to adopt the British perspective that drunkenness was not a legal defense for criminal behavior.[89]

Attempts to lure Native people into predatory exchanges and subsume them under colonial law were symptoms of another trend that Native leaders actively resisted: the rum trade threatening their autonomy. The Haudenosaunee noted that traders offered them plenty of overpriced rum for their furs but little of the ammunition, foodstuffs, clothing, or other supplies that they now deemed necessary for daily life.[90] In addition to internal disputes caused in moments of inebriation, sachems worried that disruptions to hunting and the volatility of trade caused by the amount of rum in Indian country would lead to civil wars and the breakdown in relationships between Native groups.[91] For instance, Conrad Weiser visited with Native men along the Susquehanna River who passed on the vision of a seer that "*rum* will kill us and leave the land clear for the Europeans without strife or purchase."[92]

By the mid-eighteenth century, increasing numbers of Native sachems and seers began to advocate for avoiding rum—or at least drunkenness. In June 1748, the Oneida sachem Shikellamy sent a delegation to meet with Pennsylvania authorities who worried about French advances south of the Great Lakes. When, as was common during these sorts of diplomatic missions, the British offered their counterparts rum, the Haudenosaunee delegates refused. The Council of Cayuga explained, "We have drunk too much of your rum already, which has occasioned our destruction; we will, therefore, for the future beware of it."[93] Previous experiences with rum had convinced these men to proceed with caution.

Some Native people hoped by midcentury that nonconsumption would become a collective—rather than an individual—undertaking. In the midst of the Seven Years' War, the Lenape prophet Neolin shared a series of visions. In one, an eight-day journey led to an encounter with the Master of Life. Neolin shared that the Master of Life told him, "The land where you dwell I have made for you and not for others. Whence comes it that you permit the whites upon your lands? Can you not live without them?"[94] A Quaker fur trader in Pennsylvania explained that Neolin's visions led him to warn of all the "sins and vices which the Indians have learned from the white people."[95] Neolin expected that eventually Native communities would cut off trade with the British, shutting off access to rum.[96] Yet the historian Gregory Dowd has compellingly argued that Neolin's teachings, which gained many adherents beyond Pennsylvania, "promoted reform, not rejection." While he opposed drunkenness, his vision was unlikely one of complete abstinence.[97] And Neolin's vision depended on the agency of Native people to forego rum rather than European colonists refusing to sell it.

By midcentury—less than a century after rum production began in North America—many Native people acknowledged that rum posed a threat to their existence in eastern North America. Yet most did not go so far as Native Americans would in the century that followed when the Shawnee prophet Tenskwatawa advocated for total abstinence and the Pequot intellectual William Apess described rum as "that burning, fiery curse."[98] Natives and Europeans might temporarily ban rum in the seventeenth or early eighteenth century, but the trade generally continued. Both groups recognized its social, economic, and political utility and explored ways to manage its presence to limit the very clear dangers that accompanied its use.

Managing the role of rum in colonial-Native relations required nuanced understandings that sometimes bewildered colonial authorities. Colonists expressed exasperation with what they regarded as inconsistencies on the part of Native leaders. When sachems representing the Haudenosaunee gathered in Albany in 1710, several members of the treaty party began consuming rum. New York authorities asked their Haudenosaunee counterparts to curtail the drinking, but the spokesperson replied that it was the New Yorkers' fault that they were drinking. They proceeded to repeat a request that they claimed to have made countless times: "that no rum may be hereafter sold upon any account."[99] Six years later, the Onondaga sachem Dekanissore found himself on the opposite side of the issue when he pressed to learn "who has requested the prohibition of rum." When reminded that he had in fact made the request, Dekanissore replied that they "now desired the prohibition might be now taken off."[100] Colonial officials noted the inconsistencies between requests for the abolition of the rum trade and sustained Indigenous drinking patterns. At Conestoga in 1721, William Keith declared that he "would gladly make any laws to prevent this that could be effectual, but the country is so wide, the woods are so dark and private, and so far out of my sight, that if the Indians themselves do not prohibit their own people there is no other way to prevent it."[101] By homing in on these sorts of contradictions, colonial officials myopically focused on internal divisions within Native polities or their prioritization of rum sales over social order.

However, the requests of sachems in the Northeast and beyond suggest that Native policies toward the rum trade prioritized the protection of Native spaces and economic advantage over a sustained social policy against drinking. More commonly than calling for an outright ban on Indigenous rum drinking, tribal leaders sought to limit where transactions took place. Representatives of the Haudenosaunee made this point explicit in a 1728 exchange. They stated that they did not want an outright ban on rum but rather a moratorium on the commodity being brought into their castles. Instead, Natives could fetch any unadulterated rum that they chose to buy at the Oswego truckhouse.[102] Similar patterns held true farther south in Pennsylvania. Speaking with colonial authorities after he tragically killed his uncle while intoxicated, Sassoonan begged that traders stop bringing large quantities of rum to the Lenape, suggesting instead that "if any Indians want it, they should come to Philadelphia for it."[103] By attempting to control the spaces where rum could or could not pass in these ways, Native people advanced claims of sovereignty over their own territories.[104]

Native leaders hoped that regulating where rum was exchanged would help them realize more favorable outcomes. Requests for trade to be centered in Oswego, for instance, came with hopes that the rum would remain unadulterated and the warehouse stocked with firearms, ammunition, and other "real necessaries."[105] Sachems suggested that issues would subside if a more honest and robust marketplace prevailed where consumers could expect fair exchanges for a wider array of goods.

Responses when agreed-upon restrictions failed similarly show their prioritization of community strength over an outright policy of abolishing rum. In the aftermath of Sawantaeny's death at the hands of John and Edmund Cartlidge in 1722, the Haudenosaunee sent a wampum belt depicting a small barrel and a hatchet accompanied with orders to "stave all rum they met with" down the Susquehanna.[106] Almost fifteen years later, this arrangement raised hackles, however, because colonial officials charged that "instead of taking from those who bring it and staving it, they take and drink it, which is both unjust in itself and does more mischief."[107] Contemporaries again blamed this on Native propensities for drunkenness, but acquiring rum without paying for it enriched the people who seized it. Though the language used to request such relief contributed to dialogues suggesting that Native people drank too much, Native leaders sometimes may have leveraged these emerging stereotypes and resultant policies to increase their supply of European goods at no added cost.

Colonial and Native leaders also haggled over whose responsibility it should be to regulate the rum trade. Europeans dwelt on the fact that the American backcountry was too porous for them to adequately patrol, while Native sachems insisted that those responsible for producing a commodity should also be tasked with managing its trade. As a delegation of Shawnees relayed to Alexander Johnson later in the eighteenth century, "It is you that make the liquor, and to you we must look to stop it; we find it is out of our power to do it."[108] But to many, managing the trade did not mean ending it. A Seneca leader named Kayashuta insisted in 1765 that as producers of rum, the colonists had a responsibility to make sure it was available for sale. He reasoned, "You make rum, and have taught us to drink it; you are fond of it yourselves; therefore, don't deprive us of it."[109] According to Kayashuta, colonists were duty-bound to ensure a supply of the quality rum that they made.

Colonial authorities' campaigns to regulate—or convince others to regulate—the rum trade in the North American interior were part of broader initiatives to keep individuals who were expected to perform work for them from drinking in ways that would disrupt that labor. As historian Michael Witgen observes, colonizing ventures invested in the fur trade did not incentivize assimilation because they depended on "Indians to continue living and working as Indians."[110] As a result, legal restrictions on drinking rum focused more on stabilizing Indigenous-colonial relationships and managing the supply of rum to maximize commodity production and trade than on eliminating alcohol consumption entirely.[111] Patrolling where alcohol was sold and working to steady prices in Native-claimed spaces served the economic and social goals of empire.

In the same ways that governors, legislatures, and commissioners tried to control how Native people consumed rum, they also occasionally pursued similar policies aimed at servants, slaves, iron workers, soldiers, and other laborers. Connecticut and Pennsylvania authorities heavily restricted the sale of alcohol in the vicinity of iron works.[112] Three years after a group of London Trustees founded the colony of Georgia as a bastion of exclusively free and coerced European labor in 1732, they amended the colony's charter to forbid the sale of rum and brandies, holding that it interfered with the "labor and discipline" of the earliest settlers.[113] And in 1747, New York governor George Clinton specifically forbade a man named Joseph Clements from selling liquor to "Indians or soldiers near Mount Johnson."[114] Fearing immense social changes engendered by the invention and profusion of rum, colonial authorities sometimes fought to dictate where and how subjects and nonsubjects alike drank rum.

Starting in the mid-seventeenth century, colonists and Natives in the Northeast encountered a commodity that was new to all parties. Colonists leveraged their experience consuming other alcoholic beverages, their connections to rum producers in other colonies, and the cheapness of the spirit to make inroads in trade and diplomacy. While now dependent on European trade goods, Native people gained regular access to physiological responses that could enhance traditional rituals of celebration and mourning, or inspire new ones, and which many at times sought out. Because each group of people had limited experience with the commodity, they challenged and sought to shift the social and economic meanings of rum held by the other. These efforts have often been interpreted as early evidence of a particularly destructive circumstance occasioned by Native people being unable to resist this aspect of colonialism. Most certainly, Indigenous Americans had culturally distinct understandings of alcohol, and many died from violence connected to drunkenness, starvation and overexposure caused by colonialism and uneven trade, or disease worsened by these factors. But contrary to the ethnic stereotype drawn by colonizers of unbridled consumption, Indigenous people chose to engage with—and, alternatively, forgo—rum. Moreover, the social panic that colonists predominantly located in Indian Country engulfed many parts of the Atlantic world, as an array of people, including elites and commoners in Britain itself, contended with the emergence of cheap, domestically produced, and readily available spirits for the first time.

Rum Lane

By the late seventeenth century, metropolitan entrepreneurs joined their overseas counterparts in making rum. English and Scottish sugar refineries churned out vast quantities of molasses and skimmings when refining sugar imported from the Caribbean. The decision to route these wastes to local distilleries—where they could be processed alone or mixed with grain-based distillates—pitted the economic potential of a new ingredient against traditional forms of control within the distilling industry. Initially, the economic value of molasses and sugar skimmings won out, bolstered by tax breaks and a relaxation in guild control. The rapid growth of distilling in Britain ensued. In the early eighteenth century, elites feared that the influx of molasses- and grain-based distillates led to drunkenness and a breakdown in social control. Sometimes making explicit comparisons to recent events in their colonies, these Britons joined a chorus of voices opposing the ongoing changes wrought by the invention of rum.

The emergence of rum production in England and Scotland both benefited from and accelerated the maturation of a metropolitan distilling industry. In 1637, London's distillers were incorporated as a company. A mere three years later, opponents observed the ill effects of distillates that were "so fierce and heady" that a pint could inebriate ten men and women.[115] By the end of the century, distilled spirits, including rum, held a price advantage over beer because of technological advancements in still construction, the availability of raw ingredients, and lower excise tax rates. England's lower classes decamped from alehouses to spirit sellers because distillates provided the same opportunity for sociability and inebriation that they traditionally sought out at a lower cost.[116]

When these distillers began experimenting with sugar and its by-products in the 1670s, they harnessed the economic potential of Atlantic trade to change metropolitan cultures of consumption. As in North America, the industry built on the region's economic relationship with Barbados and other burgeoning plantation societies. English and Scottish distillers only occasionally imported molasses or rum from abroad, however. Instead, sugar merchants focused their trade on buying semiprocessed sugars. To match the purity of foreign imports, refiners needed to remove additional molasses from the sugar. In response, a new industry of sugar refining took hold in port cities including London, Bristol, Glasgow, and Leith.[117] Refineries repeatedly reboiled imported sugars in a series of copper pans, extracting an additional round of skimmings and excess molasses. The leftover syrups ultimately comprised 30 percent of the volume of sugars brought into the refineries.[118] By 1679, London distillers mixed this molasses into their fermenting washes, introducing a form of rum production to England itself. According to an early eighteenth-century letter from Thomas Walduck of Barbados, embracing rum production paid dividends for the industry in Europe. As far as he was concerned, distilling had "never became a trade incorporated either in England or Holland, until sugar was made in America and they had molasses upon to make spirit."[119]

The coupled industries of sugar and rum production began their ascendance in Scotland around the same time. Between 1660 and 1707, Scotland encouraged domestic manufacturing by offering tax exemptions to qualifying businesses. Four Glaswegian merchants capitalized on favorable regulations to open the Wester Sugar house in 1667. Two years later, the Easter Sugar house began operating as a joint-stock partnership of five other merchants. In 1677, a "great promoter of manufactories" named Robert Douglas opened a sugary in nearby Leith. Each of these businesses successfully applied for a special status that allowed them to import any necessary supplies for their refineries tax-free.[120]

Sugar houses combined ingredients from around the Atlantic world. Scottish merchants carried on a direct trade with the West Indies at least as early as 1665. Around two ships per year arrived in Glasgow and Leith from the West Indies over the next twenty-five years, the majority from Barbados.[121] The owners frequently sent for other supplies and skilled sugar boilers from Rotterdam and other parts of continental Europe. Until the late 1670s, Scotland's sugar boilers shipped their refuse molasses and skimmings back to the Netherlands to acquire capital that could be used to purchase more sugar in London.[122]

Around 1680, Scottish industrialists began to ferment and distill their molasses locally rather than send it abroad. They made this change due to falling molasses prices and heightened enforcement of taxes on exported sweets.[123] The Wester Sugar house recorded forty-two sales of "Scottish" or "Glasgow" brandy in 1680, likely produced using the refinery's supply of sugary by-products.[124] In 1681, when the Glaswegian sugar houses' tax exemptions lapsed, they sent a new petition to Parliament, this time asking for their advantages to be extended to rum production as well. To the chagrin of local tax collectors, the new distilleries received their exemptions, but taxmen nonetheless seized a quantity of Scottish rum in 1684.[125]

This seizure sparked a dialogue between taxmen and producers that exposed both the concerns regarding—and potential for—the introduction of this form of commodity production transplanted from the West Indies. The tax collectors insisted that the distillers owed taxes on the rum because "the strong waters made of the molasses was unwholesome for men's health," the sugar refineries were turning usable sugars into spirits, and unscrupulous distillers were selling foreign brandy as Scottish rum in order to avoid paying taxes on the imports.

The petitioners systematically addressed these claims. First, they argued that "the molasses is looked upon as a very wholesome liquor in these countries and there is some thereof that comes near the fruit brandy . . . that it's scarce discerned or known from the finest of the foreign brandy." Second, the distillers pointed out that the rum was valuable precisely because the ingredients being distilled "will not be sugar." Finally, they vehemently denied that any foreign brandy was being sold as rum and offered to forfeit any spirits that were proven to be mislabeled in this manner. Reiterating the importance of their tax exemption, the distillers concluded by stressing that eliminating this benefit would lead Scotland's sugar and rum industry to total ruin.[126] Ultimately, the exchequer largely accepted the distillers' explanation.[127] The exchequer dictated, however, that any distillate removed from the distillery "must be marked with the word RUM."[128] The mandated label unequivocally established the linkages between the Scottish distilleries and their American counterparts in terms of what they made.

Despite producing a spirit called rum out of sugar's refuse, the burgeoning industries in England and Scotland differed from their compatriots across the Atlantic in several significant ways. Britain's proximity to and reliance on expertise and supplies from the Netherlands and Germany ensured that these sugar houses and distilleries maintained a closer relationship to continental European peers than did those in the West Indies and North America.[129] Likewise, the expense of these imported supplies led Scottish merchants to create partnerships to manage their sugar works and distilleries rather than relying on incremental growth as was the "Barbados custom." Finally, the Scottish sugar and rum producers typically depended on a hired—rather than enslaved—workforce of about a dozen men. Rum production in England and Scotland nonetheless drew ingredients and inspiration from overseas.

English political developments in 1688 and 1689 enhanced the value of molasses-based spirits produced in Britain even as they lessened the chances that the product would resemble or be called rum. Parliament outlawed the importation of French brandy in 1688. The following year, the Dutch-born William of Orange's coronation led Protestants to embrace Dutch *genever* as a replacement to French brandy. As they developed a taste for the new spirit, however, English society contended with the high costs of importing foreign-produced spirits.[130] Domestic manufacturers of distilled spirits responded by using ingredients from England and its colonies to mimic Dutch tastes while simultaneously embracing a vital lesson learned from rum: that distillation could fundamentally transform detritus into something consumable.

Replacing Dutch or French imports with domestically produced alternatives depended on a reliable base ingredient. England lacked the vineyards necessary to take on French brandy. And while the island grew plentiful amounts of grain, each boll of wheat or barley turned into alcohol could not be eaten. Farmers thus preferred to sell only low-grade grains to brewers and distillers. Distillers quickly realized that England's Caribbean colonies—and the burgeoning sugar and molasses trade that they carried on—provided another ingredient for alcohol. Distillers and merchants banded together to champion alcohol resurrected from the trash heap, and many Britons believed that sugar-based spirits held the greatest potential for the future of Britain's distilleries. Taking arguments initially applied to rum suggesting that dregs could be transformed into merchantable spirits through fermentation and distillation a step further, others suggested that mixing molasses spirits with low-grade grain spirits would mask the flavors of other damaged goods.[131] The economic benefits were vast, Thomas Tryon argued. They would ensure the "employment for many thousands in England itself," including distillers, coopers, and shop owners.[132]

Prospective rum distillers in Scotland listed other advantages. When seeking permission to set up a sugar refinery and rum distillery in 1701, Matthew and Daniel Campbell earmarked their produce "for trade for the coast of Guinea and America" because "no trade can be managed to the places foresaid or the East Indies without great quantities of the foresaid liquors."[133] Two years later, William Cochran and his business partners suggested that the "distilling of rum" would ensure a steady supply of drink for Scottish consumers despite wartime shortages.[134] By producing a waste-derived liquor that could reduce imports and bolster exports, these distillers argued that their manufacture of molasses-based spirits would enrich Scotland's economy.

Not everybody celebrated the expansion of rum production in England and Scotland. In 1690, the Company of Distillers of London lost much of its regulatory power.[135] According to Daniel Defoe, an occasional ally of the distillers' guild, untrained "petty distillers" broke into the industry with an inferior product composed of "mixed and confused trash," including molasses, "damaged sugars," soured wine, and other detritus.[136] They began to use the cheapest spirits and ingredients available to produce English gin, or geneva, which they quickly defined as a cheap spirit meant to approximate the piney flavor of Dutch genever.[137] Certain profit-minded gin producers went so far as to replace the juniper berries with oil of turpentine.[138] Some compound distillers likewise added the signature gin botanicals to molasses instead of grain spirits.[139] In response to loosening regulations, spirit production in England quadrupled between 1684 and 1714.[140] The market share for molasses spirits and rum also grew. Whereas molasses and other imported materials only made up 13.7 percent of the low wines produced in England in the 1690s, it comprised 22 percent of the distillates in the 1700s and 1710s.[141] The by-products of sugar contributed to the rapid growth of distilled spirits in Britain, as did an emerging ethos that distillers could remake superfluous matter into something valuable.

New ingredients and a vastly expanded distilling industry led to falling costs for distillates in Britain, which lured many working-class Britons to this stronger category of alcohols. One London cleric and influential critic of gin suggested in 1736 that 400,000 of approximately 650,000 Londoners drank regularly.[142] The amount of gin that they consumed had more than doubled in the preceding thirty years. By the 1720s, the average person consumed as much as a pint of gin per day.[143] Working-class people now consumed large quantities of a commodity that a generation earlier had largely been outside of their means. Guild leaders in London decried "liquors of a very mean quality," which could now be "afforded for less than half the price they had before been usually sold for."[144] Defending the ways in which affordable spirits democratized access, "A man of Kent" pointed to the hypocrisy of looking down upon laborers taking a "cheerful glass in his own way," given heavy drinking among elites.[145]

Critiques of gin (some of which amounted to juniper-infused rum) often dwelt on what writers perceived to be the harm it caused to Britain's working class. Thomas Wilson suggested that compound spirits were troubling markers of "luxury and extravagance" among working people and signs of a general decay of traditional class structures. He furthermore worried that landowners now struggled to exact rent out of a "drunken ungovernable set of people." Wealth that had traditionally filtered up to the landed elite now became waylaid in gin shops.[146] A judge named Henry Fielding worried that if "drinking this poison be continued in its present height during the next twenty years, there will, by that time, be very few of the common people left to drink it."[147] Together, these writers repeated arguments circulating throughout a drunken Atlantic world that laboring people were overconsuming alcohol, rendering them less capable of working for their social betters.

As had often been the case in both North America and Jamaica, critics singled out overindulging women. Wilson and Defoe advanced rumors of mothers and nurses feeding their children gin rather than milk. Defoe worried that tainted breast milk combined with childhood alcohol consumption would beget "a fine spindle-shanked generation" of Englishmen.[148] Stephen Hales, one of several proponents of liquor reform in England who also served as trustees for the fledgling colony of Georgia, looked toward Native North America to explain how the new raft of distilled spirits caused declining birth rates. He included excerpts of a letter from a Maryland clergyman who wrote of barren women dooming the colony's Native population. In his eyes, "a good part of their present decrease and unfruitfulness" could be blamed on the excessive consumption of rum.[149]

Hales's interests in culling evidence of the pernicious effects of rum consumption to warn against wanton gin drinking demonstrates how colonists and Britons made sense of new distillates and the social dynamics of their consumption by comparing their experiences to others in the Atlantic world. The ideas traveled the other direction, too, as evidenced by Hales's role in outlawing rum and other distillates in the fledgling colony of Georgia. Similarly, the August 2, 1736, edition of the *Pennsylvania Gazette* repurposed a parliamentary report to warn colonists of the ill effects of drunkenness. Linking moral panic in London and the North American colonies, a prefatory note from "P.P." contended that "our rum does the same mischief in proportion, as their geneva."[150]

Gin's critics also pointed out other instances of what they considered to be antisocial behavior occasioned by drunkenness. Wilson attributed a rash of murders, robberies, and arsons to this "deluge of vice and immorality."[151] Defoe worried that gin served as a gateway to greater problems. He claimed that workers spiraled downward from drunkenness to unemployment to criminality.[152] Reminiscent of Haudenosaunee tendencies to blame the rum rather than the person for crimes committed while in drink, Henry Fielding recalled defendants who entered his courtroom to answer for crimes "that the gin alone was the cause of the transgression" and expressed regret that he "was obliged to commit them to prison."[153] Along with the scene subsequently depicted in Hogarth's *Gin Lane*, these tracts joined writings from other corners of Britain's Atlantic world in claiming that new spirits conjured from low-quality ingredients made subjects ungovernable.

Many social reformers trying to downplay the wide-ranging economic ramifications of temperance attributed the rapid expansion in alcohol consumption to spirits derived from grains grown in Britain, but defenders of the distilleries consistently noted the role of molasses-based distillates in soaring consumption rates. One writer claimed that sugar bakers ultimately sold one-ninth of the volume of the sugars imported into Britain to distillers. The anonymous writer suggested that regulating distilleries risked destroying the sugar colonies as well as Britain's refining industry.[154] Likewise, a distiller's apprentice writing under the pseudonym "Jack Juniper" released a play costarring Queen Gin and her "cousins" the Duke of Rum and the Marquis de Nantes (representing brandy).[155] That same year, a defender of the British distilleries asserted that more than just gin should be outlawed if Parliament was indeed seeking to promote temperance. In his estimation, "To make the scheme complete, we must also prohibit Arrack, for the consumption of the better sort, and rum for the rest . . . without which restraint drunkenness would still have footing among us."[156] These apologists sought to improve the reputation of gin and rum by equating it to other spirits favored by wealthier drinkers.

By noting that what set gin apart was the people consuming it, however, British distillers and their defenders borrowed from a transatlantic playbook that focused attacks on the laboring class. The text of the 1736 Gin Act itself sought to generally limit alcohol consumption among "people of inferior rank" because it threatened their health, "unfitted them for useful labor, debauched their morals, and excited them to all kinds of vices."[157] Because the rum produced in England sold for just "half the price" of French brandy, it also quenched the thirst of many of the same people.[158] The so-called Gin Acts in no way spared molasses-based spirits.[159]

Critics remained silent, however, regarding the ways in which elites consumed rum in Britain. Rum was a common ingredient in medical remedies recorded in the manuscript recipe books of English housewives. A common treatment for rheumatism in the late seventeenth and early eighteenth centuries involved consuming a combination of aged rum and resin from the lignum vitae tree, while a cure for consumption entailed mixing balsam jelly, spring water, honey, warm milk, and "a glass of the best Jamaica rum."[160] The belief that one could cure "cold" illnesses by prescribing a "warm" medicine helps explain rum's prevalence in these medical treatments.[161]

British people—especially those with connections to the West Indies—often served rum at their tables too. Genteel women (or their servants) mixed rum, sugar, citrus, water, and spices in order to turn the raw spirit into punch or shrub, beverages previously made with brandy from continental Europe or arrack from the East Indies.[162] This sort of mixology offered housewives a means to create a sweeter, milder flavor that appealed to elite tastes and could be served in arresting communal punch bowls. Mixed drinks pairing rum with exotic ingredients and the finest accoutrements continued the process of transforming matter from something distasteful to something desirable. It furthermore offered a means for some metropolitan men and women to differentiate their patterns of drinking from those popular among nonelite and non-European drinkers that they decried as out of control and even dangerous.[163]

* * *

Before landholders and distillers could consolidate their power by limiting who could make and drink distilled spirits, an array of producers and consumers in many corners of the Atlantic world had responded to the invention of rum and determined their own uses for it. A Jamaican clergyman decrying Port Royal as a modern-day Sodom, a Haudenosaunee sachem complaining about rum that "stinks and is noisome," and a man from Kent imbibing "in his own way" were all reacting to a new form of commodity production and attempting to determine the place for that commodity within their existing social and economic relationships. These negotiations proceeded differently depending on local circumstances and the identity of the drinkers in question, but all three involved socially elite individuals seeking to impose ways of using—or not using—rum on the people from whom they expected deference and labor. Many men and women worked out their own relationships to the new commodity that clashed with these visions. Such collisions over where—and by whom—rum should be made and traded, and how much was appropriate to consume, were an equally vital component of makers and drinkers creating an Atlantic world with rum at its core. This extended process of creation also entailed defining how makers operating in various sites of production would interact with each other.

CHAPTER 3

Circulating Ideas in a World of Rum

Ipomoea purga is a flowery vine that grows in the American tropics. A close relative of the morning glory, it originated in Mexico but quickly spread to Jamaica and Florida in the cargo holds of European ships. Cultivators would uproot the plants and cut the black roots, shown in Figure 6, into thin slices. The dried root—called *jalap*—was sent all around the world as a purgative used in treatments for edema and to prepare patients for smallpox inoculation.[1] By the 1760s, alcohol producers found another use for the tuber, too. Distillers noted that adding jalap root to the wash boosted fermentation so drastically that you could literally hear it sizzle when added. Many believed that jalap was necessary to produce alcohol in the upstart distilleries of Britain and North America, where cooler temperatures slowed the fermentation process. But in the West Indies—the very place where jalap was harvested—the climate proved "propitious to fermentation, and precludes the necessity of gross ferments, such as barm and jalap," as the London expert Richard Shannon noted in 1805.[2] West Indies distillers therefore avoided it. How, then, did a tropical root deemed unnecessary and even detrimental to distillation in its own habitat became commonplace in production centers thousands of miles away?

In part, the addition of a new ingredient for rum in the eighteenth century built on processes underpinning its invention and consumption in the seventeenth century. Scholars suggest that Indigenous Americans and, after being forced to the Americas, enslaved people of African descent discovered the medicinal powers of jalap. As the tuber arrived in new environs, Europeans, too, learned of these properties.[3] In the hands of new groups of people, knowledge surrounding jalap and its uses grew. Through exchanges and experimentation, novel uses—including in rum—emerged and gained currency.

Figure 6. Illustration of *Ipomea Purga*. From Theodor Zwinger, *Indianische Zaunruben oder Mechoacana* (1696), 255. Courtesy of the John Carter Brown Library.

Jalap's unlikely journey from the American tropics to urban distilleries thousands of miles away also exposes several underemphasized realities regarding how rum makers acquired their expertise in the eighteenth-century Atlantic world. Makers, merchants, and drinkers had already created the beverage, determined a standard name, integrated large-scale distilleries dependent on coercive labor systems into colonial and metropolitan economies, and considered the cultural meanings of drinking rum by the end of the seventeenth century. Yet acts of creation continued as they readily tinkered with their recipes. Producers endeavored to make stronger and better-tasting rum more efficiently and in new places. This experimentation thrived on the frequent exchange of information.

Distillery operators seeking to learn from their compatriots benefited from their place within the British Empire. Rum manufactories operated and innovated in the West Indies, North America, and Britain. New industrial and record-keeping technologies born out of regulatory concerns cleared the way for more efficient production models starting around 1730. Improvements in transportation and printing in the mid-eighteenth century made it easier than ever before to carry information between continents. Moreover, the enslavement of people of African descent secured access to the labor and expertise of men and women forced to work in the industry. Finally, a seemingly insatiable demand for rum—driven by the lack of a sizable British brandy industry, priorities of traders engaged in the Indian trade and the African slave trade, and provisioning policies of the British military—convinced distillers that whatever rum they made would sell. Combined, these conditions convinced distillery operators that tweaking their recipes for rum was possible and could be advantageous. And the illusion of never-ending demand for rum encouraged these men to openly discuss their concerns and propose solutions with people engaged in similar business throughout the empire.

Geographically scattered distillers found many ways to learn from each other. They visited other distilleries. They engaged in face-to-face and written conversations. By enslaving men experienced in the industry, purchasing patents, and buying books, distillery operators swapped financial resources for access to expertise. As they transported distillery equipment, tools of measurement, and rum itself, producers—along with merchants and consumers—passed on ways of knowing and making. Appreciating how this community of practice thrived in the context of the early modern Atlantic world shows how individuals within the British Atlantic world collectively leveraged personal and business relationships to embrace change and pursue profits.[4] The steady transmission of information simultaneously served the goals of empire because standardization functioned as a form of control that could, at times, yoke distant sites of production together.[5] Yet the idea that distant distillers and the empire that connected them could collectively benefit an Atlantic world full of rum makers and merchants rested on excluding others from the advantages gained through this particular community of practice. An ethic of cooperation masked the deep inequities and even outright violence baked into a system that extracted the ideas and labor of enslaved and poorly compensated distillery workers for the benefit of distillery owners.

Migrations as Conduits of Information

People moving throughout Britain's Atlantic world carrying ideas about how to make rum linked the seventeenth-century origins of the industry to eighteenth-century innovations. Enslaved people with previous experience in the distilling industry often operated as especially significant vectors of rum-related knowledge. Seasoned European planters and overseers, or occasionally Britons traveling overseas, could also introduce new processes. At other times, distillery operators would visit distilleries with the express purpose of better understanding how they made rum. Whether permanently relocating or just passing through, rum producers' journeys were some of the most straightforward ways in which interested parties learned about how others were producing rum and introduced their own improvements. The paths that these individuals followed—within the Caribbean; from the Caribbean to Britain, Africa, and North America; and from Europe and Africa to the Americas—further highlight the many people and places involved in productive exchanges.

Colonists in established rum-producing islands often moved to upstart colonies in hopes of amassing great fortunes by building thriving rum and sugar plantations on land that they received at little or no cost. As the British continued to occupy and colonize new islands and coastal lands in the eighteenth century, they relied on planters and the individuals they enslaved from existing colonies to incorporate these islands into their imperial system by building the infrastructure necessary to produce rum. During the British occupation of Guadeloupe and Martinique in the Seven Years' War, the British taught local planters to distill spirits rather than "throwing away their molasses."[6] When Britain claimed Grenada, St. Vincent, Dominica, and Tobago in the 1760s, the island governments created provisions to attract middling residents of long-established British Caribbean islands. For established planters, settling the Ceded Islands sparked fierce debate because of fears that it would lower the price that their own produce and properties fetched. But written correspondence and financial transactions between new and established rum producers suggests that a spirit of cooperation between individuals often prevailed. Of course, these upstart planters demanded much of the actual work—building distilleries, collecting sugary wastes, mixing the wash, heating the stills, collecting the distillate, and packaging the rum in puncheons—from enslaved producers forced to new plantations.

Relocating planters sometimes uprooted entire enslaved communities from one plantation to another. At other times, fledgling planters in upstart colonies specifically sought out particular people of African descent already possessing the skills needed to make rum. In these cases, individuals were often separated from their families and communities in order to bolster rum-based profits. In 1781, a planter in Dominica sought to purchase and then forcibly relocate an enslaved cooper, carpenter, and mason from Barbados—whose labors were necessary for the construction and upkeep of the sugar works that he was managing.[7] That same year, a J. Pinnock reported from Jamaica that his "head stiller" Jeffrey was one of four enslaved men kidnapped by pirates, likely for sale in the new colonies.[8] An enslaved distiller like Jeffrey could have transmitted knowledge of the best ways to make rum and may even have been targeted for his expertise. Many migrations engineered to access knowledge integral to rum production entailed forcible removals that severed familiar connections.

Hired distillers and overseers who sought opportunities overseas often touted their experience making rum in order to secure employment in Britain or another colony. When men returned to England from the Caribbean, other planters would often send their contacts to gather information. Businessmen in England valued the hands-on experience of men who had acquired expertise on Caribbean plantations. After John Mills had "had my full share of labor and toil in this part of the world," he resolved to return to England in 1753 where several men in the sugar trade were vying for his services.[9] From that vantage he would have advised how best to make sugar and divert any wastes to nearby distilleries. Englishmen also sent Caribbean experts to Florida, India, and West Africa as they sought to expand rum production in the late eighteenth century. Two friends approached the London coppersmith William Forbes in 1773, asking him to recommend a rum distiller with experience in the West Indies to go to St. Augustine, Florida, and another to work in India.[10] Intent on setting up a rum industry worked by free labor in Sierra Leone in 1794, a Dr. Smeathman likewise advocated relocating both white distillers "and vast numbers of people of color in the West Indies" to the new colony.[11] Throughout the eighteenth century, people returning from the Caribbean provided expertise on sugar and rum plantations and brought transferrable production skills to Britain and its other colonies. Even if they themselves had never been enslaved, these men carried information that they learned from enslaved practitioners.

Migrating experts traveled in other directions, too. People born and trained in Europe frequently helped make and improve rum in the West Indies and North America by introducing new technologies. In 1774, a Mr. Fleming traveled from London to Grenada, carrying with him knowledge of "the manner of fixing" local planters' still heads.[12] Likewise, in the 1790s, the Scotsman John Campbell moved from Edinburgh to the West Indies, ready to share the "arts of my making yeast powder" with fellow sailors and government officials.[13] Just as migrants brought information derived through experience in the West Indies to North America and the Caribbean, knowledge traveled the opposite direction in much the same way. This sort of information exchange probably became more common later in the eighteenth century, as British experience in alcohol production—and manufacturing capabilities more generally—grew.

Shorter trips designed specifically to gather information became a vital way for interested parties to collect and aggregate information in a comparatively short period. Sometimes these journeys were merely a stopover on a longer journey. On his way from Britain to Jamaica in 1794, Kean Osborn briefly disembarked in Madeira and Barbados, which provided an "opportunity of seeing a great deal of the country and among other things a curiously constructed water mill and sugar work."[14] American distillers completed similar fact-finding missions to English distilleries. For instance, at a dinner party in Bristol, England, and in ensuing site visits, Daniel Roberdeau received advice from local sugar boilers and distillers about how to profitably reopen his Virginia distillery.[15] These quick trips to other distilleries often entailed rum producers calling on casual acquaintances.

Others undertook more extensive journeys of discovery through West Indies distilleries. In 1775, Nathaniel Phillips stopped in Madeira, Barbados, Tobago, St. Vincent, Grenada, Dominica, and Antigua on his way to his Jamaican plantations. On each island, he sought out the best plantations and took note of the size of the estate, equipment in use to make sugar and rum, crop yields, planting seasons, and patterns of work.[16] Men preparing to publish guides to making rum also traveled to observe many plantations throughout the Caribbean. For instance, Patrick Kein visited every parish in Jamaica in 1768 "merely for the purpose of gaining some information."[17] John Dovaston visited St. Christopher, Jamaica, Nevis, and Montserrat while preparing to write "Agricultura Americana."[18]

Free and forced migrations regularly facilitated the transmission of information and innovations useful to the rum production process. Forcing enslaved rum producers to establish commodity production in new places allowed planters to move on-the-ground experience and expertise to places where individuals were unwilling to venture on their own volition. All told, interactions made possible by long-distance travel were especially useful for individuals hoping to gather information from distant sites of production. Highly technical processes were easier to pick up when observed or explained in person.

Finally, showing up at a distillery unlocked secrets that other forms of exchange left unexposed. Published accounts rarely mentioned what was gained from observing—or even talking to—enslaved distillery workers, even though visitors would have immediately appreciated that no rum was being produced in the West Indies without their forced labor. Despite the proprietary nature of some of the information that distillers hoped to collect, very few correspondents described being kept out of any distilleries. Established distillers enjoyed the recognition of being singled out as worthy of emulation by their visitors. It is also possible that the social conventions of life in the British West Indies—where elite visitors expected a warm reception when visiting island plantations—made it difficult for established producers in that region to decline such requests even if they wanted to.[19] No matter what facilitated this culture of openness, planters and self-taught experts successfully collected expertise from established sugar and rum producers and, importantly, from the individuals they enslaved.

A World of Conversations

Traveling rum makers noted their visits to other distilleries, but they only rarely recounted the substance of their conversations. Nonetheless, while touring properties or sharing a meal, they learned from distillery operators and their neighbors. Quotidian conversations covered many subjects. Operators discussed facility and process improvements, as well as new frontiers for the expansion of production. They also gained context for their failures. Sometimes, information accessed through personal interactions circulated more widely through letters. Whether such conversations remained local or were exported elsewhere, they demonstrate the highly decentralized pathways that exchanges of information and ideas took in the Atlantic world.

When describing their visits to other distilleries, men and women highlighted their interactions with plantation owners and operators rather than with enslaved technicians, though the scant evidence suggests there were plenty of the latter, too. During her husband's tenure as the governor of Jamaica in the early 1800s, Maria Nugent accompanied island gentry to several sugar plantations. On at least two occasions, she gained a "peep at the process" of making rum before the foul odors emanating from the distillery chased her away. Although she insinuated that this work was carried out by enslaved men, Nugent made no reference to any direct conversations.[20] Dovaston similarly noted that his advice on making rum came from the "observation" of various plantations but did not mention speaking directly with enslaved workers.[21] Nugent and Dovaston described their fact-finding visits in ways that disembodied the technical processes they observed from the enslaved people motivated by threat of violence.

Caribbean rum producers used what they learned through both observation and conversations to improve how they made the spirit. The planter Clement Caines attributed the "undeniable richness" of his rum to "a gentleman of Antigua" named Mr. Lightfoot, who advocated lining his lees trough with clay.[22]

Ezekiel Dickinson similarly attributed advice about adding chalk to soften the flavor and molasses to "heighten the color" of his rum to a conversation with his nephew.[23] And Thomas Barrett resolved to "see" a Mr. Madder to learn how to prepare the plantation's rum for market.[24] In North America, the firm of Brown and Benson advised a ship captain whom they had tasked with procuring a hydrometer to call on a distiller in New York to learn which instrument would best answer their purposes.[25] In all of these circumstances, distillers found that conversing directly with other free producers could improve their own product.

Individuals intent on opening new frontiers for rum production also talked to islanders who had visited less settled lands. Of Puerto Rico, Samuel Martin observed, "Its soil is reported by everybody that have seen it, to be like that of St. Kitts, admirably fruitful."[26] Similar conversations convinced Martin to steer clear of Tobago. He had heard that "the poor settlers of Barbados know that island so well, that not one of them will accept of land there gratis."[27] Martin and his compatriots likely saw face-to-face exchanges as more accurate sources of information regarding colonization schemes because they could verify the individual judgment of the people with whom they spoke.

Word-of-mouth exchanges were particularly important if things went wrong in distilleries. After distillery yields declined or the rum proved defective, owners and operators called on neighbors in order to solve the problem. When writing absentee investors with news of subpar rum yields, plantation operators compared their experiences to that of their compatriots in an effort to troubleshoot.[28] Conversations with nearby plantations also allowed plantation managers like William Rodgers to avoid frustrations that nearby planters were experiencing. Rodgers noted in 1802 that comparing the Westmoreland Estate's recent yields with an "observation of the loss in our neighbor['s] stock" led him to the conclusion that a new variant of cane lessened the rum yield on Jamaican plantations.[29] Communicating through word of mouth allowed many distillers to understand what went wrong or to avoid the mistakes that others on the island had made.

European-descended distillers were most likely to record their exchanges with other rum producers, but they were not the only rum producers to talk. Enslaved men made up the vast majority of distillery workers in the West Indies. As they developed friendships and families, engaged in informal market activities, and drank rum as part of unsanctioned gatherings and rituals, enslaved distillers interacted with rum producers from nearby estates. It is highly likely that they talked about making rum, even though these exchanges never produced a paper trail. The lack of written record of these conversations exposes another means by which enslaved expertise was hidden: enslavers suppressed reading and writing among enslaved people as a form of control. Perhaps a producer selling illicit rum may have received feedback from enslaved consumers about the preferred taste, color, or strength of rum. Or just as likely, a distiller worried about a problem in his distillery for which he could be held responsible and punished might have sought advice from an acquaintance with more experience in that line of work. Informal conversations drew from many different groups of rum producers, almost certainly including enslaved people.[30]

When they could not meet directly with the people from whom they sought information, rum producers sometimes attempted to engage in similar exchanges through written correspondence. In the 1730s, Josiah Martin sought advice from North America to improve his Antigua rum yields. Concerned with the initially sluggish rate of fermentation when distilleries began operations each January, Martin asked a New York merchant to acquire a Mrs. Bickley's yeast recipe, which he hoped would lead to considerable savings in the distillery.[31] Two years later, he talked with a Barbadian plantation owner living in Boston who claimed to be able to produce more than twice as much rum from the same amount of sugar wastes. Martin's new acquaintance promised to write to his plantation manager in Barbados with instructions to send the improved recipe to Antigua.[32] Martin was not alone in writing letters to pursue improvements. Fifty years later, when Thomas Robison prepared to open a distillery along the Casco Bay in Maine, he received a collection of handwritten instructions and distillery records originating from a Montserrat planter named Tyrell Herbert and another Caribbean distillery owner named James Aitkens.[33] Advice flowing back and forth from the West Indies to New England suggests that producers in the eighteenth century never recognized one place or one person as the intellectual hub of the industry. Instead, they wrote to whichever family members, casual acquaintances, or complete strangers they believed could provide them with an advantage. Those contacts, in turn, represented information as their own that had been gleaned from personal experience and interactions with an array of workers.

Producers also wrote to merchants in hopes of matching the rum they made to the vagaries of local markets. North American distillers corresponded with European merchants to learn what color of rum sold best. Distillers and merchants also used letters to stay apprised of climatological events in the West Indies in order to know when prices shifted. For instance, word of "dry seasons in the West Indies" caused Nathaniel Holmes to raise his prices for North American rum in 1754.[34] Furthermore, rum's makers and merchants used letters to track how political developments affected rum prices. News of political developments such as a moratorium on fermenting grains in Britain, the closure of ports in North America, a prohibition on trading rum to West African coastal forts, and wars in continental Europe caused major price fluctuations in distant production centers.[35] By acquiring knowledge of market conditions quickly and accurately, distillery owners in the West Indies, North America, and Britain poised themselves to capitalize on the sale of their rum. If prices were high in a certain place, they could divert their rum there or try to increase production.[36] If prices for plantation produce were low across the board, planters could slow down operations or delay their sales until prices rebounded.[37] Because aged rum sold for a premium, profits in distilleries could be enhanced by such patience. Reaching out to reliable correspondents in faraway places allowed distillery operators to master the markets for rum.

Whether in one location or dispersed around the Atlantic world, distillers valued conversations with an array of other makers and sellers of rum. They used these interactions to pursue innovations, learn about alternative ways and places to make rum, troubleshoot, and match their product to market preferences. In order to do so, they placed trust in family, acquaintances, and sometimes strangers to provide them with sound advice. They likewise demanded that enslaved Africans carry out highly technical work that built the expertise the distillers claimed for themselves. When distillery operators shared their expertise with friends, family members, and outsiders either out of good will or belief in a collective benefit, or in an attempt to gain recognition as experts in their field, they were often reappropriating ideas born from the harshness of slavery.

Paid Exchanges of Knowledge

Although they continued to rely on personal relationships to access information regarding rum production, distillery operators also increasingly paid to gain access to the labor of experienced producers, newly patented inventions, and published manuals written by experts. The costs of accessing expertise in these ways varied considerably. Nonetheless, whether a large outlay to purchase an enslaved distiller—or hire a salaried one—or a small one to buy a book, the profusion of paid exchanges of knowledge in the latter half of the eighteenth century marked the consumer revolution's impact on rum production. Producers bought and sold ideas as they sought greater profits from their own enterprises.

If you owned a distillery and did not personally possess—or control the labor of enough people who did possess—the combination of skills necessary to ferment molasses, distill rum, and package the commodity, the fastest way to gain the necessary skills was to acquire the labor of one or more experts. So when Thomas Cave signed Richard Morgan up to work in his Bristol distillery and when Daniel Roberdeau hired David Jackson to superintend his Alexandria distillery, both men were paying wages for more than the physical labor of their employees: they were acquiring a system of knowledge necessary to bolster their rum production process.[38] Likewise, distillers bought and sold enslaved experts in order to access the know-how they possessed. Sensing that his Mina distiller, Robin, would be worth more to another planter on St. Christopher who needed skilled distillery workers, Robert Cunyngham included Robin in a group of eight expert and seasoned people that he traded for twelve newly arrived Africans.[39] Likewise, John Colman purchased Quacqo—an enslaved man from Barbados—for what he perceived to be an exorbitant price because he needed a highly trained cooper for his Boston distillery.[40] Once again, the transfer of expertise between producers often relied on the physical and intellectual work of enslaved or hired rum producers who did not accrue the full financial benefits of their labor.

Distillery-specific proprietary information could also be patented and offered for sale. Interestingly, the men selling their inventions often described themselves as distillers, suggesting that the industry's advancements often came from individuals actively working within it. Rum producers bought and sold recipes for improved molasses fermentation with some regularity, linking sites of production separated by the Atlantic Ocean. In 1797, a Medford, Massachusetts, rum distillery owner named Fitch Hall traveled to England in an attempt to share his improved fermentation technique with distillers there.[41] Improvements such as Hall's often involved adding specific strains of yeast to the molasses wash. Noting both the frequency of this type of improvement and its questionable effectiveness, a nineteenth-century observer in the Caribbean noted that "the employment of yeast on estates has formed the groundwork of many a delusive promise, for which our unfortunate colonists have had to pay."[42] Despite the uncertain success of these arrangements, producers continued to chase their potential.

The crown, Parliament, and American legislatures alike encouraged the monetization of innovations. As early as 1685, the English diplomat and politician William Blathwayt asserted that "if the spirit of rum could be improved, as is proposed, it would be of very great profit to his Majesty and his plantations."[43] Making clear that the ideal of improvement was long-standing, John Nasmith received a financial reward from Queen Anne in 1712 for his successful experiment in a Glasgow distillery that greatly reduced the amount of molasses needed to ferment a batch of alcohol.[44] Attempts to receive compensation for innovations increased throughout the century. Patent offices protected the intellectual property of individuals registering new technologies. Between 1752 and 1755, the Barbados Assembly passed acts providing three separate inventors the exclusive right to sell their distillery-related inventions on the island for at least ten years. John Pass and John Stalker each acquired patents for their pump designs, while William Culpepper received exclusive rights to his improvement for "the advantageous altering and making most useful stills and still heads for the distillation of rum."[45] The US Patent Office issued at least thirty-six patents for improvements in distilling and rectifying spirits between 1790 and 1808—more than they granted for most other industries.[46]

Enterprising distillers sought to thread the needle of protecting their industrial secrets while also promoting them. During his 1797 visit to England, Fitch Hall hoped to add a British patent to the American one that he already held.[47] In the wake of American independence, this legal maneuvering was the only way to ensure that non-American distillers elsewhere in the anglophone Atlantic would respect Hall's intellectual property rights. With patents in hand, inventors employed networks of agents in places where the patent was most likely to sell. In addition to selling the proprietary knowledge, they could also report any infringements. Boasting that he had devised a safer, faster, and more efficient patented still design, the Pennsylvania distiller Michael Krafft posted correspondents elsewhere in Pennsylvania as well as in New Jersey, New York, Maryland, Massachusetts, and Kentucky, "to render the access" to his prototypes "more facile."[48]

The profusion of metropolitan and colonial printing presses in the latter half of the eighteenth century supported an entire genre of how-to guides that expanded access to information crucial for distillers. Whereas patents offered one discrete piece of information for sale, these books instead collected and shared many best practices that could help distillery operators produce rum more efficiently. Distillers practicing in both Europe and the Americas wrote accounts of how to make rum that were printed in both regions and read throughout the Atlantic world. Contrary to how they have sometimes been characterized, colonial inhabitants were by no means "minor figures" in the intellectual traffic contained within these books.[49] Instead, writing these guides allowed a subset of British and colonial distillers to monetize their expertise and cement their reputations as leading figures in the transatlantic world of rum production.

Over the seventeenth and eighteenth centuries, at least three dozen experts in distillation stationed throughout the Atlantic world authored guides to their trade. While distillation guides had been written by English experts since the early seventeenth century, Caribbean planters only began to produce guides to plantership around 1750. North American distillers authored additional books detailing best distillery practices starting in the 1790s. These manuals varied in length, tone, and the expertise claimed by the author. They often detailed how and when to mix molasses wash, how to boost fermentation, when to distill, how to measure alcoholic content, and how to limit mistakes. British and North American experts interspersed their advice on how to make rum with information on producing a plethora of other spirits. Caribbean experts instead situated rum production within the sugar-refining process. Based on individual authors' experiences and interests, the advice offered in these guides varied significantly.

With plenty of competition, and intent on convincing would-be readers to follow their particular advice, these authors listed a variety of credentials that they suggested made them uniquely worthy of emulation. Some noted their training as chemists and included sections where they theorized about how fermentation and distillation worked.[50] Other experts, such as John Dovaston—who traveled to the Caribbean—and Richard Shannon—who remained in Britain—sought to combine their scientific knowledge with experience in the industry. Their writings interspersed tried-and-true recipes and tips with theories regarding miasmas and vapors.[51]

Another group homed in on practical expertise in their descriptions of distilling.[52] Samuel McHarry of Lancaster County, Pennsylvania, who exemplified this group of writers, acknowledged that distilleries were staffed by "knaves, blockheads, and conceited characters," but nonetheless preferred to share hands-on advice rather than scientific knowledge in his distilling guide. Explaining the necessity of gaining practical distilling experience, he remarked, "The professed chemist, and profound theorist may smile at my ideas, but should any one of them ever venture to soil a finger in the practical part of distilling, I venture to say, he would find more difficulty in producing good yeast, than in the process of creating oxygen or hydrogen gas."[53] With myriad experiences in different distilleries, these men offered varied perspectives on how to make alcohol.

Writers drew liberally from expertise created by others. Experts whose experience came from the Caribbean shared recipes and operating procedures that were largely deployed and refined by enslaved distillers. When they wrote about an experiment devised to improve production, that creative work again exacted labor from the unrecognized people who mixed ingredients and operated the stills. The authors also borrowed ideas acquired in one part of the world and applied them to another. Writers commonly reproduced extensive passages from other guides to distillation regardless of where the information had originally been collected. Ambrose Cooper explained that when he decided to write a book on distilling he first "read most of the treatises on the subject, and extracted from each what I thought necessary for my purpose, proposing to supply the defects from my own experience." The second edition of his book even translated from the French book *Traité raisonné de la distillation*.[54] Published experts sought to combine their own experiences with preexisting theoretical and practical descriptions of how to make rum with little concern for attributing ideas to their original source. This practice often drew together ideas pioneered in different parts of the Atlantic world.

But writers whose pamphlets and books connected rum production in different locales encountered a persistent problem: their expertise focused on a specific place even while the nature of print culture—and the fact that the vast majority of these guides were published in London—spread their knowledge elsewhere. Some writers republished ideas originating an ocean away.[55] Others, such as a Barbadian planter named William Belgrove, drew more nuanced distinctions. In a broadside that he sent to St. Christopher shortly after his *Treatise upon Husbandry or Planting* was published in 1755, he acknowledged that "soil in Barbados differs from that in Saint Kitts" and offered brief remarks on how his instructions could be adapted to a different island.[56] In these cases, authors recognized that their writings needed to account for local conditions.

Regional variations in the rum industry lent themselves to the recognition of place-specific experts whose writings further crowded this marketplace of information. The Antigua planter Samuel Martin—publishing sometimes under the pseudonym of "An Old Planter" to allude to the source of his expertise—dedicated his *Essay upon Plantership* to "all the planters of the British sugar colonies" in hopes that his acumen could improve the quality of sugar and rum production in the region.[57] Although most subsequent writers acknowledged the value of Martin's work, they sought to extend or amend his advice to other islands. Belgrove offered advice specific to Barbados in 1755; John Dovaston (1776) and Patrick Kein (1796) focused on Jamaica; and Joshua Peterkin's regional expertise concerned St. Christopher (1790).[58] Likewise, Samuel McHarry noted in 1809 that the absence of a guide to distillation produced in North America created an opening for his book because previous works were "at variance with" American "habits, customs, and mode of economy."[59] Although influenced by their predecessors, each of these authors established their distilling acumen by stressing their accumulated experience in specific places.

Despite needing to account for regional peculiarities, an array of rum producers read books and pamphlets emanating from throughout the Atlantic world. Distillers in London interested in reading more about their craft were aided by the fact that books written by Caribbean-based authors were frequently published or later reprinted in the metropole. London imprints of books detailing Caribbean rum production were probably marketed toward absentee planters or colonial consumers, but London-based distillers delved into these sources as well. Richard Shannon's description of Caribbean rum production aligns with the information that he would have gleaned from reading various guides written by Caribbean planters detailing the processes carried out by enslaved workers. Even if they accessed the information indirectly, people reading about distillation encountered rum distillery-specific expertise that originated in the hands and minds of an expansive group of Caribbean rum makers.

Unsurprisingly, guides to sugar and rum production were frequently printed and read in the Caribbean. The majority of the eight known reprintings of Martin's *Essay upon Plantership* were undertaken in Antigua between 1750 and 1802. Five hundred fifty-five subscribers from various Caribbean islands paid in advance for the second edition of Joshua Peterkin's *Treatise on Planting*.[60] Additionally, island-specific almanacs—which were a significant revenue source for many Caribbean-based printers—sometimes included articles advising improvements in the rum production process.[61] Plantation owners and overseers would have read these printed materials and then directed enslaved distillery workers to carry out any suggested adjustments.

Caribbean planters sought published advice on rum production from a variety of locales. The notorious Jamaica enslaver Thomas Thistlewood's personal collection of books included titles originating in and beyond the West Indies. He owned copies of Samuel Martin's *Essay upon Plantership* and I. P. Baker's *Essay on the Art of Making Muscovado Sugar*, and purchased a copy of the Jamaica almanac each year. He also transcribed portions of manuscript guides to plantership written by John Pulley Edwards and Richard Beckford.[62] Thistlewood consumed guides to distillation written by British experts as well. His inventory of books included Cooper's *The Complete Distiller* and George Smith's *Compleat Body of Distilling*, and he also scribbled notes next to his records of seemingly unrelated texts that included information deemed useful for distilling. Thistlewood described many of these volumes as well-worn, suggesting that he or a borrower regularly referred to them for advice.[63] Although Thistlewood may have been unusual among Jamaican planters for his level of fascination with books, his meticulous records demonstrate the extent to which distillery owners in the Caribbean could engage with published advice pertaining to distillation from different parts of the Atlantic world.[64]

At least some North American distillers had access to a relatively similar collection of rum-related books. The 1770 membership list from the Library Company of Philadelphia lists eight subscribers connected to at least one of the fourteen Philadelphia distilleries operating at that time.[65] Nonmembers could also access books from the library for a fee. By 1807, distillers visiting the library could borrow many of the same titles that Thistlewood owned, including Cooper's *Complete Distiller*. The library obtained several late eighteenth-century descriptions of sugar and rum production, including William Beckford's *Descriptive Account of the Island of Jamaica* and Clement Caines's *Letters on the Cultivation of Otaheite Cane*. Although the Library Company's collections focused on rum-related books printed in London, the nature of the information collected in these books connected readers to expertise originating in Britain, the Caribbean, and South Asia.[66]

Through subscription libraries or by borrowing from acquaintances, North American distillers in other cities could also acquire and read many books detailing how to best produce rum. Readers in smaller cities, with less-established distilling industries, faced greater challenges acquiring these sorts of books. For instance, in 1784, the Maine distiller Thomas Robison could not acquire the guide to distillation that he sought.[67] Even when they struggled to acquire the books they wanted, though, distillers such as Robison recognized the utility of this branch of print culture.

The number of titles that explained rum production increased over the latter half of the eighteenth century. Many leading distillers in Britain, the West Indies, and North America wrote down their advice in hopes of advancing the collective understanding of how to make rum. They calculated that attaching their names to a useful guide would advance their social standing. For instance, Samuel Martin insisted that he selflessly chose to share his *Essay upon Plantership* for no reward other than the "right to claim the merit of being a whetstone to sharpen the ingenuity of other men, in the service of their country."[68] There was some financial incentive to publish a popular guide to rum production as well.[69] Regardless of their motivations, the profusion of prescriptive guides suggests that publishers found eager audiences for these books. As the books passed from centers of alcohol production in Britain, North America, and the Caribbean, guides to distillation functioned as an important means by which knowledge of rum production spread between dispersed producers.

Given that producing rum entailed both knowing how to make the spirit and possessing the ability to carry out the craft practices that it entailed, there were very clear limitations to what could be learned in books and who could learn it.[70] Caribbean guidebooks systematically underrepresented the role of enslaved distillers in that region, meaning that readers gained an inaccurate view of how rum production was carried out there. Many authors even agreed that their accounts remained necessarily incomplete. Peterkin warned his readers that he chose not to burden them with details that "every young planter must be thoroughly acquainted with."[71] Conversely, other experts noted that certain things could only be learned through experience. Martin, for instance, claimed to measure when the wash was ready to be distilled by "the taste and smell, which cannot be described."[72] Even authors who had many incentives to overstate the utility of their work recognized that books did not impart all secrets.

Some distillers could not learn directly from a book, since distillery owners sought to maintain their control over enslaved workers by preventing them from learning to read. Not all hired workers were literate either, meaning that their engagement with these texts would remain mediated by the individuals who controlled their labor.[73] The cost of books furthermore precluded itinerant distillery workers of limited means from buying them. Nonetheless, printed guides to rum production constituted a relatively affordable way to gain a wealth of information. The volume and regional specificity of prescriptive literature in the second half of the eighteenth century increased who could access productive knowledge and what information they could learn, but all parties recognized that this information functioned best alongside other ways of knowing.

Objects as Sources of Information

Distillers learned immensely from migrating experts, visits to other distilleries often dependent on slave labor, conversations, letter writing, and reading. But among a community of producers who sometimes could not read or write and who possessed varied degrees of knowledge about how rum was produced elsewhere, these forms of information exchange were not always enough. Producers around the Atlantic world instead read the distilling equipment itself to try to discern best practices for the distilling process. Stills imported from Britain only worked as intended if craftsmen elsewhere installed them properly. The color and flavor of rum corresponded with certain decisions made by its producers. And new tools of measurement established standards that changed how makers, sellers, and drinkers determined quality. The power of salable goods to establish and transfer meanings to consumers in and beyond early America is well established. In similar ways, more pedestrian tools—and a commodity marketed to nearly everybody—made best practices legible to geographically scattered distillers who often had limited access to other ways of acquiring knowledge.

In rum distilleries, individuals operating in many distinct social worlds coalesced around a common goal—in this case making rum. Despite some regional peculiarities, distillers in the West Indies, Britain, and North America all relied on certain objects like stills, hydrometers, and gauges. Regardless of where they would be used, these common tools were usually made in the same workshops in England. Relying on these items wedded distillers to each other, uniting rum producers through their common use of technology despite the challenges posed by distance and rigidly enforced social hierarchies. The forms that these objects took reflected both the designs and interests of English manufacturers and improvements requested by users elsewhere in the Atlantic world.

No matter where they operated, distillers recognized stills as an irreplaceable tool of their trade. Although some were produced in North America, the vast majority of stills used throughout the British Atlantic world were produced in England. Copper production in southwestern England and southern Wales grew rapidly in the late seventeenth century in response to the surging demand for copper stills and sugar pans in Britain's Caribbean colonies.[74] New technologies formed as British industrialists sought to create uniformly thin sheets of copper to satisfy their colonial customers.[75]

The coppersmiths who turned these sheets of copper into stills also balanced the desires of distillers with their own financial and logistical considerations. For instance, in order to attach pieces of the stills together, coppersmiths used either cast or forged nails. While the cast nails were cheaper, Caribbean distillery owners' desires for more durable and leak-proof vessels led William Forbes's London shop to use only forged nails.[76] Likewise, in the late eighteenth century, some distillers wanted to purchase towering stills to make rum. Although Forbes's shop produced much larger stills for local clients, he tended not to sell stills larger than a thousand gallons abroad on the advice of merchants who noted that larger models would not fit in the cargo hold of most ocean-bound ships.[77] By negotiating the desires and realities of the copper industry, local and distant rum producers, and merchants, coppersmiths including William Forbes created an object that responded to information offered by various actors in diverse parts of the Atlantic world.

Forbes's stills in turn imparted a set of standard operating procedures on the distillers who purchased them. The majority of orders for stills that he received—including the one sketched in Figure 7—included very limited directions. For instance, Forbes received an order in August 1789 for "a still to

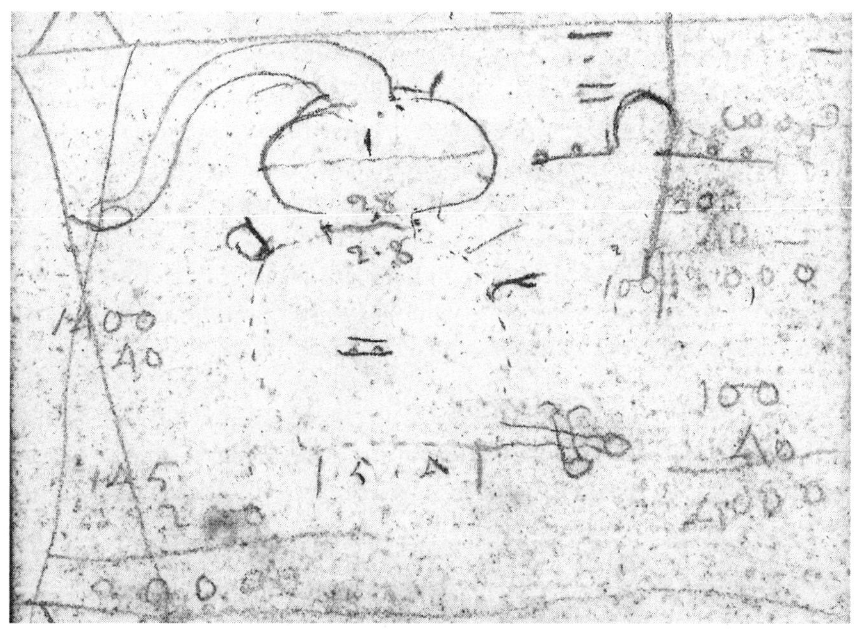

Figure 7. Sketch of a still from Note-books of William Forbes (1774). Falkirk Archives, A727.1460.

contain 300 gallons with a head and copper goose neck."[78] In this case, the purchaser entrusted Forbes to choose the dimensions of the still, the size and style of the head, and which direction the worm tube would need to be oriented. These engineering decisions ultimately shaped the work of enslaved workers installing and then using the stills in the Caribbean. They dictated how close the still would need to be placed to the fire and how efficiently it vaporized and condensed rum.

Sometimes clients asked Forbes to alter his standard design. With some regularity, Caribbean distillers would ask him to enlarge the head of the still, which may have improved the efficiency with which it recondensed alcohol vapors. In 1773 a Tobago planter ordered a still of three hundred gallons with a head proportionate to a four hundred–gallon still.[79] Even though this planter was requesting an alteration to the common design, the manner of ordering rested on a mutual understanding between him and Forbes about the standard dimensions of a still. Because he supplied stills to rum producers around the world—including in Britain, North America, the West Indies, and India—Forbes's judgment regarding the construction and ideal proportions of stills prevailed in many different places. One author of a guide to distilling claimed that coppersmiths like Forbes dictated "the whole destiny of the manufacturer."[80]

Merchants and consumers often attempted to "read" allotments of rum for clues regarding its production as well. Colonial newspapers regularly listed the current prices for rum produced in different places. In 1764, the *Georgia Gazette* listed the price of Jamaica rum at four shillings per gallon; Barbados and Antigua rum at three shillings, sixpence; New York rum at two shillings, fourpence; and New England rum at two shillings, twopence.[81] This relatively stable hierarchy of prices carried certain assumptions about how rum was produced in different places. Jamaican distillers added more cane syrup to the molasses and skimmings, which purchasers believed made the rum stronger and purer tasting. Barbadian planters emphasized the quality of ingredients and workmanship over the strength of the rum. While merchants recognized its quality, it did not fetch the prices reserved for Jamaican, or sometimes even Antiguan, rum.[82] On the other end of the spectrum, North American rums—made from months-old molasses shipped from the Caribbean—sold for a fraction of the price. By arriving at prices based on the geography of where rum was produced, makers and drinkers of rum accepted a set of common assumptions about how rum in different places was produced.

Other markers of quality such as appearance and taste also conveyed common meanings to producers and consumers alike. Rum producers and consumers often lauded rum that had acquired a caramel hue and smoother taste from the toasted barrels that it sat in for three or more years. As a plantation operator explained in 1756, "We never think our rum in Barbados in any degree of perfection under three years old, the older the better."[83] Producers and consumers in the Americas and Britain thus associated the darker West Indian rums with the premium, aged product. Before even tasting the rum, merchants and consumers assumed that this process imparted a smoother, mellower, and sweeter taste.

Sometimes the taste, strength, or color of rum diverged from what tasters expected, however. Such discrepancies could result from producers trying to emulate other styles of rum they had encountered. For instance, caramel-colored rum that did not exude the tasting notes of being aged was likely dyed with tea leaves or burnt sugar.[84] Taste testers also frequently identified shortcomings in the production process. Daniel Roberdeau complained that a parcel of Jamaican rum ended up at a vendue sale in 1766 because "most of them were still-burnt, a quality very detrimental and [that] will never suit at private sale."[85] North American distillers made similar mistakes: a buyer complained to the Massachusetts distiller Nathaniel Holmes about "exceeding ill-tasted, still-burnt" liquor in 1754.[86] By describing the rum as "still-burnt," correspondents did more than describe the taste: they identified what had gone wrong in terms legible to other makers and sellers.

On other occasions, merchants and consumers complained about deficient rum without specifying what had gone wrong. They simply expected that any other discerning palate would immediately taste the problem.[87] In this way, the circulation of rum throughout the Atlantic world in the seventeenth and eighteenth centuries depended on common expectations of how rum should be made, what the finished commodity should contain, and how it should look and taste. Producers took a leading role in these negotiations, but the circulation of rum offered merchants and consumers ample opportunity to weigh in as well.

As the eighteenth century wore on, distillers changed how they evaluated rum and began to rely on more precise numerical measurements of volume and strength.[88] In order to ascribe a value to an allotment of rum for the purposes of sale or taxation, all parties needed to agree on the amount and quality of rum involved. Throughout the seventeenth and early eighteenth centuries, the shape and approximate size of the container and its origins usually sufficed. However, tax collectors and, eventually, buyers and sellers explored new tools of measurement. When specifying a number of gallons rather than a number of containers of an approximate size, or the percentage of alcohol contained instead of a simple attestation that it was strong enough, distillers and merchants applied Enlightenment-era concepts of quantification to preexisting production techniques. These tools changed how rum was evaluated throughout the Atlantic world.

Such changes originated in the tax office. Parliament imposed heavier taxes on rum and other alcohols produced in and imported to England and Scotland starting in the 1730s. In order to accurately charge taxes, excise officers (and distillery operatives checking their work) needed to precisely measure two things: the volume of the alcohol being sold and its strength. Producers sometimes simply counted rum puncheons and assumed an average volume for them. But more precision made it easier to compute taxes, measure loss, and track sales. Makers and sellers of rum—as well as the taxmen—increasingly relied on gauging rods to measure the diagonal length of the vessel in question. They could then plug those numbers into mathematical formulas to compute the volume of the container.[89] In 1736, the Barbados Assembly passed an act requiring that rum on the island undergo this sort of mathematical gauging.[90] While rum producers and buyers noted that the calculations varied depending on who performed the measurements, gauging rods remained the go-to method for measuring the volume of vessels into the nineteenth century.[91]

Tax collectors and molasses spirit producers also sought a standard scale to measure the strength of their alcohols. Prior to the mid-eighteenth century, several techniques had been common. Distillers and merchants relied on their taste; measured the "Holland proof" by shaking a sample of alcohol and observing how long it took for the bubbles to dissipate; mixed alcohol with gunpowder and watched how it reacted when a flame was introduced; or added a drop of oil and surveyed whether it floated or sank. Each of these tests aimed to determine whether a sample was more than 50 percent alcohol by volume—or "proof." However, England's Excise Office yearned for more exact and replicable forms of measurement. Between 1746 and 1751, two relatively affordable and easy-to-use tools hit the market which measured the specific gravity of alcohol: Richard Clarke's hydrometer and Alexander Wilson's "philosophical beads."[92] Using a series of carefully calibrated weights, users determined how heavy the tool needed to be to sink in a sample of alcohol. When adjusted for the temperature of the liquid, that information made computing the precise amount of alcohol in the sample possible.

Both tools were manufactured and marketed in Britain, where excise and customs officers first adopted them, but distillers and merchants in the Americas quickly found uses for them too. In the guidebook accompanying his hydrometer, Richard Clarke acknowledged that "it is well known that the heat of the climate in the West Indies, will make all spirituous liquors, appear much stronger than they really are." His hydrometer set therefore came with an extra weight that would adjust for the warmer temperatures of the tropics.[93] Almost from the start, instrument makers understood the global reach of their tools. Improved hydrometers sold later in the century and used throughout the rum-producing world required users to measure the exact temperature and then use a chart to adjust the hydrometer reading accordingly.[94] "Philosophical beads," such as those photographed in Figure 8, were a set of small glass bubbles designed to float in liquids with different specific gravities. They could not account for different temperatures, but they nonetheless found users in the Americas.[95] Some planters, such as Nathaniel Phillips in Jamaica, subsequently calculated conversion rates between how the beads performed in the Caribbean and in Britain, and even how the beads compared to the oil test.[96]

Because measures of specific gravity fluctuate based on the temperature of a sample and the skill of the tester, regional discrepancies abounded. Producers throughout the Atlantic world nonetheless strived to use the same tools and techniques in order to standardize their judgments of volume and strength. The objects used to carry out measurements were usually devised and produced in Britain. But again, they accounted for users who lacked in-depth training in

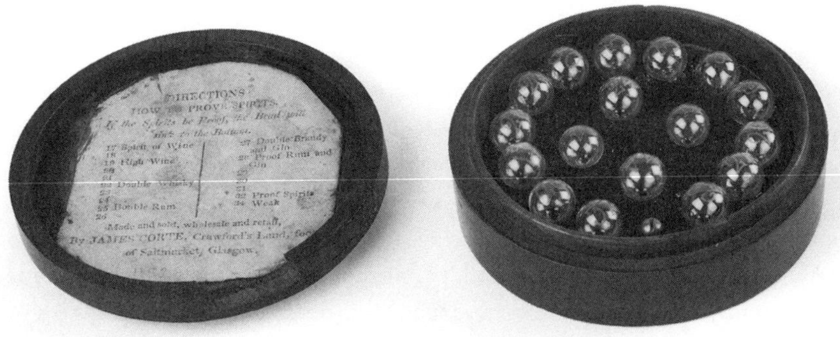

Figure 8. Hydrometer "Philosophical Bubbles" by James Corte, Glasgow (c. 1750–1805). Collection: Powerhouse Museum. Gift of Robert C. Dixson, 1954. Photo: Jules Boag.

scientific measurement and operated in tropical climates that affected how the tools functioned.

The fact that rum producers in various parts of the rum-producing world used similar tools to make comparable measurements demonstrates the emergence of a common body of distilling knowledge that manifested itself in eighteenth-century material culture. Because alcohol markets in Britain, North America, and the West Indies had been linked for the better part of a century by this point, a tool and scale of measurement initially devised for a specific administrative purpose in Britain gained currency in many other parts of the Atlantic world. In the process, a transatlantic community of distillers created a new means of establishing and sharing standards of what rum should be and, indirectly, how it was best made.

Separated from other distillers by thousands of miles, rum producers in the eighteenth-century British Atlantic world shared many material circumstances in common. They often relied on copper stills hammered out by the same coppersmiths in Britain. Distillers sold their rum for different prices in the same markets, which was only possible due to common understandings of geographic hierarchies of quality and shared beliefs of what made rum good or bad. As the century progressed, they became increasingly invested in using the same tools and scales of measurement to govern and record the quality of the spirits that they produced. Stills, rum, and the tools used to measure it all provided access points that a community of practice could teach about and learn from. Objects were yet another way in which a world of rum producers passed on and accessed the information they used to make rum and innovate. Such tools were especially important because they made complex calculations and consistent judgments possible in workshops dependent on the labor of people whose learning was heavily restricted, who could be forcibly relocated, and whose living conditions contributed to tragically short life expectancies.

The remarkable web of shared information among distillery owners and operators from near and far was neither perfect nor absolute. Despite common standards among producers of rum, people could still be tricked or make mistakes. In July 1758, Samuel Martin sent a shipment of "very fine rum" to his son in London. He promised that he had not repeated the past mistake of mixing the rum with "the grounds of beer, as I was formerly advised to do, very foolishly."[97] Other times, information that apparently worked in one place was misapplied to another. An Antigua plantation manager named Samuel Redhead reported to the Barbadian planter William Codrington that his advice for distillation was "a poor performance and not of the least advantage to us."[98] Long-distance exchanges of rum production knowledge offered important opportunities but also created scenarios where ineffective or even detrimental ideas persisted.

At other times, certain distillers chose not to share information. Fifteen years after the end of the American Revolution, the Massachusetts distiller Fitch Hall noted his surprise at the cold welcome he received when attempting to visit London compatriots. Despite his intentions to see how a new invention of his could be adapted for British distilleries, Hall explained to his brother in Massachusetts that "you cannot conceive the difficulty there is in getting a sight of their works, they are [suspicious] of everybody."[99] British distillers may have been uniquely wary of competitors, even if those distillers plied their trade nearby. In one of the many diatribes against the Excise Office written by Bristol distillers, a Mr. Perkins worried that the interlopers would "divulge and expose the secrets of trade."[100] Even in England, distillers regularly shared their expertise with other rum producers in the Atlantic world, but at least some producers worried that open exchanges could imperil the profits to be gained with proprietary knowledge. This impulse foreshadowed new business practices integral to nineteenth-century industrialization where secrecy increasingly prevailed.

* * *

Despite these hiccups, the transatlantic world of rum production was remarkable for the level of information exchange that distillers sought from other practitioners both near and far. Tied up in a volatile business that had required a substantial initial investment, distilleries in the West Indies, North America, and Britain relied on a transatlantic community of producers to inform them of practices and innovations that might be beneficial. Such cooperation was possible because producers valued ideas devised elsewhere, had personal affinities to other English-speaking distillery operators in the Atlantic world, and calculated that the incredible demand for rum could absorb whatever produce their compatriots brought to market. They shared ideas and innovations through visits, conversations, the purchase of people, patents and books, and the exchange of objects. They also sought out, purchased, forced labor from, and accessed productive knowledge through enslaved experts. Rum production exuded significant regional variety, but distillers nonetheless recognized that they shared much in common with—and could learn from—other producers. In so doing, they repeatedly bought into a vision of the invention of rum as ongoing and dependent on regular exchanges within a broader Atlantic world. The makers and movers of rum were quick to congratulate themselves on serving "the public weal."[101]

A very different reality afflicted the majority of people hired or enslaved to work in the rum distilleries of the Atlantic world. In fact, cooperation and coercion were tethered together. The individuals seeking their personal fortunes in rum distilleries staked their success to the compulsion of men and women of African descent. When visiting the rum manufactories of friends and acquaintances, they watched enslaved men make rum in order to learn what they should require of the people whom they, in turn, enslaved. Likewise, enslaved or wage-earning distillers carried out the innovations suggested by patents or prescriptive literature. These same people were sometimes moved against their will to expand rum's frontier. The fact that tools and even the liquor could be "read" for insights into rum's production meant that individuals kept from reading and writing could still access information necessary for making adjustments. The widespread circulation of information convinced distillery operators throughout Britain's Atlantic world that substantial profits lay in the extraction of labor from the enslaved, natural resources where the commodity was produced, and people living in Upper Guinea and the Gold Coast.

PART II

Extraction

CHAPTER 4

Slavery and the Work of Making Rum

In 1823, William Clark's *Ten Views in the Island of Antigua* were converted into aquatints and published in London. Drawn while he served as a plantation overseer in Antigua, Clark's prints provide some of the most detailed visual evidence of enslaved people making rum. In *Exterior of the Curing House and Stills* (Figure 9), he depicts men of African descent carrying and loading cane trash into the fireboxes of stills and beginning the arduous process of carrying puncheons of the commodity to market. *Interior of the Distillery* (Figure 10) shows another eleven bondspeople making barrels, mixing ingredients, moving rum, and receiving instructions from a plantation distiller. All told, twenty fully dressed men of African descent—and five European supervisors—directly take part in the distillery work depicted on this Antigua plantation.

Clark's prints idealize the work of making rum. They present the various spaces of forced labor as clean, spacious, and well ordered. No hint of the near-constant dangers that defined slavery can be found.[1] Clark's vision of rum production in Antigua differs considerably from the reality detailed in letters, account books, and books written, shared, and read by distillery owners and operators.

While these prints are misleading in many ways, *Ten Views in the Island of Antigua* captures the sheer amount of work that went into creating a puncheon of rum. Plantation inventories listed only a handful of enslaved "distillers," yet Clark places two dozen men in the immediate vicinity of the still house. The larger series further highlights the many connections between women and men of all ages planting and harvesting sugarcane, grinding the cane, boiling sugar, distilling rum, and shipping sugar and rum from the West Indies. Scenes of enslaved men loading ships with these commodities even hint at labor and markets elsewhere in the Atlantic basin.

Figure 9. Exterior of a Distillery. From *Ten Views in the Island of Antigua* by William Clark (1823). Yale Center for British Art, Paul Mellon Collection.

The discrepancy between descriptions of isolated plantations with a few designated distillers and visions of scores of people on hundreds of Caribbean plantations completing the dangerous tasks necessary to make rum invites further scrutiny. How did distillery owners and slaveholders operating in different parts of the Atlantic world, but often conversing with each other, construct a system of forced labor designed to maximize the production of rum? And how did the predominantly enslaved makers of rum experience and think about their work? Answering these questions demonstrates that expectations among individual rum producers that distillation knowledge should circulate "freely" shaped how enslavement functioned throughout the British Atlantic world.

The work of making rum involved coercing physical and intellectual work out of many different groups of workers. Enslavers in the British West Indies demanded that field workers, tradesmen, sugar boilers, and distillers complete their tasks in particular ways. They sought access to the reproductive labor of enslaved women in order to raise the next generation of rum producers. French planters and British merchants pioneered trade patterns that incorporated syrups made by enslaved workers on sugar plantations in Martinique, Guadeloupe, and Saint-Domingue into the supply of distillable materials processed by North

Figure 10. Interior of a Distillery. From *Ten Views in the Island of Antigua* by William Clark (1823). Yale Center for British Art, Paul Mellon Collection.

American rum manufacturers. Distillery operators in the Caribbean, North America, and Britain also traded in the bodies and minds of men they deemed valuable for the expertise gained by working in the industry.

Being forced to make rum shaped the lives of the enslaved. Certain tasks crucial for rum production elevated their risk of death or dismemberment. Fieldwork, feeding cane into sugar mills, and bearing and rearing enslaved tradesmen "in embryo" extracted much of this most dangerous work from women.[2] Moreover, possessing expertise sometimes subjected rum producers to forced removal from family and kin if enslavers deemed their skill more valuable for some other person in some other place. At the same time, men trained as coopers, sugar boilers, and distillers often found a respite from fieldwork, as well as limited material benefits. Taking part in making rum also ensured access to the commodity itself. And gaining, passing on, and deploying skills allowed some enslaved rum producers to challenge their commodification within a system seeking to make them interchangeable. Rum may have been initially produced as an afterthought—like its main ingredients, a by-product of making sugar—but by the eighteenth century, the work of making rum shaped the contours of an Atlantic-wide system of forced labor and the experiences of those caught within it.

The Work of Making Rum

Clark's *Ten Views* situated the distillery within a larger sugar plantation. In so doing, Clark acknowledged the close connection between the production of these two commodities. Rum production thrived on the inefficiencies of sugar manufacturing: damaged canes, uncrystallizable or soured syrups, and poorly refined sugars found a second life in the distillery. Even when everything went as intended in the mill and boiling house, though, the skimmings with dirt suspended in them and the molasses that oozed out of curing sugar composed the base ingredients for rum. To account for the full gamut of enslaved people forced to expend intellectual and manual labor in pursuit of rum, we must account for the women, children, and, to a lesser extent, men who cleared, planted, and cut cane fields, and then shepherded the produce through the sugar and rum works.

The first steps in this process were also some of the most labor-intensive ones. Enslaved men and women had to burn underbrush, fell trees, and remove stumps as they converted forests into fields. Holing the cane usually occupied September and October.[3] As the soil on a plantation became depleted, workers dug "large and deep holes" meant to keep topsoil and manure in place and irrigate the cane seedlings.[4] Planters expected enslaved people to dig as many as one hundred of these six-inch deep, three-by-three-foot holes each day with the assistance of only a hoe.[5]

Once the holes were dug, manure added, and small pieces of cane planted, enslaved workers spent sixteen months nurturing the sugarcane. They reinforced the holes, applied fertilizer, weeded between the sugarcane, and fended off rats and other pests. Successfully completing these tasks ensured that the largest proportion of sweets would be sent to the boiling house and distillery. However, hurricanes, infestations, and other disruptions sometimes prematurely knocked down the cane and threatened the year's yields. When disaster struck, milling damaged canes and sending the juice straight to plantation distilleries allowed operators to recoup some of their sugar losses as rum.[6]

If planting stayed on schedule and if the canes remained healthy, the sugarcane harvest usually began each January. For the next six months, field workers spent each working day cutting and bundling the cane, carrying it to the mill by hand or by cart, and feeding the cane through iron rollers that squeezed the green juice from the stalks. Owners and plantation managers attempted to maximize profit by speedily harvesting the cane before the risk of hurricanes increased. Additionally, cane would sour within a day or two of being cut, meaning that no time could be wasted before milling the sugar. Any cane that soured before processing was sent directly to the distillery.

Plantation operators collectively demanded that a subset of people they designated as field hands undertake the work necessary to grow and harvest the sugarcane. They divided this group of people into a series of gangs organized according to age and strength. Children as young as three to five were ordered to perform light weeding.[7] At the age of five or six, boys and girls were placed on the third gang, under the supervision of a female slave driver who had demonstrated experience rearing several children of her own. "The rising generation" weeded the fields and manured the maturing canes.[8] Around the age of twelve, healthy children joined the multigenerational second gang. There, adolescents, nursing mothers, the elderly, and others whom plantation managers identified as possessing "rather weakly habits" planted canes, cleaned and banked the holes, and cut smaller canes.[9] On comparatively healthy plantations, the largest group of field workers belonged to the "great gang," a collection of able-bodied men and women compelled to dig cane holes, plant canes, cut and bundle cane, and feed the mill. By embracing the gang system, planters extracted as much labor as possible from the plantation's most vulnerable populations, including children, women preparing for or recovering from childbirth, the elderly, and the disabled.

Caribbean experts who expounded on the optimum management of sugar plantations embraced Enlightenment ideals circulating in the print culture of the era as they sought to make plantation slavery more efficient. They encouraged plantation operators to keep detailed records of the labor completed and the crops produced. Some suggested providing workers with more time to themselves, better tools, and additional provisions of sugar and rum during the most arduous work.[10] They rarely questioned the underlying racial logic of slavery, however. Furthermore, the efficiency that they sought through eliminating waste and increasing the productivity of enslaved workers introduced a particular kind of brutality to the rational and modern eighteenth-century plantation.

Many of these late eighteenth-century changes placed new burdens on enslaved women. Based on two decades of work on Jamaican plantations, David Collins advised that the most capable group of enslaved workers should be organized "without any regard being had for their sex." While he acknowledged arguments that men were stronger than women, Collins countered that there were "many women who are capable of as much labor as men."[11] Though some plantation operators may have questioned this logic, other decisions made by enslavers necessitated the use of women in the most physically demanding fieldwork. Many enslaved men occupied skilled or supervisory roles as blacksmiths, carpenters, coopers, boilers, distillers, or drivers. Women rarely occupied these roles. Based on his demographic analysis of the Barham family's Mesopotamia Estate in Jamaica, historian Richard Dunn suggests that while 40 percent of the enslaved working population was female in the latter half of the eighteenth century, women made up roughly 50 percent of the field gang.[12] On the nearby Roaring River Estate, the gender imbalance of fieldwork was even more pronounced. Seventy of ninety-two—or 76 percent—of women and just twenty-eight of eighty-four—or 33 percent—of men carried the designation of field workers.[13] Planters' strategies tasked a predominantly female group of workers with some of the most exacting work on sugar plantations. These individuals who rarely entered plantation distilleries cultivated the sucrose that was ultimately fermented and distilled within them.

The potential for upward mobility reserved for enslaved boys and largely denied to enslaved girls placed another responsibility crucial for rum production on the shoulders of African and African-descended women. Even though deaths consistently outpaced births in the sugar landscapes of the Americas, slaveholders considered enslaved women's reproductive potential as a means to improve the self-sufficiency and efficiency of their plantations.[14] On Mesopotamia, 299 women of childbearing age gave birth to 420 children whose births were recorded.[15] Half of that plantation's enslaved population had been born there, while roughly one-third had been born elsewhere in Jamaica. Enslaved mothers balanced the demands of fieldwork with nursing and rearing children.[16] As they embraced pro-natal policies in the latter half of the eighteenth century in response to Enlightenment-era challenges to slavery that ultimately imperiled the future of the slave trade, enslavers attempted to incentivize reproductive labor by shortening the work day of enslaved mothers and releasing mothers of six or more children from fieldwork.[17] Pro-natal policies that were meant to adjust to dwindling overseas sources of enslaved labor pressed the exceedingly dangerous work of childbirth on enslaved women.

Slaveholders believed that the reproductive labor of enslaved mothers prepared creole sons to fulfill duties integral to sugar and rum production. John Dovaston advised that "active boys" should be singled out and trained as millwrights, joiners, wheelwrights, coopers, coppersmiths, boilers, and distillers in order to "have your business done without loss or delay, or the trouble of setting unskillful people to do what they are not accustomed to."[18] Plantation operators preferred to train creole boys for several reasons. They were already in place on a plantation at the age when apprenticeships typically began and had not just survived the ordeal of the Middle Passage, meaning that they could extract more years of labor out of them. Experts also contrasted the strength, "genius," and trustworthiness of properly reared children to stereotypes that they attached to various African ethnicities.[19]

Job assignments for enslaved children could be wielded over families as a means of control. In the 1740s in Barbados, a Mrs. Alleyne favored an enslaved boy, likely due to a connection that she shared with one of the boy's parents. While she had planned to send him to England to receive an education, she did not manumit him or provide any financial support in her will. After her death, John Alleyne explained, "We can no farther comply with her intentions then by learning him to read, and when he is old enough putting him apprentice to some trade or other necessary for the estate whereby he may be able (though a slave) to serve it in a capacity somewhat above the common hand."[20] Alleyne nonetheless saw this course of action as more desirable than the alternative.

The power of plantation owners and overseers to determine an enslaved child's job training allowed them to prey on women of childbearing age sexually. The mixed-race children of white plantation workers and enslaved women were often placed in skilled jobs.[21] Although this arrangement aimed to satisfy the white fathers of enslaved children by keeping their progeny away from the cane fields, the enhanced value attached to children trained as coopers, masons, or distillers meant that manumitting their children if they chose to would ultimately be more costly.[22] Often, mixed-race children were the product of nonconsensual relationships between enslaved women and free men, affording mothers limited choices regarding their bodies or their reproductive potential.[23] However, Maria Nugent wrote of meeting an overseer's "*cher ami*" on the Hope Plantation in 1801. The woman proudly introduced her mixed-race children to Nugent, and her interactions with other enslaved women suggested the benefits of her favored status.[24] It is crucial not to essentialize the decisions made by enslaved mothers or overstate the level of control that they possessed, but some women may have seen benefits in giving birth to and raising children who would likely be spared from the fieldwork their mothers endured.

Field workers' duties related to sugar and rum production normally ended with feeding the cane into the mill where they squeezed out the cane juice. The mill usually sat at the center of a plantation, near the boiling house, curing house, and distillery. This layout meant that workers needed to carry the sugarcane several miles from the outermost fields to the manufacturing center of the plantation. Operating these mills threatened dismemberment or death upon the men, and especially women, who fed the stalks between three vertical iron rollers. Depending on the geography of the plantation and how well capitalized it was, the rollers were powered by animal, wind, or water. Harnessing wind or water saved on human and animal labor but came with a steep cost. As Edward Littleton lamented, "If a mill-feeder be catch't by the finger, his whole body is drawn in, and he is squeezed to pieces."[25] Enslavers often kept an axe at the mill to sever an arm trapped in a mill before the rest of the body became ensnared. Such tragedies occurred most commonly when slaveholders compelled laborers to perform this task at night, after a full day of work in the cane fields.[26] Five women living on the Mesopotamia Estate in 1763 were missing one or both of their hands, likely a tragic reminder of who the victims of the unrelenting rollers tended to be.[27]

The desire to produce as much sugar and rum as possible led to the adoption of powerful machines that stopped for nothing as they turned around the clock. This reality complicates how expertise was defined on plantations. While most women spent their working lives in the cane fields, they nonetheless relied on tactile precision to produce the cane syrup destined for the boiling house and distillery and to stay alive and whole.[28] The work of making rum exacted skilled labor from a wider array of enslaved people than is often recognized.

Once the cane juice was extracted, enslaved male artisans processed it into sugar and rum in a series of nearby workshops. Carpenters and masons built and maintained sugar works, aqueducts, and piping connecting the mill, boiling house, curing house, and distillery, and supplying the water to each of those spaces. Blacksmiths repaired tools and equipment. Coopers fit together staves of wood to create the watertight containers in which the ingredients for rum fermented and which carried the finished product to market. Suggesting the indispensability of these craftsmen to the work of making rum even beyond the Caribbean, distilleries in North America and Britain often counted coopers and carpenters among their regular workforce and contracted frequently with other tradesmen.[29] These men were just as crucial for making rum as the female-dominated field gangs.

Trades were reserved for especially able or well-connected men. As teenagers, managers plucked these "distinguished" boys from the second gang.[30] Installed as "junior" craftsmen, they learned their trades from more experienced slaves.[31] While some young men were chosen for these tasks based on perceptions of their intellectual or physical abilities, others were selected because of who their parents were. Robert McAlpine, the son of an enslaved woman named Affy working on Mesopotamia's great gang and a Scottish bookkeeper named Andrew McAlpin, began his working life when he was installed as a house servant at age eleven. By the age of seventeen, he was apprenticing as an enslaved cooper.[32] Like master craftsmen in other parts of the Atlantic world, enslavers saw utility in training adolescents who would become fully accustomed to their crafts early in life.

Enslaved tradesmen who lent their expertise to turning sugar into rum gained certain material and reputational benefits from their work. Thomas Roughley recommended that plantation operators reward the various headmen with "a weekly allowance of a quart or two of good rum, some sugar, and now and then a dinner from the overseer's table."[33] James Chisholme occasionally sent his old clothing overseas to be dispensed among the enslaved.[34] Extra food or used clothing was a highly compelling motivator for men caught within a system that perpetually pushed them and their families toward the precipice of starvation and overexposure. Tradesmen may have additionally sought out the freedom of movement or recognition of skill attached to their assigned occupations. In the aftermath of the 1736 slave conspiracy in Antigua, one writer suggested that the mobility and resources afforded to "handicraft tradesmen, overseers, [and] distillers" gave them standing as community leaders who had the ability to disrupt colonial order.[35]

Plantation operators also weaponized fear to compel enslaved men to carry out their specialized tasks. Tradesmen understood that their positions shielded them from the most excruciating work of cultivating, harvesting, and grinding the cane. They likewise worried that failing to properly learn or carry out their work—or upsetting their enslavers for any number of trivial reasons—could lead to a return to the deadliest tasks of the cane fields. In the early nineteenth century, a man named Ashton Warner wrote of his experiences on a plantation in St. Vincent. Presuming himself to have been emancipated alongside his mother as an infant, he began an apprenticeship with a cooper making containers to transport sugar and rum at the age of ten. When reenslaved on the Cane Grove Estate, the plantation manager assigned Warner to the cooperage. He recalled the first enslaver he labored under, Mr. Donald, as a fair man even though he "held [Warner] unjustly as a slave." But when a more mercurial manager replaced Donald, Warner's fears grew. At least twice the manager terrorized him with the threat of a demotion to the field gang. Warner recalled the intense fear and embarrassment caused by this possibility. He later wrote, "If the sentence of death had been passed upon me, I could not have felt more stunned. I shall never forget it! I knew that if I was sent to the field it would make me destroy myself—for it is always counted by Negroes who have been above it, the worst of all punishments—the lowest step of disgrace—to be placed in the field gang."[36] Warner evocatively described the motivations compelling him to invest his body and mind in plantation production.

From tending cane fields to giving birth to and rearing the next generation of rum producers to working as a cooper or other tradesman, many different tasks that facilitated the work of making rum sapped physical and mental energy from enslaved men, women, and children. As early as the eighteenth century, observers struggled to make sense of why enslaved people lent their mental acuity—which they could conceivably withhold—to plantation production.[37] But these motivating forces are crucial to understand because they show how slaveholders used small measures of relief from violent control, overwork, and undernourishment to extract even more work out of enslaved people. Subject to unspeakable acts of violence and perpetually on the verge of starvation and overexposure, enslaved people fought to survive.[38]

Given sugar's value advantage over rum, cane syrups gathered at the mill were first destined for the plantation's boiling house. Within that building, a team of highly trained enslaved men heated a series of copper pans with a combination of firewood and the crushed stalks that had passed through the mill. They boiled the syrup until it thickened, skimming froth and detritus off the top. Boilers ladled these skimmings into a chute that conveyed them to the distillery. Once they properly clarified and reduced the syrup, workers ladled it into clay molds. If done properly, the sugar would cool and crystallize. As moisture from wet clay packed on top of the molds seeped through the curing sugar, molasses drained out and was sent to the distillery. Any mistakes in the boiling house could be devastating to a plantation's bottom line—the Antigua planter Samuel Martin warned that claying sugar too soon would limit the amount of sugar produced and "cannot be compensated by converting it into rum."[39] Whether or not everything went as planned, however, sugar boiling created additional substances for the use of the distillery.

Plantation distilleries collected injured canes, soured juices, and pans of damaged sugar from the boiling house as well as the molasses, skimmings, and lees that eighteenth-century distillers regularly converted into rum. Balancing these ingredients to account for the taste and alcoholic potential of rum was one of the many tasks demanded from enslaved Caribbean distillery workers. They also judged when the wash had properly fermented and was ready for them to load into the stills. Firemen risked life and limb to regulate the heat applied to the boiling distillate.[40] Workers also had to maintain the water-cooling system that reconstituted gaseous alcohol in its more concentrated form. Plantation distillers tasted and measured the proof of the distillate to determine whether the flavor and alcoholic content met consumer expectations. Finally, they loaded the rum into barrels that could be carted or shipped to market. Distillers called upon their expertise to adjust the final product on the frequent occasions when these processes did not go as expected. Salable rum could not be produced without the strength and skill of these producers.

As with the other parts of the sugar works, plantation distilleries overwhelmingly demanded enslaved men to mix, ferment, distill, and package rum. Distillery work frequently drew from recently imported Africans. A majority of Mesopotamia's distillers were born in West Africa.[41] A 1729 inventory from a St. Christopher plantation likewise listed the African ethnicity of distillers. The Igbo man Quamina had likely been taken from near the Niger River, while Robin was Fante, originating from the Gold Coast.[42] Several factors may explain enslavers' willingness to station African-born people in plantation distilleries. Rigorous labor in front of the intense heat required to vaporize alcohol may not have appealed to creole boys—or their parents—seeking marginally safer occupations. Alternatively, plantation operators may have deemed distilling too important a station to assign for any reason other than one's demonstrated ability to complete the associated tasks.

While experts often warned against it, some plantation operators compelled men weakened from years of forced labor in an unforgiving environment to work in distilleries. Richard Beckford warned against using "crippled ordinary Negroes for that use which requires able-bodied vigorous men."[43] Attesting to the physical toll of life and labor on West Indies plantations, bookkeepers recorded the health of enslaved distillers as "infirm," "rheumatic," "sickly and spitting up blood," "almost blind," and "lame."[44] The comparatively poor health of distillery workers might have been attributable to their age. In 1773, the Stapleton family's Nevis plantation records listed the age of thirty-three of the thirty-seven enumerated field hands between sixteen and forty, while both distillers and two of the three sugar boilers were older than forty.[45] Some enslavers stationed old and infirm people who could no longer work in the fields, but who had acquired expertise in rum making, in these roles. In turn, these bondspeople provided continuity to the rum production process: they passed on their acquired expertise to the younger men with whom they labored and lived. For instance, when the fifty-year-old distiller Cudjoe Stanley passed away in February 1799, the plantation owner John Pretor Pinney expressed his hope that the plantation manager on Mountravers Plantation in Nevis "took care to bring up one under him that the estate may not be at a loss for a proper successor."[46]

The largest group of enslaved people systematically excluded from distillery work in the British Caribbean was, of course, women. Given the restrictions placed on nonworkers entering these workshops, distilleries emerged as one of the most gender-segregated spaces in the Caribbean. However, a bookkeeper on Antigua's Jolly Hill plantation recorded the presence of a distiller named Pusk and a second distiller named Dutchess among a list of female slaves in 1783.[47] There is little indication of why Jolly Hill diverged from the standard procedures of the island and the region. These women may have been filling in as a result of a labor shortage. Jolly Hill could have alternatively been influenced by nearby French islands, where distilleries were often placed under the supervision of women.[48] Jean-Baptiste Labat explained that he preferred female distillers "because we suppose that a woman is less prone to drink than a man."[49] Regardless of why Pusk and Dutchess were put to work in a distillery, their presence highlights that women were capable of—and in one Frenchman's view better equipped for—distillery work, though British plantation owners stationed them there exceedingly rarely.

French Connections in a British Atlantic World

Labat's observations regarding the value of female plantation distillers serves as a reminder that the British sugar islands comprised just part of an interimperial constellation of plantation societies. The French and English initially settled these islands in the seventeenth century, establishing private sugar plantations possessing their own mills, boiling houses, and curing houses. They depended on the physical and intellectual work of enslaved Africans in similar ways. Like their British counterparts, planters in the French islands relied on the gang system of plantation production and trained enslaved people to fulfill specialized industrial functions. And in both places, men performed this work in exchange for privileged treatment but also under fear of maltreatment or even death.[50] Generally, British and French sugar plantations produced the same crop and demanded commensurate labor from enslaved people of African descent.[51]

One of the most notable differences between French and British plantations concerned the production of rum. Throughout the eighteenth century, sugar plantations in the British islands usually included an on-site distillery. Such distilleries were far rarer on French plantations.[52] This difference largely resulted from France's particular brand of mercantilism. Unlike British policies that allowed, and often encouraged, trade between colonies, French officials insisted that West Indies merchants transship all produce through France.[53] French brandy makers lobbied for decrees barring distillates from the West Indies from competing with domestic manufactures. In 1713, the production of sugar-based spirits in France was outlawed, as was the exportation of rum or closely related spirits called *guildive* or *tafia* made in the French West Indies. British observers suggested that the illicit trade of syrups and spirits expanded rapidly beginning the following year.[54] In 1752, the ban was renewed, though Caribbean alcohols could now be bonded in French warehouses and then sent on to West Africa as part of the slave trade. Officials relaxed these policies in 1768—allowing the exchange of rum anywhere in exchange for foodstuffs—and in 1777—when they lifted restrictions on selling the distillate outside of France. But by that time plantation operators had devised a cadence of sugar production less dependent on the sale of alcohol.[55] Coincidentally, one of the adjustments made by French planters to maximize profits without relying on rum distillation involved purifying the sugar beyond what was practiced in the British Caribbean, thereby removing an even higher proportion of the syrups that lacked a readily apparent use.[56]

French policies did allow for the consumption of sugar-based distillates on the same islands where they were produced, and these alcohols emerged as an important part of the consumption patterns and informal economies of the enslaved. About one-quarter of syrups generated in Saint-Domingue in the 1770s were distilled into a rumlike beverage called tafia in-colony.[57] The 1685 *Code Noir* forbade enslavers from furnishing enslaved people with cane brandy instead of stipulated allotments of cassava and meat.[58] Yet enslavers offered portions of rum to individuals who performed night work or other arduous tasks.[59] During his time in Saint-Domingue between 1799 and 1803, the French physician and botanist Michel Étienne Descourtilz recorded a variety of informal transactions that involved trading tafia for labor and information from the island's African-descended population. He dispensed spirits to a Congolese man who helped him spear caimans. An enslaved cook named Adonis offered a bottle of tafia to destroy a voodoo call. Likewise, Descourtilz pried medicinal knowledge from enslaved individuals and gathered the life histories of Africans over nighttime conversations fueled by tafia and tobacco.[60] For the men and women acquiring tafia from the Frenchman, the product could be consumed or resold. It also featured in certain spiritual rituals. For instance, the *danse á Don Pédre* was a voodoo dance introduced to the southern province of Saint-Domingue around 1768. After consuming tafia mixed with gunpowder, a dancer would look downward as he or she performed rapid, forceful contortions to the point of exhaustion.[61] This French Caribbean equivalent to rum was manufactured and widely valued in French islands even if it largely remained a local—or illicit—trade good.

With limited plantation distilleries, and a circumscribed market for any rumlike beverages that were produced, French planters sought to unload excess syrups. A La Rochelle merchant and defender of the wine industry's advantage named Jean-Baptiste Gastumeau responded to the seizure of smuggled guildive in 1751 with an impassioned plea for maintaining policies meant to protect French vintners. Falling back on an attitude that the makers of rum in Barbados overcame a century earlier, he argued that brandy occupied a fundamental place in the national economy while syrups left over from boiling sugar in overseas colonies were a "useless and superfluous material."[62] From his vantage in a French port city, Gastumeau probably underestimated the value of molasses to French planters. With no legal outlet for molasses or the spirits derived from it in France, Caribbean producers and merchants sought out markets in other islands where they could receive goods otherwise in short supply. Despite being a four-day journey from Martinique, St. Eustatius emerged as a common site for the trade of French plantation goods to British and American merchants.[63] During the War of Spanish Succession, French islanders also bartered molasses and tafia for beef and other provisions at St. Thomas, St. Lucia, and Barbados.[64] They even traded quantities of molasses and rum with Boston merchants in exchange for "large ships."[65] These ingredients that would be converted to rum in Britain's Atlantic colonies aided in the purchase of the more than seventy-seven thousand African slaves who disembarked from British ships on French islands. Many of those men and women ultimately died producing the volumes of sugar and its by-products that were reinvested in this illicit branch of the transatlantic slave trade.[66]

Until the 1760s, the French considered these exchanges illegal, while the British taxed them at a rate that many merchants were unwilling to pay. Traders operating in both empires collaborated to hide their transactions. Most commonly, mariners would slink into "some creek or bay in the night time," picking up illicit cargoes from nearby French plantations.[67] Enslaved mariners powered the coastal trade linking Guadeloupe and Martinique to nearby St. Lucia, St. Eustatius, and Antigua.[68] North American merchants also sent lumber, horses, and other supplies directly to French islands. Governor Worsley complained that "there is now in New York, no less than sixteen distilling houses set up, which are wholly supplied with molasses from Martinique."[69]

For their part, British traders could pick up supplies of contraband molasses at entrepôts where they were legally admitted. They could then rack molasses (or even rum) in barrels with English markings to misrepresent their provenance. Or they could feign emergencies that provided cover for them to enter and trade in foreign ports that were otherwise off-limits.[70] These forms of smuggling collectively removed large volumes of molasses from the sites where it was produced and eschewed or muddied any sort of paper trail. Illicit trade therefore ensured that molasses might flow from French to British hands, but qualitative descriptions of that commodity (or how it would be best used) rarely did.

Following the Seven Years' War, more liberal trade policies made it possible to legally—or semilegally—trade in molasses.[71] Yet these changes did not fundamentally change how or where these exchanges took place. French authorities gave their blessing for the establishment of a limited number of free ports in 1763, where foreign ships could exchange foodstuffs for molasses. These free ports, such as Le Môle St. Nicholas in Saint-Domingue, developed at the sites of well-entrenched smuggling marts.[72] Aided by the liberalization of trade policies, North American merchants imported 5.7 million gallons—or over 87 percent of the total imported volume—of molasses from the French sugar islands by 1770.[73] After the American Revolution, an even larger share of the American trade passed through Port-au-Prince. Companies specializing in the American trade streamlined this process by connecting French produce with American merchants who would have generally struggled to communicate with the planters themselves.[74] Coastal vessels and trains of mules carried sugary syrups from the sites of their production to the warehouses supplying American distilleries.[75] French producers provided raw ingredients to distillers elsewhere in the Atlantic world without ever interacting with them directly.

The limited connections between molasses producers and the individuals converting the syrups into rum led to issues of quality and trust. The Virginia distiller Daniel Roberdeau warned in 1775 that molasses in Le Môle was "ever to be had, but never free from adulteration."[76] Similar complaints followed Martinican syrups as well. Stephen Holland complained to Moses Brown in 1792 that molasses from that French island was "not what I call merchantable."[77] Each of these merchant-distillers described a central pitfall of molasses detached from the context of its production. The labor of enslaved producers in Saint-Domingue, Martinique, and Guadeloupe contributed vast quantities of ingredients destined for North America's rum distilleries, yet the circumstances of trade limited the flow of ways of knowing and making that often circulated with commodities.

Enslaved Rum Producers on the Move

At least on occasion, however, experts enslaved in the French Caribbean traveled the same routes as the molasses that they were forced to produce. Free ports relied on the movement of a multiethnic cast of sailors, engendering fears that crews offered refuge for runaway slaves.[78] Yet, just as merchants sought to move molasses through these ports without clues of its production, slave traders tried to detach African-descended people from their prior lives. According to Jennifer Morgan, "Sale was an originary moment in the destabilization of and violent disregard for Black family life."[79] The anonymity afforded by sites of transimperial trade facilitated this sort of dislocation and rendered it harder to reverse.

Both of these dynamics shaped the experiences of a man named Francis and another named Francois. In July 1749, Francis absconded from James Smith's Boston sugar refinery. Before being enslaved in Boston, Francis had lived in Martinique and at least passed through Louisbourg, Nova Scotia. Smith likely accounted for Francis's experience in the French Caribbean sugar industry when placing a bounty on him.[80] Nine years later, a man named Francois self-emancipated from Joseph Griswold's New York rum distillery. Griswold described Francois as being roughly forty years of age and speaking "little or no English, as he mostly lived with the French."[81] These two men endured linguistic and social dislocation when transported to North America. The advertisers' decisions to share these particular details in runaway advertisements aligned with their understanding that the reverse route could be appealing as a route to either freedom or reunion.

North American producers also sometimes forcibly relocated people to new frontiers of sugar and rum production. In 1771, Captain Daniel Campbell claimed ownership over a man named Boston in Grenada. The twenty-eight-year-old man coincidentally hailed from Boston, where he had been "brought up to the sugar-baking business in this town." In response to what his enslavers characterized as "his bad behavior," they forced Boston to the West Indies. Boston challenged the authority of his enslavers to relocate him by running away and seeking a return to North America.[82] Campbell had disregarded others' evaluations of Boston's behavior, Boston's own wishes, and the financial costs of a potential escape because he deemed the man's body and mind useful for advancing commodity production. Campbell's acceptance of those risks offers further evidence of the indispensability of enslaved experts to transfers of productive knowledge within the Atlantic world.

Francis, Francois, and Boston were three individuals caught up in a more extensive trade in African-descended men whose understandings of processes necessary to make rum made them desirable to distillery operators in distant colonies. When this system functioned as hoped, these men tended not to say much about the purchase or sale of distillery workers. However, mentions of enslaved distillers and sugar workers self-liberating and other breakdowns in the forced transport of experts suggests that such transactions were relatively common.

The 1729 odyssey from Barbados to Boston of a man named Quacqo offers another opportunity to understand these journeys. It unveils the risks incurred by distillery operators hoping to acquire expertise through the intra-American slave trade and explains why they took those risks. Equally important, Quacqo's story highlights the dislocation, discomfort, and opportunities for self-presentation that he experienced during his forced relocation.[83]

Sometime in 1728 or early 1729, a customs officer and cooper in Speightstown named Edward Denny decided to transport and sell Quacqo. He enlisted a merchant named Benony Waterman to facilitate the sale in Boston. Neither Denny nor Waterman provided a definitive reason for why they sold this man. Waterman told a potential buyer that Quacqo was sent "away for a small fault." Perhaps he ran away repeatedly, or gained a reputation as a thief, or otherwise refused to meet the expectations of his enslaver. Quacqo himself later suggested that "he was sent away for being drunk."

Quacqo was not the only one forced along this route. Starting a few years earlier, Waterman often transported groups of up to ten enslaved men, women, and children north to Boston during the summer. In 1729, he advertised his cargo of "likely young Negroes lately arrived from Barbados" as well as "good Barbados sugar and molasses." All were available for purchase at the foot of Scarlet's Wharf.[84] Some of Boston's approximately forty rum distillers must have read these newspaper advertisements with great interest.[85] Indeed, merchants like Waterman found a ready market for the sugar, molasses, and human chattel ferried between the two British colonies.

Less is known about how Quacqo and the people he journeyed with experienced their confinement aboard ship. In the late spring, as another sugar harvest wound down, Quacqo boarded the *Martha*, captained by Edward Cooper, and began a journey of several weeks to Boston. It is unclear if Quacqo knew the other people who boarded the ship with him. Olaudah Equiano's famed 1789 narrative of his experiences of enslavement and emancipation provides some context for this sort of journey. Equiano noted that the food on the journey from Barbados to North America was preferable to that on the Middle Passage. Quacqo likely experienced this journey a bit differently. He spoke English and worked as a tradesman, likely evidence that he was born in Barbados. He may have never before been to sea, so a foreign diet and seasickness would have been more jarring for him. Two years earlier, a pair of people forcibly transported by Cooper to be sold by Waterman had died shortly after disembarking in Boston, victims of the physical toll of being transported to North America.[86] Equiano also noted that the intra-American voyage separated him from his "countrymen," whose fellowship constituted "the small remains of comfort" that he had enjoyed.[87] Quacqo probably experienced a similar loss of friends and family as he left Barbados.

Fatigued, nauseous, and scared, Quacqo came ashore along the Boston waterfront in early July 1729. Before even taking out an advertisement in the newspaper, Waterman marched Quacqo several wharves south to the yard in front of John Colman's rum distillery.[88] While Colman and Waterman had not previously conducted business together, Waterman believed Quacqo's unique skill set should be marketed directly to distillery owners. Waterman offered Quacqo to Colman for a hundred pounds. Colman balked at the price and asked, "What is he that you ask such a price for him? What was he brought up to?" Colman assumed that Quacqo's valuation could be attributed to his considerable skill.

Waterman explained that Quacqo was a cooper by trade. At this point, Colman began to address his questions to Quacqo, who later acknowledged that he had been coached to respond in certain ways. Colman asked him if he could make molasses hogsheads and rum hogsheads. Quacqo answered affirmatively. He asked how many hogsheads he could make in a day. Quacqo answered two. He asked Quacqo if he drank heavily and Quacqo said no. Satisfied that Quacqo "must be a very good workman," Colman agreed to the purchase price and assumed ownership of Quacqo. He believed that the skill Quacqo accrued in Barbados made him a sound investment in Boston.

To this point, Quacqo's story aligns with many other victims of trans-American crossings. His owner in one part of the Atlantic world wanted to sell him and realized that Quacqo's specialized set of skills increased his value in another part of the rum-producing world. It was at this point that Quacqo's experience began to diverge from what everybody expected. A few days after assuming control of Quacqo, Colman sent him down the road to work with a cooper named Richard Barnard. Per Colman's instructions, Barnard "set him to work but found him to understand very little of a cooper." He found that it took Quacqo several days to make a fish cask and that he was wholly incapable of making the tight hogsheads necessary for storing rum. Furthermore, when pressed by one of the hired workers at Colman's distillery, Quacqo admitted that he had been transported away from Barbados for drunkenness. Colman confronted Waterman with these facts and sought to cancel the sale. Waterman insisted that Quacqo worked as a cooper in Barbados and refused to return the money. Colman sued the Barbados merchant.[89]

How did Quacqo transform from a skilled to an unskilled man as he moved from Barbados to Boston? One prevailing answer has been generally to ignore the effect of enslaved skill, thereby muting the intellectual work of bondspeople.[90] Yet enslaved expertise was more than a mirage. Forty-one percent of slave advertisements in Massachusetts advertised the skills possessed by the individuals being offered for sale, suggesting that would-be buyers found something useful about these descriptions.[91] This particular buyer—John Colman—worked in the industry, meaning that he was well-versed in the finer details of the West Indies trade. He had also bought and sold people on other occasions, and accumulated the usual trappings of a successful businessman.[92] His purchase of Quacqo may not have worked out as he hoped, but his experiences in a transatlantic market for rum—and with the people usually tasked with producing it—led him to believe that purchasing enslaved distillery workers was a risk worth taking.

Quacqo's story instead suggests the imperfection of transplanting ways of knowing and doing between rum-producing regions. Rum producers frequently sent materials, ideas about fermenting and distilling, and people back and forth between the West Indies, North America, and Britain. These exchanges were crucial for the invention and production of rum. But regional disparities also had to be accounted for. In this case, the work expected of a distillery cooper varied widely. In Massachusetts, where hired labor remained comparatively cheap, coopers fashioned barrels from rough-hewn oak staves. Alternatively, in an effort to reduce freightage and maximize enslaved labor on plantations, Caribbean merchants imported processed staves or even precut "puncheon packs" from North America.[93] As a result of this ongoing process of deskilling, Quacqo could qualify as a cooper in the Caribbean while lacking the finer skills expected of him in a Boston distillery.[94]

Quacqo also acted on opportunities to shape his own experience and displays of ability. The depositions highlight how he changed his story—claiming to be highly skilled in one context and demonstrating his incapacity to do the work required in another; sober in one and prone to drunkenness in the other. There were other opportunities for self-presentation as well. Is it possible that Quacqo acted in certain ways while toiling in Barbados, hoping to be moved elsewhere? Or, once in distant Boston, may he have thought he could return to loved ones in Barbados simply by failing to meet the expectations of his new enslaver?[95] Maybe he sought to slow down his work for Colman initially so that the expectations of his productivity would remain lower. Such questions linger, but they suggest the power that Quacqo may have exercised to limit his commodification.

Quacqo's story is so visible in legal records because he was either unwilling or unable to facilitate the transfer of expertise between two American colonies. Far more often, however, the purchase of enslaved distillery workers went smoothly enough to pass without comment.[96] In fact, distillers were some of the largest urban owners and renters of bondspeople in North America.[97] A 1772 census of Newport, Rhode Island, found that eighteen of the largest taxpayers operated distilleries and each one owned between one and ten people.[98] In Boston, Thomas Child owned three enslaved people at the time of his death in 1753, and a 1760 inventory of Andrew Johonnot's distillery recorded two enslaved workers.[99] Peter Chevalier's Philadelphia distillery began operations with "2 Negroes" named Sharp and Tom in 1761 and added a third man, the "Negro Pompey," in 1763.[100] Though not a slaveowner himself, Richard Derby rented two enslaved workers from separate owners in 1762 and early 1763.[101]

Making rum in both the West Indies and North America required many of the same tasks to be completed. The workforce procured and mixed huge vats of molasses and skimmings from nearby sugar refineries. Because temperatures tended to be cooler on the continent, North American distillers often elected to add yeast—and sometimes jalap—to the wash. After fermentation slowed, the distillers loaded molasses into stills that were, on average, twice the size of those used in the West Indies. Such stills required an even larger volume of firewood to operate, and the length of the distillation run took commensurately longer. As in the Caribbean, coopers such as Quacqo had to shave, bend, and join oak staves into watertight containers to hold the rum. Certain details of the work regime differed from other parts of the Atlantic world. For instance, enslaved distillery workers in North America tended to labor alongside owners, salaried distillers, and day laborers. The nature of some of the work also varied in important ways. Yet the many occasions where men like Quacqo were forced to migrate from landscapes of rum production in the Caribbean to distilleries in North America suggests that individuals believed that experience gained in one part of the rum-producing world could be applied elsewhere.

Distillery owners viewed the work of enslaved people as being highly skilled and thus valuable. This was, of course, why John Colman and Benony Waterman settled on such a high price for Quacqo. Such a calculus, even sometimes calculated erroneously, prevailed throughout the eighteenth century. Almost fifty years after Quacqo's journey, Cornelius Harnett sought to hire or purchase a distiller to operate his Wilmington, North Carolina, rum manufactory while he served in the Continental Congress in Pennsylvania. This was a difficult task, especially during the American Revolution. Harnett ultimately lamented that he could find "no distiller either white or Black to be got at any rate."[102] In his mind, the labor of a hired or purchased distiller could be largely interchangeable. Even Harnett's unsuccessful attempts to locate a new distiller to supervise the production of rum suggest that distillery operators continued to envision the purchase and transportation of enslaved experts from one colony to another as a viable means of acquiring the necessary expertise to conduct their business.

Enslaved and formerly enslaved rum producers in North America confronted the risks and opportunities of distillery work. Coerced workers regularly completed arduous and dangerous tasks. The nature of rum production exposed them to extreme fluctuations in temperatures and required near-constant physical exertion. Workers of African descent were often singled out for the most onerous jobs; some died in horrific accidents. For instance, in 1735, an enslaved distiller in Isaac White's Boston distillery dropped a pail of spirits on the floor, which quickly caught fire. The fire spread to the distiller's rum-soaked clothes, sending the burning man running "into the sea to quench himself." The relief came too late as the man succumbed to his burns.[103]

Although enslaved people possessed limited ability to choose which work they completed, they could gain certain benefits from making rum. They openly or clandestinely acquired some of the rum that they were producing. Individuals leased to distillery owners lived more independent lives than those working and living with their owners.[104] Likewise, free Blacks trained to work in distilleries were able to parlay their expertise into job opportunities during a period when free workers of African descent struggled to find employment.[105] Further suggesting that distilleries hired workers whose race may have precluded them from other opportunities, a Native American man named Edward Greene labored in a Rhode Island distillery over the winter of 1792.[106] Distillery work was exhausting and dangerous, and many formerly enslaved people refused to engage in it, but it provided certain openings for workers who had learned the associated skills.

The marketplace for enslaved distillery workers occasionally crossed the Atlantic Ocean, drawing in places less often envisioned as the homes and workplaces of the enslaved. At least fourteen thousand people of African descent lived in London by 1770. Although their labor was most visible in domestic settings, these coerced laborers also served in various trades in England, Scotland, and Ireland throughout the eighteenth century.[107] Prior to 1730, men of African descent could formally apprentice with London tradesmen and even attain the status of freeman. However, in that year, a Barbados-born man of African descent named John Satia completed his apprenticeship with a London joiner. While Satia was granted freeman status, the lord mayor of London resolved to keep that accomplishment from becoming precedent. On September 14, 1731, he declared "that for the future no Negroes or other Blacks [were] to be suffered to be bound apprentices at any of the companies of this city to any freeman."[108] This ruling foreclosed the opportunity for enslaved and formerly enslaved people to complete formal apprenticeships in England's capital, but some young bondsmen continued to train in these workshops.

Enslaved people worked in British distilleries and cooperages, but operators tended to only note their presence when they ran away. At least three men of African descent liberated themselves from British distilleries over the course of the eighteenth century. In 1760, John York, a twenty-six-year-old man bearing country marks and who spoke halting English escaped from John Harland's London malt distillery.[109] Fifteen years later, the eighteen-year-old Black distiller's apprentice John Otley eloped from another London distillery.[110] Otley was listed as an "apprentice," and his escape occurred three years after the Somerset decision rendered slavery legally unenforceable in England, but some Britons continued to force labor from their "servants" through custom and threats of enslavement in the colonies.[111]

At least eight men trained or training as coopers also left their sites of forced labor in Britain during the eighteenth century. Many of these coopers came from Britain's American colonies. A sixteen-year-old man of mixed-race descent named Matthew Natwit had been born in Jamaica.[112] Caeno, "brought up in Philadelphia [and] by trade a cooper," escaped the bonds of slavery in Cork.[113] Caeno probably learned his craft in North America, further demonstrating the mobility of skills often associated with the production of rum.

In other cases, slaveholders elsewhere sent bondspeople to Britain to undergo formal training. Almost 80 percent of the slaves listed for sale in British newspapers were between the ages of one and seventeen.[114] While many of those children were sent to perform household work, American enslavers occasionally sent young enslaved men to learn trades in demand in the colonies as well.[115] Governors of the Cape Coast Castle—a British slaving fort on the Gold Coast—also sent company slaves to London to apprentice in a variety of trades.[116] One of those men, Quashy, escaped from the London cooper he was training under in 1736. Trying to entice him to return—and sensing that he likely did not want to remain in England—the governors hoped to secure his cooperation by promising that he would be "sent home to his own country directly" if he came forward.[117] Perhaps the Royal African Company believed that Quashy had already acquired enough skills to help them package and dispense rum and other liquid commodities at the time of his escape. Britain could be both the terminus for tradespeople previously enslaved elsewhere and the site of training for coerced people meant to heighten the profit margins of distant slaveholders.

Some enslaved workers saw Britain as a respite from plantation societies in the Americas. Black Britons enjoyed a freedom of movement and a standard of living unlikely to be replicated on a sugar plantation or even in a New England distillery.[118] Furthermore, as the next chapter will detail, enslaved distillery workers in England and Scotland avoided the deadly plantation environments of the West Indies, which were actively being engineered to promote maximum rum production but at heavy human costs. A man named Harry went so far as to state that he was "not willing to return to his native country, Antigua" in 1771.[119] The substantial free Black population living in Britain tantalized Harry with the possibility that he could live undetected as a free man.

Other bondspeople no doubt experienced the profound dislocation of being forced to a foreign land thousands of miles from their friends and family. Perhaps that explains why the creole blacksmith Peter escaped London on a fleet headed to the West Indies, an enslaved sailor named Joe worked to "ship himself for Carolina," or an unnamed fifteen-year-old boy moved from Bristol to London, hoping to "embark for Jamaica."[120] Relocating to Britain improved the lot of some enslaved people, while motivating others to emancipate themselves.

* * *

The work of making rum consumed the labor of far fewer enslaved people in Britain than it did in the West Indies or even North America, yet the presence of coerced distillery workers and coopers in England, Scotland, and Ireland highlights how making rum expanded slavery and made its forms and conditions more flexible. Distillery operators facilitated the circulation of distillation knowledge by forcing people who gained training in one part of the rum-producing world to labor elsewhere. The expertise required for making rum increased the value of slave trading and involved a greater number of places in these transactions. While the conditions of enslavement varied, the Caribbean, North America, and Britain operated within a linked system. Throughout the eighteenth century, distillery operators—and those who supplied them—converted the bodies and minds of the enslaved into more rum and more slaves.

In the descriptions of men, women, and children making rum, we also catch glimpses of how these individuals experienced their work. They usually made rum under threat of physical violence. Some gained small concessions—a modicum of self-determination, safer workspaces, better clothing, more food or resources, or even a recognition of their ability. By making rum—or occasionally refusing to do so—the enslaved belied enslavers' attempts to treat them as interchangeable commodities. This fact is especially pronounced in the testimony of a formerly enslaved Virginia distiller named Daniel Hopkins.[121] Toward the end of a deposition taken after the US Civil War, Hopkins's inquisitors zeroed in on the fact that the man did not read or write. The attorneys sought to use this fact to discredit his expertise and his recollection. They ended by asking the man how he knew what he did about the distillery's operations. Perhaps defensively, maybe proudly, maybe defiantly, Daniel ended his testimony with five words: "Just by my own ideas."[122]

CHAPTER 5

Rum's Environmental Costs

Thomas Jefferys's 1770s map of Tobago plotted a new course for making sugar and rum. At the conclusion of the Seven Years' War, Great Britain claimed the former French colony of Grenada, as well as Dominica, St. Vincent, and Tobago, a series of islands that France and Great Britain had previously agreed not to occupy. This map, printed roughly a decade later, documented several innovations from previous, more spontaneous colonization efforts in Barbados and Jamaica. At several spots along the coastline, Jefferys acknowledged the presence of Native people governed by King Roussel or King Peter—a tacit recognition of Indigenous power in the region that remained strong enough to resist British conquest. Jefferys also computed the size of individual landholdings in each of the island's eight divisions. The average sizes of between a hundred and three hundred acres—smaller than the most capitalized plantations on previously settled islands—reflected imperial policies designed to encourage the settlement of islands like Tobago with a larger number of white, British settlers. And, most curiously, the map, reproduced as Figure 11, marked three tracts of land as "reserved in wood for rains."[1]

The presence of these plots on the Jefferys map shows that authorities invested in this scheme recognized the environmental costs of earlier colonization efforts and thought they could mitigate them on the recently ceded islands. An act of the Privy Council in the spring of 1764 dictated how these ceded lands would be apportioned. The council acknowledged that islands settled more than a century earlier, such as Barbados and Antigua, "have been distressed by the entire waste of that wood." Such islands now had to import any timber that they needed to construct sugar works or keep their stills running. Even more distressing, many experts claimed that the loss of tree cover led to a drier, windier climate that could imperil commodity production.[2] The Board of Trade advocated

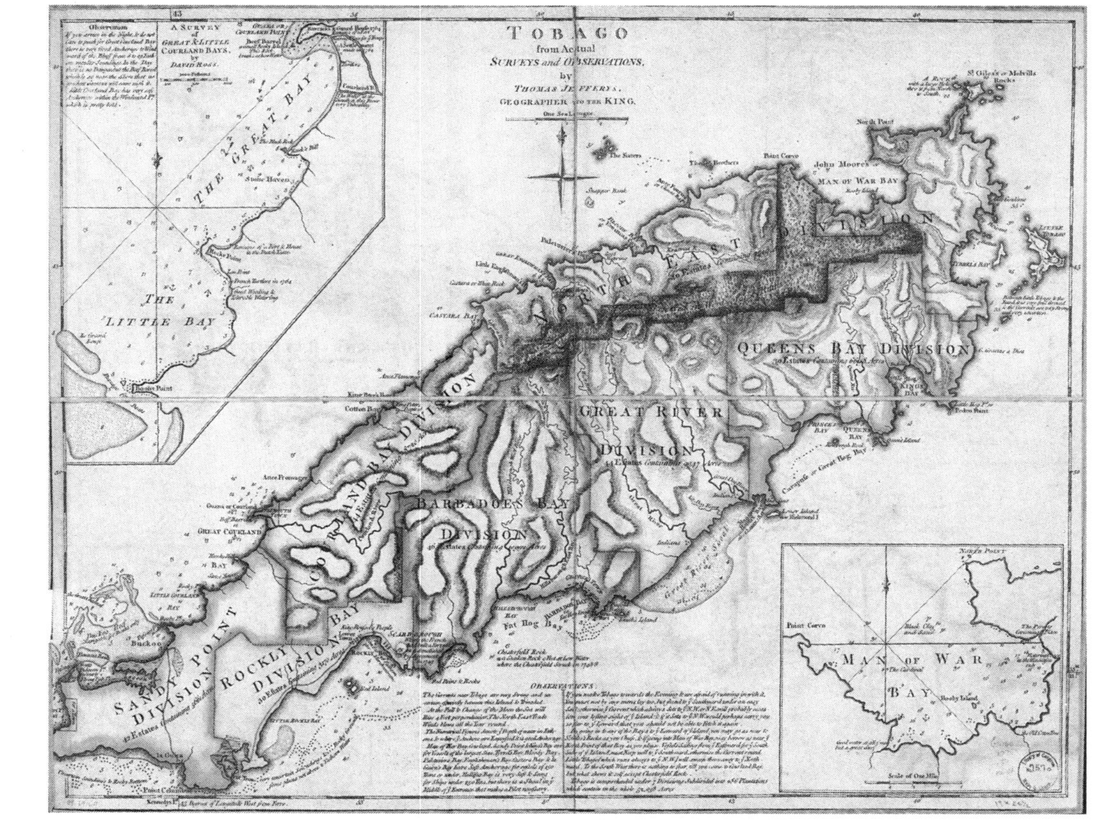

Figure 11. *Tobago from Actual Surveys and Observations* by Thomas Jefferys (1775). Library of Congress Geography and Map Division.

combating the changing climate by preserving "a proper number of acres of woodland," which would be "most useful in the preservation of the seasons."[3] Policymakers understood that past efforts to make sugar and rum in the Caribbean made islands less habitable and productive in the long run.

Other aspects of this settlement plan limited its effectiveness. The Privy Council did not specify how much land should be set aside, leaving such decisions to local officials. On Tobago, the island most successful in creating reserves, the vast majority of the preserved land was in the mountainous interior on land that would not have supported sugar cultivation anyway. Over the ensuing decades, the small reserve set aside on King's Hill in St. Vincent suffered "highly injurious" encroachments.[4] Neither Dominica nor Grenada ever formally preserved woodlands. Dominica's government heeded other parts of the settlement plan, though, such as taxing settlers for woodlands that they owned but had not yet cleared.[5] In these diverging decisions, the conflict between conservation and extraction come clearly into focus.

The fact that unbridled sugar and rum production continued to win out over policies aimed at longer-term sustainability is telling. Colonial officials knew from firsthand observation and scientific treatises that failing to protect woodlands created an environment less hospitable to humans and suboptimal for plantation production. Yet knowledge of these dire consequences had limited effects on the recently ceded islands and well-established British colonies alike. Nor were planters responsive to the effects of these plans on the enslaved people they compelled to make rum and sugar. Instead, they crafted a system of commodity production that generated wealth and shielded elite inhabitants from environmental harm by exposing hired and—especially—enslaved workers to the most insalubrious situations.

Rum's emergence as the quintessential Atlantic commodity prioritized maximizing profitability above other considerations such as future productivity. Making rum thrived on the denuding of landscapes more than producing sugar or other plantation commodities did. Nearly every step in the rum production process either promoted a clear-cut landscape or benefited from the forest products generated by that process. These behaviors kept the fires underneath stills stoked, the production and consumption of rum regulated, distilleries in working order, and puncheons of rum circulating.

Gathering this amount of timber with limited forethought led to a host of environmental changes in and beyond the Caribbean. Deforested islands experienced more volatile weather patterns, marked by periods of intense drought interspersed with harsher climatic events. When these conditions imperiled rum production, plantation operators sought to mitigate the issues affecting commodity production through innovation, often unleashing other unintended consequences. They rarely sought to solve the underlying problems they observed, however. Ultimately, distillery owners in the West Indies and North America accepted these risks as they engineered a system where nonelite, and especially enslaved, producers bore the most extreme costs of deforestation, disaster, and disease that accompanied their rum yields.

Making Landscapes Barren

The system in place to make rum in the West Indies consumed vast swaths of woodlands. In order to convert dense Caribbean forests into sugar and rum factories, many acres of land needed to be cleared. When Cary Helyar first planted sugar on his Bybrook Estate in Jamaica in 1672, he had supervised the planting of 24 acres of cane and the clearance of an additional 6 acres for pasture and provisions by a workforce of 55 enslaved Africans and 14 European servants.[6] Within a couple of decades, his nephew John reported that 400 acres had been planted with cane. The space needed for sugar works, slave dwellings, pastureland, and provision grounds meant that a significant proportion of the remaining 600 acres that the Helyars owned had also been cleared. Enslaved people, whose population on the estate had swelled to 140, slashed underbrush and felled trees to convert forests into fields. Individuals enslaved on Bybrook or rented from other slaveholders cleared far more land each year than was standard. More commonly, plantation owners would clear one or two acres of woodland each year, progressively increasing the amount of land planted in sugarcane.[7]

On smaller islands, deforestation proceeded rather quickly. When Richard Ligon lived in Barbados in the 1640s, he complimented the dense, mature forests.[8] The sugar boom led to widespread deforestation in the ensuing decades. Despite some charges that the island's forests had been cleared by the 1660s, an emphasis on locally sourcing fuel and lumber lasted longer than is sometimes suggested.[9] But settlers had largely deforested Antigua by 1750, and Montserrat lay barren in the 1770s.[10] Inhabitants of these clear-cut islands resorted to fulfilling their timber needs by cutting and shipping wood from more remote regions of the Caribbean and the Americas.[11]

British planters continued to cut down trees to expand commodity production on islands with remaining woodlands. After assuming the management of a recently purchased plot of land in Dominica in the 1770s, Robert Bruce announced that he had ordered eighteen acres of woodland to be cleared. He explained that the remaking of the natural landscape aimed to "lessen the labor of the estate" by placing cane fields contiguous to the mill, boiling house, and distillery. Acknowledging that "the trouble and risk to those who commence the settlement of a new estate out of the woods is almost incredible," Bruce assured the plantation's absentee owners that he had hired a slaveholder who operated a jobbing gang to handle this laborious task.[12] Depending on jobbing gangs to clear land outsourced the heightened risk of death that accompanied it to hired hands.[13]

The human and financial costs associated with clearing woodlands might suggest that planters would judiciously manage trees on their properties. Yet they cleared land for many reasons other than carving cane fields or pastureland out of forests. Many of these underappreciated causes of deforestation specifically served the needs of plantation distilleries. Fuelwood remained a steady need for those distilleries throughout the seventeenth and eighteenth centuries. To minimize fuel needs, planters often directed the enslaved to save and burn cane stalks that had been squeezed dry by the sugar mill.[14] This fuel was known as bagasse, and it proved remarkably efficient for boiling sugar but not for rum. Bagasse tended to burn hot and very quickly. Distillers observed that fires which burned inconsistently or at too high a temperature imparted an "empyreumatic, or disagreeable burnt flavor" to rum that must be avoided.[15]

Sourcing firewood for rum distilleries—which likely burned around one cord of wood on each day of operation—was thus an important part of a planter's or manager's job. In the months leading up to the beginning of the 1758 sugar harvest, a bookkeeper on the Chancery Hill plantation in Jamaica recorded the labor of as many as "35 hands culling wood for [the] still house."[16] These enslaved hewers of wood often focused on cutting fast-growing copperwood trees and gathering brush.[17] When land was cleared for other uses, more mature stands of trees would be converted into firewood. For instance, when John Bryce contracted to clear seven acres of the Barham family's Island Estate in Jamaica in 1780, he was instructed to deposit the cut timber outside of the plantation distillery.[18] Frequently, individual plantations might not have had enough fuel to keep their distillery going due to local rates of deforestation. On larger islands like Jamaica, such shortfalls could be solved by purchasing wooded lots elsewhere on the island.[19] Barbadian planters instead had to seek out external sources of fuel. The high costs of fuelwood may explain why planters on some smaller islands tended to produce less potent rum that was distilled only two rather than three times.

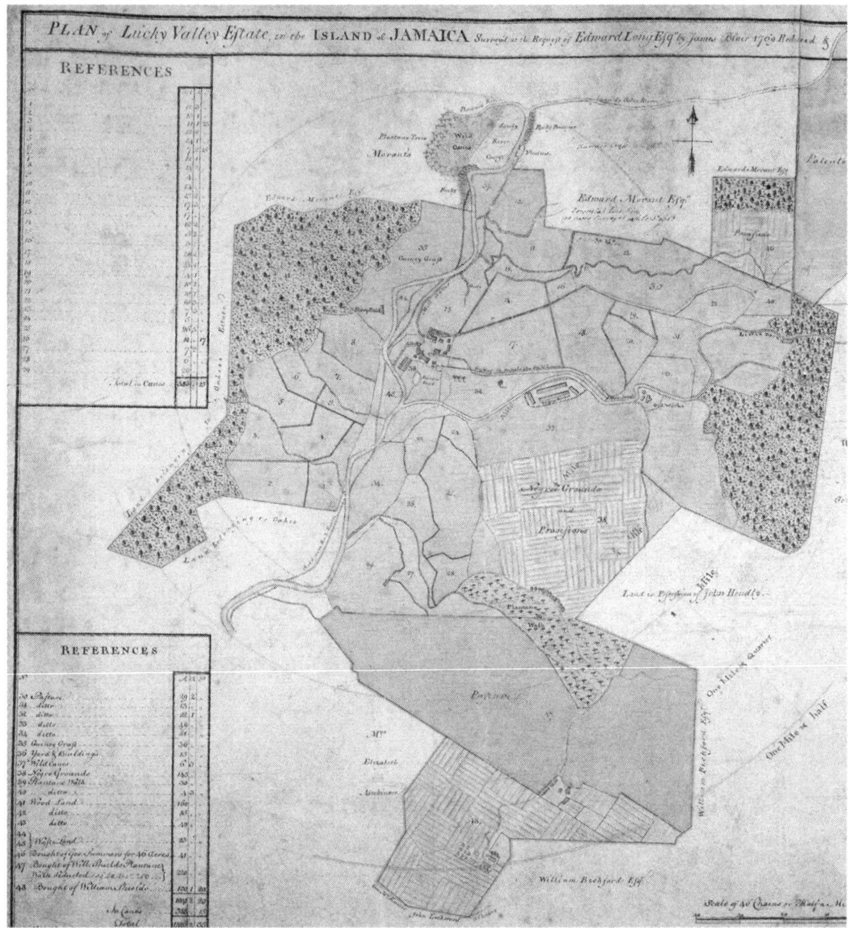

Figure 12. *Plan of the Lucky Valley Estate, in the Island of Jamaica* by William Gardner after James Blair (1769), detail. From the British Library Archive.

While clear acreage and fuelwood put heavy demands on islands like Jamaica, they did not lead to the same levels of deforestation. In fact, landowners sometimes found another reason to clear-cut their holdings before the space or fuel was necessary: surveillance. Planters and enslavers considered unobstructed sightlines as crucial to the effective management of productive landscapes.[20] In 1782, Ezekiel Dickinson detailed his plans to clear two hundred acres of woodland on his family's property. Though he had no immediate plans to plant the land in sugar, and he probably did not have a need for all of that timber at once,

Dickinson nonetheless thought that clearing land first and answering use questions later would enable "the overseer to see where to carry proper drains for laying the upper part of the estate dry."[21]

Clearing vast landholdings also made it easier for undermanned enslavers to watch the people they compelled to work. A 1769 plan of the Lucky Valley Estate, included as Figure 12, shows a typical layout for a Jamaican sugar plantation. The sugar works and housing for enslaved and free workers occupied the center of the plantation, with cane fields protruding out from those hubs. Fields were not separated by any sort of windbreaks, and woodlands only remained on the very edge of the landholdings, often on land that was too sloped or marshy to grow sugar.[22] Even denuded of trees or other sight breaks, plantations in Jamaica tended to be too large and hilly to be observed from one location. However, a plantation's workspaces—mill, boiling house, distillery, and cane fields—could usually be seen from both the sugar works and wherever the overseer lived.[23] Conversely, the hard-to-reach woodlands that stymied surveillance efforts tended to be less-regulated spaces. They often included provision grounds where the enslaved grew food to personally eat or sell. Gullies and other wooded areas also became associated with marronage and other illicit gatherings, as evidenced by the presence, in Figure 13, of both armed maroons and discarded bottles that likely contained rum.[24]

The fact that these plantations produced rum dictated the forms that surveillance took. Enslavers and enslaved alike found rum desirable for both its physiological effects and the cultural meanings it could convey. Because the individual estates produced it, procuring rum did not require a purchase on the part of the plantation owner. The cheapness and availability of the spirit meant that owners and overseers regularly dispensed it to enslaved workers as a means to coerce more work out of them. As early as 1679, Thomas Trapham advised, "If it chance to rain and wet the laborers in the field, it is agreeable if not necessary to fortify with a moderate dram."[25] Over a century later, a Jamaica planter named John Gardner Kemeys claimed that rations of sugar and rum had become so commonplace—and expected—that the enslaved would "not cut a stick without it."[26] When they dispensed rum during rainy weather or during the long days of work mid-harvest, planters acted on the belief that it could increase productivity.

Planters simultaneously fretted that the prevalence of rum on the estates that produced it also led to trouble. By the end of the eighteenth century, overseers diagnosed enslaved men as "addicted" to rum.[27] They worried how this dependency affected the labor regime necessary for its continued production. On the Phillipsfield plantation in Jamaica in the 1790s, an enslaved driver named

Figure 13. *The Maroons in Ambush on the Dromilly Estate in the Parish of Trelawney, Jamaica* by Robert Cribb after François Jules Bourgoin (1801). From the British Library Archive.

Pera began to drink more and more. Pera refused to do as his enslavers instructed, responded poorly to correction, and "was very imprudent to the whites." Other men began to follow Pera's lead by drinking heavily and declining to "work in their usual way." The plantation's operators, of course, worried most about the "loss of labor on the estate."[28] Pilfered rum and its effects on productivity contributed to these concerns. In 1777, a man named Howell absconded from John Mills's Nevis estate after stealing rum straight from a still.[29] Three years later, the distillery on Hope Plantation in Jamaica burned to the ground when an unnamed man caught a puncheon of rum on fire when trying to appropriate some of its contents.[30] As the responses of angry absentee plantation owners made clear, the fine line between rum as elixir and rum as inebriant could only be drawn through the careful supervision of workspaces.

At times, enslavers became concerned that rum consumption might grow from an individual failing to a threat to the colonial racial hierarchy. In the aftermath of a suspected plot among enslaved Antiguans to murder whites on the island, the Antigua Council's investigation placed rum at the center of the conspiracy. A man named Billy who testified at the trial detailed conspirators taking "the oath in a glass of rum mixed with grave dirt to kill man, woman, and child."[31] Jemmy remembered a toast of rum punch promising "damnation to those who failed to kill the whites."[32] By January 1737, a subset of slaveholders became concerned that the execution of dozens of enslaved people had gone too far. In arguing for an end to the violence, they suggested that many convicted conspirators only joined the cause after "being first raised, and warmed with liquor, and then flattered, threatened, importuned, and persuaded."[33] Possibly because Antiguans blamed the rum for social disorder—or perhaps simply as a result of the scarcity of lumber on a denuded landscape—authorities used the wood from nine rum hogsheads to build the scaffolding used to execute some accused conspirators.[34]

Building distilleries and distillery equipment also consumed large quantities of finite lumber, though the resulting deforestation was not always local. While they varied in size based on when they were built and the size of the enterprise, distilleries tended to be among the largest and most valuable buildings on Caribbean plantations.[35] One ordinary still house described in a 1798 inventory of an Antigua estate occupied a wood-framed stone building that was fifty-two feet long, twenty-six feet wide, and eleven feet tall.[36] Sometimes a storehouse for rum would be built underneath the distillery, and a loft created additional storage over part of the building. Inside, several dozen cedar cisterns were reserved for fermenting wash. Depending on the preferences of the owner, these cisterns were sometimes sunk into the ground. In other distilleries they sat above ground. Their size corresponded with the size of the stills—an average of about four hundred gallons apiece. Plantation distilleries might have two larger stills to initially process the rum wash, and one slightly smaller still where the low wines were redistilled to refine the flavor and further concentrate the alcohol. Worm tubes—used to condense alcohol vapors back into a liquid—often snaked outside of the building into water cisterns or ponds. Those pipes continued back into the building where rum could be collected in locked pails that limited pilfering. The floors were often made of wood, and the roof tended to be shingled with hardwood.

The specific labor required to make rum favored using timber building materials even if the Caribbean climate and risks associated with distillation did not. Planters embraced wood-framed stone buildings and shingled roofing as means to protect their investments. The wooden framing relied on tension strength, which offered increased stability during earthquakes.[37] Likewise, hardwood shingles shed rainwater more effectively than thatching, protecting expensive imported distillation equipment and ensuring that rum could be made even during periods of heavy rain.[38] Planters usually relied on wooden cisterns because they were an affordable option for creating large, watertight vessels. A 1752 guide to making sugar and rum further advised that wooden vessels best served this purpose because of their "imbibing" traces of a batch of rum, which expedited fermentation.[39] Samuel Martin worried, however, that wood "tainted" the syrups that touched it if a previous batch had spoiled.[40] Distillery operators stated their preference for cedar, in part because it was insect-resistant and "seasoned" more quickly than other materials.[41]

Lumber for the distillery was far from a one-time expense. William Beckford noted in 1790 that "as the West-India Islands are so subject to hurricanes, and the sugar works to fire, the first expense therefore cannot be said to be the last."[42] Distilleries and their contents also sometimes just wore out. A 1768 inventory of Samuel Martin's Antigua estate estimated that the newly hung stills "will probably last twenty or thirty years."[43] Neither wooden cisterns sunk into the ground nor shingles weathering rain and sun lasted so long. One writer blamed "leaky, rotten cisterns" for the loss of dozens of hogsheads of molasses each season.[44] Plantation bookkeepers regularly listed the planks, beams, shingles, and staves needing replacement. Sometimes planters tried to source lumber locally—by flooring their distilleries with mahogany or building cisterns out of indigenous mastic or santa maria woods—but more often they relied on imports from Europe and especially North America.[45]

Besides fuelwood, the most constant drain on timber was the oak puncheons and hogsheads that contained rum and molasses on its way to market. A significant amount of rum would be consumed locally, which allowed for those puncheons to be reused. However, merchants loaded thousands of puncheons for transshipment each year. In 1747, for instance, Jamaica planters exported 5,061 puncheons of rum and 3,302 hogsheads of molasses.[46] A puncheon contained around 20 curved wooden boards—or staves—which were usually shaped out of white oak. Planters preferred staves from more temperate climates because they had a tighter, more impenetrable grain.[47] One expert estimated that plantation operators expected a loss of up to half of their imported staves as enslaved people redirected them for their own use.[48] Based on these estimates, Jamaica's 1747 rum and molasses exports would have depended on a total of 202,440 puncheon staves and 132,080 hogshead staves—roughly 500,000 board feet of imported oak.[49] When stave supplies ran out, there was no alternative means to send products to market.[50]

Building, maintaining, and operating Caribbean distilleries—and the puncheons and hogsheads that they relied on—consumed millions of board feet of timber per year. Merchant-distillers in North American cities facilitated much of this trade, sending various types of lumber to British and French islands in exchange for molasses and rum.[51] In the seventeenth century, the wood could be sourced closer to these trade centers, but procuring the lumber became more challenging over time. By the end of the American Revolution, a former imperial official in North America reported that "the timber of New England and the middle states has for many years been in a great measure exhausted."[52] Answering the call for lumber from more and more distant woodlands, seventeen-year-old Lemuel Roberts traveled from his home in Stillwater, New York, to Grand Isle on Lake Champlain in 1768 to spend "a cold and dreary winter, amidst great fatigue and toil" cutting staves for a British merchant firm. Reflecting the increased pressure placed on this "complete and totally uncultivated wilderness," Roberts and his brother slept in a lumber shed previously built by Canadian woodcutters and visited with other nearby hewers of wood.[53] The timber demands of making rum depended on culling trees thousands of miles from Caribbean plantations.

Reactions to Environmental Change

The international demand for American timber had effects on local environments along North America's eastern seaboard. Benjamin Franklin explained in a 1763 letter that "when a country is cleared of woods, the sun acts more strongly on the face of the earth."[54] Likewise, the experiments of Stephen Hales earlier in the eighteenth century suggested that the moisture found in plant matter "provided in the earth against a dry season."[55] Because of the immensity of the American continent and the various land management decisions made by private landholders, deforestation proceeded less uniformly than in the Caribbean.[56] Nonetheless, historians have tracked the changing climatic and environmental conditions accelerated by North America's continuing role as a lumber supplier for the French and British Caribbean. Individual towns became drier, warmer, and windier. When rains did arrive, the storms tended to be more intense and often caused flooding. Soil that baked under the sun and was deprived of labyrinthine networks of roots washed away with those rains. The silt choked waterways necessary for trade and sustenance.[57]

While the climatic effects of deforestation in North America were noted by local residents observing changes carefully, the clear-cutting experienced in the West Indies—and its effect on the weather—was much starker. Setting aside wooded preserves in Tobago and St. Vincent explicitly responded to the increasing levels of desiccation witnessed on islands like Barbados and Antigua. When the governor and council of St. Vincent reaffirmed their protection of

King's Hill in 1791, they touted the success of their initial conservation efforts in "attracting the clouds and rain."[58] Even those individuals resistant to preserving woodlands nonetheless acknowledged that land management affected the climate. As he ordered the clearance of his property in 1782, Ezekiel Dickinson insisted that the desiccation of a newly denuded landscape "will make the estate more healthy by letting in sun and air."[59] Dickinson did not deny the effects of deforestation, but he did question whether they were undesirable.

Planters generally agreed, though, that droughts entailed one of the greatest risks to making sugar and rum. They fretted that prolonged periods of dry weather—sometimes lasting years—would impede the growth of sugarcane, producing smaller quantities of sucrose to be crystallized or distilled.[60] These same droughts imperiled the lives of enslaved people because provision grounds where they grew much of their own sustenance wilted.[61] Dry weather also disrupted the water supply to the mills and distilleries that relied on it to turn the rollers that crushed the cane, as an ingredient in the rum wash, and to condense rum vapors back into liquids. In 1761, a plantation manager explained to Roger Hope Elletson that "the current of water to your still house is too weak . . . [and] neither is the current constant owing to its sinking into the ground in dry weather."[62] Without a reliable source of water, rum simply could not be made. Finally, excessively dry landscapes endangered the largely wooden distilleries and the cane fields that surrounded them. In 1780, a fire in the Hope plantation's distillery raged, melting even the pewter necks on the stills. Together, enslavers and enslaved gave up on saving the still house and turned their attention to containing the fire. The plantation manager considered their success in averting larger disaster to be a small miracle due to "the long drought preceding the accident."[63]

Flummoxed by droughts that their own behaviors had exacerbated, planters experimented with many small innovations that they hoped could stabilize commodity production. Samuel Martin's attempts to mitigate drought conditions in Antigua in the mid-eighteenth century show the lengths that some planters would go to lessen the effects of water shortages. He experimented with planting sugarcane farther apart so that the roots would not compete for finite moisture and deployed a fire engine to water cane lands.[64] He planted provisions of black-eyed peas and Guinea corn. He even considered building a gristmill to alleviate famine conditions.[65] Other contemporaries sought to limit the risks of plantation distilleries catching on fire by roofing the buildings with fire-resistant materials such as slate tiles or copper sheathing.[66] In making each of these adjustments, planters like Martin hoped that operational changes could alleviate the pressures of drought.

Martin and his compatriots also sought to reengineer the plantation landscape to better serve the rum-making process. Water shortages left distilleries without water for mixing into the rum wash, cleaning equipment, and cooling the distillate. Unwilling to let a water shortage stall the rum-making process, planters forced enslaved people to carry water to the distillery. The weight of the water and the fact that this sort of labor was exacted on top of the standard plantation workload—and at times when potable water was likely in equally short supply—exacted a heavy human toll. Martin advised a neighbor that this added labor made those enslaved on his plantation "more sickly in crop time especially the women, by carrying water at night to cool down your worm tubs and coppers."[67] Martin's solution, which his brother had carried out on their family's Antigua plantation in the 1730s, entailed building a large water reservoir next to the distillery.[68] Distillery ponds became an irreplaceable—but dangerous—part of plantation topographies as the century wore on. John Dovaston advised that an ideal still pond should be at least thirty feet long by thirty feet wide and six feet deep. Bryan Edwards suggested that they should be considerably larger and hold twenty to thirty thousand gallons of water in reserve. Ideally, the pool's foundation would be made of flagstones or brick, which were to be covered by a thick slab of lime-based cement. Finally, a foot-thick layer of clay would keep the pond as watertight as possible.[69] When the distillery needed water, workers could deploy either a bucket brigade or a pump to move water into the worm tubs. Others even snaked the worm tubes into the still pond to lessen the labor of carrying water.[70] By storing such a large quantity of water, rum producers hoped that they could work through periods of little rainfall.

This attempt to shield rum production from the effects of climate change unleashed several unintended consequences on the health of people living and laboring near the distillery. Martin acknowledged that stagnant pits of water were "injurious to the health of the inhabitants" but dismissed those concerns on his plantation by explaining that due to the prevailing wind patterns, "exhalations can never pass to my dwelling, or the Negro houses."[71] In this context, Martin attributed unpleasant smells—of rotting animal or vegetable matter, or even foul and stagnating water—to disease-causing miasmas.[72] By the end of the distilling season, these ponds accumulated dirty water, ashes, distillery waste, and manure, making them likely sources of miasmas.[73] While Martin's attention to the threat of miasmas may have offered the enslaved some protection in their habitations, he made no such accommodation for the distillery and sugar works where people spent considerably more time laboring.

Epidemiologists no longer believe that smells alone can cause disease, but putrid, stagnating water no doubt made Caribbean plantations less healthy places. If water from still ponds was ingested, it easily could have caused the fluxes that enslaved people often dealt with. When the ponds were at their filthiest, the warm water also provided an ideal hosting ground for malaria-carrying mosquitoes. Once cleaned each July, those same ponds—especially when clay-bottomed—instead invited the *Aedes aegypti* mosquito and the yellow fever that it transmitted.[74]

Deforestation also magnified the effects of storms. Though the climate generally became drier, intermittent rainstorms may have become more intense. Planters who had clear-cut their lands could no longer rely on tree root systems to keep the topsoil in place. Those uprooted trees also ceased absorbing rainfall. Furthermore, removing tree cover caused the moist topsoil to dry out more quickly, which limited the amount of rainwater that could soak into the ground. Combined, these factors increased the risk of flooding and contributed to the impoverishment of the soil by carrying away the nutrient-rich humus and topsoil. In addition to constricting sugarcane harvests, the loss of topsoil also released large amounts of sediment into rivers and streams, which constrained water flows and navigation. Furthermore, these changes in water absorption rates caused water to pool. Resulting puddles, and the decline of habitat for insect-eating birds, provided suitable conditions for *Anopheles* mosquitoes to spread malaria.[75]

Planter responses to climate unpredictability heightened the issues caused by excessive rains. In order to harness the power of gravity to move water and the ingredients for rum into the still house, plantation distilleries tended to sit at the bottom of hills, often on low-lying land. For plantations bisected by rivers, the optimum site for distilleries often sat near the stream. While convenient during droughts, this placement became a liability during storms. Flooding was the most serious immediate cause of death and property damage when hurricanes struck.[76] Rising waters infiltrated plantation distilleries, destroying rum and the equipment used to make it.[77]

Rum production increased the likelihood of adverse weather events, and, in turn, weathering natural disasters was a unique experience for Caribbean rum producers. In addition to imperiling lives and damaging sugar works, hurricanes and other severe storms brought with them gusts of wind and storm surges that could ravage cane fields. When those cane fields were destroyed, the ability to create rum out of waste increased in importance. Planters directed the enslaved to harvest the damaged cane forthwith, grind it, and send the juice to the distillery. In these trying times, plantation operators reconceptualized rum as a means to recoup some of the financial losses wrought by tempests.[78] But frequently, the associated flooding seeped into the underground fermenting cisterns and the winds ripped off the roofs and even toppled the distilleries themselves.[79] Attempting to salvage some profit in the midst of calamity, overseers directed the enslaved to complete makeshift repairs or even build temporary shelters so that making rum would continue unabated.[80] The same storms no doubt led to deaths in enslaved communities, the destruction of cabins that tended to be less solidly built than the distilleries, and devastation of provision crops. Yet the paired system of slavery and rum production that Caribbean plantation owners had carefully constructed meant that their attention often dwelt on the spaces where rum was made more than the people tasked with making it.

The heavy environmental costs of making rum defined the industry in North America as well, even if some of the specific stresses of the system varied. By 1770, roughly 140 rum distilleries operated in British North America. Most of these distilleries were located in port cities like Boston, Newport, New York, and Philadelphia. The fact that this work was undertaken in cities meant that distilleries were far more concentrated than in the West Indies. For instance, in Philadelphia, fourteen distilleries (operating on a much larger scale) coexisted in a city similar in size to one or two large Jamaica plantations. Interspersed among houses and other industries, these distilleries encountered a fuelwood scarcity that only intensified as the century wore on. Observers worried that the loss of tree cover made the city hotter and disease prone.[81] Like their compatriots in the Caribbean, Philadelphians also fretted over wooden distilleries and their propensity to catch fire.[82]

The close quarters of American cities introduced unique concerns, especially regarding the disposal of industrial wastes. Peter Chevalier's distillery, which opened in 1761, was likely distilling over 17,000 gallons of molasses per year.[83] If that constituted an average output, Philadelphia distilleries alone—merely the fourth-largest distilling center in British North America—could have churned out up to 240,000 gallons of rum per year. But only one-quarter to one-third of the molasses wash ended up as rum. Contemporaries described 480,000 to 720,000 gallons of leftovers each year as "foul and stinking liquors."[84] Philadelphians worried that miasmas emanating from distillery by-products and other industrial waste caused disease outbreaks including yellow fever.[85] Modern science corroborates the danger associated with molasses-based effluent. When drained from stills, the waste is high in temperature, acidic, and full of dissolved solids and ash. The lead used in manufacturing eighteenth-century stills seeped into the waste, releasing dangerously high levels of the heavy metal wherever it drained.[86] In certain circumstances and doses, raw stillage has been shown to devastate aquatic environments, killing over 50 percent of fish within four days.[87]

Urban American distillers tended to dispose of this poisonous slurry in two troubling ways. They often dumped it into drains on the side of the street, relying on gravity and other wastewater to slowly carry it into streams and rivers. This technique choked some of those waterways, including the Dock Creek, and contributed to horrible stenches. When city officials imposed fines on this sort of behavior, many distillers instead sought to store their effluvia within their urban properties. With limited space, they burrowed down. Petitioners alleged that the wastage in these purpose-built pits seeped into the groundwater and rendered neighboring wells "entirely unfit for common use."[88] Complainants repeated these claims in newspapers and legal decrees throughout the eighteenth century, suggesting that changes in distillers' behavior were hard to enforce.

Uneven Exposures

Distillery owners who profited from practices causing the degradation of the urban environment generally concerned themselves more with the short-term profits generated by their distilleries than the wide-ranging implications of their business decisions. Their disinterest resulted in part from being able to remove themselves from the path of diseases that their business decisions might foster. In the aftermath of yellow fever outbreaks in the 1740s, elite Philadelphians increasingly built country estates right outside of the city where they could quarantine in the summer and fall.[89] At least eight men who partnered in or outright owned a Philadelphia distillery also kept one of these country houses. After the death of Philadelphia distiller Edward Croston, his widow, Ann, sought to sell the family's "plantation" in Northern Liberties. She boasted that it was "in a very healthy air," with access to a "fine stream of water" and "well-timbered."[90] According to Croston's description, the most notable aspects of the property—its healthfulness and resources—aligned with the very things that making rum had helped sap from Philadelphia proper.

The divergence between the environmental conditions deemed suitable for elite and nonelite Americans came into conflict in the 1780s and 1790s as a result of both politics and disease. After the ratification of the US Constitution in 1788, Philadelphia temporarily became the capital of the United States.

A correspondent for the *Pennsylvania Gazette* worried how the "unwholesome effluvia of dirty streets" would jeopardize the health of congressmen, foreign ministers, and other government officials unaccustomed to them.[91] Roughly a month after the government arrived in July 1790, another writer accused the "offensive, stinking and destructive waters" unleashed by distillers and other industrialists like tanners and butchers of inviting a miasma "which lay the foundation of dangerous diseases, especially in hot weather." In this essay and a subsequent response, Philadelphians advocated either outlawing distilling in Philadelphia or removing these sorts of industries to a less populated part of the city, farther from the halls of power.[92] These regulatory measures were never enacted, but they show how the need for elites to occupy Philadelphia during the disease-infested summers prompted renewed calls to reverse the despoliation caused in part by making rum.

The yellow fever epidemics of the 1790s further exposed how environmental disasters shaped by human decisions were experienced differently based on legal status, race, and financial means. Epidemiologists then and now believe that these outbreaks had to do with Philadelphia's distilleries. Benjamin Rush blamed the filthiness of the city. Scientists now recognize that while the environment in Philadelphia may have allowed *Aedes aegypti* and yellow fever to thrive, the disease was likely imported each year by the ships that carried Mid-Atlantic grains and timber to the Caribbean and brought back commodities including the molasses that would be distilled into rum. During the outbreaks of 1793 and 1798, those who could afford to fled the city when the outbreaks began. In 1798, as many as three-quarters of the inhabitants living within two blocks of Dock Street—the epicenter of rum distilling and complaints lodged against its makers—left the city.[93] Believing incorrectly that their race conferred immunity to the disease, Philadelphians hired people of African descent to care for the sick and dying.[94] More generally, those who lacked the resources to stop working and find housing outside of the city tended to remain. Referring in 1798 to the class-based system of suffering that resulted, authors of one report explained that "after most of the citizens, whose circumstances would permit, had fled to the country, the poor began, generally, to suffer, and the disease sustained no abatement."[95] As disease raged in Philadelphia, the white and Black men who would have carted firewood and molasses, built puncheons, mixed ingredients, and run the stills likely had to stay put in the contagious city.[96]

Those who owned Caribbean plantation distilleries also recognized that the environment they had, in part, built was incredibly unhealthy, and they often tried to limit their exposure to its most deadly aspects. While their understanding of the causes of many diseases was incomplete, planters nonetheless correlated drought conditions, reservoirs of putrid water, malnourishment, and natural disasters with disease. The most common conditions that they encountered included malaria, yellow fever, measles, tuberculosis, syphilis, yaws, hookworm, schistosomiasis, and smallpox.[97] Between one-eighth and one-twelfth of white settlers in Jamaica died each year between 1730 and 1770, and the white population was only able to sustain itself during the era of slavery through near-constant immigration.[98] The inability of Europeans and their few surviving descendants to stay alive in the tropics was frequently used to justify the enslavement of Africans—who, they argued, were better able to labor in hot conditions—in the Caribbean.[99] Many of these same afflictions—coupled with overwork, undernourishment, and workplace accidents—also claimed the lives of African-descended slaves with tragic constancy.

Observers furthermore noted that the rum made on these plantations played a prominent role in the deadliness of the Caribbean. In a 1684 pamphlet, Thomas Tryon advised planters of the risks of "superfluous drinking" in the hot Caribbean climate. He warned that overindulging in the "pernicious drink called PUNCH" had been associated with a deadly stomach disorder called dry bellyache.[100] By the eighteenth century, planters recognized that this disorder was caused by the particles of lead infused into rum through pewter distilling equipment.[101] Experts advised aging the spirit, which gave some of the heavy metals time to settle at the bottom of the cask. Nonetheless, dry bellyache continued to cause the death of free and enslaved people in the Caribbean.[102] Because aged rum carried a higher value and was more esteemed among elites, this source of lead poisoning may have afflicted property owners in the Caribbean less often.

Owners of sugar and rum plantations sidestepped many risks by doing the same thing that their counterparts in Philadelphia did: removing themselves from harm's way. Owners of 111 of the 4,006 Jamaican plantations inventoried between 1732 and 1786 lived off the island, usually in Britain. While a small minority of all property owners, this group of planters tended to own larger-than-average estates and may have been responsible for the majority of all sugar exported from Jamaica.[103] The tendency for the architects and owners of the largest sugar and rum manufactories to profit off of Caribbean plantations while living in Britain only intensified as the eighteenth century unfolded.[104] Their successes within a community of practice that prioritized information sharing probably led other aspiring absentee distillery owners to adopt strategies less concerned with the local environmental impact of large-scale rum production out of a hope that they too would eventually decamp for healthier climes.

Even when they were not in a position to permanently remove themselves from the Caribbean, plantation owners still capitalized on their freedom of movement. While living in Jamaica, John Campbell frequently wrote to family members in Britain regarding the healthiest place to live. Although he acknowledged in 1793 that "the times have been rather sickly for the white people," he stayed put and four years later boasted that "this is the finest climate in the world for an old man."[105] Campbell's correspondence details his preoccupation with health and an acknowledgment that he could migrate as necessary while many others could not.

Many of the planters who remained in the Caribbean kept houses in island cities, which served as havens from less salubrious plantation microclimates. Elite sugar planters were overrepresented in island assemblies. During the legislative season, which extended from October to February in Jamaica, they decamped to the capital city of Spanish Town. In 1754, 107 of 411 heads of household in that city were listed as planters, and 27 carried the distinction of being sugar planters.[106] Although the legislative season was scheduled around the agricultural calendar, it also meant that leading planters lived and socialized in the city in the months when the mortality rates for free and enslaved Jamaicans tended to be highest.[107] These planters and their allies recognized the relative health of Spanish Town. When opposing an attempt to remove the capital to nearby Kingston, planters criticized the move on the basis of healthfulness. One sympathetic doctor went so far as to suggest that Spanish Town was "always a healthy place."[108] Planters built urban oases in Barbados too, and the high rates of absenteeism in the Ceded Islands can partly be ascribed to the slow development of cities there.[109] Such cities had economic and social draws, but they also appear to have had healthful ones.[110]

Whether permanently moving, considering relocation, or temporarily decamping for a nearby city, the men who controlled the means of rum production made such calculations based on their ability to hire a team of plantation operators to carry out supervisory work. Authors of guides to plantership set high standards for this supervisory class. Samuel Martin suggested that plantation managers needed to master skills including math, bookkeeping, architecture, and engineering, as well as sugar boiling and distilling.[111] Based on his experiences in Barbados, William Belgrove further believed that whoever was hired to manage plantation distilleries should be efficient in setting their fermenting molasses, exact in determining when to start and stop collecting distillate, and adept in managing distillery fires. They also needed to diligently record the output of the distillery and carefully watch their enslaved workers to minimize carelessness and theft.[112]

Planters often struggled to employ and retain such well-rounded employees. Populations in the Caribbean rarely sustained themselves in this era, which left planters reliant on migrants from Britain. High risks of mortality tied to disease, natural disaster, and enslaved resistance deterred many men from relocating for this work. Alarmed by paltry white settler populations, island assemblies repeatedly passed deficiency laws that required planters to employ a number of white workers in proportion to the number of people that they enslaved.[113] While many planters found it more cost-effective to pay the associated fine and chronically underman their plantations, these laws nonetheless shaped who was hired to manage, oversee, and keep records of plantations and their distilleries. In 1774, Samuel Martin hoped to find an English orphan he could bring to Antigua and train in plantership.[114] Similarly, by 1803, a J. Shand noted that decreasing mortality rates among enslaved people in Jamaica resulting from amelioration, combined with continuing high mortality among white islanders, was making it hard for him to satisfy the conditions of the Deficiency Act. He asked a correspondent in England for help locating four men who were "sober, young without habits formed."[115] New migrants were especially prone to certain illnesses like yellow fever and malaria endemic within island societies. They also lacked the specialized set of skills that planters desired.

The demand for hired workers gave those Britons who relocated to the Caribbean and cheated death considerable negotiating power. One writer suggested that in Jamaica even "the poorest white person seems to consider himself nearly on a level with the richest, and, emboldened by this idea, approaches his employer with extended hand, and a freedom, which in the countries of Europe, is seldom displayed by men in the lower orders of life toward their superiors."[116] Owners and managers blamed this dynamic for problems in the stillhouse. In 1790, a plantation manager named Charles Rowe wrote to his employer that the shortfall in his St. Elizabeth Plantation's rum yield should be blamed on the "mere carelessness and inattention of the person that had the direction of the distillery," and Rowe's successor blamed a subsequent rum drought in 1799 on "the want of good distillers."[117] Yet these men received salaries far higher than they could have expected in England and could usually find another job even if they gained a reputation on one plantation for subpar work or deficiencies in character.

This supervisory class of white plantation workers needed to stay on plantations to complete their work, but they nonetheless enjoyed far greater freedom of movement than the people they compelled to work. Plantation owners fretted that their bookkeepers, distillers, and managers left their workstations and allowed sugar cultivation and rum production to progress unsupervised.[118] The transient nature of this workforce meant that they often sought out new sites of employment between harvests. More generally, these migrating plantation employees tended to imagine their stay in the Caribbean as temporary, yearning for the day when they could return home to Britain with fortunes secured.[119] Realizing this dream was rarer, but it nonetheless motivated decisions to prioritize short-term profits.

* * *

Distillery owners, and to a lesser extent the men they hired to oversee the spaces and people they claimed as their own, exercised their freedom of mobility in ways that enslavement denied others. In the context of a dangerous and, many believed, deteriorating environment, such decisions placed the burden of living through and troubleshooting the threats of deforestation, drought, disaster, and disease squarely on communities of enslaved people. Plantation operators understood that their pursuit of efficiency in making rum exacerbated these threats. They even adjusted to improve the productivity of their distilleries when environmental threats imperiled outputs. But they rarely considered broader changes—such as reforming or limiting commodity production—that would have lessened these effects.

Distillery owners understood that their pursuit of rum and the profits it unlocked exposed enslaved and hired workers to increased risks of death at the hands of natural disasters, famines, and epidemic disease. They made such calculations, in part, because makers and movers of rum were prepared to redirect some of the produce of their distilleries to fuel the transatlantic slave trade. Decisions made to prioritize rum production contributed both to the tragically high mortality rates of the eighteenth-century Caribbean and the market-driven solution of repopulating the region through the enslavement of millions of West Africans.

CHAPTER 6

Manufacturing Demand and Supplying Slavers

Around 1802, the rum producer and former slave-ship owner Thomas Robison put his distillery and surrounding buildings in Portland, Maine, up for sale for twenty thousand dollars.[1] He or his agents plotted the land and its buildings in order to attract would-be buyers. That map, included as Figure 14, offers a rare glimpse of New England rum distilleries and their facility for constructing thriving businesses around two long-distance trades—one with the West Indies and another with Africa. In so doing, Robison and his collaborators profited from converting molasses produced in the Caribbean at high human and environmental costs into rum that would be exchanged for captured Africans to be resold in the Americas.

Robison and his compatriots represented his distillery (labeled A on the map) as a cutting-edge enterprise in myriad ways. Initially built in 1784, the building itself measured sixty feet by seventy feet. The sellers described it as "the first in America of its size." Fresh water, which Robison earlier touted as the secret to his rum's quality, flowed into the distillery through a series of pipes. Distillers manufactured the rum in four stills ranging from 50 to 1,600 gallons. They could churn out as many as 400 gallons of rum per day.[2] Rum distilleries had dotted the American coast for over a hundred years by this point, but Robison embraced technological improvements to operate on a much larger scale.

Several outbuildings supported the distillery's endeavors. Across the wharf, artisans in the cooper's shop (D) transformed Maine's hardwood forests into barrel staves and, ultimately, some of the strongest puncheons crisscrossing the Atlantic Ocean. Further down the wharf, a fifty-by-twenty-five-foot storehouse (C)

Figure 14. Thomas Robison's Distillery. *Plan of Ann (now Park) Street, Portland* (c. 1802), detail. Collections of Maine Historical Society, MaineMemory.net, item 11989.

extended three stories high. It could store three hundred hogsheads of molasses—enough to make over thirty thousand gallons of rum.

The wharf (B) jutting out past these buildings was most important for Robison's business plan. It measured eight hundred feet long, allowing ships that drew up to eleven feet of water to safely dock. The length of the wharf reflected Robison's understanding that making it easy to supply the distillery with molasses and departing ships with rum was the key to financial success. As he explained to associates in 1790, he had extended the wharf to "accommodate those who do me the favor to load their vessels. If any of your friends should want rum shipped them to Guinea I could supply them with good rum on very reasonable terms."[3] Robison made easing the frictions of Atlantic trade a priority.

Robison's distillery complex evoked modernity. It operated on a larger scale than distilleries earlier in the century. The operators organized several integrated manufacturing processes on one property. They connected centers of production and consumption around the Atlantic world. And they responded efficiently to specific—and sometimes shifting—consumer tastes.

To Robison, modern business practices also entailed supplying slavers. When he outfitted the *Eagle* in 1790, Robison carried over ten thousand gallons of rum to Upper Guinea. Like other merchants and distillers who joined him, he believed that his cargo closely matched the distinctive tastes of African slave traders in the region who preferred the taste, strength, and attractive pricing of North American rum. Furthermore, he expected that as they neared Africa the captain of the ship, Henry Skinner, and Robison's son-in-law and business partner, Thomas Hodges, would diversify their cargo by trading some of the rum to fellow slave traders carrying supplies originating from other parts of the world. With a wider assortment of goods in hand, the rum could be paired with textiles, weapons, beads, tobacco, and other wares in exchange for captive Africans. Rum was also frequently offered as gifts to traders, political leaders, and laborers in order to unlock as many exchanges as possible. Robison hoped that the rum—and 188 rolls of Brazilian tobacco soaked in rum and packed alongside it—would be converted into 200 bondspeople to be sent to Cuba.[4] Many Africans, Britons, and Americans were challenging the slave trade in new ways by the late eighteenth century, and Robison was ultimately convicted under Massachusetts law for outfitting the *Eagle*.[5] Yet men like Robison saw making rum and trading slaves as mutually constitutive.

Distillery owners and slave traders wrote about their rum and the markets it opened up in abstract numbers of commodities bought and sold, but that does not adequately capture the human dimensions of the trade. Around 1738, a young boy named Broteer Furro, who was enslaved during a violent attack that killed his father, was marched from his home and imprisoned at Anomabu. When the *Charming Susanna* encountered Broteer, a crewman named Robertson Mumford exchanged four gallons of rum and a piece of calico fabric for the boy he renamed Venture. He carried him to Rhode Island in hopes of turning a profit.[6] In a narrative that he dictated that was published in 1798, Venture Smith spoke for hundreds of thousands of Africans whose commodification in the eighteenth century rested in part on being exchanged in Upper Guinea and the Gold Coast for rum and other goods.

The paired experiences of Smith and Robison gesture at the transatlantic tentacles linking North America and West Africa. All told, historians have counted sixty-four distilleries in Massachusetts, twenty-six in Rhode Island, eighteen in New York, and fourteen in Pennsylvania by 1770, with 5.5 percent of all slaving voyages—and 12.7 percent of British voyages—originating in North America.[7] Merchants outfitting their ships in New England carried 85 percent to 90 percent of the value of their cargo in rum. Their transactions concentrated in the West African regions of the Gold Coast and Upper Guinea.[8] Given that twelve million people were taken against their will from Africa, understanding how rum was made in North America and routed to West African consumers is crucial to understanding how hundreds of thousands of people were forcibly transported and enslaved on Caribbean plantations.

Transregional trade brought together highly experienced merchants from North America, Europe, and Africa. At times, contemporaries and historians alike have underestimated the agency of West African participants in the trade. The American abolitionist Anthony Benezet blamed "the introduction of those infernal spirits" for many West African leaders' decisions "to captivate their unhappy country people in order to bring them to the European market."[9] In turn, leading Caribbean intellectuals of the mid-twentieth century, including Fernando Ortiz and Eric Williams, argued that slave-ship captains "corrupted and weakened" African polities, "bribed" local leaders, overserved African merchants "until they lost their reason," and purchased slaves with rum.[10] Subsequent scholarship—which has found that African traders often prioritized the acquisition of luxury products like imported textiles—emphasizes that slave trading entailed haggling between savvy merchants of European and African descent.[11] Traders chose to accept rum because they preferred its taste, psychoactive properties, portability, cost, and purchasing power when compared to competing liquors of African and European provenance. They acted in their own interests when they acquired allotments of rum in exchange for captives or for services rendered in support of the slave trade.

There is a lot of rum to account for. All told, around 22 percent of the rum produced on the North American continent in 1770 was destined for West Africa.[12] Between 1709 and 1807, 10.9 million gallons of Rhode Island–produced rum supplied the slave trade.[13] That rum, as well as additional cargoes from Massachusetts and other North American colonies-turned-states, were used to purchase hundreds of thousands of captives who were carried largely to the Caribbean against their will. Although captives were sometimes exchanged for rum alone, it was more often one of several trade goods sorted together to purchase these humans.[14] The significance of rum to the transatlantic slave trade is often reduced to its purchasing power, but it also functioned as gifts and diplomatic overtures necessary for cross-cultural business relationships to flourish. The combined social and economic appeal of the spirit resulted from the fact that New England distillers went out of their way in the eighteenth century to design a product highly desired by African traders and laborers in Upper Guinea and the Gold Coast. These regions, stretching from modern-day Senegal down to Ghana, were geographically the closest coastal trading regions to the distilleries that supplied them. By cultivating a market for their rum, American producers and merchants doubled down on their investment in the transatlantic slave trade despite growing dialogues concerning its immorality.

African Drinkers, American Makers

Rum, English American colonies, and the transatlantic slave trade flourished together beginning in the mid-seventeenth century. Although the English had participated in earlier slaving voyages, they reengaged in a more organized and intensive way in the mid-seventeenth century. This timing coincided with the expansion of their colonies in the Caribbean—and to a much smaller extent, North America—that consumed unfree laborers.[15] For the most part, European and American traders relied on West African middlemen to provide them with their cargoes while they remained aboard ship or in forts. Those traders dictated the goods they were willing to accept for the gold, ivory, and humans they parted with: textiles, metal wares, beads, weaponry, and alcohol. All told, textiles constituted 55 percent of the merchandise shipped by English trading companies to Africa between 1662 and 1713. Alcohol, some of which was produced by enslaved rum makers, complemented these other trade stuffs. Upper Guinea accepted 8 percent of the incoming goods in spirits, while the value of distilled alcohols received along the Gold Coast hovered around 2 percent. Despite appearing to be a comparatively minor part of the slave trade at this point, one historian estimates that West Africa consumed around sixty thousand gallons of imported spirits a year between 1680 and 1713, forty thousand of which went to the Gold Coast.[16]

African merchants and drinkers in these regions chose the spirits they would buy carefully. They initially preferred brandy over grain spirits and rum. A Lutheran minister named Wilhelm Johann Müller observed in the 1660s that when the Fetu people of the central Gold Coast were offered "French brandy, they lay into it as if it were water, and enthusiastically thank the whites, in order that their throats may again be washed with brandy." Conversely, the discerning consumers "despised" grain-based spirits, referring to them as "stink-jar." When an early shipment of "spirits made in Barbados in the West Indies (called kill devil by the English)" appeared on the coast, the Fetu would not even "take this drink in their mouths."[17] At midcentury, Fetu preferences were likely shared by Englishmen exploring and trading in West Africa. A 1661 account of a voyage up the Gambia River suggested that Royal African Company workers would benefit specifically from brandy because "in this climate it is the most needful for their health."[18] An array of discerning consumers preferred sweet, refined brandies over other distillates.

By the 1680s, Englishmen made headway in influencing West African tastes. Jean Barbot noted that during his first stint at the Cape Coast slave castle in 1678–79, traders easily converted brandy into gold and slaves. Only three years later, though, he "found a great alteration" as English traders flooded the Gold Coast with rum from the West Indies. In 1683, an English ship parted with 8,000 gallons of rum in exchange for "120 slaves plus gold" bound for the sugar plantations of Barbados.[19] By now accepting the English substitute for brandy, African merchants "obliged all to sell cheap."[20] English slave ships gained an upper hand when consumption patterns evolved because French brandy derived from wine cost three times what rum produced from sugary wastes in England's colonies did.[21]

While explaining early modern tastes and preferences can be challenging, rum appears to have won out in Upper Guinea and the Gold Coast for several reasons. Imported distilled spirits held allure in Upper Guinea and the Gold Coast because they were strong, portable, and stable. Francis Moore ventured from the Gambia River to the Guinea Highlands while employed by the Royal African Company in the 1730s. Moore listed an array of locally produced alcohols but observed that when rum or brandy could be had, the people of Joar "drink but a small quantity of the others."[22] The demand intensified during the annual rainy season of May to November. Jean-Baptiste Gaby observed that palm sap in Upper Guinea was useless for making wine during the wet months.[23] In turn, rum became "one of the best commodities we can have to trade with in the rainy season," according to Moore, because African consumers welcomed a seasonal replacement for their traditional alcohols.[24] Later in the eighteenth century, trades for imported brandy and rum had turned a season of dearth into a season of plenty. One French adventurer characterized liquor and tobacco as the "preservatives which they employ against the deleterious qualities of the air and water, during the four rainy months."[25] At times when local alcohol supplies dried up, West Africans consumed even more imported distillates.

Local preferences for brandy and especially rum came down to the taste, appearance, and affordability of various spirits. By nature of their base ingredients, brandy and rum are normally sweeter than grain-based whiskeys and gins. For consumers accustomed to sweet palm wines, the residual sugar in these spirits may have been an asset.[26]

Furthermore, Barbot suggested that consumers along the Gold Coast "prefer the brown color in" French brandies.[27] Rum could pick up a similar hue as a result of its long-distance transport in oak barrels whose staves had been heated and bent over an open flame. The coloration may have carried spiritual significance for buyers in the region. Akan, Ga-Andagme, and Ewe people shared beliefs tied to the spiritual potency of liquids including water, blood, and alcohol. Social upheaval in the seventeenth and eighteenth centuries that corresponded with the expansion of the transatlantic slave trade increased the importance of war gods in these societies. War deities demanded blood sacrifices. Adjudging the golden hue of aged spirits to be "red," many people living near the Gold Coast deployed this alcohol in their martial rituals. For instance, if a warrior brought home the head of a defeated enemy, he was given rum (sometimes mixed with drops of blood) to make him braver and to avenge the spirit of his vanquished foe.[28] Rum met local expectations of taste and strength and typically at a lower cost. Attention quickly shifted to maintaining a consistent supply.

The earliest casks of rum to arrive on the Upper Guinea and Gold Coasts originated in Barbados. In December 1693, Thomas Phillips, a sea captain working for the Royal African Company, encountered an "interloper" sailing off the Guinea Coast from Barbados with a cargo predominantly composed of rum. He found a favorable trade for five hundred gallons, which he subsequently sold "to good advantage."[29] Twenty years later, pressure mounted for the Royal African Company to supply rum directly. A Reverend Gordon advised in 1714 that "the company would do very well to direct the buying and fitting out of sloops loaded with rum from Barbados, where it is always cheapest, for the coast."[30] This proved more challenging than anticipated. By 1721, Royal African Company agents in Barbados, St. Christopher, Nevis, and Antigua had been tasked with anticipating and meeting African demand for rum on the Gold Coast.[31] Tastes for rum in West Africa were initially developed over drams of Caribbean rum, though supply issues abounded.

Europeans and Africans intermittently proposed alleviating rum shortages by setting up distilleries in Africa, much as they had in other corners of the Atlantic world. In 1708, the Dutch planned to import two hundred slaves from Ouidah to staff a sugar and rum manufactory along the Gold Coast in Butre. Barbot suggested that the economic advantage to be gained by the Dutch through this enterprise was "much to be feared" by the French.[32] Ten years later, William Johnson wrote from the Cape Coast asking for a half dozen "persons that are well known in nature of boiling sugars with coppers, stills and all other sorts of vessels necessary and useful for distilling rum."[33] By the middle of the eighteenth century, the Asante king (*Asantahene*), Opoku Ware, also attempted to set up a distillery of his own, ostensibly to limit his dependence on Atlantic trade for the commodity. He lured four Dutch soldiers to Ashanti with large sums of gold, and they set up clay stills with bamboo worm tubes. Before distilling could commence, however, the Dutch governors paid Opoku Ware's "big men" for the return of the soldiers and immediately hanged the would-be distillers for abandoning their countrymen.[34]

North American rum producers increasingly entered the trade in hopes of undercutting their competitors. Rhode Island merchants later claimed that "some merchants in this colony first introduced the use of rum" along the coast of Africa in 1723.[35] They overemphasized Rhode Island's role in introducing rum to the region as it had been present for at least four decades by that point, but they correctly noted that rum from their colony became commonplace in Upper Guinea and the Gold Coast during the 1720s.[36] Rhode Island's rapid rise as a distilling center engaged with the slave trade likely resulted from the economic advantage afforded to communities where entrepreneurs engaged in the same business shared supply networks, a labor force, and expertise. In addition, Rhode Island's monetary policy made large expenditures comparably affordable in the early eighteenth century.[37] Within fifteen years, these "rum men" created intermittent gluts of rum that affected the exchange rate. Captain John Cahoone wrote back to Rhode Island in 1736 that seven ships laden with rum were "ready to devour one another" at Anomabu.[38]

The embrace of American rum on the African coast incentivized continued expansion of distillation in early eighteenth-century North America. Around

1700, colonists who previously undertook distilling part-time and in their homes began to specialize in the business. They constructed purpose-built distilleries and purchased enslaved laborers.[39] Augustus Lucas aimed to sell one such distillery in New York in 1704. The 50-by-22-foot building housed two stills measuring 140 and 100 gallons apiece. This distillery was far smaller than that listed for sale by Thomas Robison a century later. The square footage measured one-quarter the area of the later manufactory, and the largest still held just one-tenth of the capacity. Nonetheless, the stand-alone distillery represented a departure from the intermittent production that preceded it. Attesting to the source of expertise powering early industrial growth, Lucas advertised "a stout lusty Negro man, who understands stilling," alongside the distillery itself.[40]

In Massachusetts and Rhode Island, the most successful of these emerging rum producers tended to pair trade and distillation. According to a Boston customs officer named Archibald Cumings, Massachusetts distillers were churning out 2,000 hogsheads of rum from British, French, and Dutch molasses by 1717.[41] Early in the 1720s, a merchant named Thomas Amory joined the distillers' ranks.[42] The Limerick-born man spent time in Barbados, South Carolina, England, the Azores, and on the coast of Africa before opening a distillery at the foot of a wharf on Boston's South End in 1722.[43] Until his untimely death in a distillery accident in 1728, Amory progressively built up his rum-making operation. He requested a 350-gallon still to expand his operations in the fall of 1722.[44] Amory also added a 300-gallon still "for rum" by January 1725 and put up a still of 640 gallons in the summer of 1727.[45]

Motivating Amory's distillery expansions was an observation that rum "is now in demand and will always be when that from Barbados fails."[46] Ships laden with Caribbean molasses docked at Amory's wharf. Once unloaded, his distillery processed around three hundred gallons of molasses per week into a commensurate volume of rum.[47] Amory sought out several venues for his rum. He carried on a brisk trade through family contacts in South Carolina. He accepted beeswax, tallow, hides, rice, and barrel staves for the rum sent south.[48] Amory directed other shipments of Boston rum to Ireland.[49] Based on his familiarity with the itinerary of the sloop *Africa* in 1725, it is also possible that some of the rum carried aboard that slave ship also originated in the Amory distillery.[50]

Amory's business, and that of an increasing number of other distillers, relied heavily on enslaved people of African descent as both laborers and purchasable property. When he initially moved to Boston, he brought with him two African-descended people: a twelve-year-old enslaved boy named John and a "free man" named Balthazar whom he subsequently chose to "send away" to South

Carolina.[51] By 1719, Amory no longer personally claimed possession of these young men but resolved to send for a couple of enslaved women he owned in Terceira.[52] Amory bought additional men to work in his distillery once resettled, including an enslaved man named Ambrose who was forcibly relocated from Antigua in 1724.[53] Amory averred that his "own slaves" were the ones making the rum.[54] Slavery and distillation were deeply enmeshed.

The Newport distiller Godfrey Malbone was even more deliberate in pairing rum production and the transatlantic slave trade. By 1728, Malbone had both opened a rum distillery and financed his first slave voyage.[55] His ships imported over 50,000 gallons of molasses from the Caribbean in 1729, some portion of which fed his distillery.[56] Over the next dozen years, Malbone sent at least a half dozen ships to Africa. When it departed in the spring of 1738, the *Diamond* carried 3,662 gallons of Malbone's New England rum in hogsheads and another 2,372 gallons of "French" rum in smaller barrels.[57] The people purchased by this rum may have met an especially swift fate. That summer, newspaper readers learned that a sloop belonging to Malbone "was totally consumed by the lightning on the coast of Guinea" with many unfortunate people already confined on board.[58] Integrating the West Indies trade, distillation, and the slave trade paid dividends for men like Malbone, but at steep costs for the people he sought to commodify.

West Africa was the largest market among many for rum departing America. Merchant-distillers exported approximately 44 percent of the rum produced in New England distilleries. In the immediate aftermath of the American Revolution, one writer explained that "the greatest part" of the exports were "sent to Africa, to Nova Scotia, to Newfoundland, and to Canada."[59] In 1770, an estimated 1.766 million gallons of North American rum were exported from the mainland colonies, with 590,000 gallons shipped to other colonies; 313,000 gallons sent to Africa; 234,000 gallons supplied to Newfoundland; and 231,000 gallons sent to Quebec.[60] Smaller volumes filtered to Native polities and European markets. More than one-fifth of the rum leaving the North American colonies in 1770 supplied the transatlantic slave trade.

North American merchant-distillers believed that their ability to engage in the triangular trade was crucial to their success. Merchants engaged in this trade readily acquired molasses from British, French, and Dutch ports in the West Indies in exchange for American-harvested fish, wheat, and lumber. This molasses supplied colonial distilleries. Rhode Island merchants explained that the distilleries were "the main hinge upon which the trade of the colony turns" and the margins between the price of molasses and the price of rum served as the lifeblood for "many hundreds of persons."[61] Distillers in Massachusetts, New

Hampshire, and New York adapted a similar mindset. Colonial distillers relied on the rum industry for their livelihood. So too did laborers who seasonally cut firewood and barrel staves, carpenters and masons who built and maintained distilleries, rope makers and ship builders who supplied the merchant marine, and seamen who sailed these ships.[62] Furthermore, by vending a commodity of their own manufacture in West Africa, rum men from New England enjoyed a trade advantage over British and foreign traders who sold other, more expensive-to-obtain products like brandy or Caribbean rum.[63] Historians generally compute the standard profitability of slave-trading voyages at 10 percent, which was moderately higher than other forms of trade.[64]

Petitioners representing Rhode Island and Massachusetts extolled the value of the slave trade for the British imperial project and warned of the dire consequences of any challenge to their distilleries. Shortly after passage of the Sugar Act, Joseph Maudinit claimed that Massachusetts "rum, carried to the coast of Guinea, is employed in the purchase of gold, to pay the balance of their trade to England; and of slaves, to be carried to the West Indies."[65] According to Rhode Island petitioners, "two-thirds of our vessels will become useless, and perish upon our hands" if the molasses and rum trades were disrupted. They also warned that a decline in American rum on the African coast would reopen coastal African markets to the French brandy trade.[66] In stressing how the rum-fueled slave trade accumulated specie, balanced trade, opened slave markets to underresourced colonies, and kept French traders at bay, these writers staked out a claim for the integral place of the American rum-for-slave trade in the British Empire. The triangular trade may not have dominated the larger transatlantic slave trade or the balance of payments between North America and Britain to the extent that the petitioners suggested, but it played an outsized role in the economic and political decision-making of colonial Americans.

Reacting to Consumer Desires

Because of its perceived importance to their economic well-being, North American distillers modified their rum to satisfy prospective buyers more readily than their counterparts in the British Caribbean. Generally, those buying and consuming Caribbean rum set values—and made assumptions about strength and quality—based on the island of origin.[67] Although colonial newspapers sometimes listed prices current for "New England" or "continental" rum, such price listings left unsaid the many ways in which individual producers designed spirits to satisfy specific and varying tastes. In a 1769 advertisement, Charles Thomson advertised "Philadelphia rum" that "is freed from the disagreeable tang which usually accompanies continent rum, and is so much improved in smell and flavor, as to be little inferior to, and scarce distinguishable from, that made in the West Indies."[68] On other occasions, producers mixed in cherries, juniper berries, snakeroot, cloves, and anise to satisfy buyers who preferred to mask the flavor of neat rum.[69] They also matched their exports to regional assumptions of what rum should look like. Through conversations with trade partners, the Rhode Island merchant firm of Brown, Benson, and Ives learned that in Copenhagen "yellow" or "colored" rum sold for two to five rigsdaler less than white rum, and demand for colored rum lagged accordingly.[70] In response, they sent a shipment of "all white which we observe has the preference at your market."[71] One of the greatest strengths of North American distillers and merchants was their facility with matching rum to the desires of consumers.

Sometimes distillers' mastery of the marketplace stretched the truth. Some discerning consumers preferred "a full amber color"—and the accompanying flavor that came from aging rum for a period in toasted barrels.[72] Satirizing how some distillers approximated this appearance, a 1771 broadside offered "the invaluable secret of changing the quality of Philadelphia and New-England RUM to the [aesthetics] of West-India [rum]; at the trifling expense only of your honor and veracity."[73] This advertiser mocked the many producers who seriously pursued a similar goal. Distillers advised soaking used tea leaves, wheat-flour dough balls, or even old bread in a hogshead of rum to adjust its color and harshness.[74] Other experts suggested mixing molasses or burnt sugar to make new rum appear old.[75] Many of these tricks probably went undetected.

In 1789, however, Thomas Robison got caught. Convinced that his Maine rum equaled spirits from the Caribbean in quality, Robison initially boasted that his product fetched the same price in Boston as Caribbean rum.[76] Robison then began packaging his Maine rum in casks marked as originating in the West Indies. Rumors promptly spread in New York about his ruse. Consumers responded by avoiding his product entirely.[77] Robison's decision to misrepresent where his rum originated sparked a crisis in consumer confidence.

Reeling from the New York market shunning him, Robison next turned his gaze across the Atlantic. He reached out to acquaintances in St. Eustatius, Canada, and England, offering to fill their cargo holds with American rum that could be sold in Africa.[78] In concert with his son-in-law, Robison outfitted the *Eagle* with 11,070 gallons of rum and 188 rolls of tobacco for the African coast.[79] Robison estimated that the cargo could be exchanged for as many as 200 captive people.[80] With Hodges on board but under the command of Captain Henry Skinner, the *Eagle* departed on August 14, 1790 for Upper Guinea. At Gorée, Hodges "sorted" the cargo by trading rum and tobacco for firearms, which he hoped would provide more flexibility in subsequent exchanges.[81] Continuing south, they stopped at Îles de Los, where Hodges and 30 Africans he had purchased with the ship's cargo parted ways with the *Eagle* and set off to Saint-Domingue on board *La Jeromee*.[82] After Hodges departed, the *Eagle* continued south to Sierra Leone, purchasing 15 more captives before setting sail for Cuba in June.[83] The *Eagle* fell short of its lofty ambitions, but nonetheless converted its cargo of rum and tobacco into 45 captives destined for excruciating labor on Caribbean plantations.[84]

When they broke into the transatlantic slave trade, American merchant-distillers like Robison manipulated the taste and appearance, transportability, strength, and cost of their rum to satisfy African merchants and consumers. Drinkers generally compared North American rum unfavorably to Caribbean rum. Scottish traveler Janet Schaw, who spent time in the West Indies and North America, described the American distillate as "the most shocking liquor you can imagine," while the vice admiral in command of the British Navy's North American Station lamented that sailors consuming New England rum imbibed "the most pernicious of all liquors and all too often in its very worst state."[85] Producers and consumers alike recognized that fermenting and distilling months-old molasses limited the upside of North American distilleries' output. Nonetheless, distillers aimed to deliver a consistent product. They tried to avoid scorching the wash in their stills, which left the distillate with a burnt flavor.[86] They also mixed batches of rum together, ensuring a consistent flavor profile across hogsheads.[87] Convinced that he had done his best to deliver a quality product, distiller Daniel Tillinghast wrote to the slave merchant Aaron Lopez in June 1770 that "I have been as careful to make it all alike as possible, and as good as any I ever made for Guinea."[88] Distillery operators and slave traders emphasized the quality of their produce even if their rum did not appeal to all consumers.

The choice of barrels also affected the flavor and appearance of rum destined for Africa. When Rhode Island distillers racked rum in "exceeding foul" casks in 1768, it had to be sold at a discount.[89] Distillers generally hoped that oak containers would improve the taste of the contents. For instance, the Rhode Island distilling partners Brown and Benson tied the aging of their rum for "some months" to its enhanced quality.[90] When it sat in warehouses in New England or sloshed below deck on ships sailing east to Africa, rum also picked up a caramel hue and a smoother flavor from the toasted oak staves that contained it.

Of course, the most straightforward function for hogsheads was to contain the commodity as it made its way to market. Even well-built hogsheads leaked if staves broke or the hoops holding them together burst.[91] To mitigate losses, distillers loaded rum destined for Africa in casks hooped with iron rather than wood.[92] Given their sturdy construction, William Ellery charged a premium of twenty shillings for the "Guinea" hogsheads holding part of the cargo of the *Success*.[93] Distillers and merchants invested in premium casks in order to mitigate a loss leader for the trade.

North American distillers also packaged their rum in ways that made transportation easier. Generally, Guinea hogsheads were larger than those used in other exchanges, which offered savings to merchants.[94] However, for some transactions, smaller, easier-to-move containers prevailed. In 1762, the *Whydah* carried rum in hogsheads, tierces, and barrels.[95] Sometimes, traders requested even smaller containers like ankers. One trader suggested that additional staves should be sent to Africa unassembled so that the ankers could be "made up large or small as the times are."[96] American manufacturers could most easily adjust to these sorts of preferences because the staves of different sizes were hewn locally and the distilleries often included on-site cooperages.

The strength of American rum contributed further to African demand. Selling particularly potent rum cut down on transportation costs and satisfied African tastes for high-proof spirits. Timothy Fitch's orders to Captain William Ellery for the voyage of the *Caesar* in 1759 predicted that his New England rum would sell well because it was secured in strong casks and above the usual strength.[97] Daniel Tillinghast understood that below-proof rum led to the opposite problem. When notified that three hogsheads delivered to Aaron Lopez were deficient in that regard, Tillinghast promised to send along twelve gallons of "high wines" that could be mixed in to boost its proof.[98]

Slave traders rarely enumerated the exact strength of their rum, but a Danish trader who regularly encountered the British on the Gold Coast in the mid-eighteenth century warned of its potency. Ludewig Ferdinand Rømer recollected occasions when "our sailors thought that they could tolerate just as strong doses of West Indian brandy as they could of Danish brandy, but one can see it is poison for them." Overindulgences of this sort left the Danes with hangovers that lasted a fortnight.[99] In line with Rømer's description, an employee of the African Company of Merchants calculated that rum was usually 10 percent stronger than grain-based distillates from Britain and therefore "of more value to the natives."[100]

In order to cut down on transportation costs, merchant-distillers transported American rum in this highly concentrated form and then mixed it with water once they approached the West African coast. Rømer suggested that Royal African Company employees mixed an equal portion of rum and water together in the bottles that they dispensed to African workers.[101] Europeans also normally drank the rum with water added.[102] In 1750 and 1751, William Chancellor recorded his experiences as a surgeon aboard the New York slave ship the *Wolf*. He explained that while coasting between Upper Guinea and the Gold Coast, African merchants came aboard looking to trade for rum. As it had not yet been mixed, the captain made up an excuse to delay the transaction until the following day.[103] Diluting rum that had been shipped in concentrated form was common practice.

Some participants in the slave trade presented this mixology as evidence of white traders getting the better of their African counterparts. The Dutch West India Company merchant Willem Bosman recalled Dutch traders watering down spirits and then adding soap to it so that it would react to proofing tests as if it were stronger.[104] Later in the eighteenth century, the slave trader–turned–abolitionist John Newton suggested that unscrupulous merchants would refill half-consumed bottles of rum with water so that they appeared "full as they were before." In turn, "The Blacks, who buy the liquor, are the losers by the adulteration."[105] These representations presented Africans as inept merchants either ripe for exploitation by European traders or needing the protection of abolitionists.

Frauds no doubt occurred, but it is imperative to recognize African merchants as the sophisticated consumers and businessmen that they were. In Accra in 1760, an Akyem leader named Bang required brandy produced in Flensborg. Though Danish traders regularly "tested him," Bang always tasted the deceit.[106] Barbot likewise averred that the West Africans he encountered "will presently discover whether it is not adulterated with fresh or salt water, or any other mixture."[107] Experienced traders expected specific qualities in their spirits and their engagement with makers and traders of rum from around the Atlantic world imparted them with the expertise to determine when their demands were not being met.

In light of these considerations, New England distillers weighed many factors when preparing a shipment of rum for Africa. As a merchant based in Anomabu named John Ashley summarized to his Boston contacts in 1793, "I must beg your particular attention to this cargo, that the liquor is good and strong: and that the casks be all strong and well iron bound. I also wish as many ankers put on board as you possible can procure."[108] In one regard, American distillers enjoyed an advantage over Caribbean or British distillers. Centers of rum production in New England were also leading producers and exporters of barrel staves. Continental distillers could procure strong, appropriately sized, and fresh containers more easily, quickly, and cheaply than others. However, the greatest advantage realized by the American rum men was due to their willingness to answer the varied requests of distant consumers. They manufactured demand for their rum by adjusting the taste, appearance, and strength of rum to best suit markets in Upper Guinea and the Gold Coast at an attractive price.

Some but certainly not all consumers in West Africa expressed a preference for the taste of North American rum. African consumers occasionally complained that rum of other provenance was "peculiar tasting."[109] Akan people in particular stated a preference for American rum over West Indies rum. An African Company of Merchants employee worried in 1787 that American merchants held an upper hand over their British competitors because the Fante accepted American rum "in preference to any other liquor."[110] But the preference for New England rum was not universal. Thomas Rogers reported from Îles de Los in 1764 that he could not sell his cargo of rum loaded in Newport because traders waited "in daily expectation of a vessel from Antigua."[111] Consumers in these particular outposts expressed a general preference for rum over brandy, but their regional partialities differed.[112]

North American distillers often captured the alcohol market in Upper Guinea and the Gold Coast because they met the desires of consumers at a lower cost. Customer demand around the Atlantic world generally sustained lower prices for a New England product that was at times described as "ill-flavored."[113] New England merchant-distillers' acuity with smuggling foreign molasses into colonial America and American rum out of the colonies furthermore offered an opportunity to deliver rum at costs less affected by tax burdens. British and Caribbean distillers did not always find it worthwhile to compete with American prices. Except during periods of heightened customs enforcement, such as in the immediate aftermath of the 1764 Sugar Act, British slavers preferred to trade for rum through the Isle of Man rather than relying on domestic distilleries to supply the slave trade.[114] They also re-sorted cargoes with American merchants when their paths crossed in African waters. Caribbean slave traders intermittently sold rum in West Africa, but they found greater success selling mixed cargoes that included textiles and luxury goods. With limited access to desired goods other than alcohol and smaller quantities of tobacco, American merchants were singular in peddling a cargo largely centered on rum regardless of the economic climate.[115]

African consumer preferences and a willingness of American traders to supply rum at a lower cost than competitors help to explain this anomaly, but it is also likely that American merchant-distillers acquiesced to certain conditions that chased other suppliers away. American slave traders noted the volatility of the market in humans. Much of this unpredictability resulted from routines of shortages and gluts. For instance, when twenty Rhode Island ships carrying nine thousand hogsheads of rum descended on the coast of Africa in 1763, the price of the human cargo ballooned to two hundred gallons of rum per person.[116] Then, in 1771, Captain John Duncan wrote from Anomabu that "there is so many of our countrymen here that does not look upon rum better than water."[117] Too many rum traders flooded West Africa with greater volumes of rum, lowering the profitability for American slave traders.

The rum men saw little recourse other than to accept what was offered when prices fell. At times they lingered on the African coast for six or more months in hopes of obtaining a more favorable exchange.[118] But waiting carried considerable human and financial costs. The people forced onto the slave ships quickly sickened and died while incarcerated and fed rations designed to keep them barely alive.[119] The ships themselves could be consumed by worms in the tropical waters.[120] In 1750, the captain and crew of the *Wolf* attempted to force the price of slaves lower by refusing to trade any more rum to their African counterparts. The traders responded in kind by refusing to allow the *Wolf* to replenish its water or food stores. William Chancellor predicted that "they will weather us out, for they can go better without rum than we without corn or water."[121] These realities greatly limited the options of rum traders.

While at least one partner in a slaving voyage hoped that printing an account of the state of the trade in Newport's newspaper would "prevent many vessels from pushing that way this fall," American slave traders proved hard to scare off.[122] In spite of heavy risks, New England financiers gambled on the slave trade because of its potential, though elusive, profitability.[123] To stand a chance, the rum men engineered workarounds for their homogenous cargoes and the limited demand for them. A majority of slave traders added variety to their loads by "sorting" their cargo or trading rum for other goods in demand at their intended destinations.[124] They tried to keep haggling over prices to a minimum, too. John Fletcher implored his captain, Peleg Clarke, to "strike immediately for your cargo of rum (for dispatch sake) and not higgle about it too long as generally the first offer most likely will be as much as you will get after from the number of rum vessels going on the coast."[125] In many cases, this entailed trading directly with European-controlled coastal forts rather than engaging directly in exchange with independent African or European traders.[126] When trading solely in rum, these traders often found themselves accepting "very bad slaves" who were most likely to succumb quickly to the hardships of the Middle Passage and plantation slavery.[127] American slave traders sorted their cargo, emphasized haste over cost, and sometimes exchanged in particularly vulnerable people as means to adjust to a low—and inconsistent—price point and demand for their rum.

Caribbean-based rum merchants normally guided the bulk of their rum elsewhere except for moments when they saw financial advantages in sending rum directly to West Africa. For instance, the American Revolution disrupted the flow of molasses to American distilleries and rum to West Africa. In response, "6 rum men from the West Indies" stepped into the breach in July 1776.[128] That December, a "rum brig from Grenada" exchanged at the far more advantageous rate of 120 to 140 gallons of rum per slave at Cape Coast.[129] When explaining the issue with the supply chain disruption and rising costs, the governor of Cape Coast Castle, Richard Miles, noted that "an African chief's profits arises principally by his connections with the Americans."[130] While Gold Coast consumers preferred rum for its taste, their concern with where it originated largely came down to price. When American rum was available, it made engaging in the slave trade more profitable for African political leaders and merchants.

Preferences for American rum along the Gold Coast outlived disruptions wrought by the American Revolution. In 1778, African traders responded to wartime disruptions by paying 50 percent more for rum than for brandy.[131] Following the Treaty of Paris in 1783, New England merchants returned to the region and supplied traders and independent merchants with their distillate. However, the African Company of Merchants continued to prohibit American rum in their forts.[132] In the spring of 1784, the Boston-based *Commerce* sailed around Anomabu seeking to trade with the Fante, who had previously agreed to trade solely with the British. According to the governor, Captain Saltonstall "used every argument to inflame the minds of the Blacks and instill into them that spirit of republican freedom, and independence." He suggested, however, that the more powerful argument was the "plentiful supply of rum." When reminded by the British of their agreement, the Fante asserted their sovereignty by insisting that "the country belongs to them" and they would engage with "any nation they please."[133] A British warship ultimately chased the *Commerce* away and enforced the Fante-British trade monopoly. In 1788, however, company policy changed to once again allow for the sanctioned exchange of American rum. As British and American slave traders raced against the impending abolition of the slave trade, they once again did so with cargoes of rum distilled in the newly independent United States.

Rum on the African Coast

In the late eighteenth or early nineteenth century, an Igbo woman named Akeiso was captured, bound, and marched to the coast. She later remembered, "The enemies of our country seized and sold us to the white people, for the love of drink." Stripped naked, chained belowdeck, and fed sparingly, Akeiso's Middle Passage ended with disembarkation in Jamaica, where she was renamed Florence Hall and forced to work by the "dread of punishment."[134] Her short narrative shares her understanding that the commodification, suffering, and enslavement that she experienced resulted from enslavers' attempts to valuate human lives in quantities of alcohol.

Quantitative records that often obscure people like Akeiso nonetheless suggest the commonality of her experience even beyond the Bight of Biafra. Between 1772 and 1780, Richard Miles recorded the purchase of 2,218 slaves from Akan traders along the Gold Coast. Liquor of colonial manufacture made up just 9 percent of the volume of trade goods. However, rum was present in 70 percent of the barters. While it may not have been the most valuable good exchanged, Akan traders expected rum as a part of the parcels of goods received in exchange for their human merchandise.[135] This reality suggests that rum facilitated the enslavement of a greater number of people than one might expect simply by computing a standard exchange rate from rum to people.

Rum on its own factored into exchanges for some of the most vulnerable people removed from West Africa. In fact, it was somewhat rare for North American traders to simply exchange rum for slaves. As early as 1715, employees of the Royal African Company at Cape Coast Castle noted the "difficulty of a cargo of rum purchasing a cargo of Negroes."[136] Usually, traders would only accept unsorted rum for captives they deemed less valuable. Miles generally only purchased aged or infirm slaves with rum alone.[137] People purchased for an unsorted cargo of rum were so suspect that William Moore had to go out of his way to convince Aaron Lopez and Company that the individuals he sought to sell were first-rate and that only a small percentage suffered from maladies that would affect their sale.[138]

In other exchanges, the rum men began their time in Africa by exchanging parcels of spirits for firearms, textiles, or other dry goods to diversify their cargo. A Mr. Eldrid of Rhode Island explained how sorting a cargo worked for Upper Guinea markets: "They carried from Rhode Island rum and tobacco, and exchanged part of these goods, either at the English factories, or with English ships on the coast, and with the remaining tobacco, and with the goods so taken in exchange, they purchased their slaves."[139] Sorting provided American slavers with the array of goods needed to access markets for human beings. British and other European traders transacted with the Americans precisely because they, too, needed to include rum in their assortments. In 1756, for instance, Thomas Taylor hoped to send rum from Anomabu to Ouidah because he had heard that "they have no vessels there but Portuguese and they can't trade without some spirits."[140] American rum may not have been enough to singlehandedly unlock all trade opportunities in West Africa, but it was a vital component of converting commodities produced by slave labor into more enslaved laborers.

Additional quantities of rum were consumed through activities that supported the slave trade. A cooper named William Raymond who sailed on the *Minorca* in 1774 certified that the ship's captain frequently dispensed rum as part of sailors' rations. Some crew were furthermore punished for "pillaging or stealing of the cargo."[141] When a barrel of rum on the *Mary* was found half empty and missing its bung, the captain likewise supposed that the missing spirits had been "drunk by the sailors."[142] Perhaps crewmen surrounded by the anguish and death that they perpetuated on the Middle Passage numbed their compunctions with rum.

Slavers also consumed rum in their attempts to turn people into commodities. Olaudah Equiano recalled the terror of being taken aboard a slave ship in Benin for the first time, convinced that the crew planned to eat him. Attempting to settle the terrified boy, one of the African traders gave Equiano a taste of liquor. While it was meant to calm him, it instead sent him "into the greatest consternation at the strange feeling it produced" because he had never tried spirits before.[143] Rum was a constant presence on slave ships that sought to reduce African people to merchantable goods.

African slave traders associated slave ships with rum, too. They often expected a *dashee*, or gift, of rum before commencing trade. William Smith wrote that "the natives will make no bargain with us till they receive a present, after which we must give every man in the canoe a large dram of rum, or *English* Spirits."[144] John Atkins similarly averred that African traders "never cares to treat with dry lips."[145] Captains and crews sometimes spoke derisively of these encounters, but they ultimately recognized the necessity of gifts for facilitating productive exchanges and acquiesced to the demands of their counterparts in trade.[146]

Traders and company employees joined ship captains in dispensing rum as part of their efforts at diplomacy. An independent white slave dealer named Nicholas Owen who operated in Sierra Leone in the mid-eighteenth century explained that when somebody died in the vicinity of Sherbro, Europeans in the area were "obliged to send some small matter" like rum "to show he's concerned."[147] When visiting or negotiating with dignitaries, Europeans often offered gifts of rum as well.[148] Disputes regularly developed between Europeans and Africans invested in the slave trade, and rum once again factored into restoring the peace. For instance, when the British fort at Anomabu was being built in 1756, native builders became disillusioned and began to tear down the half-completed walls. The correspondent for the African Company of Merchants noted that such work stoppages were relatively common, but once again required an outlay of spirits during the resulting palaver. Parties settled disputes at palavers, but according to the company employee, "if we would gain our point we must expend great quantities of liquor."[149] Dashees and palavers sealed with rum were so important for diplomacy between Africans and European slave traders that Thomas Melville wrote from Cape Coast Castle in 1751 that "a fort here may as well be without guns as without rum or brandy."[150]

Rum could be used to purchase an array of goods and services in West Africa. In 1750, the *Wolf* purchased fresh meat in the form of a two-hundred-pound turtle for five gallons of rum.[151] Slave-trading forts often paid wages in rum. Mixed-race soldiers protected the forts for ten bottles of rum per month.[152] In its description of resources surrounding the Tantumquerry Fort in Otuam, the African Company of Merchants catalogued a supply of ironwood two miles away. They estimated that nearby townspeople would transport eighteen-foot-long joists of the lumber for no more than "2 or 3 gallons of common spirits."[153] In the vicinity of slave trading forts, the payments in rum could either be consumed by the laborers or sold for other goods including gold.[154] Exchanges of rum for goods and services helped spark the transition from a patronage-based financial system to a market economy on the Gold Coast during the era of the transatlantic slave trade.[155]

Not all merchants, political leaders, or workers in Upper Guinea or the Gold Coast accepted gifts or payments in rum, however. This was especially the case in Upper Guinea as Islamic clerics converted locals starting in the 1720s and expanded their influence over the ensuing decades. Conflict that surrounded the spread of Islam increased the availability of captives taken during war, but Muslim traders would not accept rum as payment. It became progressively harder for American merchants to trade in the region as a result.[156] As Nicholas Owen observed, devout Muslims "drink no strong liquor and are moderate in their diet."[157] It was not for lack of exposure. Rum was so instantiated in the region that Muslims there believed that "rum is the liquor with which they are to be solaced" in the afterlife for their earthly temperance.[158] Although some African consumers chose to diverge from standard business practices, their actions should not distract from the centrality of the invention of rum to the transatlantic slave trade of the eighteenth century. North American rum loomed large in the calculus of those involved.

* * *

The millions of gallons of rum made and shipped by American distillers and merchants to ports including Gambia, Sierra Leone, Anomabu, and Cape Coast demonstrate several realities regarding rum's role in the transatlantic slave trade. First, the destination of these voyages was not happenstance. Rum sold in limited regions of West Africa and that is where American traders overwhelmingly focused their energies. Demand for American rum among African consumers dispels more traditional notions of unbridled demand for North American spirits or subsequent suggestions that tastes for this spirit were generally inconsequential.

Instead, eighteenth-century traders from America, Europe, and Africa agreed that rum offered a valuable trade good to parts of West Africa that also enriched the colonial American economy. American distillers and merchants were so invested in this trade, in fact, that they adjusted the taste, strength, appearance, packaging, and price to captivate the Upper Guinea and Gold Coast markets. These regions were the closest journey from New England and faced less competition from Portuguese and Brazilian slavers and their rival spirits. Focusing on these particular markets to supply British plantations in the Caribbean served the empire especially well because it positioned the New England traders to meet stated preferences for speakers of Akan from the Gold Coast, or "Coromantees."[159] For their part, Africa-based traders recognized the enthusiasm of American traders and pushed for progressively larger allotments of rum in exchange for people. The rum that they received changed economic relationships and consumption patterns in West Africa in ways that many West African elites found beneficial. Individuals making and selling rum carefully calibrated and monitored the desires of slave buyers and sellers. Far less care was taken with the millions of people consumed by this system in West Africa, along the Middle Passage, and in American landscapes of slavery.

The business ethos of North American distillers fit comfortably within the essential qualities of the rum industry in terms of its emphasis on innovation, reliance on hyperextractive processes, and focused pursuit of profits. These distillers concentrated on manufacturing—rather than harvesting—a commodity.

They invested profits to expand their scales of production. They also ventured into other parts of the commodity chain. While other alcohol producers held onto ideas of where alcohol should be made, what it should taste like, or how much it should cost, North American distillers generally saw each of these questions as negotiable.

Yet turning a profit was not so easy. North American distillers were one of many groups in the Atlantic world trying to mold their relationships to rum to their own benefit. Indeed, many rum men lost fortunes to failing American distilleries or disastrous voyages to Africa, quickly replaced by neighbors who thought they could do better. However brief, these forays into the rum business were waystations for some New Englanders embracing emerging capitalist enterprises of the late eighteenth and nineteenth centuries, including, in the case of the Brown family, trade to Asia and South America, a spermaceti factory, and an iron foundry.[160] The often short-lived relationships between various makers and movers of rum suggest one final defining characteristic of rum in the eighteenth century: many people whose lives touched rum yearned for connection and, more often than not, found conflict as they sought to mobilize rum for economic and political gain.

PART III

Connection and Conflict

CHAPTER 7

Whose Profits?

A sailor's life's a life of woe,
He works now late, now early,
Now up and down, now to and fro,
What then? He takes it cheerly;
Bless'd with a smiling can of grog,
If duty call
Stand, rise, or fall,
To fate's last verge he'll jog;
—Charles Dibdin, "The Flowing Can"

The prolific English songwriter Charles Dibdin wrote and arranged dozens of songs in the 1790s and 1800s that celebrated the average British sailor. Largely silent on the political implications of Britain's sea power, Dibdin instead offered a vision of Jack Tar as brave, adventurous, and profligate.[1] At sea and in port, Dibdin's heroic sailors sustained themselves on a "smiling can of grog." If his lyrics were to be believed, it was the pleasant mixture of water and rum (sometimes with lime and sugar added in) that kept seamen upright and responding to the Admiralty's orders. By the turn of the nineteenth century, rum powered the navy, and the navy protected the makers and traders of rum.

Rum producers welcomed the subjects of Dibdin's music with open arms. They called for naval vessels to protect the landscapes where rum was made, traded, and consumed. Military campaigns in the West Indies shielded sugar and rum manufacturers from foreign attack and occasionally expanded where Britons could build plantations. In periods of war, naval convoys facilitated the secure transfer of these commodities, defending the makers and traders of rum from catastrophic losses or higher insurance rates. Even in times of international peace, those conducting business in the West Indies relied on an armed British presence to guard the institution of slavery from African-descended people intent on toppling it.

The thousands of soldiers and seamen in the Caribbean increased the market for rum as well. Those sailors could have consumed an ocean's worth of English gin, Scottish whiskey, or Indian arrack. They could have stuck to beer or imported wine or brandy. But they mostly drank Caribbean rum. The choice of intoxicant was carefully orchestrated by Britons controlling the means of rum production. It centered highly lucrative provisioning contracts on Caribbean planters and collaborating merchants. The rum ration transformed the British government into the largest single purchaser of rum in the world.[2]

When it came time to foot the hefty bill, however, rum makers and merchants throughout Britain's Atlantic World schemed to circumvent taxation. Policymakers envisioned rum as a prime source of tax revenue because at best it was nonessential and at worst it could be downright harmful. These taxes raised considerable revenue for the government. From 1788 to 1792, imports of rum were taxed at 60 percent, and taxes on all foreign spirits generated £990,000 per year.[3] When accounting for domestically produced beer and spirits (sometimes made with molasses), as well as imported wines and brandies, £4.3 million of £7 million collected in customs duties in 1800 came from alcoholic drinks.[4] However, enforcement remained a significant problem. Those who derived profit from colonies and commodities maintained by British naval supremacy smuggled, bribed, and counterfeited their way around paying the duties placed on rum. The ways in which makers of rum sought to profit off of imperial power while evading the full costs associated with it unveils how commodity producers sought to leverage the colonial apparatus for personal financial gain in new ways. Inhabitants of Britain and its colonies found value in both embracing imperial support for the rum industry and contesting official attempts to manage its production, trade, and consumption, often concurrently.

Protecting Rum

British colonies in the West Indies depended on the military might of the English to protect plantation production from Native, European, and African challengers. Jamaica itself had been conquered by Britain through war with Spain, and St. Christopher changed hands several times in the seventeenth century as the

English, French, and Kalinago fought for sovereignty over the island. In the aftermath of one of those conflicts, officials in the West Indies debated whether resettling the island would leave other colonies exposed to capture. Reflecting a viewpoint that would dictate policy in the region for the next century, the governor of the Leeward Islands, Christopher Codrington, explained, "All turns upon the mastery of the sea. If we have it, our islands are safe however thinly peopled: if the French have it, we cannot, after the recent mortality, raise men enough in all the islands to hold one of them."[5] According to this logic, Britain's navy held the key to protecting sites of rum production in the Caribbean.

The exponential growth of the British military over the course of the eighteenth century solidified Britain's control over its Caribbean colonies and ability to wage war in the region. Parliament funded this precipitous increase in military spending through increased taxes and a more interventionist public administration.[6] A significant proportion of Britain's resources went toward protecting the landscapes that made rum. The size of fleets fluctuated, but during the Seven Years' War, 17 percent of the navy's "ship days" occurred in the West Indies and 14 percent in North American waters.[7] A smaller, though still substantial army occupied many individual islands. Edward Long complained in 1774 that only about 900 soldiers remained on Jamaica in 1764, reasoning that the smallest suitable number of soldiers cantoned on Jamaica would be 1,035 men.[8] Five years later, during the American Revolution, over 7,500 soldiers occupied the British Caribbean.[9] The general strategy underpinning this system was that undermanned armies, possibly aided by notoriously unreliable local militias, could hold out in battle long enough for reinforcements to arrive by ship.[10]

The greatest surge in the West Indies fleets corresponded with periods of war with France and Spain. At the height of the Seven Years' War in 1760, thirty-four ships patrolled the region. Responding to Europe's entry into the American Revolution, the British fleet in the Caribbean swelled to seventy in January 1782. This outlay of ships and troops placed the defense of Jamaica behind only Britain itself as far as British military expenditures were concerned.[11] Whether defending its own sugar islands or threatening to invade those claimed by other European powers, Britain recognized the strategic value of the Caribbean.

The landowners and merchants invested in making Caribbean rum welcomed this military presence insofar as it safeguarded their personal and economic well-being. In 1774, Long explained that "the men of property in this island [Jamaica] pay an ample contribution, in order that it may be protected, not so much from the French or Spaniards, as against the machinations of the many thousand slaves."[12] Planters had invested in a system of production that vested the work of making rum and sugar in the hands and minds of enslaved people of African descent. The work was intensive and deadly, requiring a constant influx of newly enslaved Africans to keep sugar and rum plantations fully operational. By midcentury, 150,000 enslaved people and only 10,000 whites inhabited Jamaica, which led planters to fear the power that enslaved people held to resist their enslavement.[13] Because planters regularly flouted deficiency laws—regulations aimed to ensure a minimum proportion of white workers (some of whom worked as distillers) on each plantation—colonial militias generally remained smaller than desired. Furthermore, islanders complained that crown-appointed governors dispensed—and rescinded—militia commissions as political favors, leading to an undisciplined force.[14] As a result of their distrust of militias, planters often became convinced of impending slave conspiracies whenever the military prepared to draw down troops.[15]

Makers and sellers of rum expressed other fears and priorities as well. They asked the military to protect or expand their dominion over lands suitable for growing sugar but claimed by internal enemies such as the Maroons on Jamaica and the Kalinago on St. Vincent. Partly in response to the threat of the Maroons in the 1730s, the Admiralty briefly moved its Jamaican shipyards to Port Antonio.[16] And during the 1772–73 Carib War, 2,200 soldiers stationed in Britain, North America, and the Caribbean descended upon St. Vincent.[17] Elite islanders occasionally withdrew their financial support for foreign invasions, fearing that it would leave their properties vulnerable and that any conquered islands would lessen the value of their plantation produce.[18] Nevertheless, they supported naval ventures outside of the Caribbean when they bolstered the trade in rum. Worried about the revenue lost from North American merchant-distillers violating the Navigation Acts to import duty-free molasses from French islands, West Indies interests supported calls in 1763 to station sloops off the coast of Rhode Island to prevent smuggling.[19] They also relied on convoys to safely convey their commodities to market during conflicts.[20] Caribbean planters were remarkably successful at shaping British military policy in the Atlantic.

Despite lobbying for policies that protected rum-making interests, planters and merchants sometimes defied the law to enhance their profits. In 1742, Vice Admiral Vernon complained to the Custos of the Parish of Westmoreland that plantations near the rendezvous point for naval convoys were using rum to lure the king's seamen onto their plantations and eventually into the merchant marine. Vernon admonished "any gentlemen of the island [who] could be guilty of so much ingratitude to the crown . . . that after the crown's sending strong squadrons hither for their protection and security . . . they should countenance any measures to render the king's ships useless to them."[21] Once convoys approached Britain, captains acting on behalf of unscrupulous merchants faced another decision: they could remain with their escorts as legally required but then suffer lower prices due to a sudden glut of sugar and rum once the convoy landed. Or they could peel off and race to port. Once again, many merchants prioritized profit over abiding by the finer points of the law.[22]

Military power and private enterprise faced off in the Caribbean once more when Horatio Nelson arrived in Antigua in 1785. Nelson quickly became disgusted with Admiral Richard Hughes for not deterring American ships from sneaking into British ports in pursuit of cheap molasses for their distilleries and rum for their markets. Over the ensuing two years, Nelson prohibited the entry of American ships and even boarded and seized offending vessels. Nelson explained his motivations in a 1786 memorandum: "I thought that men-of-war were placed in this country in times of peace, not merely to guard against any sudden attack, but for the more especial purpose of taking care that our trade was carried on through those channels which the legislature had ordered." By the time he returned to England in early 1787, Nelson predicted that customs officers and his own officers in the Caribbean "will not be sorry to part with me" and the planters and merchants would "give a *bal champêtre* upon my departure." By loudly decrying the lack of customs enforcement in the Caribbean, Nelson forced William Pitt's hand and ushered in a new set of Navigation Acts in 1786.[23] The episode once again showed how those who profited from Caribbean rum production at once relied on state power and subverted it when other courses promised greater fortunes.

Britain's ballooning military presence in North America and the Caribbean carried with it a challenge—provisioning thousands of men—and an opportunity—creating consumers of colonial products—seized upon by those making and selling rum. As early as the seventeenth century, soldiers and sailors in the West Indies enjoyed rum rations. Although no standard ration existed into the 1730s, sailors in the West Indies came to expect a half-pint of rum per day to replace beer that could not be procured in the region.[24]

Profligate rum use in ports of call sparked concern among naval commanders. In June 1740, two of Vice Admiral Vernon's subordinates expressed their anxiety regarding the fleet's rendezvous in Port Royal. They worried that sailors would flock to the city's punch houses and catch a "sickness by drinking too much rum," much of which had not been properly aged to give lead particles a chance to settle.[25] The Admiralty even suggested that the fleet should ride out the dangerous hurricane season cruising the Spanish Main rather than setting sailors loose in port.[26]

Vernon remained equally concerned with how the rum ration was consumed aboard ship. Sailors received their full portion at once, and many downed it immediately. Equivalent to five or six modern-day servings of alcohol, Vernon adjudged this dose to be "sufficient to intoxicate and gradually destroy them."[27] His solution ultimately confirmed the rum ration as a sailor's right even as it regulated how it would be consumed. Vernon insisted that one quart of water be added to each half-pint of rum and that the ration be split up into two servings—one administered before noon and the other between 4:00 p.m. and 6:00 p.m. He encouraged sailors to improve the flavor by purchasing limes and sugar to mix with their grog. While aiming to combat drunkenness and improve the health of his sailors, Vernon directed that the mixology must happen publicly "to see that the men are not defrauded in having their full allowance of rum."[28] In response to the consumption habits of his sailors, Vernon created an unofficial set of regulations that would later be codified and expanded beyond the Caribbean.

The British Navy supported the use of rum because it helped to solve several problems. Over the first half of the eighteenth century, improvements in naval planning and technology meant that ships which previously struggled to stay at sea for two weeks would now remain away from port for as long as six months.[29] Supplying a gallon of beer per day for each sailor took up too much cargo space. The beer also spoiled quickly.[30] If they sought to victual with brandy or wine by stopping in Madeira en route to the Caribbean, the British fleet lost valuable time and leaked money outside of their empire.[31] Furthermore, by bringing an alcohol that sailors were bound to drink anyway onto the ship, naval command hoped to control consumption. They began to wield the rum ration as a form of discipline, withholding the half-pint for many "trifling occasions."[32] Rum helped to make the eighteenth-century navy nimbler and more disciplined.

Distillers and merchants quickly recognized the potential of the rum ration to benefit them individually and collectively. Between August 1740 and January 1741, Vernon's navy amassed 127,459 gallons of rum at Jamaica. Leading planters including William Beckford and Edwin Lascelles sold directly to Vernon.[33] Most of all, however, the fleet in Jamaica contracted with the merchant firm of Mason and Simpson to keep its sailors well provisioned. Contractors bought from an array of local rum producers to fulfill such large contracts. Because the steepest demand for rum came during wartime, the ration boosted sales for the makers and traders of rum when traditional markets were least accessible and Atlantic trade carried the highest risks.

Jamaica's planters, merchants, and bureaucrats schemed to keep these profits on the island. In 1726, Mason and Simpson incurred a loss when they had to fulfill a naval contract for an expedition despite the price of rum tripling. Concerned that the local rum sellers would price-gouge again, the contractors inserted a clause into their 1740 contract that allowed them to import rum from surrounding islands duty-free. The Jamaica Assembly instead interpreted the clause as allowing other rum onto the island only when it was unavailable in Jamaica. Because overpriced local rum could still meet demand, they charged the contractors' agent £5,328 in customs duties. Then, in 1742, the Jamaica governor's naval officer, Archibald Bontein, seized two cargoes of brandy shipped from Madeira when the price of Jamaican rum spiked again. While this seizure was reversed on appeal years later, island elites had made their point: they would use every tool at their disposal to secure local profits from the rum ration.[34]

The value of rum contracts to well-connected islands, and their planters, merchants, and appointed government officials, only grew by the time of the American Revolution. Given the size of the navy and the provisions required on a regular basis, the Victualling Board sought to procure and warehouse victuals for most naval ships in London. During the American Revolution, they contracted with forty-six men who delivered food and drink there for military use. These men were well connected and wealthy. Twelve owned a plantation in the West Indies or carried on substantial trade with the region, providing them easy access to the rum that factored prominently in victualling.[35] They found these contracts to be lucrative. While Parliament spent much of the war questioning costs, the navy remained largely above the fray by limiting information on the cost of supplies until the money was owed and Parliament had little choice but to pay.[36] Some critics derided the "enormous fortunes made by contractors" and calculated profits as high as 60 percent, but earnings hovered around 15 percent to 20 percent until 1780, when they fell to 10 percent.[37] Contracts were dependable and, as part of a varied investment portfolio, enriched most holders.[38]

Once the American Revolution began, the rum ration expanded to cover the army as well. One retired army officer and member of Parliament named Isaac Barré noted in May 1777 that he "never understood that there was any reason for rum to be served to the troops." In fact, Barré remembered that Jeffrey Amherst had limited rum supplies in the American backcountry because he did not want to "spoil the troops."[39] Yet in 1775, the adjutant-general of the army advised that rum had become a "necessary" supply. Military leaders believed that an allotment of one-sixth of a quart per man would lessen their reliance on unpotable water and make it possible to keep soldiers from surreptitiously buying spirits. It would also help cushion the loss of trade to the thirteen colonies for Caribbean planters and merchants. The 1776 order for Caribbean rum equaled one-sixth of the volume carried by merchants to North America in times of peace.[40]

As usual, well-connected merchants stood at the ready to supply rum. Over a three-year period, a West Indies merchant named Richard Atkinson entered into a series of contracts worth £154,096 to source and deliver spirits from Jamaica to North America. Lord North initially defended these contracts, insisting that they "left little or no profit for the contractor."[41] However, when the case was examined by four other Caribbean merchants in 1777, the jury determined that "the contract in question *might at the time have been reasonably made cheaper*."[42] They suggested that the contracts overpaid Atkinson by about 30 percent, but Barré, ever distrustful of collusion between West Indies interests, estimated an overage of 50 percent.[43] After more legal wrangling, 6 percent of the contracted amount was eventually withheld, though Atkinson recouped most of it in interest.[44]

In buying and dispensing hundreds of thousands of gallons of rum, the British government carried out a program that enriched Caribbean planters during a time of incredible uncertainty. Although these rum contracts were centered in the hands of a relatively small group of planters and merchants, those men bought the rum from a wider circle of distillers selling rum in the British Caribbean. Speaking to this phenomenon, an opponent of the Atkinson contracts wrote in 1780 that rum prices had been set in such a way that left "a profit in the belly of each."[45] Whereas wars had often been times of want in much of the Caribbean, military contracts steadied Jamaica's markets during the American Revolution.[46] Colonial governments made sure to extract their profits too. By resisting proposals to allow the duty-free transfer of the rum ration, colonial governments collected tax revenue from the military.[47] This set of legalized kickbacks to Caribbean merchants, producers, and even colonial governments met limited resistance because victual contracts were usually settled well before observers had a chance to review supplies or prices.

Some men in the West Indies collected purely illegal profits as well. In 1749, the Victualling Board in London found that its two Jamaica agents were demanding a 5 percent to 6 percent commission on any rum or fresh meat contract that they awarded in-colony.[48] By the 1780s, the fraud had reached another level. Just before leaving Antigua in 1787, Horatio Nelson received a tip that merchants were marking up the prices of victuals that they sold to the navy and crediting a pseudonymous account for the king's naval storekeeper to pay for his collusion. According to Nelson, the fraud amounted to £1,000,000 in Jamaica,

£500,000 in Antigua, £300,000 in St. Lucia, and £250,000 in Barbados.[49] All types of profits from the rum ration abounded in the Caribbean.

Free and enslaved people of African descent also sought to capitalize on this market by plying sailors and soldiers with rum. When ships arrived in the harbor, women and men rowed or swam to the ships offering rum and other wares for sale. They sometimes accepted gunpowder in exchange for rum, even delivering the spirit directly to the garrisons.[50] Some free women of color, such as Rachael Pringle Polgreen in Barbados, operated punch houses, taverns, and hotels where military men paid for rum and often for sexual access to enslaved women.[51]

On Sundays, soldiers ventured to markets operated by enslaved people to "chiefly supply themselves" beyond the gaze of island elites.[52] While the navy victualled with rum aged for at least six months, these sellers introduced military men to the cheaper and stronger unaged rum that left some with dry bellyache.[53] Speaking to a taste developed in unregulated spaces, one sailor declared while in Antigua that he did not care if "new rum was a bad article . . . if it fractured the brain it was all he wanted."[54] At other moments, African-descended purveyors of rum suffered due to the racial hierarchies structuring Caribbean society. One evening in 1782, two seamen on the *Shrewsbury* came ashore in Choque Bay, St. Lucia, and knocked on the door of a "Black man" named John Low asking to buy rum. Low refused, and one of the sailors threatened that "he should lose more than ten times the value of rum" before setting a nearby house ablaze.[55] Such experiences show the rewards and substantial risks facing people of African descent who augmented the rum ration.

Whether procured through official or unregulated means, the rum consumed by the navy contributed to a growing demand for the spirit in Britain. Memoirists recounting their experiences in the eighteenth-century navy regularly described fellow sailors as liking "a cup of grog as well as ever" or being "fond . . . of their half-pint of rum."[56] Such descriptions—as well as Charles Dibdin's lyrics—hinted at common stereotypes of over-imbibing sailors choosing rum over other intoxicants. Sailors furthermore deemed it their right to bring rum back with them into Britain. While Horatio Nelson sought to curtail this practice among his fleet, he nonetheless carried some premium rum from his wife's family in Nevis to his brother who had previously served the fleet as chaplain.[57] Sailors' affinity for the taste and strength of rum may explain why naval vessels began dispensing the rum ration in waters beyond the Caribbean. Rum carried by returning sailors and consumed by their families and friends also likely factored into a broadening taste for rum in England. Between 1752 and 1769,

51.8 percent—or over 3.4 million gallons—of rum recorded leaving Jamaica was shipped to London or Liverpool.[58]

The greatest indication that soldiers and sailors could shape the demand for rum comes from the North American colonies in the 1770s. As war broke out, American consumers still wanted to drink rum, but the British occupation of American cities and the naval blockade offshore caused regular shortages. The Boston Port Act, issued as a response to the Boston Tea Party, closed the port in that city, which had been the beating heart of American rum distilling. Further legislation forbade the importation of molasses elsewhere.[59] By April 1776, Daniel Roberdeau noted that his Virginia distillery had run out of molasses and would need to close.[60] Of course, merchant-distillers continued to smuggle some molasses into North America, but as Samuel Barrett noted from Boston in 1777, "Rum and molasses are exceeding scarce and the chances of introducing more much against us."[61]

American soldiers and sailors demanded rum rations despite these shortages. The "Rules for Regulation of the Navy of the United Colonies" approved by the Continental Congress in November 1775 promised sailors a "half-pint of rum per man every day," plus more for overtime or during combat.[62] Congress apportioned one gill of rum per soldier per day, though some states offered allotments of rum above that standard issue to their militiamen.[63] Speaking to the belief that rum was seen as a right for American forces, one observer went so far as to complain that Americans imprisoned by the British were only receiving "a gill of rum a day . . . which is not so strong as sailor's grog."[64]

Merchants imported rum and molasses from the Caribbean and welcomed shipments captured by privateers to meet this demand. While most rum distilleries closed at least intermittently, those supplying the military found ways to stay open. In 1776, a Connecticut commissary officer and distillery owner named Andrew Huntington petitioned that several coopers be released from their assigned military duties in order to make barrels for rum distilleries.[65] He also wrote to Joseph Trumbull a month later asking him to release "a distiller from the army—as I want him very much to make your rum."[66] Demand for rum among American soldiers warranted special dispensations for cooperating distillers.

When they could not source molasses, some distillers tried to use other base ingredients. Roberdeau attempted to sell a cache of homemade whiskey, calvados, gin, and cordials in the summer of 1781.[67] Replacing molasses with grains was problematic, however, because it consumed foodstuffs that could otherwise alleviate shortages.[68] Enterprising distillers instead desired a substitute waste product to ferment and distill "rum" from. Some turned to the practice of harvesting sweetness from unripened cornstalks, a technique they attributed to Indigenous Americans.[69] By substituting cornstalk juice for molasses, one Middletown producer named Thomas Goodwin "distilled 1,435 gallons of good proof rum in 1777," which could not be distinguished "either by the flavor or taste from new West India rum."[70] Intrigued by the potential of making entirely domestic rum, Jed Huntington passed on the article to George Washington, who forwarded it to friends in Virginia.[71] Cornstalk rum never really caught on—likely because it ideally involved uprooting the plant before the corn itself could be harvested. Nonetheless, the lengths to which distillers went to supply American soldiers and sailors with a spirit labeled as rum demonstrates how ingrained the ration had become in martial life.

Much as soldiers and seamen understood access to rum to be their right, those profiting from the production and trade of the spirit in the West Indies declared that the lucrative contracts for victualling belonged to them. Despite the existence of a highly developed gin industry in England, the domestic spirit was almost never used for victualling. In 1806, West Indies interests successfully lobbied Parliament to prioritize rum rations over brandy unless the brandy was a full shilling cheaper.[72] Eventually, proponents of Britain's domestic spirits industry went so far as to characterize the rum ration as a West Indies "monopoly."[73] The makers and traders of rum understood the value of this arrangement and acted to instantiate it.

Taxing Rum

Protecting colonial centers of rum production militarily and economically consumed a significant portion of Great Britain's annual budget. Parliament enacted new taxes to raise the needed revenue. Indirect taxes—levies placed on goods rather than property or income—made the taxes more palatable because consumers could ostensibly choose whether to buy many of the goods with duties attached to them. Elites embraced this system because it spread the burden to a wider swath of Britons who now bought colonial products such as tobacco, sugar, or imported spirits but were less likely to profit directly from their trade or production. Between 1670 and 1810, the real national income rose threefold while taxes increased to sixteen times the initial rate. In 1770, 10.5 percent of the national income was appropriated as taxes.[74]

Tax rates in American and Caribbean colonies were comparatively minuscule. While Britons paid £10 million into public coffers in 1770, the six largest

American colonies paid a total of £125,207.[75] The annual per-capita outlay of £10.57 in Britain was twenty times higher than the most highly taxed continental colonies of Massachusetts and South Carolina and one hundred times greater than New Hampshire.[76] Caribbean colonists paid greater duties than North Americans but still only a fraction of what was paid in England. In 1774, per-capita taxes were £2.30 in Jamaica and £1.66 in Barbados.[77] Colonial legislatures also exacted their own internal taxes that they could choose to disburse to or withhold from Parliament when requested.[78]

Regardless of their willingness to enact and enforce high taxes, metropolitan and colonial legislatures alike taxed rum with a frequency and at a rate higher than almost any other product of the British Empire. The Caribbean colonies other than Jamaica paid a 4.5 percent export duty on any product leaving their islands. This tax heavily impacted rum because of its centrality to island economies. A 1729 political compromise vested total authority in the Jamaica Assembly—predominantly made up of planters and merchants—to tax islanders and disburse the proceeds, but this body nonetheless also charged an excise on rum.[79] In fact, although the continental colonies are most famous for generally refusing to comply with the Molasses Act, each colonial assembly experimented with levying rum and molasses taxes of their own in the eighteenth century. A 1721 act passed by the Connecticut General Assembly stipulated that revenue generated by an impost on rum would finance the construction of a rectory for Yale College.[80] In New York in the 1720s, roughly one-eighth of the value of imports were taxed, and two of the highest profits came from rum (£5,100) and molasses (£2,500). Likewise, North Carolina's most lucrative tax in the 1750s was its levy on rum.[81] Parliament also subjected foreign and domestic spirits to excise taxes and imports to customs duties. The combined charges hit rum especially hard, adding up to a 60 percent tax rate from 1788 to 1792. In that window of time, duties on rum and other foreign spirits generated only £9,000 less than duties on sugar and over £300,000 more than taxes on domestic spirits.[82] Taxes on alcohol, and especially rum, in both colonies and the metropole fueled the fiscal-military state.

The very nature of rum and how it was made placed it at the center of eighteenth-century fiscal policy. The unparalleled strength of a relatively new class of distilled spirits and Atlantic-wide negotiations over who should consume them led to early eighteenth-century efforts to limit consumption by artificially raising the price of alcohol through taxation. Furthermore, French, Danish, and Dutch colonies all produced molasses as they made sugar, but generally only British colonies in North America and the Caribbean built up the infrastructure and expertise necessary to make and export rum from all of their sugary wastes. The abundance of raw ingredients available from foreign colonies and the relative paucity of rum-making expertise outside of British territories triggered questions about how to regulate transimperial trade. The most ardent defenders of Britain's sugar colonies and England's distilleries supported high taxes on foreign imports of molasses and rum in order to ensure strong prices for British sugar and grain-based distillates. However, they rarely succeeded in regulating trade or discouraging vice as was often intended. Levies designed to generate revenue showed greater promise.

Passing taxes on rum proved easier than collecting them. As early as March 1662, the Virginia Assembly enacted a six-pence-per-gallon duty on any rum that entered into the colony, citing "the excessive abuse of rum" and its "propensity to bring diseases and death to diverse people." Two years later, they rescinded the tax because it did not serve the intended purpose, proving too difficult to collect.[83] This pair of colonial laws anticipated by seventy-four years the goals and limitations of England's Gin Act. Alarmed by wanton consumption of grain- and molasses-based spirits among working-class Britons, Parliament passed the 1736 act to limit both the production and sale of gin and other distillates. The act instituted a duty of twenty shillings per gallon on all spirits and charged distillers a prohibitive duty of fifty pounds per year if they wished to sell it in quantities less than two gallons.[84] Both initiatives sought to effectively prohibit distillation by pricing out the lower classes from buying spirits. Initially, distillers produced less alcohol, but they eventually began to circumvent the law. One observer wrote around the time of the law's repeal in 1743 that "this law was so far from effecting a prohibition, that it really heightened, and spread the evil; for one distiller's shop that was shut up, ten places were open for the sale of drams."[85] Subsequent legislation in 1743 and 1751 changed tack by treating gin as a legitimate commodity but taxing it heavily.

Parliament's evolution from unsuccessfully leveling taxes to eliminate vice to taxing vice to generate revenue shaped fiscal policy for the rest of the eighteenth century. Activists and government officials agreed that the excessive consumption of spirits was a social ill that needed to be fixed. Yet prohibitive taxes did little to rein in drunkenness. Legislators calculated that hefty but enforceable duties could be powerful revenue generators though. Given previous collection issues, new taxes directed enforcement at alcohol producers, believing that they would then pass on the costs to consumers. As Lord North later observed, the spirit could—and should—bear higher duties because of an insatiable demand for the alcohol and its status as "not only luxuries, but pernicious luxuries."[86]

Another goal of taxes levied on alcohol producers was to regulate commerce between Britain, its colonies, and the rest of the world. For instance, Parliament charged customs on French brandy that ensured it would be more expensive than rum or other domestic or colonial distillates.[87] Throughout the eighteenth century, West Indies planters lobbied for a preferred status for molasses and rum of their own manufacture. Perceiving their profits from sugar and rum production to be falling, and facing growing competition from North American distilleries, they sought to stop the importation of French, Dutch, and Danish products into competing distilleries.[88] Officials proposed several solutions to the issue. In 1722, a customs official in Boston named Archibald Cummings proposed a duty of five pounds per hundred gallons of foreign rum and twenty shillings per hogshead of foreign molasses imported into North America, as well as three pounds per hundred gallons of rum distilled on the continent. While such duties were designed to reverse any advantage realized by North Americans flouting mercantilist protections, Cummings also believed that their enforcement would generate enough revenue to maintain an army of five to six thousand troops in North America.[89] By 1730, Parliament considered banning the trade of non-British sugar and rum to North America entirely. However, the bill stalled in the House of Lords. Two years later, Parliament instead passed the Molasses Act, levying a nine-pence duty on rum and a six-pence duty on molasses imported into North America from foreign colonies. Although the House of Lords refused to outright ban the molasses trade, they accepted a tax that opponents decried as "a total prohibition."[90] The levy fit within the right that Parliament claimed to regulate colonial trade.

Customs officials initially collected revenue owed through the Molasses Act. These collection efforts led to a temporary decline in the North American rum industry. The number of distillers operating in Boston fell by 12.5 percent between 1733 and 1735.[91] But revenue from the act steadily went down from £330 in 1734 to an average of £249 in the middle of the decade to £76 by the late 1730s.[92] Despite some initial success, the tax proved too unpopular and the colonial customs office too understaffed to enforce the Molasses Act. The Caribbean colonies that had initially requested the intervention of British authorities remained largely silent about nonenforcement after Parliament liberalized their ability to ship sugar directly to Europe beginning in 1739.[93] While Parliament made it easier to regulate trade with the Molasses Act, opposition from North America rendered this sort of tax unenforceable.

Though taxes on rum and other spirits that sought to control vice and regulate colonial trade quickly proved ineffective, the stability of demand for these products showed that placing excise and customs on alcohol could be an effective way of raising money for military and other expenses. In fact, the seemingly unquenchable thirst for rum regardless of the tax rate later caused Lord North to question the prevailing economic theory that taxing rum at exceedingly high rates would diminish demand for it.[94] As Parliament took out new loans to pay for rising expenses, they often sought to raise additional revenue by simply tacking another duty on an already-taxed good. Ultimately, some goods ended up with as many as fourteen different duties attached to them.[95]

The case of the 1764 Sugar Act offers a prime example of how taxes with other expressed purposes were also envisioned as revenue generators. The Molasses Act remained on the books but was wholly ineffective. In the wake of the immensely costly Seven Years' War, Prime Minister George Grenville came to two conclusions: colonists were wealthier than they claimed, and taxes were the most straightforward way to access that wealth. The comptroller of customs in Boston, Nathaniel Ware, advised Grenville that the rum industry was a good place to begin. He estimated that 117 American distilleries imported 38,625 hogsheads of molasses per year, rarely paying the regulatory taxes that they owed. Instead, they paid one penny "to the [customs] officer for connivance" and another four to eight pence in local excise taxes.[96] Following Ware's advice, Grenville proposed lowering the duty on molasses and increasing customs enforcement. When approached with the proposal to lower the protective tariff on foreign molasses, West Indies interests acquiesced. The agents representing the North American colonies likewise agreed and proposed a two-pence tax. That rate was slightly higher than the costs of smuggling, but politicians believed that such costs could easily be passed on to either French merchants supplying the molasses or West Africans purchasing the rum. At the last minute, Grenville decided to raise the rate to three pence to collect extra revenue, which he promised would be reserved for colonial defense.[97]

The range of taxes—and varied justifications for them—show how rum proved especially taxable over the eighteenth century. Alternatively, and often concurrently, rum needed to be priced out of the hands of nonelite consumers, protected from cheaper foreign ingredients or charged extra for using them, and levied against to fund a costly imperial apparatus. Such taxes ebbed and flowed, but the nature of rum as an inebriant made it exceedingly hard for its producers and consumers to offer effective arguments against taxing it at a uniquely high rate.

These taxes were heftiest and easiest to collect in Britain for several reasons. Questions concerning the authority of Parliament to directly levy taxes were muted. Furthermore, the efficacy of the excise and—to a lesser extent—customs offices in Britain explain much of the efficiency.[98] Technological innovation also supported the work of tax collectors. In order to levy taxes, officers needed to create a means to measure the quality of the alcohol being made. While consumers often thought about quality in terms of taste or color in addition to strength, the excise and customs officers instead based their judgments on alcoholic content alone. In 1746, a highly affordable hydrometer came onto the market in response to the request of one of the general surveyors of the distillery. By measuring the specific gravity of the alcoholic brew, the gauger was for the first time able "with great exactness, to show the different degrees of strength."[99] In turn, it became easier to accurately compute duties based on the amount of alcohol produced or purchased. Although designed for use in England, hydrometers sold in colonies as well and helped to create an ocean-spanning system of defining what made rum and other spirits more or less merchantable.

For the Excise Office, dispersing officers to measure the strength and volume of spirits was more effective if there were fewer distilleries to supervise. Parliament created laws that benefited larger distilleries, which, in turn, centralized production. For instance, distilleries were required to pay their excise duties before they sold their spirits, which proved challenging for businesses with limited capital.[100] Joseph Manesty encountered this conundrum in Chester in 1758 when he wrote that when he "could not raise cash to pay the excise of rum & some other demands pressing I had no remedy left but to shut my door."[101] In London, where these wastes were often redirected, a remarkable process of centralization of primary distilleries unfolded. Thirty primary distilleries operated in London in 1750, declining to twelve in 1760, and eight by the 1780s.[102] In an era when spirits production expanded under little regulatory oversight in the Caribbean and North America, the opposite took place in England.

Careful supervision and an emphasis on defining and quantifying alcohols also led the Excise Office to record what spirits were made of. This was necessary because the high sucrose content in molasses meant that fermenting it produced a higher proportion of alcohol than was the case with malted grains. The Excise Office accounted for these differences by adjusting duties based on what an alcohol was fermented and distilled from. Because they computed excise duties based on the volume of goods put into the still (rather than after distillation), secretly mixing sucrose-rich molasses into ferments became a common means of fraud.[103] Even according to official records, between 1737 and 1784, English distillers produced 9.5 percent of distillates—a total of 17,929,524 gallons—from molasses.[104] In the seventeenth and early eighteenth centuries, at least some of these molasses-based spirits might have been called rum. Now, the Excise Office's emphasis on specificity reserved that category for colonial products.

Circumvention

Despite the hefty taxes and intricate collection mechanisms in place, producers, traders, and drinkers of rum sought to lower their individual tax burdens by evading duties placed on the spirit. Speaking to the extent of this fraud, a committee appointed by Parliament calculated that the excise on tea, coffee, brandy, and rum in England generated £1 million per year. If fraud, which tended to most commonly center on tea and spirits, could be prevented, the committee estimated that the revenue would triple.[105] Evasion took many forms but generally fit into three categories: unsanctioned production, smuggling, and counterfeiting.

Excise collection depended on the ability of officers to observe the production of spirits. In England, where excise enforcement was carried out by a highly professionalized corps, one way to evade levies was to produce spirits where officers were not patrolling. Some observers believed that unregulated distilleries tended to specialize in making spirits from molasses because it could easily be produced on a small scale and because domestic sugar refineries produced plenty of wastes without another intuitive use.[106] Molasses spirits were also produced on stills unknown to the Excise Office.[107] Other stills were approved for home use, but complainants asserted that their produce was instead sold at taverns.[108] Finally, another group of distilleries were licensed as "rectifiers," which allowed them to mix different ingredients with already distilled spirits to create an array of merchantable products. Sometimes they secretly carried out primary distillations as well. For instance, excise officers detected a Bristol rectifying distillery that was not licensed to carry out primary distillations "working molasses wash in one of their stills" in 1779.[109]

At other times, legitimate primary distilleries used a variety of techniques to produce more spirits than they paid taxes on. In 1781, Richard Ellison caught the manager of Thomas Cave's molasses distillery using a set of "false keys" to unlock the charging pipe of a still while it was operating in an attempt to add more unregistered wash. When he tried to seize the keys, the distillery workers "got them from him by superior strength."[110] Distillery regulators also incessantly worried about producers counterfeiting the seals that they put on movable pieces to ensure that they had not been adjusted or, alternatively, using secret pipes to clandestinely fill or drain stills.[111]

Excise officers even claimed fraud when they could not determine how it was being carried out. In April 1777, General Danton of the Excise Office seized several puncheons of molasses spirits on the streets of London that the Langdon and Company Distillery in Bristol had sold to a local rectifier. The puncheons lacked the necessary permits. Convinced that the Langdon distillery was likely producing more illegal spirits, Danton and his compatriots headed for Bristol. Once in the distillery, they set up round-the-clock surveillance but found no direct evidence of fraudulent behavior. According to one of the deposed distillers, "Finding no private pipe, no open lock, no broken seal nor disturbed fastening, they became sullen through disappointment and like an enraged adder began to swell with revenge." After taste-testing dozens of containers of fermenting molasses, they alleged that two batches tasted "new" and charged the defendants double taxes on the wash. Langdon and Company disputed the excise officers' findings. In his deposition, Mr. Perkins blasted "those wise men from the east" who found Bristol's distillers to be "too great adepts in the art of necromancy to be confined by locks, fastenings, or seals." The deponents claimed that the "new" taste of the supposedly months-old wash resulted from an improved method of slower fermentation that they had pioneered.[112] That the Excise Office found them guilty without explaining how the conspiracy worked shows their confidence that distillery owners were executing sophisticated distillery frauds that even extensive surveillance could not detect.

In colonial America, smuggling ingredients from Caribbean islands not colonized by the British into distilleries emerged as another major form of fraud. In a 1763 set of instructions to the captain of the *Sally*, Melatiah Bourne advised Captain Ebenezer Frost to speak to no other ships and "put into no harbor on your voyage if there is a possibility to avoid it." On arriving back in Massachusetts Bay, the *Sally* should strike its sails and "run in undiscovered under the Gunnet Head" near Plymouth. Tipped off by a "broad blue vain," a coconspirator would dispatch "a vessel or vessels to take out [the] cargo."[113] The following year, the *Betsey* surreptitiously stopped in Guadeloupe after leaving Dominica and loaded a cargo of illicit molasses and rum. The ship sneaked into Maryland's Nanticoke River and offloaded the cargo before claiming to have sailed from Dominica in ballast. The Admiralty condemned the *Betsey* for violating the Molasses Act—one of only two times that authorities officially sanctioned Maryland conspirators for smuggling distillery ingredients.[114] But the larger pattern is clear: North American merchants and makers of rum slinked into inlets and darted between islands to evade tax collection.

At times, customs enforcement was so unpopular in colonial North America that merchants importing molasses for distilleries could openly land their cargo without paying the requisite taxes. Instead, they colluded with customs officers, paying duties on a small portion of their cargo along with a bribe to the officer.[115] Even after Parliament expanded the corps of customs officers in North America in the mid-1760s to fight back against such irregularities, local tax evaders maintained the upper hand. In July 1768, for instance, thirty men boarded a schooner in Boston that the customs office seized for carrying thirty hogsheads of unentered molasses. They locked the two officers in the cabin and removed the molasses. Massachusetts governor Francis Bernard complained that this use of force had accompanied every seizure over the past three years.[116]

Tax evaders violently resisted customs and excise enforcement in the eighteenth-century British Atlantic world with regularity. Between 1723 and 1730, more than 250 customs officers sustained injuries, six fatally, in an era where customs and enforcement expanded rapidly in England.[117] In June 1778, a mob converged at a Bristol distillery when excise officers attempted to seize a batch of rum shrub that had been mixed without their oversight. The crowd wrested the confiscated rum from the excise officers and rolled the barrels into the River Avon. They jumped in after them, "desirous of disappointing those minions of power of their booty." Once out of sight of the excisemen, they pulled the barrels ashore, staved the containers, "and drank some until many were unable to move." In using force to steal back the legally questionable rum and then drinking it, the rabble-rousers destroyed six hundred gallons of evidence of the distillery's indiscretions.[118] Violence, or at least the threat of it, often accompanied tax evasion.

Following the American Revolution, North American smuggling continued even as its purpose changed. Freed from British mercantilist policies, American merchants sought out molasses in sugar-growing regions of Martinique, Guadeloupe, Saint-Domingue, Trinidad, and Suriname. But American merchant-distillers also wanted to continue trading in the British islands. Within months of the signing of the Treaty of Paris, for instance, Daniel Roberdeau rekindled his business relationship with Jamaica merchants in order to trade Virginia wheat for Caribbean molasses.[119] Much to the chagrin of residents of both places, Parliament prohibited trade between the United States and their Caribbean colonies in American ships.[120] In response, sea captains got creative. Some American ships claimed distress in order to enter ports from which they were barred so they could fill their holds with molasses.[121] Alternatively, a Grenada correspondent named George Shand advised Thomas Robison to create a set of fake ships' papers in Shand's name to avoid seizure of American ships by Britain's navy, as well as strict customs enforcement by the French at Martinique.[122] A year later, Robison instructed a captain of one of his ships to "show no American colors papers or log books, nor even your letters," and to await instructions from Shand before proceeding into port.[123]

Incentives abounded to move rum clandestinely even when it remained within the empire. In fact, some observers suggested that smuggling was so common in Britain that even honest merchants had to break the law to stay solvent.[124] One of the most common ways to illicitly enter rum into England and Scotland was to offload cargoes on the islands surrounding Britain. The Isle of Man, in particular, became a popular point of disembarkation.[125] By 1765, however, the British government sought to limit this smuggling route.[126] Though the Isle of Man may have been closed to illicit trade, shipping goods through the Channel Islands remained one way for British distillers to augment their supply of untaxed ingredients. One complainant reported as late as 1787 that "3,000 puncheons and upwards of Danish rum are now annually imported into Guernsey and Jersey" for unapproved reexport into Britain.[127]

Even when rum was legally bonded in Britain, further opportunities for smuggling abounded. An export distiller in Bristol named William Shorland was caught in October 1780 selling his liquor in England despite averring that it would be exported. Shorland had hoped to circumvent heavier excise taxes imposed on spirits sold locally to a rectifier. However, an excise agent reported Shorland "for taking away export spirits and hiding them in an unentered cellar."[128] Likewise, because merchants were not charged taxes on spirits bound for Ireland, they sometimes marked their rum for reexport but instead sold it within Britain.[129] By shifting their rum between legal and illegal ports, men tasked with moving rum created loopholes to muddy its provenance and therefore its tax burden.

Customs officers often involved themselves in smuggling operations. When seeking to reform the office in the 1780s, a member of Parliament named Henry Beaufoy suggested that enforcement could be improved by halving the number of customs officers to remove the corrupt ones and doubling the pay of the honest men. He claimed that for every puncheon of rum traveling up the Thames, eight gallons were underreported, costing the treasury £40,000 per year.[130] London merchants and customs officers also conspired to underreport the contents of incoming barrels of rum for their own profits. One observer alleged that local gaugers and merchants misrepresented volumes of rum by as much as 7 percent and proof by as much as 5 percent. In this way, London buyers could receive more alcohol for lower prices, and customs officers profited from a kickback paid on the unmeasured rum.[131] Many parties sought profit in the margins between the volume of rum imported and the volume recorded by the taxman.

Producers and merchants also hoped to lessen their burden by misrepresenting what spirits they were making or selling. Customs and excise rates were calculated based on three qualities: the type of alcohol, where it was made, and its strength. By misrepresenting any of those three categories, one could evade certain duties. These schemes also affected consumers who overpaid for counterfeit, and sometimes outright dangerous, alternatives.

To profit from illicitly produced or imported spirits, unscrupulous businessmen needed to find a way to sell their unlicensed alcohol. They commonly did so by mixing English molasses spirits with imported rums. Some West Indies planters accepted this reality. For instance, Samuel Martin noted that British markets preferred rum from Jamaica because it had "a stronger tang and [was] therefore more capable of adulteration."[132] One published expert suggested that Caribbean rum could withstand the addition of as much as 25 percent British molasses spirits to create "made-up rum."[133] Others, however, worried that "shameful adulteration" negatively affected the taste of rum, lessening demand for the spirit.[134] As Thomas Robison's frauds discussed in Chapter 6 attest, North American distillers likewise approximated the taste, strength, and color of highly esteemed West Indies rum in their locally produced, and thus less taxed, distillates.

Alternatively, rectifiers mixed various other ingredients to convert rum and molasses spirits into more profitable liquors. A typical rectifier's laboratory included botanicals like "caraway, aniseed, peppermint, [and] noyan," and other ingredients including sugar, spirit of nitre, and silver nitrate.[135] Rectifiers would, for instance, mix and redistill molasses spirit, malt spirit, mace, cloves, nuts, cinnamon, coriander seed, ginger, cubebs, raisins, dates, licorice, English saffron, and sugar to make a "fine usquebaugh."[136] Because of the high customs duties charged on French brandies, rectifiers often sought to replicate those flavors in their laboratories. As with "made-up rum," some writers advised mixing a small proportion of brandy into a large vat of cheaper spirits. Other rectifiers carried out more sophisticated—and possibly dangerous—schemes to counterfeit French brandy with locally produced alcohol. Ambrose Cooper suggested that nitric acid would add "vinosity" to molasses spirits and thereby "pass on ordinary judges for French brandy."[137] For this concoction to pass as brandy, however, it also needed to look the part. Cooper advised rectifiers to add either molasses or burnt sugar to approximate the caramel color of oak-aged French brandy. Rectifiers needed to choose their coloring agent carefully: lower classes of people preferred the sweetness imbued by the molasses, while "nicer palates" appreciated the "agreeable bitterness" of burnt sugar.[138] Using molasses spirits and rum to counterfeit other beverages emerged as a popular means to profit from illicitly produced or entered alcohols.

* * *

The expansion of the British state both sheltered and benefited from rum production in the eighteenth century. Officials prioritized the protection of the landscapes where sugar and rum were made over many other places. Military leaders fueled their presence, in part, by feeding soldiers and sailors rum. By purchasing more rum than any other entity, the Victualling Board offered economic protection to West Indies interests during tumultuous periods. Of course, funding these new initiatives required revenue raised through taxes. Rum filled that need better than any other commodity. Parliament recognized that rum was nonessential, cheap, intoxicating, and highly desirable, which made it possible to tax the spirit at very high levels. Rum was of paramount concern for the British Empire's military priorities and funding streams.

On an individual level, those whose livelihoods depended on rum sought to benefit from these new policies while limiting how much they had to pay for them. Colonial distillers and merchants acted out of self-interest in resisting how much they paid in taxes and what those taxes supported. Individuals with a financial stake in the rum industry could also evade taxes to demonstrate their political opposition to the duties they were charged.[139] Yet opposition to taxes levied against the rum industry did not necessarily correspond with opposition to the British state more generally. North American distillers expressed almost uniform opposition to the Molasses Act, and then the Sugar Act, but they took different tacks in response to the imperial schism. Of a subset of twenty-six Boston merchants who also owned rum distilleries in the 1760s and 1770s, fifteen supported independence, seven remained loyalists, and four maintained neutrality.[140] Alternatively, a wide swath of Caribbean merchants and planters who chose not to join their American compatriots in declaring independence drew the ire of Horatio Nelson in the 1780s for openly flouting the Navigation Acts to trade with the United States. Many leading merchants and sellers of rum might have resisted policies that negatively affected them while acknowledging that they benefited from Britain's fiscal and military policies.

This reality helps to explain who gained the most economically from policies concerning rum in the latter half of the eighteenth century. Historians have long debated how profitable the sugar islands were for the British Empire. Their estimates range from the suggestion that the sugar islands constituted a financial drain to the islands being relatively profitable.[141] Yet individuals—many of whom owned rum distilleries, fulfilled government contracts, and traded in the commodity—amassed great fortunes through their agile investment in the Caribbean and workshops that converted its produce into rum. The many ways that they sought profit demonstrate the great capacity of rum's makers and movers to benefit from state interventions while sidestepping less favorable directives often at a moment's notice. In the 1790s, these same beneficiaries of British imperial policy built on plantation slavery encountered new challenges lodged by both enslaved people and white abolitionists intent on toppling the system.

CHAPTER 8

Defining Rum by Challenging Slavery

Sometime in the 1790s, the Herculaneum Pottery in Liverpool fashioned a creamware punch bowl teeming with contradictions. The English manufacturer decorated the bowl for American audiences, reproducing the likenesses of George Washington and Benjamin Franklin, as well as the seal of the United States. They also adorned the bowl with four lines of poetry, visible in Figure 15, that had been associated with the antislavery cause since they were printed on a Wedgwood teapot in the 1760s:

> Health to the Sick;
> Honour to the Brave;
> Success to the Lover;
> and Freedom to the Slave.[1]

These antislavery sentiments sat uncomfortably. The verses—painted in a manufactory located in the port city that dominated the British slave trade—adorned the same surface as a celebration of the American president whose properties enslaved over three hundred people.

The anticipated contents of the bowl add to the incongruity. Even when consumed in British or American households that did not themselves own slaves, the rum, sugar, citrus, and spices mixed together in a bowl of punch drew heavily from Caribbean plantations. By the late eighteenth century, abolitionist slogans painted on a creamware bowl could not mask the unsavory backstory of its contents' production and trade.[2]

Some devotees to rum—likely including whoever purchased this bowl—nonetheless sought opportunities to disentangle rum and slavery in an age of Atlantic revolutions. Their optimistic goals made a certain amount of sense. For

Figure 15. Creamware punch bowl attributed to Herculaneum Pottery (c. 1796–1800). Museum of the American Revolution, 2017.13.01.

150 years, makers and drinkers of rum separated by racial, economic, and political divisions—as well as the Atlantic Ocean itself—negotiated what rum was, how it should be made and consumed, and who should benefit from its creation. It was logical to wonder whether they could reinvent rum once more. As others had done before them, abolitionists sought connection and cooperation with other makers and drinkers. They embraced the political power of the commodity by working alongside people with complimentary goals.

The makers and drinkers of rum sympathetic to the message of the contradictory punch bowl responded to the challenges posed by slavery in several different ways in the final decades of the eighteenth century. Some antislavery advocates, many of whom were themselves enslaved, struck against the sites making rum, thereby bringing attention to rum as a morally compromised commodity. In the same years, hundreds of thousands of consumers tried to retrain their taste buds and purchasing decisions by doing without. Aware that nonconsumption campaigns were hard to maintain, a subset of producers experimented with sources of rum unsullied by slavery. Efforts at commodity substitution and transplantation attempted to draw North American stands of sugar maple trees, the fledgling colony of Sierra Leone, and even eastern India into a community of commodity makers tethered together by free-labor rum.

A coordinated strike against sugar and rum offered opponents of slavery considerable hope in the 1790s before falling well short of its goal. In addition to a raft of locally specific challenges, these efforts suffered from a perpetual discrepancy between the need for expert rum producers and elite proposals for who should perform the work. They also tended to lack the financing and patience that would be necessary to defeat established producers whose political connections often shielded their profits. Such tensions expose the limits of political unifications around rum in an age of antislavery activism.

Foundations of Resistance

From the earliest years of rum production, enslaved people resisted the coercion of their labor. With regularity, the forms of resistance struck against the very commodities that they were being forced to make. In his mid-seventeenth-century directions to the manager of a Barbados plantation, Henry Drax observed that the workers he enslaved "are more generally addicted to thieving" sugar, molasses, and rum. Recognizing—as everybody on the plantation would have—that these goods were "our money and the final product of all our endeavors," Drax demanded that the working buildings and the commodities be kept under careful supervision.[3] A few decades later, an Englishman named John Taylor detailed new and unsavory methods of control in use in Jamaican distilleries designed "to keep the Negroes from drinking it."[4] Taylor and Drax presented the appropriation of rum as personal failings among the enslaved that hurt their bottom line and required adjustments in how rum was made. When enslaved workers seized some of the produce of their labor for themselves, they struck at the profitability of plantation production.

As early Quaker activists began to oppose slavery in the first half of the eighteenth century, then, their opposition to slavery and decision to target sugarcane-based commodities themselves joined a movement already pioneered by enslaved producers in the Caribbean. Early Quaker activists differed from their predecessors, however, in resisting slavery by avoiding morally tainted goods altogether. Nonconsumption began as a personal action among a small group of individuals especially well versed in the work of making sugar and rum. In the 1730s, an English Quaker named Benjamin Lay, who had spent time in Barbados as a merchant before relocating to Pennsylvania, began to act on his belief that eating sugar and drinking rum was tantamount to stealing from coerced producers.[5] In a printed attack on Quaker slaveholders in an era when many of his coreligionists both continued to drink and continued to enslave people of African descent, Lay emphasized rum's origins in the waste pile to mark the commodity as an especially immoral product. He detailed how the "grease, dirt, dung, and other filthiness, as, it may be limbs, bowels, and excrements of the poor slaves, and beasts . . . serves exceeding[ly] well to make rum of, and molasses."[6] By arguing that the rum literally contained its unfortunate producers, he suggested that consuming it amounted to cannibalism.

John Woolman took up Lay's cause a decade later. By the time that he became an outspoken opponent of slavery in the 1750s, slave ownership among Quakers in Pennsylvania had fallen to less than one in three households. Nonetheless, Woolman distinguished himself by avoiding a full gamut of products made by enslaved people. After visiting slaveholders in the southern colonies of North America, conversing with individuals who had firsthand knowledge of the slave trade and Caribbean slavery, and reading books about slavery and commodity production, he resolved to avoid goods that he understood to be tainted by the institution of slavery.[7] Even among a religious community coming to terms with the ethical implications of slave ownership, Woolman found relatively few coreligionists willing to jettison all commodities that touched the hands of the enslaved. In his community, one could be properly pious and opposed to slavery yet consume rum and other compromised goods.

Woolman's principled nonconsumption coexisted—and at times intersected—with similar consumer choices of others who did not share his faith. In 1760, a Munsee leader from Wyalusing named Papunhank visited Philadelphia and met with Quaker reformers including Woolman. Papunhank had had contact with several Moravian missionaries in the 1750s before formal baptism in 1763. Previously a regular consumer of rum, Papunhank underwent a revelatory experience that caused him to commit his life to God and preach abstinence from alcohol to his Indigenous followers. Woolman later visited Papunhank's settlement in Wyalusing in 1763. Although he did not directly connect his nonconsumption to the evils of slavery, Papunhank criticized the rum trade and colonial violence that were part and parcel of the same Atlantic trade networks. For Woolman, this reasoning offered yet another reason to resist rum.[8]

Four thousand miles away in West Africa, certain African merchants especially in Upper Guinea also chose not to accept rum as payment, possibly as a form of protest. The Quran forbade Muslims from drinking alcohol, which caused many Muslim leaders in West Africa to abstain. At least as early as 1782, the region of Futa Toro accepted no payments in rum. Historian Bronwen Everill draws a connection between the rise of Islam in the area and growing concerns about the ramifications of the Atlantic trade. She explains that "beyond blocking the sale or purchase of enslaved people, consumers could avoid buying the products those enslaved people were forced to make, or abstain from goods 'tainted' by association with the slave trade."[9] Although many American colonists, Indigenous people, and African political and religious leaders continued to trade and drink rum, individuals shaped by various faith traditions—who often identified personal experiences that revealed the harm caused by rum—occasionally resisted colonialism and slavery by targeting the goods generated by the system.

Ideas concerning the political and economic power of nonconsumption circulated throughout the Atlantic basin, but forgoing rum remained a personal rather than a collective decision until the last quarter of the eighteenth century. Personal beliefs about slavery rarely coalesced into popular, actionable sets of convictions prior to 1775. Instead, it took the American Revolution—which the Declaration of Independence connected to a desire to protect "inalienable" human rights—to change the nature of antislavery in Britain and its colonies. The conversations about rights attached to American independence helped position antislavery advocates as "moral exemplars rather than utopian fanatics," according to historian Christopher Leslie Brown. Religious leaders—and especially a subset of Evangelical Christians—now found it easier than before to mobilize their followers in opposition to slavery and the slave trade.[10]

Long-standing ideals honed by the Enlightenment and popularized during the Age of Revolutions shaped new forms of antislavery activism. So too did the emergence of rum as a commodity of global importance and the highly visible circulation of information that accompanied this development. Inhabitants of the Atlantic world were now saturated with mentions of rum. Books, pamphlets, and private letters penned in distant sites of production but circulating widely shared details of how to make rum. These texts also included details regarding how workers were affected by the production process. A reader of a North American newspaper in the eighteenth century would encounter gruesome reports of (mostly enslaved) distillers dying in explosions and other industrial accidents.[11] Guides to Caribbean plantership likewise provided details on the fragility of life on a Caribbean plantation.[12] More so than a generation earlier, common consumers encountered harrowing descriptions of the human costs of their buying habits.

The extent of enslaved opposition to the conditions of sugar and rum production also infiltrated the print culture of the late eighteenth century. For instance, the *Boston Gazette* provided notice in July 1771 that a man well versed in the sugar business sought freedom by absconding from Grenada. The advertiser offered a twenty-dollar reward for his reenslavement.[13] English readers would have likewise learned that a man and a woman claimed by Samuel Gregory of Jamaica ran away while in London in 1763.[14] In fleeing sites of enslavement, individuals demonstrated to newspaper readers that they preferred dislocation and substantial risk to the danger and unfreedom represented by Caribbean sugar and rum colonies. Free Blacks on Jamaica made their perspectives clear as well. When Parliament studied whether plantations in the colony could be staffed by emancipated workers, an agent for the island named Mr. Fuller averred that "in Jamaica no free Negro was ever yet known to hire himself, or be employed in agriculture upon the sugar plantations."[15] Collectively, the print culture of the mid-eighteenth century stipulated that slavery remained crucial for the production of rum and that when given the choice people avoided this dangerous work.

Antislavery advocates crafted sensationalized accounts from this set of facts. A rumor spread that the blood of enslaved Africans was literally used to cure sugar. Some refiners drained cow's blood through sugar pots in order to purify the sugar, a fact that opponents of slavery mobilized as a metaphor for the human costs of consumption. By the 1790s, William Fox quantified the amount of human flesh that a British family consumed: by using five pounds of sugar per week, one family caused "the murder of one fellow creature" every twenty-one months.[16] In one response written by Andrew Burn, claims of cannibalism became even more hyperbolic. He averred that a British consumer literally consumed the blood and pus and sweat of the people who made it, saving the most gruesome story for rum. Seizing once again on the common understanding that rum repurposed the unpotable, Burn recounted how British consumers quickly downed a hogshead of rum that they later realized contained "the body of a roasted Negro."[17] That rum production took place in colonial and metropolitan workshops decried for regular frauds made such arguments all the more compelling.

Many constituencies agreed by the 1780s that plantation slavery carried an immense human cost that the British government had the ability to mitigate, but the path forward remained uncertain. William Cowper's 1788 poem "Pity for Poor Africans" exposed a level of complacency despite growing concerns about the morality of slavery. Cowper explained,

> I own I am shocked at the purchase of slaves,
> And fear those, who buy them and sell them are knaves;
> What I hear of their hardships, their tortures, and groans
> Is almost enough to draw pity from stones.
> I pity them greatly, but I must be mum,
> For how could we do without sugar and rum?[18]

Armed with greater context and concern for the human costs of plantation production, a wider swath of slavery's opponents began to draw up plans to topple the system. When William Wilberforce's bill to abolish the slave trade failed in Parliament in 1791, activists wondered how large groups of ordinary commodity consumers could force change. For long-standing and emerging opponents of slavery alike, three courses of action presented themselves: striking against slavery directly, forgoing slave-produced commodities like rum, or finding alternative sites for its production that remained unsullied by slavery. These courses of action combined to challenge how profit was normally derived in the late eighteenth century.

Attacks on a Compromised Commodity

Enslaved people resisted their enslavement for longer than rum had been produced, but in the final decades of the eighteenth century their attacks on spaces connected to its manufacture took on new potency. Sometimes these attacks were isolated, such as on December 10, 1785, when a group of runaway slaves attacked William Stuart's plantation in Rosaly, Dominica, killing four white servants and several enslaved people who joined the defense. Before departing, they set fire to the entire sugar works, including the distillery.[19]

At other times they were highly coordinated. In August 1791, revolutionaries in Saint-Domingue attacked plantations and their owners and operators. Thousands of slaves formed an army that marched from plantation to plantation, setting sugarcane and the tools used to convert it into merchantable commodities ablaze. In the first ten days of the uprising, rebels burned 184 sugar plantations. When a French officer later asked an unnamed prisoner about the revolutionaries' methods, he emphatically declared, "We have a right to burn what we cultivate because a man has a right to dispose of his labor." In this man's mind, fire functioned as a means to reassert his control over the proceeds of his own work.[20]

Haitian revolutionaries eventually defeated both slavery and monarchy in Saint-Domingue, but even halting resistance to slavery could alter landscapes of slavery and draw attention to the morally compromised nature of plantation produce.[21] A 1795 rebellion in Grenada offers insight into the many functions of rum as enslaved and free islanders waged war over the future of enslaved commodity production. On March 2, free men of mixed French and African descent led attacks on the towns of Grenville and Gouyave. As they retreated to their base of operations, Julien Fédon's Belvidere Plantation, they took roughly forty British captives, including the island's lieutenant governor, with them. Fédon ordered all but three of the captives executed in retaliation for an attempted assault of Belvidere. Linking their actions to the future of the slave trade to this island, at least one of these prisoners was held in the cargo hold of a slave ship.[22] Until their defeat fifteen months later, the revolutionaries controlled most of the island, allowing very little sugar or rum to be manufactured or sold. They actively recruited enslaved men and women to their cause, promising emancipation in return. Contemporaries estimated enslaved casualties of the rebellion—in which they fought on both sides—at seven thousand.

Fédon's rebellion responded to several distinct political issues.[23] Some French inhabitants (including Fédon) who had remained on the island after British dominion was established in 1763 resisted the usurpation of previously held rights. Others were swayed by the ideals of the French Revolution. Witnesses described revolutionaries—including one of the raconteur's own "servants"—wearing liberty caps and cockades and unfurling flags pronouncing "liberty, equality, or death."[24] One of the commissioners of Guadeloupe, Victor Hugues, went further to connect insurrections in British islands to the "genius of liberty" emanating from France. He wrote in early June that he had overseen the shipment of "a plentiful supply of arms and ammunition, together with a few men" to Grenada.[25] Commissions of rank signed in the French islands and given to some leaders touted the Rights of Man, decried kings as "robbers and tyrants," and—merely a year after the National Assembly's 1794 decree of abolition—called for the overthrow of the "edifice of slavery."[26]

African-descended revolutionaries in Grenada accepted parts of this ideology, but they also pursued their own goals uniquely focused on destroying the spaces of their enslavement. While they often highlighted the loyalty of their own bondspeople who mobilized to protect British interests, slaveholders noted moments when other people they claimed to own joined Fédon's camp on their own volition.[27] They attributed this decision to promises of emancipation offered by Fédon.[28] However, enslaved people casting their lot with the revolutionaries would have had good reason to hedge their bets. Fédon himself continued to own slaves until the revolution began.[29] And his ally in Guadeloupe, Hugues, coerced unpaid labor from nominally free *cultivateurs* even after abolition.[30] Freedom was anything but a guarantee.

Enslaved participants in Fédon's rebellion thus acted in ways that defined freedom and buttressed claims to it on their own terms. This often involved the appropriation of their enslavers' possessions, especially rum. John Hay recollected that shortly after being detained he encountered a number of men and women whom he had formerly claimed as his own carrying liquor and other supplies toward Belvidere.[31] Another man captured by Fédon's forces, Francis McMahon, recollected fears that first night regarding "the effects of intoxication with the rebel Negroes" that might end in a massacre of British inhabitants.[32] Immediately after refusing their enslavement, revolutionaries seized and freely drank rum that slaveholders had dispensed only sparingly to the enslaved among the insurgents. Rum consumption that flouted societal norms heightened fears among Grenada's white inhabitants.

Unlike some other opponents of slavery, the Grenada rebels did not stop drinking rum. Instead, they used it as a tool of war. Plantation rum that could not be put toward the war effort was quickly destroyed, keeping British planters from accruing any profit from its sale.[33] Most rum was instead consumed or dispensed as rations by the men and women in rebellion. At one point a rumor spread at Belvidere that British colonists poisoned all of the rum on the island. One revolutionary named Le Riche proposed that "to revenge ourselves" against this attack, they should poison the rivers and "endeavor to extirpate from the face of the earth such a race of monsters."[34]

It is also possible that Fédon and his followers used rum to weaken fighting forces intent on assaulting their base of operations. British planters criticized the government for not attacking Belvidere quickly when the number of revolutionaries had not yet swelled. In a letter defending the delay, Captain Gordon insisted that he had been unable to prevent soldiers from overconsuming alcohol, rendering them unfit for combat. He reported a curious source for that liquor: "Contrary to my expectation, I found that the Negroes brought rum to the men from every house or hut that I passed."[35] In this case, teeming supplies of rum bogged the army down.

Despite their embrace of rum, the revolutionaries pursued an especially destructive campaign against the island's refineries and distilleries. One observer described how soldiers recruited from plantations and made "the Negroes of each estate burn those of their respective masters, and plunder the curing-houses and rum-cellars."[36] As a plantation owner and political leader courting support from the French colonial government in Guadeloupe, Fédon did not sanction this level of destruction. Less than two weeks into the insurrection, he outlawed "plunder, murder, and burning of estates."[37] But some of his allies continued to fight with fire. Two months later, a plantation owner named Samuel Cary reported in a letter that the insurgents "burn at least one estate in some part or other every night, sometimes two or three."[38] Only in August did he report that the burning had slowed.[39]

Plantations invested in making sugar and rum were most likely to be targeted by these attacks. When hostilities ceased, sixty-five plantations claimed that their "sugar and rum works" had been destroyed, while sixty-one more sustained considerable damage. In comparison, only thirty-five coffee estates were destroyed.[40] Furthermore, the fires did not spare the sugar plantations owned by supporters of the revolution. When the government confiscated the property of accused revolutionaries in the aftermath of the rebellion, many of the seized sugar plantations had been burned to the ground.[41] As landholders observed early in the rebellion, this campaign of destruction had the potential to strike at the profitability of slavery long after conflict ceased. Samuel Cary wrote, "Whether we shall beat them out, however, is doubtful, and if we do, we get but a ruined island."[42] Such an island would no longer possess the infrastructure to quickly force the enslaved back into the especially onerous tasks integral to making sugar and rum.

The robust coverage of Fédon's rebellion in American and British newspapers and pamphlets laid bare the centrality of sugarcane-derived commodities to political developments in Grenada that likely would have scared most readers still grappling with shocking news emanating from Saint Domingue. The supply shortages—and thus price shocks highlighted in Table 1—that accompanied this news forced an even wider swath of rum drinkers to pay attention. In the first half of the 1790s, prices for rum produced in the United States skyrocketed. The specific upticks in 1791 and 1792 and again in 1795 coincided with these moments of social unrest that disrupted the production and trade of molasses and rum. As Brown, Benson, and Ives wrote to trade partners in Copenhagen in 1792, several factors including "the disturbances in the French West Indies and destruction of a great number of plantations has rendered molasses extremely scarce and in some places not to be obtained which will operate to keep rum very high in this country."[43]

Emergent moral opposition to Caribbean slavery in Britain and parts of the United States gained new adherents due to the unusually high prices for sugar and rum that followed. A merchant in Bristol suspected that protesters' "real motive for leaving off the use of it is its being at such an enormous high price and I believe that as soon as it falls, it will be used as freely as ever it was."[44] The East India Company's Committee on Warehouses likewise reported that "many persons abstain altogether from the use of sugar, rather than submit to the enormous price to which it is now advanced."[45] The success of nonconsumption at a moment of

Table 1. Average Monthly Price in Shillings per Gallon of New England Rum

Year and Location of Sale	*Minimum Shillings/Gallon*	*Maximum Shillings/Gallon*
1740, Philadelphia	1.67	2.17
1750, Philadelphia	2.25	2.75
1760, Philadelphia	3.28	4.28
1770, Philadelphia	2.08	2.33
1776, New York	2.5	5.0
1783, Boston	1.96	4.75
1784, Philadelphia	2.5	3.22
1790, Philadelphia	2.67	3.17
1791, Philadelphia	3.04	4.0
1792, Boston	3.42	3.75
1793, Boston	3.08	3.67
1794, Boston	3.5	4.5
1795, Boston	3.93	4.5
1795, Philadelphia	5.75	6.5
1796, Charleston*	4.17	4.33
1797, Charleston*	3.75	4.17
1798, Charleston	4.0	4.0
1799, Charleston	4.0	4.0
1800, Charleston	3.25	4.0

* Denotes rum listed as "American rum."

Source: Adapted from Arthur Harrison Cole, *Wholesale Commodity Prices in the United States, 1700–1861: Statistical Supplement* (Cambridge, MA: Harvard University Press, 1938).

record prices does not mean that participants were insincere in their choices to forgo consumption. Rather, inflated costs for an everyday item forced consumers to confront why the labor costs factored into the cost of a dram of rum were on the rise, creating deeper connections between abolitionist makers and drinkers.

From Nonconsumption to Transplantation

In the midst of antislavery revolts in the Caribbean, British antislavery advocates pushed for a complete pivot away from sugar and rum. William Fox's 1791 essay, *An Address to the People of Great Britain, on the Propriety of Abstaining from West India Sugar and Rum*, emerged as the foremost articulation of the reasons for not consuming rum and sugar. It went through at least 26 editions, and roughly 130,000 copies were printed in London alone.[46] The ideas contained within it spread widely. Around a dozen other pamphlets sprang up in its wake, extending and revising Fox's ideas to reach new audiences.[47]

Even slavery's apologists contended with Fox's arguments. In 1792, a tobacco merchant in central Virginia named Francis Jerdone read in a letter from his nephew, George Braikenridge, in England that "many ignorant people here have left off the use of sugar on the foolish supposition that every pound that is consumed costs the Negro that makes it an ounce of blood."[48] Braikenridge's criticism emphasized the circumstances of plantation commodity production to repeat one of Fox's most dramatic claims.

At a moment when a critical mass of Caribbean bondspeople made the extent of their opposition to slavery undeniable, British writers responded by presenting nonconsumption as the only moral response to plantation slavery. William Bell Crafton plainly argued that consumers must take responsibility for exploitation caused by their tastes. He explained, "If we purchase the commodity, we participate in the crime. The slave-dealer, the slave-holder, and the slave-driver, are virtually the agents of the consumer, and may be considered as employed and hired by him to procure the commodity."[49] Ignorance no longer sufficed as an excuse either, because the print culture of the era offered plentiful examples of the abuses rampant in slavery and the slave trade. Samuel Bradburn confessed that he had previously consumed slave-produced goods because he had not fully understood the circumstances of their production. But those days were over. He insisted that now people "must sin with our eyes open" if they continued to seek out commodities derived from sugarcane.[50]

The goals of the movement were not entirely consistent. Cotton fell outside of the consumer action in order to protect the livelihoods of textile workers in England.[51] Likewise, leaders of the Sierra Leone Company believed that they could only defeat the slave trade by offering in-demand, though morally dubious, trade goods including alcohol in exchange for what they deemed "legitimate" produce from Upper Guinea.[52] Concerns of practicality also shaped the expressed goals of the anticonsumption campaign. Based on the information included in these pamphlets, nothing less than an immediate end to plantation slavery could wash the blood out of sugar. Likely worried that anticonsumption could not be maintained for long enough to accomplish this ambitious goal, activists often set the more moderate objective of abolishing the slave trade. Of course, any outcome allowing plantation slavery to continue would have ameliorated few of the issues described by William Fox and others. Nonetheless, abolitionists embraced inconsistencies in order to make the campaign as likely to succeed as possible.

These compromises initially worked, as anticonsumption quickly gained an immense following in Britain. In 1793, when Thomas Clarkson undertook an exhaustive tour of England, he met many enthusiastic supporters. He estimated that three hundred thousand people in Britain had ceased using sugar and its by-products.[53] Women crucially adapted household consumption patterns to support the collective action.[54] Momentarily, at least, the implications of plantation production concerned British consumers enough that a significant portion of the population voluntarily went without sugar and rum.

Nonconsumption campaigns rarely last long, however. Anticipating this reality, some leaders hoped that nonconsumption would provide a runway for the transplantation of commodity production to sites of free labor. Crafton contended that Britons could return to their past consumption habits if they found a way to "obtain the produce of the sugarcane in some other mode, unconnected with slavery, and unpolluted with blood."[55] His emphasis on sugarcane rather than sugar once again reiterated that any collective action must also account for rum. Responding to antislavery sentiment and supply shortages in the West Indies, British consumers increased their use of East India sugar tenfold between 1791 and 1793.[56] However, there was simply not enough free produce to replace slave-produced sources of sugar and rum. Recognizing this shortfall, dozens of businessmen, sometimes propped up by government and company officials, explored new commodity frontiers.

Some transplantation attempts doubled down on sugarcane, but many other projects sought alternative sources of both sucrose and ethanol. William Wilberforce wondered in a 1793 letter to Zachary Macaulay if a peculiar set of "free laborers"—meaning honeybees—could be colonized in Sierra Leone to such a degree that they could replace sugar.[57] Writers also suggested the utility of stands of birch in Britain, hickory and sugar maples in North America, and date palms in India.[58] Still committed to the pairing of sugar and rum, one observer proudly stated that the *gur* from Indian date trees yielded "a spirit scarcely distinguishable" from the finest rums.[59] The noted American abolitionist and early temperance advocate Benjamin Rush begrudgingly acknowledged the same alcoholic possibility for sugar maple sap.[60] Many ideas circulated about setting up free-produce sugar plantations or harvesting sweetness from other sources, but only a few of them amounted to much.

Activists arranged many of the resulting far-flung colonial ventures to appear as a unified campaign to moralize commodity production. An article that first appeared in the *General Advertiser* in August 1791 praised the possibilities of both maple sugar and Sierra Leone sugar to "alleviate the miseries of the unfortunate Africans, who hitherto have, with their blood and their tears, watered the sugarcane."[61] One month later, a proslavery writer in Jamaica acknowledged that these projects combined with revolution in Saint-Domingue to provoke anxiety among planters. He explained that "the planters here were kept in fear by the account of East India manufactured sugar, and the growing importance of the maple sugar of America."[62] In these renderings, maple sugar and free-labor sugarcane—and the rum replacements distilled from their by-products—jointly comprised a response to humanitarian concerns about enslaved commodity production that connected "the friends of liberty all round the globe."[63]

Ultimately, three replacement schemes for sugar and rum gained the most traction in the 1790s: the rapid expansion of the maple sugar industry in the United States, the transplantation of formerly enslaved individuals and plantation agriculture to Sierra Leone, and the intensification and modernization of sugar production—as well as the introduction of rum distillation—to India.[64] Each proposed frontier sought to replace slavery with labor that the projectors deemed "free." They also accompanied broader colonization schemes seeking to expand the political and economic influence of the United States and Britain. Whereas the initial settlement of sugar and rum plantations happened slowly and somewhat organically, establishing new commodity frontiers relied on institutional and economic support from politicians and elite businessmen. Large, highly capitalized landowners, along with the political figures who cleared legal hurdles for them, took leading roles in these commodity substitution efforts. While they were in a position to finance new ventures, these projectors tended to have limited practical experience within the industry that they were trying to reform. They often lacked the expertise (or means to acquire it) necessary to thrive in this line of work. In fact, many of the eventual downfalls of the new commodity frontiers—an overestimation of the sugar maple's potential, the unwillingness of formerly enslaved people to produce these commodities, or unfamiliarity with the climate of eastern India—can be attributed to the ways that fledgling producers often pursued novel plans without accounting for whether there were enough skilled producers willing to perform the work.

"The Woods of America Forward the Cause"

Indigenous Americans produced maple sugar long before sugar plantations emerged in the Americas. When the English first settled New England in the seventeenth century, they learned how to tap trees, collect the sap, and reduce it into sweet syrups and cakes of sugar from Native people.[65] During his voyage into the Carolina interior in the early 1700s, John Lawson observed the southern limits of the sugar maple range. He watched as Indigenous people in the Southeast cut a V into the side of a tree to tap it, inserted a pipe, and then collected the sap in gourds before they boiled it into granular sugar.[66] The Haudenosaunee—whose territories in New York and Pennsylvania were praised as prodigious sugar maple habitats in the 1790s—also produced large quantities of sweets from a tree they called *ozekéhta*.[67]

Eighteenth-century colonists and travelers appropriated an originally Indigenous knowledge system of maple sugar production, while simultaneously discounting the expertise of its Native purveyors. Pehr Kalm described its production in the hands of both Native Americans and European-descended farmers in primitive terms.[68] He specifically took issue with Native people who adulterated the sugar with flour and chose not to refine it into a product that resembled what he thought sugar should look like. By the 1790s, this process of appropriation progressed even further. Neither of the major promotional pamphlets on the virtues of the sugar maple acknowledged the initial inventors. Instead, writers condensed the history of the sugar maple to roughly "thirty years," while furthermore contending that innovation had only just begun.[69] They wrote Native people out of their story of sugar production altogether.

Proponents of maple sugar—and, increasingly, maple-based rum—instead drew attention to how commodity substitution could advance an American project of independence and territorial expansion. As colonists bristled at the Sugar Act in 1765, a Boston newspaper announced that one man had produced upward of six hundred pounds of maple sugar the previous year and that the accompanying syrups were "very little, if anything, inferior to our West-India molasses."[70] Following the Treaty of Paris, advocates continued to peg saccharine independence to American maple stands. Proponents hoped that forested lands expropriated from Native people could yield enough sugar maple to replace sugar and molasses imported from the Caribbean and possibly even become a significant export product.[71] They argued that producing domestic versions of sugar and rum could serve the political and economic goals of the fledgling United States.

This attempt at economic independence also connected to antislavery actions of the early 1790s. After revolution broke out in Saint-Domingue in 1791, Thomas Jefferson and a correspondent exchanged letters directly tying increased optimism around sugar maple investments to "the insurrections in the islands."[72] Both men hoped that American commodity frontiers could benefit from the disruptions wrought by revolution, even if some of the project's most enthusiastic supporters continued to invest in slavery.

As antislavery debates gripped Parliament in the late 1780s and the Haitian Revolution raged in the early 1790s, a "maple sugar bubble" explicitly tied to divesting from centers of commodity production dominated by plantation slavery began to form.[73] After the publication of an article noting that farmers could produce sugar, molasses, and various alcoholic beverages from the maple tree appeared in the 1788 edition of *Poor Richard Improved*, a group of prominent Philadelphia Quakers began to discuss the possibilities of supporting the industry.[74] Several of them entered into conversations with a New York land speculator and proponent of maple sugar production named William Cooper.[75] The following August, Benjamin Rush met with a group of prominent men who agreed to establish an association that would purchase five hundred barrels of maple sugar each year in order to "lessen or destroy the consumption of West India sugar, and thus indirectly . . . destroy Negro slavery."[76] That evening, Rush shared his idea with the Philadelphia politician and political economist Tench Coxe. The following day, Rush and Coxe convinced another Quaker businessman named Henry Drinker to join with them. In short order, Drinker reoriented his business holdings to capitalize on the possibilities of this new venture. He directed his iron forge in New Jersey to produce sugar pans for maple syrup, and he sent his employees to survey the potential of his speculative landholdings in northeastern Pennsylvania.[77]

Though Drinker's impulse to "derive profit from virtue" was connected to his Quaker faith, he regularly collaborated with other less likely champions of the maple sugar movement, including Jefferson and Cooper. Both men invested in slavery even as they touted the abolitionist outcome of the project. Such outcomes were powerful advertising tools. A correspondent in England whose letter was first reprinted in a Philadelphia newspaper in 1791 connected the proponents of maple sugar to British abolitionists including Wilberforce, Cowper, and Fox. With the rise of new commodities derived from the tree, he continued, "now, even the woods of America forward the cause!"[78]

Landowners speculating on large swaths of sugar maple forests in Pennsylvania and New York insisted on the economic promise of this endeavor.[79] When clearing the land, settlers would preserve the sugar maples on their land. With only thirty to fifty trees per acre standing, landowners could plant crops around the valuable trees. Then, late each winter, families would spend three to six weeks tapping the trees, collecting the sap, and boiling it into sugar. Cooper predicted that each properly managed tree would annually yield around five pounds of granulated sugar and a commensurate portion of liquid sweetener that could be fermented and distilled into rum.[80] This work would occupy the winter months when farmers were less busy. And because individual families only needed wooden troughs, an iron pot in which to boil the syrup, and a few utensils, start-up costs were minimal.

Proponents presented the transition from enslaved labor to family labor as both morally and financially superior to existing production strategies. The president of the French Society for Emancipating Slaves observed that a man and four children could make 1,500 pounds of sugar in a four-week period.[81] Others noted the preeminence of women in the industry. One observer wrote idyllically of young women who "might justly be styled woodland nymphs" harvesting maple sugar in Otsego County, New York.[82] The proponents of the industry repeatedly alluded to the possibility that the labor of families could render plantations in the West Indies obsolete. As Jefferson declared in a 1790 letter, "What a blessing to substitute a sugar which requires only the labor of children, for that which it is said renders the slavery of the Blacks necessary."[83] Romanticized visions of young women or children participating in commodity production hinted in yet another way at how attempts to open new commodity frontiers circumvented questions of consent among replacement workforces.

Projectors fully understood that the success of the maple sugar industry also depended on supplanting rum produced by enslaved workers. Some innovators hoped that they could limit Americans' consumption of strong spirits like rum as the need for trade with the West Indies subsided. Rush noted that individuals could make a spirit from maple sugar molasses but hoped that Americans would simply stop drinking rum. And Drinker, who had expended considerable effort weaning his ironworkers and other employees off liquor, never mentioned the possibilities of maple sugar rum in his published writings.[84] However, distillation went hand in hand with the harvest of sugar maple on the Pennsylvania and New York frontiers. The widespread attempts to improve maple sugar refining so that the salable product looked, tasted, and felt like muscovado sugar depended on additional refining. This process included skimming detritus from the top of maple sugar pans and ensuring that syrups drained from the crystallizing sugar in centralized refining houses. Doing so released waste products analogous to what Caribbean, North American, and British distillers were accustomed to fermenting and distilling into rum, though the volume of these products may not have been enough to match Caribbean yields.[85]

Leading maple sugar projectors constructed centralized distilleries alongside the boiling houses they built to collect and process individual families' maple sugar outputs. Although the promise of free-labor maple sugar rested on a vision of small, private landholders, placing the boiling houses and distilleries beside each other in a central location replicated the spatial layout of West Indian sugar plantations in American frontier communities. When a Dutchman visited the backwoods of Pennsylvania, New York, and Vermont in 1791, he noted that John Nicholson planned to add a distillery to his sugar works in northeastern Pennsylvania.[86] That same year, "a gentleman from Ireland" named Alfred Noble joined William Cooper in Otsego County with the purpose of "establishing a distillery of spirits from the juice of the maple."[87] Noble and Cooper proudly sent a sample of the resulting spirit to Jefferson in the hopes of gaining his support for their endeavors. Jefferson explained in a letter to Washington that the maple syrup rum reminded him of whiskey.[88] General quiet surrounding the taste of maple sugar rum, and the volumes produced, may have been a concerted effort by speculators and their allies to emphasize similarities—instead of notable differences—between West Indies produce and their proposed replacements.[89]

Zealous lobbying alone was not enough to establish a successful sugar and rum industry amongst American maple stands. Settlers quickly realized that Cooper had exaggerated the average number of sugar maple trees per acre.[90] Purchasers found that the product did not resemble the West Indian goods that they aimed to produce as closely as had been suggested.[91] During a frigid spring in 1790, the majority of settlers could not produce enough sugar or molasses to even cover the costs of the equipment they received from Cooper on credit.[92] When landholders ran out of money or became disillusioned, they began burning their trees to make potash. As more white settlers populated northern Pennsylvania and western New York, the abolitionist possibilities of America's forests receded.[93]

Over the ensuing decade, public celebrations of this substitute commodity became less common. But they never ceased. Some Americans continued to harvest and process maple syrup for sugar and rum for personal and local consumption.[94] When Bryan Edwards's *History of the West Indies* was published in 1800, the *Gazette of the United States* hypothesized that the chapter on sugar production would be beneficial to Americans "engaged in the maple sugar manufacture."[95] These interested parties were increasingly carrying out America's colonization of the Northwest Territory. In 1803, Anishinaabe near Fort Michilimackinac produced "many tons" of maple sugar and offered it for sale to American settlers at reasonable prices.[96] And according to Tench Coxe's census of American manufactures, Ohio alone produced over three million pounds of maple sugar in 1810.[97] Into the nineteenth century, the sugar maple, and its potential to derive profit from newly expropriated Indigenous territories, remained a powerful justification for American expansion westward but did not supplant plantation slavery in the Caribbean.

Free-Labor Plantations

Rum and sugar derived from free-labor sugarcane drew the attention of many British abolitionists. Sierra Leone became one site for this imagined imperial project. Unsuccessfully colonized by the British in 1787 and resettled with mostly Nova Scotian refugees in 1792, the expressed purpose of the Sierra Leone colony was to resettle free people of African descent on the continent. However, the success of the colony's antislavery mission depended on creating an economic engine for the settlement.

As leaders organized the 1792 recolonization efforts, they invested in jump-starting tropical commodity industries. The Sierra Leone Company hired James Watt, who had previously worked as a plantation overseer in Dominica, to supervise this work. Upriver from Freetown, he managed a square-mile tract of land set aside to produce commodities including sugar and rum.[98] Watt paid free native workers three shillings and sixpence per month—in addition to prodigious allotments of rum—to work from sunup to sundown on what was dubbed "Clarkson Plantation." Others hoped that sugar boilers and distillers from the Americas who resettled in Sierra Leone would join him. One writer insisted that "when the sugarcane comes to be cultivated, some instruction from a person well skilled in the boiling of sugar, and the distillation of rum, will be absolutely necessary."[99] Formerly enslaved migrants to Sierra Leone who gained experience on West Indian plantations might have been best equipped to lend their expertise to these technical processes, though they showed little predilection to resume the work that marked their enslavement.

Visions of sugar and rum plantations in Sierra Leone appealed to abolitionists for several reasons. They offered the possibility of opening up a new source for the commodities untarnished by slave labor. In 1791 and 1792, London's Sugar Refiners Committee proposed supporting fledgling industries in Sierra Leone as a means to lower sugar prices that were spiking in part due to enslaved resistance in the Caribbean.[100] Furthermore, in a diplomatic mission to Timbo, Watt explained to Fula leaders that the Sierra Leone Company planned to disincentivize slave trading in the region by offering "all those articles for rice, ivory, etc., which the slave traders will give only for slaves."[101] Given the long-standing centrality of rum to the slave trade in Upper Guinea, a local, free-labor substitution could be highly lucrative.

Despite their initially high hopes, plantation production in Sierra Leone underperformed for several reasons. Observers noted that sugarcane grew naturally on many parts of the African coast, but the subpar, clay soils surrounding Freetown were not conducive to its cultivation.[102] Many emancipated slaves who relocated to Sierra Leone also actively avoided work in cane fields, boiling houses, and distilleries. C. B. Wadstrom suggested that these individuals were reluctant to work on plantations but might be more willing to embrace sugar and rum production if it occurred on land that they personally owned. However, the costs of private land ownership, as well as building small mills, boiling houses, and distilleries stunted this enterprise.[103] Finally, representatives of the Sierra Leone Company in London lobbied to have free-labor sugar admitted with the same tax advantages as West Indies produce, but to little effect.[104] Despite the potential for replications of Caribbean plantations to emerge as a profitable part of this new colonial endeavor, Clarkson Plantation was mostly abandoned by 1796. Free-labor sugar and rum from Sierra Leone never materialized.[105]

Other efforts to find free-labor alternatives to slave-produced sugar and rum—especially in the Indian Ocean basin—progressed further than this failed attempt in West Africa. Renewed efforts by the British East India Company (EIC) to colonize eastern India starting in the 1770s included initiatives designed to transplant Caribbean-inspired commodity industries to the East. However, during subsequent efforts in the early 1790s, enterprisers responded to heightened demand for free-labor sugar and rum by placing new emphasis on combining ingredients and expertise culled from the Atlantic world with the techniques of small local farmers devised during the region's precolonial past.

The Indian subcontinent may initially appear to have been an odd location for the development of free-labor plantations, but many observers touted its potential in the late eighteenth century. The slave trade and forms of domestic slavery structured life and labor in early colonial India.[106] On the Malabar Coast, enslaved Indians even engaged in agricultural work.[107] However, the work of enslaved Indians was not tied to any major product being made in India for export to Britain.[108] And repeated efforts to ban the slave trade and slavery itself in Bengal in the 1780s and 1790s suggested to those observing from afar that commodity production carried out by free workers was a realistic possibility. When a longtime EIC official named Charles Grant returned from India in 1790 and joined the London Abolition Committee the following year, he and his colleagues had reason to hope that plantation operators in Bengal could undercut the slave system by employing paid and family labor.[109] In many ways, however, abolitionists' valorization of free labor in India was based more on an imagined ideal than on-the-ground conditions.

Following the EIC's formal takeover of the government of Bengal in 1772, Britons with varying levels of experience in the sugar and rum industry attempted to reform sugar and alcohol production in India, which had existed for millennia but they claimed had grown moribund.[110] At least five separate groups built Caribbean-style sugar works in the 1770s. The Bengal Commercial Society combined the capital and expertise of five Britons, three of whom also worked for the EIC. With an initial investment of £50,000 they rented 3,300 acres of land in 1775 in the hope of planting sugarcane and building a state-of-the-art sugar works.[111] Similarly, a partnership of the merchants Rumbold, Charlton, and Raikes formed in 1777 with the purpose of producing sugar, rum, silk, and indigo.[112] Joseph Hodgson, John Levett, and Peter Touchet each imported stills and other equipment to produce rum, albeit on a smaller scale, in Bengal.[113]

These entrepreneurs chose to import equipment from Europe rather than using techniques and materials originating in India. In 1773, John Levett purchased two 850-gallon stills from the London coppersmith William Forbes.[114] The following year, he transported four more stills, worms, and pump systems from London to India.[115] Similarly, rather than using the bags that traditionally contained sugar and molasses in Bengal, these businessmen imported staves and iron hoops from England in order to construct European-style barrels.[116] Many of these supplies came from the same British workshops supplying distillers in the Atlantic world.

Standard commodity production techniques also traveled to India from the Atlantic basin, especially the Caribbean. According to a letter from the court, Joseph Hodgson "erected sugar works on the best plan of those in the West Indies," complete with a plantation distillery, by 1776.[117] Cane fields approximating—or even surpassing—the size of Caribbean plantations depended on workforces with a variety of specialized technical skills. And again, the British proprietors hoped to borrow from their experiences in the Atlantic world. John Levett wrote to the still maker William Forbes to ask if he could recommend a British distiller to staff his Bengal distillery.[118] Rumbold, Charlton, and Raikes gained permission in 1778 to hire and ship a group of twenty expert commodity producers from England. The group was to include "two overseers used to the planting, cultivation and boiling of the sugarcane," as well as seven indigo producers trained in the West Indies.[119] At least one plantation even hoped to install the major labor system of the West Indies in Bengal: African slavery. The Bengal Commercial Society unsuccessfully petitioned for the right to import "twenty Negroes from the West Indies" for the plantation to use as carpenters and blacksmiths.[120]

These initiatives failed spectacularly despite the infusion of capital and ideas from the British Atlantic world. The would-be planters observed that "the soil of Bengal is perhaps the richest in the world," but lambasted the small-scale Indian farmers who grew sugar and made spirits as "averse to innovation, ignorant, and timid."[121] The Bengal Commercial Society successfully produced small amounts of refined sugar and rum from neighboring Indians' sugarcane but could not save their own sugarcane from "an unconquerable enemy"—termites.[122] For many, financial distress and even bankruptcy followed.[123] Critics claimed that these plantation owners' plans were doomed by their failure to account for the local economics of labor and lending. The Bengal Board of Trade concluded that the high cost of borrowing money combined with the low cost of free labor meant that expensive sugar mills, boiling houses, and distilleries would rarely cover the initial investment. Attempts by elite businessmen and company officials to quickly install a West Indian model of plantations in the East Indies failed to live up to its promise in the 1770s. Sugar production in Bengal never ceased entirely, and European rum production continued, but neither Europeans nor Indians appear to have heavily invested in the sugar and rum industries over the next fifteen years.[124]

Despite previous struggles, sugar and rum from India received a boost from the anticonsumption movement. Consumers who swore off slave-produced sugar and rum purchased inferior—yet more expensive—Indian sugar in an attempt to align their consumer activities with their values. A recently relocated Caribbean plantation overseer named William Fitzmaurice reported from India that "the failure of the West-India crops, the rage of abolishing the slave trade, and the combinations consequent thereon, concurred in rendering the first importations of India sugar, such as was sold in England these two years past, peculiarly successful."[125] Consumer action breathed new life into Bengal's sugarcane.

EIC officials, in turn, threw the might of the company behind endeavors to revitalize sugar and alcohol production. The company pursued four sets of policies in support of this goal: they lobbied for Bengal produce to gain the tax advantages reserved for West Indian sugar; they ensured that their fleet could carry the commodities produced in Bengal; they financed the migration of experts—but not bondspeople—from the West Indies to the East Indies; and, unlike in the 1770s, they attempted to learn from local commodity producers.

One of the EIC's first goals was to negotiate a more favorable tariff on East Indian products. In the early 1790s, taxes on West Indian sugar hovered at around

25 percent of the value.[126] By comparison, Bengal sugar, which was subject to the same taxes as other foreign-produced sugar, was taxed at a rate of 37 percent.[127] Worried that these higher taxes were "prohibitive," the EIC did everything in its power in the 1790s to gain a similar advantage for themselves. They enlisted the help of the London Sugar Refiners Committee in 1791 to "defeat the monopoly possessed by the West India Planters."[128] Despite continued pleas that Parliament encourage sugar production in the East Indies as it had in the West Indies, the higher levy on Bengal sugar remained.[129]

Though the EIC failed to secure a reduction in sugar duties, they leveraged the company's infrastructure to support the production and transfer of sugar and rum. They greatly expanded the carrying capacity of their fleet to ensure that salable produce could be moved from Bengal to European and other markets. By 1797 the company reserved 7,000 tons of space on their ships for Bengal sugar and another 6,400 tons for other products including rum.[130] Some plantation products were destined for Europe, but the EIC also opened up markets elsewhere. Military and merchant marine rations for soldiers and sailors passing through Bengal often consisted of the local distillate.[131] Significant quantities of rum were also shipped to St. Helena and British colonies in Australia throughout the 1790s.[132] Most of all, Indian sugar and rum ended up outside the British Empire. The EIC estimated that more than ninety thousand gallons of Bengal rum were shipped to Hamburg and the United States in 1796 and 1797.[133] Taking yet another cue from the Atlantic world, this trade relied extensively on smuggling to avoid British tariffs.[134] By facilitating legal trade with other British ports and doing little to stop trade outside the empire, the EIC ensured that sugar planters in eastern India could find outlets to sell their products globally.

The EIC also actively invested in commodity production. At times, the company itself operated rum distilleries in Mirzapur and Visakhapatnam.[135] While the enterprises themselves often lost money, the company funded various experiments to improve production more generally. By 1791, Lieutenant John Paterson arrived in India "perfectly conversant in the nature of the sugar trade, and of the most approved methods adopted in the cultivation of the article in the West Indies." Paterson insisted that the "attention, and encouragement" of the EIC would result in increased success in producing both sugar and rum.[136] The committee agreed. They offered Paterson the financial support necessary to create a model plantation in Sonamukhi.[137] In a contract that commenced on 1 January 1792, the company signed on to help him procure nearly two thousand acres of land rent-free. Furthermore, the company agreed to allow Paterson to import mill equipment, as well as rum- and sugar-making supplies, from Britain duty-free. He was also welcome to "take out three Europeans at his own expense for the sole purpose of being employed in his sugar works."[138]

The EIC agreed to invest money in, and forgo profits from, Paterson in order to support the establishment of his plantation for two reasons. First, as the contract stipulated, the company was entitled to buy all of Paterson's sugars at the Calcutta warehouse for a set price.[139] The sugar could then be shipped to Europe where it would encourage the consumption of tea from the East Indies. Officials anticipated that the quality of this produce might also improve the reputation of Bengal sugar. Additionally, the EIC envisioned Paterson's plantation as a laboratory for the creation of productive knowledge. The Bengal Board of Trade made clear in a 1792 missive that they hoped to "draw some inferences of the advantages he may derive from his West-Indian skill," even though he was not obliged to provide it.[140]

Although they continued to stake their rum- and sugar-making credentials on their experience of working on plantations in the West Indies, EIC employees and private distillers alike differed from their forerunners in the 1770s by considering and actively incorporating expertise created in Bengal and other parts of the East Indies. The EIC sent out a questionnaire to employees stationed in different districts of Bengal. These reports allowed the company to gather information on European and Indian cultures of commodity production in India. For instance, the report from Calcutta reported that sugar was alternately produced using both the "West-India manner" and traditional Indian cultivation techniques. Some local producers (and European converts) also distilled fermented gur, using a still made of clay and bamboo.[141] By the early 1790s, EIC employees paid attention to varied sugar-boiling and distilling techniques and considered what each might contribute to a revitalized industry within Bengal.

These investigations into the different ways that sugar and rum could be produced in Bengal rehabilitated certain traditional Indian production techniques in the eyes of the EIC.[142] Rather than developing large plantations with expensive sugar works, Bengal agricultural landholders, called *raiyatts*, farmed smaller lots of land, largely relying on the labor of their families.[143] When their sugarcane matured, these farmers assembled temporary mills and boilers on the edge of their fields. Portable sugar works reduced the distance that unprocessed cane needed to be carried, required less labor to operate, and were easier to replace in the event of natural disasters.[144] Fitzmaurice reported that the men he hired were able to construct a "country" mill and boiling house in an hour and quickly processed "very fine strong-grained sugar, which upon claying appeared equal to the best St. Kitts sugar."[145]

In light of swirling abolitionist arguments, observers of East Indian production celebrated how the work was performed. They extolled free labor on both economic and moral terms. Henry Thomas Colebrooke acknowledged that slavery existed in India, but the low costs of food, clothing, and housing in Bengal meant that wages were eminently affordable. He estimated the daily pay of an agricultural worker at twopence. In his sanguine calculations, Colebrooke speculated that the wages for these workers only amounted to 10 percent to 15 percent of the costs of relying on slave labor in the West Indies when the initial buying price, provisioning, and medical costs of enslaved Africans were accounted for.[146] Free-labor crusaders further argued that small landholders and wage holders were motivated to work harder and seek out improvements in ways that plantation slavery discouraged. One writer explained, "The Bengal peasant is actuated by the ordinary wants and desires of mankind. His family assist his labor and sooth his toil, and the sharp eye of personal interest guides his judgement."[147] Beyond the economic advantages of relying on highly motivated and low-paid workers, William Fitzmaurice saw a humanitarian advantage in participating in Bengal's existing labor market. He wrote that "inasmuch as the cultivation of the sugarcane destroys annually in the West thousands of men, women and children, by incessant toil, it will save the lives of thousands of the East, by giving them employment and sustenance."[148] These proponents did not comment, however, on the extent to which "free laborers" were compelled to work due to their caste or economic condition, or any other implications of their meager wages.

For Fitzmaurice and other British colonists in Bengal, rum was far more than an afterthought: it was the industry most primed to benefit from British innovation and supervision. Fitzmaurice accused Indian distillers of using "contaminated jaggery which is collected from far and near for those distilleries." This carelessness produced "rum equally sour and unwholesome as the very ingredients from which it is distilled." He argued that Britons trained in distilling in the West Indies would pay closer attention to the quality of ingredients fermented and would process the sweets before they soured because they already prioritized the manufacture of both sugar and rum.[149] Lessons learned in the Atlantic world, including emphasis on cleanliness and attention to time, would now enrich a new commodity frontier.

Ultimately, the EIC, British experts, and Indian landowners and laborers arrived at a system of sugar and rum production in Bengal that incorporated ideas from the Atlantic world and from South Asia. Unlike earlier attempts in the 1770s, company officials and private British entrepreneurs accepted that sugarcane could be cheaply and efficiently grown and processed by small landholders, their families, and local wage workers. They reformed this process by transplanting production techniques from the Atlantic world designed around centralization, time discipline, and ingredient quality. In 1800, the Board of Trade approved a plan to expand the annual distilling capacity of the Mirzapur rum distillery from 100,000 to 240,000 gallons, double that boasted by Thomas Robison's preeminent American distillery.[150] By the end of the eighteenth century, European and South Asian expertise combined to create a nominally free-labor alternative to the British plantation system with incredible potential. As in North America and Sierra Leone, however, Indian rum and sugar did not mount a credible challenge to the dominance of Caribbean plantations because the slave-produced, West Indian alternative remained cheaper and more readily available. Slavery, too, as the tried-and-true means to coerce expert labor in a demanding industry, continued largely unabated in the British Caribbean.

* * *

Late eighteenth-century opponents of slavery who unified around sugarcane and the commodities that it yielded challenged slavery and gravely threatened the future of rum in the Atlantic world. Evolving ideas about consumer responsibility—and their power to force change on exploitative commodity industries—led to a nonconsumption movement that temporarily diminished demand for goods produced by enslaved workers. Enslaved people contributed to the movement by visibly declaring their opposition to the institution and resisting their bondage in ways that increased the cost of rum. Intent on maintaining profit, governments, companies, and elite individuals briefly attempted to transplant commodity industries dependent on slavery in and beyond the West Indies to new colonial ventures around the world that sought to capitalize on free labor. Their efforts generally fell short of the stated goals.

To a greater level than could have been fathomed a century before, the financial interests of governments, companies, and elite individuals infiltrated almost any attempt at grassroots reform. Once again bolstered by the British military, distillery owners in the Caribbean united in protecting their interests against enslaved resisters. Fledgling competitors and investors in free-labor rum struggled to match the taste or production efficiency of slave-produced rum. Innovation would simply take longer than the movement had to give.

Actions of makers, traders, and drinkers over the previous 150 years set the stage for this emerging stasis. The preferred taste, strength, color, and price of different rums had been negotiated in the sugar plantations of the West Indies, urban distilleries in Britain and North America, a transatlantic web of taverns and stores, the decks of slave ships, and the halls of Parliament. But by the 1790s, producers and consumers participating in these exchanges settled on several defining characteristics for rum. It was made from sugary wastes; it was strong; it was cheap; and, for at least another generation, it would be inseparable from plantation slavery. Something innately fluid now proved resistant to wholesale change.

Epilogue

Global-Caribbean Legacies of an Atlantic History

Mount Gay's Barbados distillery sits within a few of miles of the former site of the Castle Estate, one of several possible sources of the "oldest" rum that opened this study.[1] Many invocations of history and heritage ornament the company's rum bottles. In letters on the label almost as large as the brand name, consumers are reminded that rum production has continuously been carried out there since 1703. Should the sticker fade, the year is molded into the glass bottle itself. Labels for Mount Gay rums designed for every taste and price point connect past to present with descriptors such as "hand-crafted," "heritage," "pot still," and "navy strength."

This is the rum that one might have predicted this book would conclude with. Produced on the island where rum emerged by the 1640s and a plot of land that included a plantation distillery throughout the eighteenth century, Mount Gay is undoubtedly part of the history I have set out to understand. Moreover, its present-day market ties together the geographic breadth of this project. Distilled from sugarcane harvested in Barbados and other parts of the Caribbean, the rum sells locally. It also exports to Britain and the United States. Americans purchase 1.35 million liters of Mount Gay rum each year.[2] Within these bottles, an Atlantic history of creation and extraction in pursuit of profit comes into focus.

But understanding how the invention of the quintessential Atlantic commodity reshaped broader economies and societies requires a review of other parcels in the liquor cabinet as well. When the makers, traders, and drinkers of rum continued to create rum, extract ingredients, and connect with and challenge each other in the nineteenth and twentieth centuries, their geographies morphed. Distilleries and markets in North America and Britain closed or retooled, and rum became overwhelmingly associated with a transimperial—and then postcolonial—Caribbean. In the twentieth and twenty-first centuries, however, rum also globalized, attracting new makers and drinkers beyond its traditional domain. While it may be tempting to focus on change over time, these adjustments instead offer clear evidence of the impact that the seventeenth- and eighteenth-century shift to a new type of commodity had on the economies and societies that sprang forth. "New" ideas within the industry can instead be seen as redistillations of seventeenth- and eighteenth-century ideas.

Shortly after a subset of makers and drinkers tried and failed to sever the bond between rum and slavery in the 1790s, rum began to shift from an Atlantic commodity to a Caribbean one. George Washington mulled over his next move as an entrepreneur three months after retiring from the presidency in 1797. The farm manager of Mount Vernon urged Washington to open a distillery.[3] Signaling a retreat from the wide-scale conversion of sugary wastes into rum that had occurred in North America's port cities for over a century, however, Washington's distillery would instead turn excess rye, corn, and barley into whiskey. His distillery—and many others like it—would produce grain spirits within sight of the fields that supplied it in order to sate the thirsts of predominantly local consumers in a rapidly expanding United States.

As he prepared to enter the distilling business, Washington reached out to an acquaintance in nearby Alexandria, who owned and operated the rum distillery established by Daniel Roberdeau a quarter of a century earlier. He asked the industry expert whether a profit could be made in this line of work.[4] John Fitzgerald assured the former president that "as to a sale of the whiskey there can be no doubt if the quantity was ten times as much as he can make provided it is of a good quality."[5] A seasoned rum producer in North America recognized that whiskey was America's distillate of the future.

Fitzgerald knew that the United States clung to an increasingly precarious place in a world of rum. The American Revolution made it harder to acquire molasses and other supplies from Britain and its remaining colonies. And while trade outside of the British Empire offered some new opportunities, revolution in the Caribbean further disrupted the international trade necessary to make rum. Abolitionist activism of the 1790s also reminded Americans that rum production relied on international producers heavily invested in slavery and the slave trade. Fitzgerald certainly realized that the relationship between his distillery and the Caribbean plantations he relied on was in flux.

Dozens of rum producers in the early United States including Fitzgerald remained committed to the industry in which they had heavily invested. They continued to make rum and even pursue innovations in their distilleries. In 1792, rum producers in the United States distilled 4.2 million gallons of rum—roughly 85 percent of the volume that had been produced before the American

Revolution.[6] And Rhode Island distillers capitalized on a surge in slave trading to Africa by shipping 5.7 million gallons of rum to that continent between 1784 and 1807.[7] Although many distilleries remained in operation, fewer new ones opened. When distillers died or retired, it became harder to find somebody to take over their businesses. For instance, Fitzgerald's distillery—which the executor of his estate later described as "the most uphill and unprofitable work"—languished after his 1799 death.[8]

Political developments in the first decade of the nineteenth century further constricted opportunities for distillers who outlasted Fitzgerald. Both Great Britain and the United States responded to decades of activism by outlawing the transatlantic slave trade at the end of 1807. Almost overnight, one of the largest outlets for rum made outside of the West Indies contracted sharply. Adding to the effects of the abolition of the slave trade in the United States, the Embargo Act of 1807 sought to stanch all trade with British and French metropolitan and colonial ports, thereby cutting Americans off from their primary sources of molasses. Estimates suggest that this legislation shrunk the United States' gross national product by as much as 5.8 percent in 1808.[9] Though the embargo only lasted until early 1809, it created yet another impediment for producers struggling to keep their stills running.

In the twenty-five years following the Treaty of Paris, then, a combination of political, economic, and ideological factors reduced North America's role in the transatlantic circuit of rum production. Many Americans—including George Washington, but also smaller farmers who embraced fruit brandies, whiskey, and maple spirits production on their family farms far removed from deep-water ports—pursued other forms of alcohol production, which local consumers increasingly accepted. The maple sugar rum proselytizer–turned–census taker Tench Coxe quantified the changing nature of American alcohol production in his 1810 survey of American industries. Distillers produced 2.8 million gallons of rum in the United States, which constituted only 57 percent of the amount distilled forty years earlier. By comparison, the United States now produced 22.9 million gallons of fruit- and grain-based spirits. Many Americans had extracted themselves from the Atlantic-facing world of rum, refocusing on cultivating land recently expropriated from Indigenous nations. Nearly two-thirds of this volume was produced in states and territories that had begun the process of abolishing slavery. American orchards and fields of grain overtook rum in ways that free labor sugar and maple sugar never did.[10]

Britain's standing as a rum producer substantively changed in the early nineteenth century as well, as new tax structures and technological innovations crowded the domestically produced spirits market. From 1803 to 1825, Parliament imposed high tariffs on rum imported from the West Indies, stunting demand on the British market. When those taxes were reduced, Parliament concurrently lowered the gin duty.[11] This renewed support for domestic British distilleries came at an opportune time for British alcohol producers. They were able to leverage new innovations such as the continuous still in 1801 and the column still in 1831 to make the manufacture of grain-based spirits more efficient and profitable.[12] This business environment increased the production and consumption of gin and whiskey, likely at the expense of both imported and domestically produced molasses spirits. By midcentury at the latest, the building holding Glasgow's Easter distillery—which made rum starting in the late seventeenth century—had fallen into disuse.[13]

Rum's association with Britain continued, however, because the largest single buyer of rum in the world—the Royal Navy—codified its reliance on the rum ration. In 1818, the Royal Navy established a precise alcohol content that sailors' rum needed to match.[14] And in 1844, the Admiralty confirmed the rum ration as a "sailor's right."[15] Despite some critiques of a monopoly that harmed domestic producers, these new policies stipulated that a colonial Caribbean commodity would continue to be transported to the metropole and dispersed to sailors worldwide.[16]

Rum distillers—and individuals interested in joining them—responded to political realignment, antislavery activism, and technological improvement by establishing new centers of production in the Caribbean in the early nineteenth century. Between 1776 and 1826, rum exports from most of Britain's West Indian colonies fell, a process that intensified after emancipation in 1834. Jamaica's exports grew slightly, and two new colonial ventures—Demerera and Trinidad—now combined to export over 850,000 gallons of rum per year by 1826.[17] Producers in the British West Indies confronted new and ongoing challenges including environmental degradation, the choice of many recently emancipated slaves not to work in the industry, constricting markets in North America and Africa, and increased competition from emerging centers of production.

One significant innovation in the industry entailed building new distilleries in non-British islands and embracing free trade. Some of the early infrastructure and enslaved experts necessary for expanding rum production to these islands flowed from British islands during the occupations of Martinique and Cuba in the 1760s.[18] The French lifted restrictions on exporting rum from their islands in the late eighteenth century, and the industry took off in Martinique. Rum exports from the island increased from 56,314 gallons in 1820 to 3,964,875 in

1898.[19] Newly independent Haiti also embraced rum production in the early nineteenth century.[20] Current and formerly French colonies had become makers and movers of rum.

Cuba emerged as the world's foremost producer of cane sugar following the outbreak of the Haitian Revolution, and colonists eventually invested in rum production as well. The growth of the industry followed earlier patterns that connected slavery, innovation, and profiteering. Cuba's incorporation of new strains of sugarcane and steam-powered machinery increased the efficiency of sugar production at the expense of the by-products traditionally converted to rum. Cubans nonetheless processed these excess syrups into rum. Following an economic downturn in 1852, the Spanish crown turned its attention to the Cuban rum industry in an era when slavery continued to prevail in the colony. The government offered prizes for the successful development of recipes for fine-tasting rum, and at least a half-dozen rum production manuals were printed in Cuba between 1851 and 1856. Bacardi, Bouteiller, and Compañía and other rum manufacturers in Cuba experimented with techniques borrowed from other islands. They eventually began to blend various rums produced in Cuba in their distilleries, creating a smoother-tasting distillate. This Cuban recipe for rum caught on by the 1890s as the island emerged as a leading producer and exporter of rum, even supplying some of the British Navy's rum ration.[21]

Despite being produced and sold in Cuba—a marginal rum producer in the seventeenth and eighteenth centuries—a four-hundred-milliliter carton of Tumbao Silver Dry is one of many inheritors of lessons learned through the invention of rum. In just about any store in Havana, Cuba, passersby can buy it for a little less than a dollar. The contents are packaged in small, white, rectangular boxes resembling juiceboxes that are frequently found emptied and discarded on the street. The rum itself is clear and unaged, its flavor straightforward, with 36 percent of its volume composed of alcohol. This rum is cheap and unassuming, carrying forward much of the tradition of rum as a highly disposable commodity.

Although Tumbao Silver Dry is a newer offering, other brands became synonymous with individual Caribbean islands and their diasporas over the course of the twentieth century. Since at least the 1960s, Mount Gay labels have featured a large map of Barbados and multiple assertions of the rum's provenance. In his autobiography, the Jamaican immigrant Colin Powell fondly recalled his family celebrating New Year's Day in the South Bronx with "much drinking of Appleton Estate rum, dancing of the chotisse and singing of calypso songs."[22] At special events at the Haitian embassy in Washington, DC, diplomats pass out punch made with Barbancourt rum. When one tastes any of these rums, their minds likely wander to the Caribbean rather than the Atlantic world that facilitated its invention or the global currency that it now enjoys.

Caribbean-based rum companies, including many flagship brands of individual islands, continued a long-standing practice of embracing cutting-edge financial tools throughout the twentieth century. Many iconic brands were acquired by multinational conglomerations that have extended their market reach through global supply chains and advertising. Yet the branding holds on to a distinctly Caribbean identity. Some well-established products, such as Appleton Estate, retain the colonial-era names of the former plantations occupied by their modern distilleries.[23] Newer brands with substantial followings around the globe invoke the names of pirates, sailors, and places of the early modern Caribbean.

Consumers may continue to think of rum as distinctly Caribbean, but rum and rum distilleries abound globally. In 2021, 339 million liters of rum were purchased in India, making it one of the largest markets for the spirit in the world.[24] Much of this rum is produced locally, though India now ranks as Bacardi's second-largest importer. You can also find premium rums distilled in Switzerland, the Philippines, and Australia. Some of these distilleries take advantage of the global reach of sugarcane, much like a subset of would-be distillers in the late eighteenth century attempted, by finding local sources of sugar products to convert into rum. Others, like Macardo Señor Rum—a premium Swiss brand that prides itself on processing sustainably grown molasses purchased "from small farms in India and Nicaragua"—rely on modern supply chains to bring tropical ingredients to their faraway distilleries. A similar business model has recently motivated many craft distilleries in the United States to produce rums, some of which tout geographic or genealogical connections to colonial-era makers. The branding once again ties the era of the invention of rum to the present.

Yet some things presented as premodern appear differently on closer inspection. Most notably, slavery—the dominant labor system in the Caribbean cane fields and constellation of distilleries around the Atlantic world in the seventeenth and eighteenth centuries—has been replaced by new labor regimes. Many of them remain highly exploitative.[25] A 2022 US Department of Labor report lists twenty countries—including the three largest producers—whose sugar industries rely on child labor or forced labor.[26] While distinct from the forms of enslavement that defined rum in the seventeenth and eighteenth centuries, coercion remains an important ingredient in many rum recipes.

Modern distilleries have also embraced technological innovations of the past several centuries to modernize production. Advancements in growing and harvesting sugarcane and refining sugar have mechanized and automated processes formerly carried out by humans. Sugar has become cheap enough—and molasses yields small enough—that rum is now often made from sugar itself. Most distilleries employ column stills rather than pot stills, increasing the efficiency with which they can extract high volumes of alcohol. When a rum such as Macardo Señor processes molasses wash and relies on wood-fired stills as was the norm two hundred years ago, it is now a marker of distinction.

Nonetheless, the connection between past and present extends well beyond marketing campaigns. Lessons learned through rum's emergence as the quintessential, modern Atlantic commodity centuries ago continue to shape the industry. In 2023, one of the leading data analytics companies serving the alcoholic beverage industry released a list of six growth strategies for fledgling alcohol brands.[27] Three of them bear notable similarities to issues that the inventors of rum regularly contended with. The consultants first advised customers to "use premiumization wisely." Here market research corroborated what the makers and movers of rum determined hundreds of years ago: that while some individuals sought out products that had been made from premium ingredients or aged to improve its flavor, one of rum's defining attributes was its ubiquity and availability for many different groups of consumers.

Modern analysts also implored distillers to "focus on innovation," advising that "even small changes can pay dividends." Today there is value in connecting adventurous consumers to products that better suit their tastes and may eventually catch on with broader segments of the market. Echoes of British distillers adding botanicals to molasses-based spirits to approximate gin or American distillers adjusting to meet the tastes of West African consumers reverberate. These negotiations were just some of the many interactions between the makers of rum and those selling and drinking it in the early modern period. The invention of rum—a process and not just a moment—depended on the sorts of tinkering that remain integral to modern production and profit making.

Alcohol companies were finally counseled to take seriously issues of "authenticity and sustainability" because modern consumers "are not afraid to dump the brands and retailers who do not live up to their standards and ideals." The history and contemporary nature of rum production collide within this recommendation. In terms of sustainability, modern distillers may be encouraged to consider the environmental and human implications of large-scale agriculture, deforestation, and coercive labor regimes dating back to the colonial period.[28] Authenticity, of course, furthermore means telling the truth about what a producer is making or selling. This is a lesson that Thomas Robison learned the hard way when his deception led New York rum markets to shun his product.

Authenticity also entails reexamining some of the stories that are told about the commodity and its history. Heritage is at the heart of how many rums market themselves. Mount Gay, for instance, is often touted as "the rum that invented rum." Exploring the connections between past and present can meaningfully highlight local contributions to globally significant developments and boost interest in a homegrown product. But this proffered advice would suggest that invoking the heritage of colonial rum production should include accounting for the complexities of the seventeenth- and eighteenth-century Atlantic world. This book has sought to join that conversation by rigorously questioning who devised the information necessary to make rum, deployed that knowledge, passed it on, and controlled its application, and documenting who benefited from the invention of rum and who bore the related costs. An ongoing reappraisal of this sort will likely entail covering additional places and chronologies to unveil a far more accurate, interesting, and expansive history of rum.[29]

The Invention of Rum has implications for how readers think about a modern commodity that continues to create immense wealth and serve as a gustatory representation of the cultures of the Caribbean that circulates worldwide. It also encourages a reassessment of how we think about the early modern Atlantic world writ large in two key ways. First, rum's emergence as a commodity of significance on four continents and the ocean that connected them shows the wide-ranging changes experienced by societies linked by the Atlantic Ocean in the seventeenth and eighteenth centuries. People made and consumed things that never before existed, that were sometimes extracted from items previously deemed unfit for human consumption, and that could unlock both new experiences of consumption and forms of profit-making. The novelty of what these individuals made invited regular adjustment for over 150 years. Many workers carried out innovations while bearing the brunt of labor practices shaped by colonization, the transatlantic slave trade and plantation slavery, and the ill effects of inhabiting spaces in the midst of ecological crisis. Those individuals who owned the distilleries in question were more likely to benefit financially by calling for and then selectively following regulations that enriched a comparatively small group of property owners. Understanding these processes through the lens of rum uncovers how transformative upstart commodities emerging from the Atlantic world truly were. Rum and other things like it ushered in a new era of production and consumption that infiltrated nearly every aspect of daily life.

Second, this study should cause us all to think differently about how things change. It is tempting to suggest that a commodity can revolutionize the world, ultimately losing sight of the people inventing, making, resisting, profiting, and suffering. Those people experimented; they cooperated; they fought; they coerced and were coerced; they lied, cheated, and stole; they strove for something else. Ultimately many more groups of people than we usually envision took part in conjuring a product and series of systems that continue to shape the modern world. Understanding human choice and creativity in these terms is crucial at a moment in time when many wonder whether technology can take on the most human of functions.

GLOSSARY

Anker: A wooden vessel of approximately ten gallons, also sometimes listed as a *cag*. Container sizes varied, but estimates included in this glossary are calculated from volumes listed in distillery records.

Barrel: A container of around thirty gallons.

Cane juice: The raw liquid extracted from milled pieces of cane, which would subsequently be boiled into sugar. It was extremely prone to spoiling.

Cask: Containers of approximately 150 gallons. Sometimes this term was used generically and did not correspond with a specific size.

Cisterns: Large vats in which various ingredients were mixed and the molasses wash underwent fermentation. The size of these containers varied widely depending on the size of the distillery. Some were built into the foundation of distilleries, while others sat above ground.

Coopers: Craftsmen trained to make barrels, hogsheads, buckets, and other vessels out of wood staves.

Distillation: The process by which the alcohol in a fermented beverage is concentrated. It involved heating fermented matter in a still, vaporizing alcohol (which has a lower boiling point than water), and recondensing those concentrated alcohols.

Fermentation: The chemical process through which much of the sucrose present in a substance is broken down into ethyl alcohol by yeast.

Gauger: An Excise Office official responsible for measuring quantities of spirits for the purposes of taxation.

Gauges: Measuring rods inserted diagonally into a piece of cooperage and used to calculate the volume of liquids that a barrel, hogshead, or puncheon contained.

Gin: A distilled spirit with botanicals (usually including juniper) steeped in it. Although gin was usually made with grain-based spirits, it could be made with molasses spirits.

Gur: A term used to describe both low-grade sugar and an analogue to molasses (*cootrah gur*) in India. Both substances were fermented and distilled.

Grog: Rum mixed with water, sometimes with citrus or sugar added in, as part of the British Navy's rum ration.

Head of still: The bulbous top of a still where vapors from the distillation process gather. The head was traditionally made of pewter or, more commonly, copper. Examples are visible in Figures 2, 7, and 9.

Hogshead: A container of roughly 110 gallons. In records pertaining to the Caribbean, hogsheads more often contained sugar or molasses, while similarly sized vessels of rum were recorded as puncheons.

Hydrometer: A weighted cylinder calibrated to measure the proof of an alcohol based on the density of the liquid.

Jaggery: Semiprocessed, brown sugar usually produced by independent sugar producers in the Indian subcontinent.

Jalap root: A root usually grown in the West Indies that was used to improve the fermentation process in some British and American distilleries. See Figure 6.

Lees: Molasses wash that had already been distilled. It usually contained residual alcohol, sucrose, and yeasts. In the West Indies, lees were often refermented along with additional molasses and skimmings.

Low Wines: Distillate that has passed through a still but is not yet as concentrated as desired. Molasses-based low wines were redistilled into rum.

Molasses: A brown syrup that oozed out of sugar as it crystallized and cured. Though it could not be efficiently turned into granular sugar, the sucrose could ferment into alcohol.

Molasses spirits: Distilled alcohol produced from molasses. This term was often used instead of *rum* in eighteenth-century Britain to denote distillate derived from sugar by-products domestically.

Proof: A scale for measuring the alcoholic content of various beverages. The proof of a spirit equals two times the percentage of its alcoholic content.

Primary distillery: A term used in Britain to identify centralized distilleries licensed to create distillates.

Proof spirits: The standard strength of a spirit, often calculated to be a hundred proof. The relative strength of the spirit was often expressed by how much "under" or "over" proof a sample was.

Punch: A rum-based drink that included citrus, spices, and sugar. Often served in bowls such as the one photographed as Figure 15, it was popular in Caribbean and North American homes and taverns.

Puncheon: The standard vessel used to ship rum. It contained around 110 gallons.

Rectifier: An individual in Britain who purchased distillates from primary distilleries and then mixed alcohols, botanicals, and other ingredients, and sometimes even redistilled them, into a variety of drinks including gin.

Rum: A distilled spirit derived from the waste products left over from the process of making sugar. Rum was traditionally different than cachaça or cane brandy, which were instead distilled from cane syrup that could have alternatively been processed into sugar. Other names for rum or analogous beverages in the Atlantic world included kill devil, guildive, rumbullion, rhum, tafia, and gerebita.

Shrub: A beverage mixed by some distilleries that usually combined rum, sugar, and fruit.

Skimmings: The froth and other sugary imperfections that float to the top when cane juice is boiled into syrup. Skimmings were saved and used in many Caribbean recipes for rum.

Staves: Planks of wood that have been cut and shaped and can be assembled into hogsheads or puncheons.

Still: The copper pot that molasses wash is put into and that is heated as part of the distillation process. The word is also sometimes used to describe the entire distilling apparatus, including the head, neck, and worm. Sometimes referred to as an alembic.

Sugarcane: A species of grass that could be harvested and manufactured into sugar and rum.

Sugar works: The complex of buildings on a Caribbean sugar estate where the work of grinding sugarcane (sugar mill), boiling cane syrup (boiling or sugar house), curing sugar, and distilling (distillery or still house) takes place. Sometimes the sugar works were referred to as an ingenio. They occasionally were located in one building but more often included a number of single-purpose structures built in proximity to each other—like those mapped in Figure 12.

Wash: The mixture of ingredients including water, molasses, skimmings, and lees that was fermented before being distilled into rum.

Worm: A serpentine tube usually made of pewter or copper that was connected to the still and submerged in water. The cool water condensed the distillate inside the tube into a liquid that was collected.

ABBREVIATIONS

AHR	*American Historical Review*
AICRJ	*American Indian Culture and Research Journal*
AN	Archives nationales de France, Pierrefitte-sur-Seine
ANA	Antigua National Archives
BDA	Barbados Department of Archives
BL	British Library
BOD	Bodleian Library, University of Oxford
BPL	Barbados Public Library
BRBL	Beinecke Rare Book and Manuscript Library, Yale University
BRO	Bristol Record Office, Bristol, England
CHS	Connecticut Historical Society
CSP	*Calendar of State Papers Colonial, America and West Indies*
DRO	Derbyshire Record Office
EAS	*Early American Studies*
EHR	*Economic History Review*
ELH	*English Literary History*
EUL	Edinburgh University Library
FA	Falkirk Archives, Falkirk, Scotland
FO	Founders Online, National Archives
FSL	Folger Shakespeare Library, Washington, DC
GL	Guildhall Library, London, England
GUSC	Georgetown University Special Collections
HBS	Baker Library, Harvard Business School
HL	Huntington Library, San Marino, CA
HOUGH	Houghton Library, Harvard University
HSP	Historical Society of Pennsylvania
JBMHS	*Journal of the Barbados Museum and Historical Society*
JBS	*Journal of British Studies*
JCB	John Carter Brown Library, Brown University

JEH	*Journal of Economic History*
JER	*Journal of the Early Republic*
LCP	Library Company of Philadelphia
LMA	London Metropolitan Archives
LOC	Library of Congress
MED	Medford Historical Society, Medford, MA
MEHS	Maine Historical Society
MHS	Massachusetts Historical Society
MOL	Museum of London, Docklands
MSA	Massachusetts State Archives
NAS	National Archives of Scotland
NEQ	*New England Quarterly*
NLJ	National Library of Jamaica
NLS	National Library of Scotland
NLW	National Library of Wales
NYHS	New-York Historical Society
OI	Omohundro Institute of Early American History and Culture, Williamsburg, VA
PEM	Phillips Library, Peabody Essex Museum, Rowley, MA
PGWDE	*Papers of George Washington Digital Edition*
PMHB	*Pennsylvania Magazine of History and Biography*
PP	*Past and Present*
RIHS	Rhode Island Historical Society
SA	*Slavery and Abolition*
SHC	Southern Historical Collection, University of North Carolina, Chapel Hill
SOM	Somerset Heritage Centre, Taunton, England
TNA	National Archives of the United Kingdom, Kew
UMSC	University of Manchester Special Collections
WMQ	*William and Mary Quarterly*
WMSC	Swem Library Special Collections Research Center, College of William and Mary

NOTES

INTRODUCTION

1. Wills Robinson, "Yo-Ho-Ho and a Bottle of £8,000 Rum! 12 Mouldy Bottles of 18th Century Spirit Sell for £80,000 After Being Discovered Languishing in Cellar of Harewood House Since 1780s," *Daily Mail*, 4 March 2014, https://www.dailymail.co.uk/news/article-2572936/Yo-ho-ho-8-000-bottle-rum-12-mouldy-bottles-18th-century-spirit-sell-80-000-discovered-languishing-cellar-Harewood-House-1780s.html; "The Harewood Rum 'Dark' 1780," https://www.christies.com/en/lot/lot-5757070.

2. I recognize the importance of writing about all historical actors in ways that emphasize their humanity. In the case of Indigenous and African-descended individuals who often enter the historical record in ways that dehumanized them, this can be accomplished by using their names, centering their thoughts and experiences, and practicing considerable care when reproducing historical descriptions of them. Some scholars have advocated avoiding words such as "slave" and "slaveholder" that can reduce people to a legal status. While I aim to be attentive to language throughout, I am swayed by Vanessa Holden's contention that "the terms enslaved person and slave are not interchangeable" and Leslie Harris's belief that "Black history needs more language, not less." While I often refer to "enslaved" individuals as one of many ways to acknowledge their personhood, I continue to use "slave" or "slaveholder" when such terms add nuance to how we think about processes of enslavement, colonialism, and commodification. Vanessa Holden, "'I was born a slave': Language, Sources, and Considering Descendant Communities," *JER* 43:1 (Spring 2023): 75–83; Leslie Harris, "Names, Terms, and Politics," *JER* 43:1 (Spring 2023): 149–54; Sarah L. H. Gronningsater, *The Rising Generation: Gradual Abolition, Black Legal Culture, and the Making of National Freedom* (Philadelphia: University of Pennsylvania Press, 2024), 19–20.

3. Wealth Solutions, "Rum Watch," https://en.wealth.pl/our projects/rumwatch/.

4. Lance Surujbally, "The 'Harewood House' 1780 Barbados Rum ('Light'): Review," Lone Caner, 16 September 2018, https://thelonecaner.com/r0549/.

5. Jason Wilson, "We Need to Talk About Rum: 'The Rum Tasting of the Century,' a 200-Year-Old Rum, and Uncomfortable Conversations About the Spirit's Legacy," Everyday Drinking, 23 May 2023, https://www.everydaydrinking.com/p/we-need-to-talk-about-rum.

6. M. Pietrik, "Two Centuries in a Bottle: Drinking the Harewood House 1780 Rum," Cocktail Wonk, 23 September 2018, https://cocktailwonk.com/2018/09/drinking-the-harewood-house-1780-rum.html.

7. Surujbally, "Review."

8. Rum prices varied considerably based on myriad factors including location of distillation, product quality, transportation costs, and the size of the transaction, but "the finest old Jamaica

rum" was sold in London in early 1780 for £7/6 per gallon: *Gazetteer and New Daily Advertiser*, 29 February 1780. The auctioned bottles appear to be approximately one-fifth of a gallon. The sale price is the average auction price of this allotment, as reported by the *Daily Mail*. Inflation adjustments were computed with British National Archives' currency calculator: https://www.nationalarchives.gov.uk/currency-converter/#currency-result.

9. Wilson, "We Need to Talk."

10. For a recent synthesis following this chronology, see Ulbe Bosma, *The World of Sugar: How the Sweet Stuff Transformed Our Politics, Health, and Environment over 2,000 Years* (Cambridge, MA: Belknap, 2023). One reviewer asked whether sugar is "modern capitalism's original sin": Bronwen Everill, "Sugar as Modern Capitalism's Original Sin," *Foreign Policy*, 21 May 2023. Bosma builds on a considerable literature locating modern production techniques and, ultimately, capitalism in American sugar plantations in the seventeenth and nineteenth centuries. Eric Williams, *Capitalism and Slavery*, 3d ed. (Chapel Hill: University of North Carolina Press, 2021); Richard S. Dunn, *Sugar and Slaves: The Rise of the Planter Class in the English West Indies*, 2d ed. (Chapel Hill: University of North Carolina Press for the OI, 2000); Manuel M. Fraginals, *The Sugarmill: The Socioeconomic Complex of Sugar in Cuba, 1760–1860*, trans. Cedric Belfrage (New York: Monthly Review Press, 1976); Sidney W. Mintz, *Sweetness and Power: The Place of Sugar in Modern History* (New York: Penguin, 1985); Daniel B. Rood, *The Reinvention of Atlantic Slavery: Technology, Labor, Race, and Capitalism in the Greater Caribbean* (Oxford: Oxford University Press, 2017); Stuart B. Schwartz, *Sugar Plantations in the Formation of Brazilian Society: Bahia, 1550–1835* (Cambridge: Cambridge University Press, 1986); Phillip D. Curtin, *The Rise and Fall of the Plantation Complex: Essays in Atlantic History* (Cambridge: Cambridge University Press, 1990); *Tropical Babylons: Sugar and the Making of the Atlantic World, 1450–1680*, ed. Stuart Schwartz (Chapel Hill: University of North Carolina Press, 2003); Trevor Burnard and John Garrigus, *The Plantation Machine: Atlantic Capitalism in French Saint-Domingue and British Jamaica* (Philadelphia: University of Pennsylvania Press, 2016).

11. Marcy Norton, *Sacred Gifts, Profane Pleasures: A History of Tobacco and Chocolate in the Atlantic World* (Ithaca: Cornell University Press, 2008); David Hancock, *Oceans of Wine: Madeira and the Emergence of American Trade and Taste* (New Haven: Yale University Press, 2009); Kris Lane, *Colour of Paradise: The Emerald in the Age of Gunpowder Empires* (New Haven: Yale University Press, 2010); Jennifer L. Anderson, *Mahogany: The Costs of Luxury in Early America* (Cambridge, MA: Harvard University Press, 2012); Andrea Feeser, *Red, White, and Black Make Blue: Indigo in the Fabric of Colonial South Carolina Life* (Athens: University of Georgia Press, 2013); Zara Anishanslin, *Portrait of a Woman in Silk: Hidden Histories of the British Atlantic World* (New Haven: Yale University Press, 2016); Molly A. Warsh, *American Baroque: Pearls and the Nature of Empire, 1492–1700* (Chapel Hill: University of North Carolina Press for the OI, 2018); Ben Marsh, *Unravelled Dreams: Silk and the Atlantic World, 1500–1840* (Cambridge: Cambridge University Press, 2020).

12. Hancock, *Oceans of Wine*, 73–104.

13. Anderson, *Mahogany*, 64–88.

14. Norton, *Sacred Gifts*; Warsh, *American Baroque*, 78–127.

15. Peter H. Wood, *Black Majority: Negroes in Colonial South Carolina from 1670 Through the Stono Rebellion* (New York: Knopf, 1974); Daniel C. Littlefield, *Rice and Slaves: Ethnicity and the Slave Trade in Colonial South Carolina* (Champaign: University of Illinois Press, 1981); Judith Carney, *Black Rice: The African Origins of Rice Cultivation in the United States* (Cambridge, MA: Harvard University Press, 2001).

16. David Eltis, Philip Morgan, and David Richardson, "Agency and Diaspora in Atlantic History: Reassessing the African Contribution to Rice Cultivation in the Americas," *AHR* 112:5 (Dec.

2007): 1329–58. On "multiple, conflicting, and 'sticky' traditions" coexisting and overlapping in the Atlantic world, see also Pablo F. Gomez, *The Experiential Caribbean: Creating Knowledge and Healing in the Early Modern Atlantic* (Chapel Hill: University of North Carolina Press, 2017), 144.

17. On technical skill among the enslaved in a world of sugar, see Eric Otremba, "Inventing Ingenios: Experimental Philosophy and the Secret Sugar-Makers of the Seventeenth-Century Atlantic," *History and Technology* 28:2 (2012): 119–47; Simon P. Newman, *A New World of Labor: The Development of Plantation Slavery in the British Atlantic* (Philadelphia: University of Pennsylvania Press, 2013), 189–215; Sasha Turner, *Contested Bodies: Pregnancy, Childrearing, and Slavery in Jamaica* (Philadelphia: University of Pennsylvania Press, 2017), 112–50; Rood, *Reinvention of Atlantic Slavery*, 10–11, 32–35; Kevin Dawson, *Undercurrents of Power: Aquatic Culture in the African Diaspora* (Philadelphia: University of Pennsylvania Press, 2018), 135. On new chronologies of innovation, see Russell R. Menard, *Sweet Negotiations: Sugar, Slavery, and Plantation Agriculture in Early Barbados* (Charlottesville: University of Virginia Press, 2006); Justin Roberts, *Slavery and the Enlightenment in the British Caribbean, 1750–1807* (Cambridge: Cambridge University Press, 2013).

18. Bosma, *World of Sugar*, 70.

19. Referencing "invention" in the title builds on efforts to interpret invention as incremental and cooperative. Adrian Johns, "How to Acknowledge a Revolution," *AHR* 107:1 (Feb. 2002): 106–25; Marcy Norton, "Subaltern Technologies and Early Modernity in the Atlantic World," *Colonial Latin American Review* 26:1 (2017): 18–38; Pamela Smith, *From Lived Experience to the Written Word: Reconstructing Practical Knowledge in the Early Modern World* (Chicago: University of Chicago Press, 2022). On the need to account for the relationship between knowledge production and "sometimes violent interventions into the lives and knowledges of others," see Vera Keller, *The Interlopers: Early Stuart Projects and the Undisciplining of Knowledge* (Baltimore: Johns Hopkins University Press, 2023), 12; Lukas Rieppel, Eugenia Lean, and William Deringer, "Introduction: The Entangled Histories of Science and Capitalism," *Osiris* 33 (2018): 21–22; Zachary Dorner et al., "Roundtable: Entanglements of Coerced Labor and Colonial Science in the Atlantic World and Beyond," *Labor* 21:1 (2024): 11–26.

20. Frederick H. Smith, *Caribbean Rum: A Social and Cultural History* (Gainesville: University Press of Florida, 2005), 86–87.

21. For major academic studies centered on rum, see John J. McCusker Jr., "The Rum Trade and the Balance of Payments of the Thirteen Continental Colonies, 1650–1775" (PhD diss., University of Pittsburgh, 1970); Jay Coughtry, *The Notorious Triangle: Rhode Island and the African Slave Trade, 1700–1807* (Philadelphia: Temple University Press, 1981); Peter C. Mancall, *Deadly Medicine: Indians and Alcohol in Early America* (Ithaca: Cornell University Press, 1995); José C. Curto, *Enslaving Spirits: The Portuguese-Brazilian Alcohol Trade at Luanda and Its Hinterland, c. 1550–1830* (Leiden: Brill, 2004); Smith, *Caribbean Rum*; Bertie Mandelblatt, "Atlantic Consumption of French Rum and Brandy and Economic Growth in the Seventeenth- and Eighteenth-Century Caribbean," *French History* 25:1 (2011): 9–27. McCusker's dissertation was subsequently republished "essentially unrevised" as *Rum and the American Revolution: The Rum Trade and the Balance of Payments of the Thirteen Continental Colonies* (New York: Garland, 1989), i. Rum has also been the subject of several popular commodity histories, including Wayne Curtis, *And a Bottle of Rum: A History of the New World Cocktail in Ten Cocktails* (New York: Three Rivers, 2007); Richard Foss, *Rum: A Global History* (London: Reaktion Books, 2012); Marco Pierini, *American Rum: A Short History of Rum in Early America* (2017) and *French Rum: A History 1639–1902* (2020), self-published.

22. Increase Mather, *Wo to Drunkards* (Boston, 1712), preface.

23. Anthony Benezet, *The Mighty Destroyer Displayed* (Philadelphia, 1774), 8.

24. Benezet, *Mighty Destroyer*, 46.

25. Matthew Warner Osborn, *Rum Maniacs: Alcoholic Insanity in the Early American Republic* (Chicago: University of Chicago Press, 2014), 19. For social, moral, and health-related arguments against overconsumption in the late eighteenth century, albeit as a minority viewpoint, see also W. J. Rorabaugh, *The Alcoholic Republic: An American Tradition* (New York: Oxford University Press, 1979), 25–57.

26. For a criticism of biological determinism as an explanation for the emergence of commodities now seen as addictive, see Norton, *Sacred Gifts*, 7–9. For interpretations of the allure of addictive commodities, see Wolfgang Schivelbusch, *Tastes of Paradise: A Social History of Spices, Stimulants, and Intoxicants* (New York: Knopf, 1993); David Courtwright, *Forces of Habit: Drugs and the Making of the Modern World* (Cambridge, MA: Harvard University Press, 2002).

27. Francis Rawle, *Ways and Means for the Inhabitants of Delaware to Become Rich* (Philadelphia, 1725), 28–29.

28. On the repurposing of tea fannings and dust into "'Indian tea' for the poorest consumer," see Erika Rappaport, *A Taste for Empire: How Tea Shaped the Modern World* (Princeton: Princeton University Press, 2017), 209–10. On descriptions of low-grade tea (often steeped in racist depictions), see Rappaport, *Taste for Empire*, 129–30; Robert Hellyer, *Green with Milk and Sugar: When Japan Filled America's Tea Cups* (New York: Columbia University Press, 2021), 124–42. On the rise of cheap cigarettes rolled from cut tobacco that did not meet older standards of quality in terms of leaf size, ripeness, curing technique, or color, see Barbara Hahn, *Making Tobacco Bright: Creating an American Commodity, 1617–1937* (Baltimore: Johns Hopkins University Press, 2011); Nan Enstad, *Cigarettes, Inc.: An Intimate History of Corporate Capitalism* (Chicago: University of Chicago Press, 2018), 7, 154–86. On chicken nuggets composed of bone, tendons, and other offal, see Patrick Dixon, *Nuggets of Gold: Further Processed Chicken and the Making of the American Diet* (Athens: University of Georgia Press, 2024).

29. Smith, *From Lived Experience*, 12.

30. Alyssa Mt. Pleasant, Caroline Wiggington, and Kelly Wisecup note that "early American studies necessarily and fruitfully engages with these sources, but doing so uncritically can risk retransmitting the biases and assumptions encoded in colonists' language and worldviews": "Materials and Methods in Native American and Indigenous Studies: Completing the Turn," *WMQ* 75:2 (April 2018): 217. See also Michel-Rolph Trouillot, *Silencing the Past: Power and the Production of History* (Boston: Beacon, 1995), 26–27; Marisa J. Fuentes, *Dispossessed Lives: Enslaved Women, Violence, and the Archive* (Philadelphia: University of Pennsylvania Press, 2016), 4–8; Sara E. Johnson, *Encyclopédie Noire: The Making of Moreau de Saint-Méry's Intellectual World* (Chapel Hill: University of North Carolina Press for the OI, 2023), 8–9.

31. "Propositions of Minissink Indians and Answer Thereto," 12 September 1681, in *Documents Relating to the History and Settlements of the Towns Along the Hudson and Mohawk Rivers, from 1630 to 1684*, ed. B. Fernow (Albany, 1881), 551.

32. Mintz, *Sweetness and Power*; *The Social Life of Things: Commodities in Cultural Perspective*, ed. Arjun Appadurai (Cambridge: Cambridge University Press, 1988); T. H. Breen, "'Baubles of Britain': The American and Consumer Revolutions of the Eighteenth Century," *PP* 119 (May 1988): 80–81.

33. For a commodity study centering elite producers, see Mintz, *Sweetness and Power*. For a consumer-driven study, see Norton, *Sacred Gifts*. For a commodity history arguing for the preeminence of merchants, see Hancock, *Oceans of Wine*.

34. Enstad, *Cigarettes, Inc.*, at 8. Enstad attends to experiences of work in greater detail than many other "new" histories of capitalism which have been criticized for not adequately attending to the social conditions of labor and of slavery in particular; James Oakes, "Capitalism and Slavery and

the Civil War," *International Labor and Working-Class History* 89 (Spring 2016): 195–220; Stephanie McCurry, "Plunder of Black Life: The Problem of Connecting the History of Slavery to the Economics of the Present," *Times Literary Supplement*, 19 May 2017, 23–26.

35. Recent scholarship on the history of capitalism in the nineteenth century details the formation of a highly profitable global economy, underwritten by the state and dependent on racial capitalism: Sven Beckert, *Empire of Cotton: A Global History* (New York: Knopf, 2014); Rappaport, *Taste for Empire*; Rood, *Reinvention of Atlantic Slavery*; Enstad, *Cigarettes, Inc.*; Jeremy Zallen, *American Lucifers: The Dark History of Artificial Light, 1750–1865* (Chapel Hill: University of North Carolina Press, 2019). For examples of scholarship reading these trends back into the eighteenth century, see Anderson, *Mahogany*; Zachary Dorner, *Merchants of Medicines: The Commerce and Coercion of Health in Britain's Long Eighteenth Century* (Chicago: University of Chicago Press, 2020).

36. Stephanie M. H. Camp, *Closer to Freedom: Enslaved Women and Everyday Resistance in the Plantation South* (Chapel Hill: University of North Carolina Press, 2004), 60–92.

37. Smith, *Caribbean Rum*, 56–71.

38. Linda M. Rupert, *Creolization and Contraband: Curaçao in the Early Modern Atlantic World* (Athens: University of Georgia Press, 2012), 93, 124; Wim Klooster, *The Dutch Moment: War, Trade, and Settlement in the Seventeenth-Century Atlantic World* (Ithaca: Cornell University Press, 2016).

39. Richard Sheridan boiled this argument down most succinctly: "The New World plantation represented a combination of African labour, European animal husbandry, and American soil and climate." In *Sugar and Slavery: An Economic History of the British West Indies, 1623–1775* (Baltimore: Johns Hopkins University Press, 1974), 306. See also Alfred W. Crosby Jr., *The Columbian Exchange: The Biological and Cultural Consequences of 1492* (Westport, CT: Greenwood, 1972). For rejoinders see Norton, *Sacred Gifts*, 4; Judith A. Carney and Richard Nicholas Rosomoff, *In the Shadow of Slavery: Africa's Botanical Legacy in the Atlantic World* (Berkeley: University of California Press, 2009), 4.

CHAPTER 1

1. Alice Bonner McGinty, "Stradanus (Jan Van Der Straet): His Role in the Visual Communication of Renaissance Discoveries, Technologies, and Values" (PhD diss., Tufts University, 1974).

2. For Brazil as the birthplace of rum, see McCusker, "Rum Trade," 63n1; Mandelblatt, "Atlantic Consumption," 15. For Martinique and Barbados as the "cradles" of Caribbean rum, see Smith, *Caribbean Rum*, 13. For English planters as the inventors see Dunn, *Sugar and Slaves*, 196.

3. *Certaine Inducements to Well Minded People* (London, c. 1644), 3–4; Richard Ligon, *A True & Exact History of the Island of Barbados* (London, 1657), 31–33; Charles Rochefort, *The History of Barbados, St Christophers, Mevis, St Vincents, Antego, Martinico, Montserrat, and the Rest of the Caribby-Islands* (London, 1666), *passim*.

4. Stuart B. Schwartz, *Sugar Plantations in the Formation of Brazilian Society, Bahia 1550–1835* (Cambridge: Cambridge University Press, 1985), 51–72.

5. Quoted in João Azevedo Fernandes, "Liquid Fire: Alcohol, Identity, and Social Hierarchy in Colonial Brazil," in *Alcohol in Latin America: A Social and Cultural History*, ed. Gretchen Pierce and Áurea Toxqui (Tucson: University of Arizona Press, 2014), 47.

6. Fernandes, "Liquid Fire," 48.

7. The term was not generally used to denote a distilled spirit until the eighteenth century: Fernandes, "Liquid Fire," 52.

8. Fernandes, "Liquid Fire," 47.

9. Fernandes, "Liquid Fire," 49. Fernandes finds that "cachaça" described a fermented beverage in the seventeenth century, while a contemporary publication defined "cagassa" as "slightly more dreggy and copious scum" skimmed from a sugar pan and, ostensibly, unfermented: Willem Piso et al., *Historia naturalis Brasilae* (Amsterdam, 1648), 51. Thank you to Christopher Brunelle, Julia Geisser, and Lawrence Buck for translation help.

10. Quoted in Rafael Chambouleyron, "The 'Government of the Sertões and Indians': Aguardente, Sugar, and Indians in Colonial Amazonia," *Americas* 77:1 (Jan. 2020): 32.

11. Chambouleyron, "'Government of the Sertões,'" 18–23.

12. Joseph C. Miller, *Way of Death: Merchant Capitalism and the Angolan Slave Trade, 1730–1830* (Madison: University of Wisconsin Press, 1988), 465–68; Curto, *Enslaving Spirits*, 70–75; Luiz Felipe de Alencastro, *The Trade in the Living: The Formation of Brazil in the South Atlantic, Sixteenth to Seventeenth Centuries* (Albany: State University of New York Press, 2018), 308–13.

13. Stewart Mims, *Colbert's West India Policy* (New Haven: Yale University Press, 1912), 29–35; Christian Schnakenbourg, "Note sur les origines de l'industrie sucrière en Guadeloupe au XVIIe siècle (1640–1670)," *Revue française d'Histoire d'Outre Mer* 55 (1968): 270–73.

14. "Du mercredi troisième jour d'août 1639," in Éric Rouler, *La compagnie des îles de l'Amérique 1635–1651, Une entreprise colonial au XVIIe siècle* (Rennes, France: Presses Universitaires de Rennes, 2017), 693–94. For interpretations that suggest the edict concerned sugarcane brandy, see Mims, *Colbert's West India Policy*, 25; Mandelblatt, "Atlantic Consumption," 15.

15. Melissa N. Morris, "Cultivating Colonies: Tobacco and the Upstart Empires, 1580–1640" (PhD diss., Columbia University, 2017), 177–89; Dunn, *Sugar and Slaves*, 120–23.

16. Maurile de Saint-Michel, *Voyage des isles Camercanes: En l'Amerique—Qui font partie des Indes Occidentales* (Mans, 1652), 65.

17. Jean Baptiste Du Tertre, *Histoire generale des Antilles habitées par les François* (Paris, 1667), 1:463.

18. Schnakenbourg, "Note sur les origins," 287. For a similar argument about the Dutch carrying knowledge, equipment, and capital necessary for sugar and rum production to Barbados, which has since been disputed, see Dunn, *Sugar and Slaves*, 19; Menard, *Sweet Negotiations*; Klooster, *Dutch Moment*, 166–70.

19. Du Tertre, *Histoire generale*, 2:124.

20. Neil Safier, "Beyond Brazilian Nature: The Editorial Itineraries of Marcgraf and Piso's *Historia naturalis Brasiliae*," in *The Legacy of Dutch Brazil*, ed. Michiel van Grosen (New York: Cambridge University Press, 2014), 168–86.

21. Piso, *Historia naturalis Brasilae*, 51, see also 84. Distillation for medicinal purposes is described on p. 52.

22. Some scholars note circumstantial evidence pointing to distillation in pre-Columbian Mexico: Daniel Zizumbo-Villarreal et al., "Distillation in Western Mesoamerica Before European Contact," *Economic Botany* 63:4 (Dec. 2009): 413–26; Ana Valenzuela-Zapata et al., "'Huichol' Stills: A Century of Anthropology—Technology Transfer and Innovation," *Crossroads* 8 (2013): 157–91.

23. Klooster, *Dutch Moment*, 169.

24. Ivor Noël Hume, "Roanoke Island: America's First Science Center," *Colonial Williamsburg: The Journal of the Colonial Williamsburg Foundation* 16:3 (1994): 14–28; Ivor Noël Hume and Audrey Noël Hume, *The Archaeology of Martin's Hundred* (Williamsburg, VA: Colonial Williamsburg Foundation, 2001), 2:314–16; John J. McCusker, "The Business of Distilling in the Old World and the New World During the Seventeenth and Eighteenth Centuries: The Rise of a New

Enterprise and Its Connection with Colonial America," in *The Early Modern Atlantic Economy*, ed. John J. McCusker and Kenneth Morgan (Cambridge: Cambridge University Press, 2001), 190.

25. Henry Colt letter to George Colt (1631), in Vincent Todd Harlow, ed., *Colonizing Expeditions to the West Indies and Guiana, 1623–1667* (London: Hakluyt Society, 1924), 65.

26. Dalby Thomas, *An Historical Account of the Rise and Growth of the West-India Colonies* (London, 1690), 13.

27. Arch. Hay letter to Capt. Fletcher, 27 March 1640, Hay of Haiston Papers, GD34/922/13, NAS. For contemporary advice for "adventurers" to bring "alembics to still," without a clear indication of what was to be distilled, see *Certaine Inducements*, 22.

28. This appears to be the earliest reference to a sugar mill in Barbados: Indenture between Capt. Francis Steele and Reynold Allen and David Bix, 10 March 1642, Recopied Deed Books, RB 3/1/293–99, BDA.

29. Deed from Jonathan Friessenbock to William Williamson, 1 February 1643, Recopied Deed Books, RB 3/1/289-90, BDA.

30. Inventory of Nicholas Phillips, 30 September 1648, Recopied Deed Books, RB 3/3/495–96, BDA; William Hilliard, "An Inventory of all the Christian servants negroes cattel horses coppers suger potts and other utencils on Henly Plant," 12 March 1653, Recopied Deed Books, RB 3/2/641–42, BDA.

31. Ligon, *True & Exact History*, 27; Journal of the Assembly of Barbados, 15 April 1679, *CSP Volume 10, 1677–1680*, ed. W. Noel Sainsbury and J. W. Fortescue (London, 1896), 346–56.

32. Deposition of John Powell, October 30, 1660, *Papers Relating to the Early History of Barbados*, Foreign and Commonwealth Office Collection, 1891, 3–4, https://jstor.org/stable/60229014; Ligon, *True & Exact History*, 23–24. For precolonial Indigenous habitation of Barbados, see *Pre-Colonial and Post-Contact Archaeology in Barbados: Past, Present, and Future Research Directions*, ed. Maaike de Waal et al. (Leiden: Sidestone, 2019).

33. "Petition of Captain Henry Powell" [c. 1648], in "Papers Relating to the Early History of Barbados," 5.

34. "Henry Powell's Examinacion," February 20, 1656, in "Papers Relating to the Early History of Barbados," 8.

35. "Petition of Captain Henry Powell" [c. 1648], in "Papers Relating to the Early History of Barbados," 5–6. Powell could have misrepresented this migration narrative, though Indigenous people regularly traversed the Caribbean. Tessa Murphy, *The Creole Archipelago: Race and Borders in the Colonial Caribbean* (Philadelphia: University of Pennsylvania Press, 2021), 23.

36. "Henry Powell's Examinacion," February 20, 1656, in "Papers Relating to the Early History of Barbados," 8.

37. "Petition of Captain Henry Powell" [c. 1648], in "Papers Relating to the Early History of Barbados," 6–7.

38. Henry Winthrop to Emmanuel Downing, August 22, 1627; Henry Winthrop to John Winthrop, October 15, 1627, *The Winthrop Papers Digital Edition*, Massachusetts Historical Society.

39. "A German Indentured Servant in Barbados in 1652: The Account of Heinrich von Uchteritz," ed. Alexander Gunkel and Jerome S. Handler, *JBMHS* 33 (1970): 92.

40. John Tuckerman deposition, March–April 1647, *Papers Relating to the Early History of Barbados and St. Kitts*, Foreign and Commonwealth Office Collection, 1891, 5, https://www.jstor.org/stable/60229022.

41. Ligon, *True & Exact History*, 54.

42. Stéphane Mazières et al., "Genetic Studies in French Guiana Populations: Synthesis," *American Journal of Physical Anthropology* 132 (Feb. 2007): 292–300; François Rose, "Borrowing of

a Cariban Number Marker into Three Tupi-Guarani Languages," in Martine Vanhove et al., *Morphologies in Contact* (Berlin: Akademie Verlag, 2012), 37–69.

43. Jean de Léry, *History of a Voyage to the Land of Brazil, Otherwise Called America*, trans. Janet Whatley (Berkeley: University of California Press, 1990), 73–77.

44. Jacques Bouton, *Relation de l'establissement des francois depuis l'an 1635 en l'isle de la Martinique* (Paris, 1640), 54–55.

45. Thomas Verney to Edward Verney, January 9, 1639, in *Letters and Papers of the Verney Family Down to the End of the Year 1639*, ed. John Bruce (London, 1853), 195.

46. Ligon, *True & Exact History*, 32.

47. *The Memoirs of Père Labat, 1693–1705*, trans. John Eden (London: Frank Cass, 1970), 98–101.

48. Sarah E. Barber, "Indigeneity and Authority in the Lesser Antilles: The Warners Revisited," in *The Torrid Zone: Caribbean Colonization and Cultural Interaction in the Long Seventeenth Century*, ed. L. H. Roper (Columbia: University of South Carolina Press, 2018), 48–50.

49. Douglas Taylor, "Kinship and Social Structure of the Island Carib," *Southwestern Journal of Anthropology* 2:2 (1946): 180–212; Taylor, "The Interpretation of Some Documentary Evidence on Carib Culture," *Southwestern Journal of Anthropology* 5:4 (1949): 379–92.

50. Marc de Civrieux, *Watunna: An Orinoco Creation Cycle*, trans. David M. Guss (Austin: University of Texas Press, 1997), 136.

51. Quoted in Douglas Taylor, "The Meaning of Dietary and Occupational Restrictions Among the Island Carib," *American Anthropologist* 52:3 (1950): 344.

52. Raymond Breton, *Dictionaire Caraibe-François* (Auxerre, 1665), 344; Douglas Taylor, "The Caribs of Dominica," *Smithsonian Institution Bureau of American Ethnology Bulletin* 119 (1938): 154.

53. Ligon, *True & Exact History*, 31–32; Smith, *Caribbean Rum*, 7.

54. Thomas Verney to Edward Verney, January 9, 1639, *Papers of the Verney Family*, 194.

55. Charles de Rochefort, *Histoire naturelle et moral des iles Antilles de l'Amerique (Rotterdam, 1658)*, 446.

56. John Cleere deposition, March–April 1647, in "Papers Relating to the Early History of Barbados and St. Kitts," 5–6.

57. Linda M. Heywood and John K. Thornton assert that while these figures concern Dutch privateers, they are applicable to English privateers who preyed on the same ships: Heywood and Thornton, *Central Africans, Atlantic Creoles, and the Foundation of the Americas, 1585–1660* (New York: Cambridge University Press, 2007), 41. See also Ligon, *True & Exact History*, 23.

58. Curto, *Enslaving Spirits*, 24, 37; Alencastro, *Trade in the Living*, 302–4.

59. Menard, *Sweet Negotiations*, 31; Hilary Beckles, *A History of Barbados: From Amerindian Settlement to Caribbean Single Market* (Cambridge: Cambridge University Press, 1990), 18; Jerome S. Handler and Lon Shelby, eds., "A Seventeenth Century Commentary on Labor and Military Problems in Barbados," *JBMHS* 34 (1973): 118.

60. Charles Ambler, "Alcohol and Disorder in Precolonial Africa" (unpublished manuscript, Boston University Africa Studies Center, Working Paper no. 126, 1987), 5; J. D. La Fleur, *Fusion Foodways of Africa's Gold Coast in the Atlantic Era* (Leiden: Brill, 2012), 127–28.

61. Curto, *Enslaving Spirits*, 35.

62. Joseph C. Miller, *Kings and Kinsmen: Early Mbundu States in Angola* (Oxford: Clarendon, 1976), 178.

63. On the risk of mistaking familiarity for connections, see Chris Evans, "The Plantation Hoe: The Rise and Fall of an Atlantic Commodity, 1650–1850," *WMQ* 69:1 (Jan. 2012): 74–75.

On treaties and oath-making see Barbara Klamon Kopytoff, "Colonial Treaty as Sacred Charter of the Jamaican Maroons," *Ethnohistory* 26:1 (Winter 1979): 49. On funerary traditions see Vincent Brown, *The Reaper's Garden: Death and Power in the World of Atlantic Slavery* (Cambridge, MA: Harvard University Press, 2008), 60–91.

64. Ligon, *True & Exact History,* 80–81. See also *Certaine Inducements*, 2–3.

65. John Hapcott, "Estate plan of 300 acres of land near Holetown, Barbados" (1646), Shelf Et647 1 Ms., JCB.

66. Rochefort, *Histoire naturelle*, 447.

67. Elsewhere, Ligon described African men scaling palm trees. Ligon, *True & Exact History*, 69, 76.

68. The "prickly palms" do not resemble coconut trees, the one palm species usually associated with the Pacific basin. Rochefort, *Histoire naturelle*, 60–61, 65–67.

69. Jerome S. Handler, "Life Histories of the Enslaved in Barbados," *SA* 19:1 (1998): 133.

70. "The Voyage of Sir Henry Colt," in Harlow, *Colonizing Expeditions*, 65.

71. Jerome S. Handler, "Father Antoine Biet's Visit to Barbados in 1654," *JBMHS* 32 (1967): 62, 68.

72. Judith M. Bennett, *Ale, Beer and Brewsters in England* (Oxford: Oxford University Press, 1996), 9, 79–85.

73. Peter Clark, *The English Alehouse: A Social History 1200–1830* (London: Longman, 1983); Bennett, *Ale, Beer and Brewsters*, 92–94.

74. Arnold Hunt, "The Lord's Supper in Early Modern England," *PP* 161:1 (Nov. 1998): 39–83.

75. Peter Mathias, *The Brewing Industry in England, 1700–1830* (Cambridge: Cambridge University Press, 1959), 6–7.

76. Bennett, *Ale, Beer and Brewsters.*

77. For analysis of where English servants to Barbados originated, see Alison Games, *Migration and the Origins of the English Atlantic World* (Cambridge, MA: Harvard University Press, 1999), 15–17; John Wareing, *Indentured Migration and the Servant Trade from London to America, 1618–1718: "There Is Great Want of Servants"* (Oxford: Oxford University Press, 2017), 53–66.

78. Schedule of Gibbs to Hill, Young & Sanders, September 4, 1640, Recopied Deed Books, RB 3/1/698, BDA. Thanks to Sarah Barber for sharing her transcription. For the gender imbalance of migration, see Wareing, *Indentured Migration*, 151.

79. Clark, *English Alehouse*, 212, 238–40.

80. I found no reference to West Indies planters apprenticing their sons to London distillers: London Distillers Company Apprentice Bindings, 1659–1709, GL.

81. T. M. Devine, "The Rise and Fall of Illicit Whisky-Making in Northern Scotland, c. 1780–1840," *Scottish Historical Review* 54:2 (Oct. 1975): 156; Vivien E. Dietz, "The Politics of Whiskey: Scottish Distillers, the Excise, and the Pittite State," *JBS* 36:1 (Jan. 1997): 35–69.

82. John Chartres, "No English Calvados? English Distillers and the Cider Industry in the Seventeenth and Eighteenth Centuries," in *English Rural Society 1500–1800: Essays in Honour of Joan Thirsk*, ed. John Chartres and David Hey (Cambridge: Cambridge University Press, 1990), 313–42.

83. "German Indentured Servant," 93.

84. Ligon, *True & Exact History*, 32.

85. Rochefort, *Histoire naturelle*, 447.

86. Breton, *Dictionaire Caraibe-François*, 344.

87. "A Swiss Medical Doctor's Description of Barbados in 1661," ed. Alexander Gunkel and Jerome S. Handler, *JBMHS* 33 (1969): 10.

88. Indenture between Walter Fenton and Thomas Rowse, December 10, 1641, Recopied Deed Books, RB 3/1/314–316, BDA; Inventory of Eleanor Bedell, January 1, 1654, Recopied Deed Books, RB 3/7/368–9, BDA.

89. Order from Mr. Fraser, April 16, 1781, A727.1691, FA.

90. "Swiss Medical Doctor's Description," 10.

91. Ligon preferred that enslaved Indigenous women make mobbie because they were "better versed" in the process than Africans. Ligon, *True & Exact History*, 54.

92. Saint-Michel, *Voyage des isles Camercanes*, 67–68. For New World substitutes in communion as a doctrinal difference, see Andrea Frisch, "In a Sacramental Mode: Jean de Léry's Calvinist Ethnography, " *Representations* 77:1 (2002): 83–90; Rebecca Earle, *The Body of the Conquistador: Food, Race and the Colonial Experience in Spanish America, 1492–1700* (Cambridge: Cambridge University Press, 2012), 154.

93. Thomas Verney to Edward Verney, January 9, 1639, *Papers of the Verney Family*, 194–95.

94. "German Indentured Servant," 93.

95. Carolyn Arena, "Indian Slaves from Guiana in Seventeenth-Century Barbados," *Ethnohistory* 64:1 (Jan. 2017): 69–71; Linford Fisher, "'Dangerous Designes:' The 1676 Barbados Act to Prohibit New England Indian Slave Importation," *WMQ* 71:1 (Jan. 2014): 117–18.

96. Ligon, *True & Exact History*, 32-33.

97. Rochefort, *Histoire naturelle*, 106.

98. Du Tertre, *Histoire generale*, 2:124.

99. Saint-Michel, *Voyage des isles Camercanes*, 65. Palm wines were being distilled in Bermuda in the 1650s. Keith Pluymers, *No Wood, No Kingdom: Political Ecology in the English Atlantic* (Philadelphia: University of Pennsylvania Press, 2021), 150. For a later example from Barbados, see Griffith Hughes, *The Natural History of Barbados in Ten Books* (London, 1750), 228.

100. "A schedule of all the goods moveable and immoveable which Christopher Thompson is to deliver unto Adam Thompson," June 20, 1644, Recopied Deed Books, RB 3/1/680–2, BDA. Similarities in design between the Thompson estate and those described by later planters suggest that rum had emerged as a distinct product that could add value. See Ligon, *True & Exact History*, 55–56; Peter Thompson, ed., "Henry Drax's Instructions on the Management of a Seventeenth-Century Barbadian Sugar Plantation," *WMQ* 66:3 (Jul. 2009): 565–604.

101. George Baynton, "An Oration in Praise of Rum, Delivered at a Commencement Held in the University of Pennsylvania on the 30th of July, 1789," in *The Universal Asylum and Columbian Magazine* (Philadelphia, 1790), 1:215.

102. Beauchamp Plantagenet, *A Description of the Province of New Albion* (London, 1648), 5.

103. Ligon, *True & Exact History*, 93

104. "German Indentured Servant," 93.

105. Sir Anthony Ashley Cooper to Robert Hooper, 30 April 1652, PRO 30/24/492, TNA.

106. Ligon, *True & Exact History*, 93.

107. Smith, *Caribbean Rum*.

108. "An Act to prevent frequenting of taverns by Seamen," 10 January 1652, and "An Act for preventing the selling of Brandy and Rum, in Tipling-houses near the broad-paths and high-ways within this land," 29 April 1668, CO 30/1/19, 63, TNA.

109. Governor Joseph West to Lord Ashley, Sir Geo. Carteret, and Sir Peter Colleton, 21 March 1671, *CSP Volume 7, 1669–1674*, ed. W. Noel Sainsbury (London, 1889), 178–89.

110. Ligon, *True & Exact History*, 56.

111. *Great Newes from the Barbadoes* (London, 1676), 6–7.

112. Thompson, "Drax's Instructions," 593.

113. Samuel Martin, *An Essay upon Plantership*, 4th ed. (Antigua, 1765), 55; John Dovaston, "Agricultura Americana, or improvements in West-India Husbandry considered wherein the present system of husbandry used in England is applied to the cultivation or growing of sugar canes to advantage," 1774, Codex 60 ENG, 180–81, JCB.

114. Thompson, "Drax's Instructions," 594.

115. Ligon, *True & Exact History*, 92–93.

116. The father of the overseer who Drax addressed, Richard Harwood, was sentenced to servitude after being captured at the first Battle of Newbury (1643). Harwood's opportunities for upward mobility in the seventeenth century remained limited because he was a "suspected papist": Thompson, "Drax's Instructions," 570n5; Newman, *New World of Labor*, 71–108.

117. Thompson, "Drax's Instructions," 594–95; Richard Pares, "Barbados History of the Records from the Prize Courts," *JBMHS* 6:3 (1939): 18.

118. Ligon, *True & Exact History*, 22.

119. Ligon, *True & Exact History*, 93. See also Edward Littleton, *The Groans of the Plantations* (London, 1689), 19.

120. Governor Kendall to the Earl of Shrewsbury, 26 June 1690, *CSP Volume 13, 1689–1692*, ed. J.W. Fortescue (London, 1901), 276–91.

121. Handler and Shelby, "Seventeenth Century Commentary," 120.

122. Thompson, "Drax's Instructions," 584.

123. "An Act to prevent persons tradeing with Negroes and Stealeing Potts and Jarrs," 14 November 1685, CO 30/5/135, TNA; "An Act for prohibiting the selling of Rum, or other strong Liquors, to any negro or other slave," 27 October 1692, CO 30/1/131, TNA.

124. "A General List of the Laws that have been enacted," 3 December 1651, in "A General List of the Laws that Have Been Enacted," Colonial Office Records, CO 30/1/459, TNA.

125. "Extract from the Record of Assize, May 1653,"and "At the Assizes, held 20 November, 1655," in *Memorials of the Discovery and Early Settlement of the Bermudas or Somers Islands 1515–1685*, ed. J. H Lefroy (London, 1877), 2:42, 63–64.

126. "Editorial: Barbados Rum," *JBMHS* 37 (1984): 97.

127. "From Leyden, 3 February 1652," in *Mercurius Politicus Comprising the Summ of All Intelligence* (London, England), 19–26 February 1652, 1345.

128. Darnell Davis, "The Etymology of the Word Rum," *Timehri: The Journal of the Royal Agricultural and Commercial Society of British Guiana* 4 (1885): 76–81.

129. *The Blue Laws of New Haven Colony* (Hartford, 1838), 109; Inventory of Eleanor Bedell, May 1655, Recopied Deed Books, RB 3/7/368–9, BDA.

130. David Eltis, "New Estimates of Exports from Barbados and Jamaica, 1665–1701," *WMQ* 52:4 (Oct. 1995): 638, 642.

131. Eltis, "New Estimates," 644.

132. Eltis, "New Estimates," 641.

CHAPTER 2

1. Drunkenness among elites was seen as a "private vice," but drunkenness among working people was a social threat: Dana Rabin, "Drunkenness and Responsibility for Crime in the Eighteenth Century," *JBS* 44:3 (Jul. 2005): 457–77.

2. Stephanie M. H. Camp, "The Pleasures of Resistance: Enslaved Women and Body Politics in the Plantation South, 1830–1861," *Journal of Southern History* 68:3 (Aug. 2002): 568–72; Gilbert

Quintero, "Making the Indian: Colonial Knowledge, Alcohol, and Native Americans," *AICRJ* 25:4 (2001): 57–71. On "bigoted humor" among eighteenth-century soldiers describing Native people drinking rum, see Gregory Evans Dowd, *War Under Heaven: Pontiac, the Indian Nations, and the British Empire* (Baltimore: Johns Hopkins University Press, 2002), 103–4.

3. Philip A. May, "The Epidemiology of Alcohol Abuse Among American Indians: The Mythical and Real Properties," *AICRJ* 18:2 (1994): 121–43; Cindy L. Ehlers and Ian R. Gizer, "Evidence for a Genetic Component for Substance Dependence in Native Americans," *American Journal of Psychiatry* 170:2 (Feb. 2013): 154–64; Roxanne Dunbar-Ortiz and Dina Gilio-Whitaker, *All the Real Indians Died Off and 20 Other Myths About Native Americans* (New York: Beacon, 2016), 130–36.

4. Carla Gardina Pestana downplays the significance of Barbadian migrants, though they numbered in the hundreds: Pestana, *The English Conquest of Jamaica: Oliver Cromwell's Bid for Empire* (Cambridge, MA: Belknap, 2017), 13.

5. Charles Lyttleton, "Reasons Proposed by the King's Command for His Majesty's Settling a Plantation in Jamaica," 3 October 1664, *CSP Volume 5, 1661–1668*, ed. W. Noel Sainsbury (London, 1880), 235–50; Klooster, *Dutch Moment*, 103–5.

6. J. Harry Bennett, "Cary Helyar, Merchant and Planter of Seventeenth-Century Jamaica," *WMQ* 21:1 (Jan. 1964): 53–76.

7. "Copy of 1669 Grant of 150 Acres," William Helyar Jamaica Papers, DD/WHh/1089/4/5, SOM.

8. Cary Helyar to William Helyar, 15 April 1671, Helyar Papers, DD/WHh/1090/3/18, SOM.

9. Cary Helyar to William Helyar, 10 September 1671, Helyar Papers, DD/WHh/1090/3/22, SOM.

10. Cary Helyar to William Helyar, 7 March 1672, Helyar Papers, DD/WHh/1090/3/24, SOM; Cary Helyar to William Helyar, 4 June 1672, Helyar Papers, DD/WHh/1090/3/29, SOM.

11. Helyar carried on a long-standing sexual relationship with a mixed-race woman from Barbados: William Whaley to William Helyar, 6 November 1675, Helyar Papers, DD/WHh/1090/2/1, SOM.

12. Cary Helyar to William Helyar, 10 September 1671, Helyar Papers, DD/WHh/1090/3/22, SOM; Cary Helyar to William Helyar, 7 March 1672, Helyar Papers, DD/WHh/1090/3/24, SOM.

13. Cary Helyar to William Helyar, 4 June 1672, Helyar Papers, DD/WHh/1090/3/29, SOM.

14. John Taylor, "Multum in Parvo," 1689, MS 105 v.2/520, 523, NLJ.

15. Eltis, "New Estimates," 639.

16. Robert Hall to William Helyar, 1 July 1702, Helyar Papers, DD/WHh/1090/3/33, SOM.

17. Smith, *Caribbean Rum*; Kathryn Benjamin Golden, "'Very Fond of Spirituous Liquors': Alcohol and Fugitive Black Life in the Slaveholding South," *SA* (2023): 1–22.

18. Vincent Brown, *Tacky's Revolt: The Story of an Atlantic Slave War* (Cambridge, MA: Belknap, 2020), 86.

19. Carl Christian Reindorf, *History of the Gold Coast and Asante* (Basel, 1895), 265–66.

20. Raymond E. Dumett, "The Social Impact of the European Liquor Trade on the Akan of Ghana (Gold Coast and Asante), 1875–1910," *Journal of Interdisciplinary History* 5:1 (Summer 1974): 69–101; Emmanuel Kwaku Akyeampong, *Drink, Power, and Cultural Change: A Social History of Alcohol in Ghana, c. 1800 to Recent Times* (Portsmouth, NH: Heinemann, 1996), 25–40.

21. Reindorf, *History of the Gold Coast*, 267. Nsã may have only referred to alcohol when spiritual beliefs were attached to its consumption: Akyeampong, *Drink, Power, and Cultural Change*, 45.

22. Reindorf, *History of the Gold Coast*, 73; Ray A. Kea, *Settlements, Trade, and Politics in the Seventeenth-Century Gold Coast* (Baltimore: Johns Hopkins University Press, 1982), 302; Charles

Ambler, "Alcohol and the Slave Trade in West Africa, 1400–1850," in *Drugs, Labor, and Colonial Expansion*, ed. William Jankowiak and Daniel Bradburd (Tucson: University of Arizona Press, 2003), 85.

23. Kenneth M. Bilby, *True-Born Maroons* (Gainesville: University of Florida Press, 2005), 239.

24. *Barbot on Guinea: The Writings of Jean Barbot on West Africa, 1678–1712*, ed. P. E. H. Hair et al. (London: Hakluyt Society, 1992), 2:591.

25. Hans Sloane, *A Voyage to the Islands Madera, Barbados, Nieves, S. Christophers and Jamaica* (London, 1707), 1:xlviii.

26. Melville Herskovitz, "A Footnote to the History of Negro Slavery," in *The New World Negro*, ed. Frances Herskovitz (Bloomington: Indiana University Press, 1966), 86–87.

27. "Trans-Atlantic Slave Trade – Database," SlaveVoyages.org, https://www.slavevoyages.org/voyages/pDuUHJGy.

28. Taylor, "Multum in Parvo," MS 105 v.2/524–525, NLJ.

29. Camp, "Pleasures of Resistance," 538.

30. John Taylor, *Jamaica in 1687: The Taylor Manuscript at the National Library of Jamaica*, ed. David Buisseret (Kingston: University Press of the West Indies, 2008), 267–69. On origins of prisoners, see Margaret Ellen Newell, *Brethren by Nature: New England Indians, Colonists, and the Origins of American Slavery* (Ithaca: Cornell University Press, 2015), 142.

31. Bybrook Account Book 1671, 23 December 1671, Helyar Papers, DD/WHh/1090/7/119, SOM.

32. Minutes of Jamaica Council, 11 May 1685, CO 140/4, TNA.

33. Minutes of Jamaica Council, 9 September 1689, CO 140/4/287, TNA.

34. Minutes of Jamaica Council, 12 January 1686 and 2 February 1686, CO 140/4/104–06, TNA.

35. Mavis C. Campbell, *The Maroons of Jamaica 1655–1796* (Granby, MA: Bergin and Garvey, 1988), 73–81.

36. Brown, *Tacky's Revolt*, 51.

37. Kopytoff, "Colonial Treaty as Sacred Charter," 49; Kenneth Bilby, "Swearing by the Past, Swearing to the Future: Sacred Oaths, Alliances, and Treaties Among the Guianese and Jamaican Maroons," *Ethnohistory* 44:4 (Autumn 1997): 655–89; Helen McKee, "From Violence to Alliance: Maroons and White Settlers in Jamaica, 1739–1795," *SA* 39:1 (2018): 45.

38. "The relation of Collonel D'Oyley," Add MS 11410/22, BL; Minutes of Jamaica Council, 28 June 1668, CO 140/1/177, TNA.

39. Nuala Zahedieh, "'The Wickedest City in the World': Port Royal, Commercial Hub of the Seventeenth-Century Caribbean," in *Working Slavery, Pricing Freedom: Perspectives from the Caribbean, Africa and the African Diaspora*, ed. Verene Shepherd (New York: Palgrave, 2002), 5–20.

40. Charles Leslie, *New and Exact Account of Jamaica*, 3d ed. (Edinburgh, 1740), 105.

41. John Style to Principal Secretary of State, 4 January 1670, *CSP Volume 7, 1669–1674*, ed. W. Noel Sainsbury (London, 1889), 50.

42. John Style to Principal Secretary of State, 4 January 1670, 49–51.

43. Taylor, *Jamaica in 1687*, 222, 239–40.

44. Taylor, *Jamaica in 1687*, 188.

45. Mary Carleton, *News from Jamaica in a Letter from Port Royal Written by the German Princess to Her Fellow Collegiates and Friends in New-Gate* (London, 1671), 3; Janet Todd, "Mary Carleton," *Oxford Dictionary of National Biography*.

46. Lieutenant Governor Molesworth to William Blathwayt, 8 August 1687, *CSP Volume 12, 1685–1688*, ed. J. W. Fortescue (London, 1899), 407–26.

47. Thomas Lynch to the Committee, 2 November 1683, CO 1/53/114–117, TNA; Depositions Concerning Charles Morgan, 3 October 1683, CO 1/53/4–15, TNA.

48. Deposition of Roger Burton, 3 October 1683, CO 1/53/2–3, TNA; Deposition of John Hayward, 3 October 1683, CO 1/53/3, TNA.

49. John Style to Principal Secretary of State, 4 January 1670, *CSP Volume 7*, 49–55.

50. *The Truest and Largest Account of the Late Earthquake in Jamaica, June the 7th 1692* (London, 1693), 9. See also *A Full Account of the Late Dreadful Earthquake at Port Royal in Jamaica* (London, 1692), 2.

51. Zahedieh notes that the "wickedness" ascribed to Port Royal abounded elsewhere: Zahedieh, "'Wickedest City in the World,'" 4.

52. Leslie, *New and Exact Account of Jamaica*, 32–33.

53. Christopher Eck, "The Spirits of Massachusetts: Distillers and Distilling in Seventeenth- and Eighteenth-Century Boston," (Master's thesis, University of Massachusetts at Boston, 1993), 29–30.

54. Kiliaen van Rensselaer to Johannes de Laet, 27 June 1632, 200; Kiliaen van Rensselaer to Wouter van Twiller, 23 April 1634, 267–88; Contract between Kiliaen van Rensselaer and Jacob Albertsz Planck, 4 March 1634, 250, all in *Van Rensselaer Bowier Manuscript: Being the Letters of Kiliaen Van Rensselaer, 1630–1643, and Other Documents Relating to the Colony of Rensslaerwyck*, ed. A. J. F. van Laer (Albany: University of the State of New York, 1908).

55. Samuel Stearns, *The American Herbal, or Materia Medica* (Walpole, 1801), 283.

56. Eck, "Spirits of Massachusetts," 30, 42–43.

57. "None to Still or Retail Liquors Without Licenss," 1661, in *The Colonial Laws of Massachusetts: Reprinted from the Edition of 1672, with the supplements through 1686* (Boston, 1887), 84.

58. Letter to John Winthrop, 1 February 1674, in *Proceedings of the Massachusetts Historical Society* 2:7 (1891–1892): 16–17.

59. Eck, "Spirits of Massachusetts," 54–56. In colonial Virginia, distillation remained focused on grains and fruits and remained in the hands of women until the middle of the eighteenth century: Sarah Hand Meacham, *Every Home a Distillery: Alcohol, Gender, and Technology in the Colonial Chesapeake* (Baltimore: Johns Hopkins University Press, 2009).

60. Cotton Mather, *Sober Considerations, on a Growing Flood of Iniquity* (Boston, 1708), 3.

61. C. Mather, *Sober Considerations*, 11.

62. C. Mather, *Sober Considerations*, 14.

63. I. Mather, *Wo to Drunkards*.

64. C. Mather, *Sober Considerations*, 16, 18; I. Mather, *Wo to Drunkards*, 47.

65. Henry J. Bruman, *Alcohol in Ancient Mexico* (Salt Lake City: University of Utah Press, 2000), 3–9.

66. Kea, *Settlements, Trade, and Politics*, 301; Adam Smyth, ed., *A Pleasing Sinne: Drink and Conviviality in Seventeenth-Century England* (Martlesham, Suffolk: D. S. Brewer, 2004), xviii.

67. George Washington to Anthony Whitting, 26 May 1793, *PGWDE*.

68. Jose C. Curto, "Alcohol Under the Context of the Atlantic Slave Trade," *Cahiers d'Études Africaines* 201 (2011): 51–85. Studies of colonial American taverns often focus on the interaction (or lack thereof) between white colonists of various social standings: David W. Conroy, *In Public Houses: Drink and the Revolution of Authority in Colonial Massachusetts* (Chapel Hill: University of North Carolina Press for the OI, 1995); Peter Thompson, *Rum Punch and Revolution: Taverngoing and Public Life in Eighteenth-Century Philadelphia* (Philadelphia: University of Pennsylvania Press, 1999); Sharon V. Salinger, *Taverns and Drinking in Early America* (Baltimore: Johns Hopkins University Press, 2002); Vaughn Scribner, *Inn Civility: Urban Taverns and Early American Civil Society*

(New York: New York University Press, 2019). Recent scholarship increasingly attends to how multi-ethnic, working-class customers coexisted and interacted in early American taverns: Serena R. Zabin, *Dangerous Economies: Status and Commerce in Imperial New York* (Philadelphia: University of Pennsylvania Press, 2009), 57–80; Fuentes, *Dispossessed Lives*, 46–69; Erin Kramer, "'That She Shall Be Forever Banished from This Country': Alcohol, Sovereignty, and Social Segregation in New Netherland," *EAS* 20:1 (2022): 3–42; Kirsten Wood, *Accommodating the Republic: Taverns in the Early United States* (Chapel Hill: University of North Carolina Press, 2023). Hancock cautions against overemphasizing public drinking at the expense of home consumption, in *Oceans of Wine*, 277.

69. For interpretations of rum being grafted onto existing spiritual structures, see Daniel K. Richter, *The Ordeal of the Longhouse: The Peoples of the Iroquois League in the Era of European Colonization* (Chapel Hill: University of North Carolina Press for the OI, 1992), 86; Peter C. Mancall, *Deadly Medicine: Indians and Alcohol in Early America* (Ithaca: Cornell University Press, 1997), 76–78. On experimentation "with 'new' ritual in 'traditional' ways," see Gregory Evans Dowd, *A Spirited Resistance: The North American Indian Struggle for Unity, 1745–1815* (Baltimore: Johns Hopkins University Press, 1992), 2. For an influential example of reframing "indigenous people as the active agents of global exploration, rather than the passive objects of that exploration," see David A. Chang, *The World and All the Things upon It: Native Hawaiian Geographies of Exploration* (Minneapolis: University of Minnesota Press, 2016), 1.

70. My framing of Native encounters with alcohol is, in part, informed by Ned Blackhawk's insistence that "to build a new theory of American history will require recognizing that Native peoples simultaneously determined colonial economies, settlements, and politics and were shaped by them": Blackhawk, *The Rediscovery of America: Native Peoples and the Unmaking of U.S. History* (New Haven: Yale University Press, 2023), 5. Brett Rushforth argues that Indigenous slavery in eighteenth-century New France similarly functioned as a "double-edged sword": Rushforth, *Bonds of Alliance: Indigenous and Atlantic Slaveries in New France* (Chapel Hill: University of North Carolina Press for the OI, 2012), 252.

71. 18 April 1671, in *Minutes of the Court of Albany, Rensselaerwyck and Schenectady, 1668–1685*, ed. A. J. F. van Laer (Albany: University of the State of New York, 1926), 1:237–38.

72. *Minutes of the Provincial Council of Pennsylvania*, 1:47, 51, 63, 64, 151, and 2:16; Mancall, *Deadly Medicine*, 107. For the complicated nature of "liquid diplomacy" in colonial Pennsylvania, see Nicole Eustace, *Covered with Night: A Story of Murder and Indigenous Justice in Early America* (New York: Liveright, 2021), 120–21. For a similar law in Connecticut, see 6 April 1654, in *The Public Records of the Colony of Connecticut*, ed. J. Hammond Trumbull (New Haven, 1850), 1:255.

73. "Conserning the bounds and limitts betwixt the English united collonies and the Duch provence of New Neatherland," 11 April 1653, in *Records of the Colony of New Plymouth, in New England: Acts of the Commissioners of the United Colonies of New England*, ed. David Pulsifer (Boston, 1859), 2:23; Jenny Hale Pulsipher, *Subjects unto the Same King: Indians, English, and the Contest for Authority in Colonial New England* (Philadelphia: University of Pennsylvania Press, 2006), 34–35.

74. Thomas Mayhew Letter, 24 June 1678, in Pulsifer, *Records of the Colony of New Plymouth*, 2:404–6.

75. *Papers Relating to an Act of the Assembly of the Province of New-York, for Encouragement of the Indian Trade* (New York, 1724), 18.

76. 18 March 1726, in "Minutes of the Commission of Indian Affairs—Albany," ed. Ann Hunter, albanyindiancommissioners.com, 1:253.

77. 19 July 1736, in *An Abridgment of the Indian Affairs: Contained in Four Folio Volumes, Transacted in the Colony of New York, From the Year 1678 to 1751*, ed. Peter Wraxall (Cambridge, MA: Harvard University Press, 1915), 197–98.

78. 30 July 1736, in Hunter, "Minutes of the Commission of Indian Affairs," 2:78.

79. *The Treaty Held with the Indians of the Six Nations, at Lancaster, in Pennsylvania, in June, 1744* (Philadelphia, 1744), 33–38.

80. 4 October 1728, in Hunter, "Minutes of the Commission of Indian Affairs," 1:507.

81. 4 July 1730, in Hunter, "Minutes of the Commission of Indian Affairs," 1:603.

82. Charles T. Gehring and Robert S. Grumet, eds., "Observations of the Indians from Jasper Danckaerts's Journal, 1679–1680," *WMQ* 44:1 (Jan. 1987): 116; 8 September 1733, in Wraxall, *Abridgment of the Indian Affairs*, 187–88.

83. 7 September 1726, in Wraxall, *Abridgment of the Indian Affairs*, 166.

84. "Moxes & Indians W. H. & G recd by Mrs Hamond," 1 July 1677, in *Documentary History of the State of Maine,* ed. James Phinney Baxter (Portland, 1900), 6:177–79.

85. "A Relacion of the Indyan War, by Mr. Easton, of Roade Isld., 1675," in *Narratives of the Indian Wars, 1675–1699*, ed. Charles H. Lincoln (New York, 1913), 11. See also Increase Mather, *A Brief History of the War with the Indians in New-England* (London, 1676), 13–14.

86. Baxter, *Documentary History of the State of Maine*, 6:177–79; Pulsipher, *Subjects unto*, 225–28.

87. Samuel Drake, *The History of King Philip's War; Also of Expeditions Against the French and Indians in the Eastern Parts of New-England, in the Years 1689, 1690, 1692, 1696 and 1704* (Boston, 1825), 59–60.

88. 13 September 1680, *Documents Relating to the History of the Dutch and Swedish Settlements on the Delaware River*, ed. B. Fernow (Albany, 1877), 658–59.

89. 4 July 1730, in Hunter, "Minutes of the Commission of Indian Affairs," 1:603. See also 10 March 1684, in *Minutes of the Provincial Council of Pennsylvania* (Philadelphia, 1852), 1:51.

90. July 4, 1727, in *Minutes of the Provincial Council of Pennsylvania*, 3:274.

91. 13 and 15 June 1716, 113, and 20 September 1735, 195, in Wraxall, *Abridgment of the Indian Affairs.*

92. *Narrative of a Journey from Tulpehocken, in Pennsylvania, to Onondago, the Headquarters of the Six Nations of Indians, Made in 1737 by Conrad Weiser* (Philadelphia, 1853), 17. See also 1 February 1726, in Hunter, "Minutes of the Commission of Indian Affairs," 1:246.

93. 13 June 1748, in *Minutes of the Provincial Council of Pennsylvania* (1851), 5:284–85.

94. *Journal of Pontiac's Conspiracy, 1763*, ed. M. Agnes Burton (Detroit, 1912), 28.

95. "Journal of James Kenny, 1761–1763 (continued)," ed. John W. Jordan, *PMHB* 37:2 (1913): 171.

96. For interpretations of Neolin as more concerned with severing trade relationships than advocating complete abstinence, see Charles E. Hunter, "The Delaware Nativist Revival of the Mid-Eighteenth Century," *Ethnohistory* 18:1 (Winter 1971): 39–49; Alfred A. Cave, "The Delaware Prophet Neolin: A Reappraisal," *Ethnohistory* 46:2 (Spring 1999): 265–90.

97. Dowd, *War Under Heaven*, 94–105, at 104; On the Mohegan-Brothertown minister Samson Occom's comparable views, see Ryan Carr, *Samson Occom: Radical Hospitality in the Native Northeast* (New York: Columbia University Press, 2023), 204–5.

98. Dowd, *Spirited Resistance*, 126–27, 138; William Apess, "An Indian's Looking-Glass for the White Man," in *On Our Own Ground: The Complete Writings of William Apess, A Pequot*, ed. Barry O'Connell (Amherst: University of Massachusetts Press, 1992), 155.

99. 6 June 1710, in Wraxall, *Abridgment of the Indian Affairs*, 71.

100. 14 September 1716, in Wraxall, *Abridgment of the Indian Affairs*, 115.

101. 8 July 1721, in *Minutes of the Provincial Council of Pennsylvania*, 3:129.

102. 5 October 1728, in Wraxall, *Abridgment of the Indian Affairs*, 174–75. Susan Sleeper-Smith notes similar attempts to keep problematic drinking out of Native villages in the Ohio River

Valley: Sleeper-Smith, *Indigenous Prosperity and American Conquest: Indian Women of the Ohio River Valley, 1690–1792* (Chapel Hill: University of North Carolina Press for the OI, 2018), 162–63.

103. 12 August 1731, in *Minutes of the Provincial Council of Pennsylvania*, 3:405.

104. Sami Lakomäki, "'Tell Them Not to Bring Any Rum Here': Alcohol Regulation, Authority, and Sovereignty Among the Shawnees, 1700–1860," *History and Anthropology* (2019): 1–20; Kramer, "Alcohol, Sovereignty, and Social Segregation," 24–25.

105. 5 October 1728, in Wraxall, *Abridgment of the Indian Affairs*, 174. See also Samuel Hopkins, *Historical Memoirs, Relating to the Housatunnuk Indians* (Boston, 1753), 169.

106. 21 March 1722, in *Minutes of the Provincial Council of Pennsylvania*, 3:154.

107. 13 October 1736, in *Minutes of the Provincial Council of Pennsylvania*, 4:91. For a similar dynamic between the Yamasee and South Carolina colonists, see 27 July 1711, in *Journal of the Commissioners of the Indian Trade of South Carolina, September 20, 1710–April 12, 1715* (Columbia: Historical Commission of South Carolina, 1926), 12–13; Alan Gallay, *The Indian Slave Trade: The Rise of the English Empire in the American South, 1670–1717* (New Haven: Yale University Press, 2002), 249–51.

108. "Speech of the Shawnees," July 1771, in *The Papers of Sir William Johnson*, ed. Milton Hamilton (Albany: University of the State of New York, 1957), 12:914–15.

109. 10 May 1765, in *Minutes of the Provincial Council of Pennsylvania*, 9:261.

110. Michael John Witgen writes about the Northwest Territory, but the general labor patterns of the fur trade observed there were consistent with centuries prior: Witgen, *Seeing Red: Indigenous Land, American Expansion, and the Political Economy of Plunder in North America* (Chapel Hill: University of North Carolina Press for the OI, 2018), 9–10.

111. Mancall, *Deadly Medicine*, 19–23.

112. 10 May 1666 in Trumbull, *The Public Records of the Colony of Connecticut*, 2:37; 24 February 1726, in *Minutes of the Provincial Council of Pennsylvania*, 3:247.

113. Julie Anne Sweet, "'That Cursed Evil Rum': The Trustees' Prohibition Policy in Colonial Georgia," *Georgia Historical Quarterly* 94:1 (Apr. 2010): 1–29; Katherine Johnston, *The Nature of Slavery: Environment and Plantation Labor in the Anglo-Atlantic World* (Oxford: Oxford University Press, 2022), 45–74. Similar dynamics surrounded palmetto-based alcohols in Bermuda as early as the 1620s that were exacerbated by the advent of distilling in the 1650s: Pluymers, *No Wood*, 147–51.

114. "Order of George Clinton Forbidding Joseph Clements from Trading in Spirituous Liquors with Indians or Soldiers Near Mount Johnson," 2 July 1747, in *The Papers of Sir William Johnson*, ed. James Sullivan (Albany: State University of New York, 1921), 1:102.

115. Quoted in Clark, *English Alehouse*, 96.

116. Clark, *English Alehouse*, 212, 238–40.

117. T. C. Smout, "The Early Scottish Sugar Houses, 1660–1720, *EHR* 14:2 (1961), 240–53; McCusker, "Rum Trade," 42–27; Kenneth Morgan, "Sugar Refining in Bristol," in *From Family Firms to Corporate Capitalism: Essays in Business and Industrial History in Honor of Peter Mathias*, ed. Kristine Bruland and Patrick O'Brien (Oxford: Clarendon, 1998), 139–69; Mona Duggan, *Sugar for the House: A History of Early Sugar Refining in North West England* (Stroud, UK: Fonthill Media, 2013).

118. Morgan, "Sugar Refining in Bristol," 143; Charles Bambridge, *The Case of Charles Bambridge, and Other Distillers, with Regard to Their Use of Molasses Made and Manufactured in This Kingdom* (London, 1679).

119. Thomas Walduck, "Letters from Barbados," 29 October 1710, Sloane MS 2302/9, BL.

120. Quoted in Smout, "Early Scottish Sugar Houses," 240–43.

121. Glasgow Customs Books, 1665–1696, E72, NAS.

122. Da. Forrester to Andrew Russell, 2 May 1679, Andrew Russell Papers, RH15/106/341/8, NAS; Robert Baird & Comp. to Andrew Russell, 28 February 1680, Russell Papers, RH15/106/377/5, NAS.

123. Robert Cumming to Andrew Russell, 1680, Russell Papers, RH15/106/381/6, NAS; Robert Cuming to Andrew Russell, 2 October 1678, Russell Papers, RH15/106/302/23, NAS.

124. Accounts of Wester Sugary, 1680–2, CS96/3265, NAS. See also Merchant Waste Book, 1675–1678, CS96/1575/2, NAS.

125. "Information from the masters of the manufactorie of the sugar workes of Glasgow Against the Tasksmen of the impositione upon wyne and brandie att Edinburgh" [1684], Laing MSS, 2, 566.1, EUL.

126. "Information from the masters of the manufactorie of the sugar workes of Glasgow." Laing MSS, 2, 566.1, EUL.

127. John Porse Letter, 4 May 1698, E79/19/9, NAS.

128. "Extract Report off the Committie Annount the Suggar Works of Glasgow," 18 April 1684, Laing MSS, 2, 566.2, EUL.

129. Dutch and German refiners continued to manage Scotland's sugar houses. In London, six "foreign distillers" took on at least eight apprentices between 1674 and 1708: London Distillers Company Apprentice Bindings, 1659–1709, GL.

130. Jessica Warner, "The Naturalization of Beer and Gin in Early Modern England," *Contemporary Drug Problems* 24:2 (Summer 1997): 388.

131. *The Case of the Company of Distillers of London, in Reference to a Bill, Intituled, A Bill for Incouraging the Distilling of Brandy from Corn* (London, 1690).

132. Thomas Tryon, *The Merchant, Citizen and Country-man's Instructor: Or, a Necessary Companion for all People* (London, 1701), 218.

133. "Act Mathew and Daniell Campbells [for] a sugar manufactory in Glasgow," 6 February 1701, in Privy Council Decreta, PC2/28, NAS. Daniel Defoe also suggested that slave traders stocked the Guinea trade with domestically produced spirits in the seventeenth century: Defoe, *A Brief Case of the Distillers and of the Distillers Trade in England* (London, 1726), 49–50.

134. "Act in Favour off William Cochran & others for a suggar manufactory in Leith," 17 August 1703, in Privy Council Decreta, PC2/28, NAS.

135. George Porter, *At a Court of Assistants of the Company of Distillers* (London, 1708); *The Case of the Company of Distillers of the City of London: With Proposals for Reforming the Abuses Practised in the Distilling Trade* (London, c. 1726); Chartres, "No English Calvados?" 316–17.

136. Defoe, *Brief Case of the Distillers*, 18–20.

137. Chartres, "No English Calvados?" 328.

138. Ambrose Cooper, *The Complete Distiller* (London, 1757), 248.

139. British distillers later held "that rum may be converted into gin, whilst gin cannot be converted into rum." John Innes, "Equalization of Duty on Rum and British Spirits," July 1846, 31644/1/16–17, BRO; *The True State of the British Malt-Distillery: Being a Defense of Mr.M[a]wb[e]y's Queries* (London, 1760), 28–29; Chartres, "No English Calvados?" 328.

140. William J. Ashworth, *Customs and Excise: Trade, Production, and Consumption in England, 1640–1845* (Oxford: Oxford University Press, 2003), 225.

141. Chartres, "No English Calvados?" 329.

142. Thomas Wilson, *Distilled Spirituous Liquors the Bane of the Nation* (London, 1736), 14–15. Jessica Warner questions the veracity of numbers fabricated by participants in the gin debates: Warner, "Faith in Numbers: Quantifying Gin and Sin in Eighteenth-Century England," *JBS* 50:1 (Jan. 2011): 91.

143. James Nicholls, *The Politics of Alcohol: A History of the Drink Question in England* (Manchester: Manchester University Press, 2009), 36–37.

144. *Case of the Company of Distillers*, 2.

145. *A Collection of Letters Published in the Daily Papers Relating to the British Distillery* (London, 1736), 30.

146. Wilson, *Distilled Spirituous Liquors*, 7–8; Jonathan White, "The 'Slow but Sure Poyson': The Representation of Gin and Its Drinkers, 1736–1751," *JBS* 42:1 (Jan. 2003): 35–64.

147. Henry Fielding, *An Enquiry into the Causes of the Late Increase of Robbers*, 2d ed. (London, 1751), 34.

148. Daniel Defoe, *Augusta Triumphans, or the Way to Make London the Most Flourishing City in the Universe* (London, 1728), 45; Wilson, *Distilled Spirituous Liquors*, 38–39.

149. Stephen Hales, *A Friendly Admonition to the Drinkers of Gin, Brandy, and Other Distilled Spirituous Liquors*, 4th ed. (London, 1751), 37–39. On the connections between reformers in England and the colonization of Georgia, see Sweet, "Cursed Evil Rum," 3–4.

150. *Pennsylvania Gazette*, 2 August 1736.

151. Wilson, *Distilled Spirituous Liquors*, vi.

152. Defoe, *Augusta Triumphans*, 50–51.

153. Fielding, *Causes of the Late Increase of Robbers*, 29.

154. *Collection of Letters*, 16–19; Lee Davison, "Experiments in the Social Regulation of Industry: Gin Legislation, 1729–1751," in *Stilling the Grumbling Hive: The Response to Social and Economic Problems in England, 1689–1750*, ed. Lee Davison et al. (New York: St. Martin's, 1992), 31–32.

155. Jack Juniper, *The Deposing and Death of Queen Gin, with the Ruin of the Duke of Rum, the Marquee de Nantz, and the Lord Sugarcane* (London, 1736).

156. *An Impartial Enquiry into the Present State of the British Distillery*, 2d ed. (London, 1736), 53.

157. Charles Leadbetter, *The Royal Gauger* (London, 1750), 286.

158. *Collection of Letters*, 18.

159. Nicholls, *Politics of Alcohol*, 38–48. Laws in 1736 and 1742 limiting the importation of Caribbean rum into Britain coincided with the Gin Acts: McCusker, "Rum Trade," 486.

160. "Receipt Book," V.a.680/147, FSL; "Cookery and Pharmaceutical Recipes of the Malet Family, ca. 1700–1740," W.a.303/93, FSL; "Mrs. Knight's Receipt Book, 1740," W.b.79/65, FSL. Rum could replace Hungary water in compounds: Sloane, *Voyage to the Islands*, 1:xxx.

161. Meacham, *Every Home*, 10.

162. "Receipt Book of Jane Staveley, 1693–94," X.d.457, FSL; "Lor Chatham's Rectt for Punch," in "Cookeries, Late seventeenth century," V.a.561, FSL.

163. One doctor suggested that mixing aged rum with water, sugar, and vegetable acid—the principal ingredients in punch—rendered it "less pernicious": John Bell, *Inquiry into the Causes Which Produce and the Means of Preventing Diseases Among British Officers, Soldiers, and Others in the West Indies* (London, 1791), 25.

CHAPTER 3

1. Sloane, *Voyage to the Islands*, passim; Bernard Romans, *A Concise Natural History of East and West Florida* (New York, 1775), 154–56; Dr. Lewis, *The Edinburgh New Dispensatory* (Edinburgh, 1796), 176–77; Mrs. M. Pearson Acct. to Samuel Dickinson, 1786, Hayes Collection, Johnston Family Series, 324, Folder 108, SHC.

2. R. Shannon, *A Practical Treatise on Brewing, Distilling, and Rectification with the Genuine Process of Making Brandy, Rum, and Hollands Gin* (London, 1805), 2:57–59.

3. Londa Schiebinger, *Secret Cures of Slaves: People, Plants, and Medicine in the Eighteenth-Century Atlantic World* (Palo Alto: Stanford University Press, 2017), 47.

4. Scholars have often focused more on the tensions among commodity producers than the affinities—voluntary and forced—that facilitated remarkable commonalities in geographically dispersed sites of production. Smith, *Caribbean Rum*, 45. For other interpretations of commodity producers in the Atlantic world pursuing competition rather than collaboration, see Rhys Isaac, *The Transformation of Virginia, 1740–1790* (Chapel Hill: University of North Carolina Press for the OI, 1982), 88–114; Anderson, *Mahogany*, 108–9, 128–29. On secrecy being rarer than written texts would suggest, see Smith, *From Lived Experience*, 120.

5. Smith, *From Lived Experience*, 176.

6. Memorial of agent of Massachusetts Bay, Mr. [Joseph] Maudinit, abt. Duties on molasses, 27 February 1764, T 1/430/228–29, TNA.

7. John Mair to Ascanius William Senior, November 1781, Nassau Family Papers, E051, NLW.

8. "20 October 1781," J. Pinnock Diary, Add MS 33316, BL. Gregory E. O'Malley argues that illicit trades carried out by pirates and privateers were crucial for supplying underdeveloped parts of the Americas with enslaved people: O'Malley, *Final Passages: The Intercolonial Slave Trade of British America, 1619–1807* (Chapel Hill: University of North Carolina Press for the OI, 2014), 85–113. See also Arne Bialuschewski, "Pirates, Black Sailors and Seafaring Slaves in the Anglo-American Maritime World, 1716–1726," *Journal of Caribbean History* 45:2 (2011): 143–58.

9. John Mills to John Mills, 1 June 1753, Mills Papers, Volume 1, MOL.

10. "Wanted by J. Levett Esqr in Bengal," 24 September 1773, Forbes Family Papers, A727.1455/2, FA; 2 May 1774, William Forbes Order Book 1772–1775, A727.1442, FA.

11. C. B. Wadstrom, *An Essay on Colonization, Particularly Applied to the Western Coast of Africa* (London, 1794), 204.

12. "7 May 1774," William Forbes Orders, Forbes Family Papers, A727.1455/29, FA.

13. John Dalrymple to the Chairman of the India House, 30 March 1796, GD51/3/236/2, NAS.

14. Kean Osborn to Nathaniel Phillips, 8 October 1794, Slebech Estate Records, 9236, NLW.

15. Daniel Roberdeau to Isaac Winn, 15 December 1783, Daniel Roberdeau Papers, MMC-3586, LOC, microfilm. See also Fitch Hall to Benjamin Hall, 9 August 1797, Hall Family Papers, 267, MED; Ephraim Bowen to Benjamin Bourne, 8 March 1798, Benjamin Bourne Papers, MSS 11/1, RIHS.

16. Nathaniel Phillips, "Voyage to Jamaica, Sept 14 to Nov 26 1775," Slebech Estate Records, 9402, NLW.

17. Patrick Kein, *An Essay on Pen-Keeping and Plantership* (Kingston, Jamaica, 1796), 70.

18. John Dovaston, "Agricultura Americana," Codex 60 ENG, JCB.

19. Trevor Burnard, *Mastery, Tyranny, and Desire: Thomas Thistlewood and His Slaves in the Anglo-Jamaican World* (Chapel Hill: University of North Carolina Press, 2004), 71.

20. Maria Nugent, *Lady Nugent's Journal: Jamaica One Hundred Years Ago*, ed. Frank Cundall (London, 1907), 39–40, 86.

21. Dovaston, "Agricultura Americana."

22. Clement Caines, *Letters on the Cultivation of the Otaheite Cane* (London, 1801), 14–15.

23. Ezekiel Dickinson to Edward East, 15 November 1782, Dickinson Family Papers, SOM, microfilm.

24. Thomas Barrett to Nathaniel Phillips, 9 January 1793, Slebech Estate Records, 8409, NLW.

25. Instructions to Capt. James Brown, 15 December 1789, Brown Family Business Records, BFBR 101/6, JCB.

26. Samuel Martin to Samuel Martin, [1767], Martin Family Papers, Add MS 41347/138, BL.

27. Samuel Martin to Samuel Martin, 8 February 1767, Martin Family Papers, Add MS 41347/259, BL.

28. Henry Plummer to Joseph Foster Barham, 23 September 1799, Barham Papers, MS Clar Dep c. 357/2, BOD. My thanks to the Eighth Earl of Clarendon for permission to quote from this collection.

29. William Rodgers to Joseph Foster Barham, 5 July 1802, Barham Papers, MS Clar Dep c. 357/3, BOD. See also Thomas Barritt to Nathaniel Phillips, 23 September 1799, Slebech Estate Records, 11605, NLW.

30. For scholarship examining local and transregional communication among enslaved people, see Roderick A. McDonald, *The Economy and Material Culture of Slaves: Goods and Chattels on the Sugar Plantations of Jamaica and Louisiana* (Baton Rouge: Louisiana State University Press, 1993); Philip D. Morgan, *Slave Counterpoint: Black Culture in the Eighteenth-Century Chesapeake and Lowcountry* (Chapel Hill: University of North Carolina Press for the OI, 1998), 524–30; Alexander X. Byrd, *Captives and Voyagers: Black Migrants Across the Eighteenth-Century British Atlantic World* (Baton Rouge: Louisiana State University Press, 2008); Julius Scott, *The Common Wind: Afro-American Currents in the Age of the Haitian Revolution* (New York: Verso, 2018).

31. Josiah Martin to Stephen Bayard, 21 February 1735, Martin Family Papers, Add MS 41352/84, BL.

32. Josiah Martin to Barry Anderson, 10 October 1737, Martin Family Papers, Add MS 41352/129, BL.

33. "Robison Papers (James Aitkens) Distillery Records Tyning Plantation," 1775–1782, Robison Family Papers, Coll. #5, Vol. 5, MEHS.

34. Samuel Thomas Smith to Nathaniel Holmes, 12 March 1754, Bourn Papers, MS Am 579/6/131, HOUGH.

35. Maynard Clarke to Samuel Walter, 22 October 1757, Walter v. Evans, C 104/248 (II), TNA; Simon Pearce to Isaac Winslow, 29 May 1774, Winslow Family Papers, Ms. N-486/1, MHS; Phyn and Ellice to Thomas Robison, 11 June 1784, Robison Family Papers, Coll. #5/1/4, MEHS; Head & Amory to Brown Benson & Ives, 22 May 1793, Brown Family Business Records, BFBR 170/3, JCB.

36. Edward Ireland to William Fitzherbert, 11 March 1785, Fitzherbert Papers—Turner's Hall Plantation, E20547, DRO, microfilm; Edward Blanchard to Daniel Dunham, 20 June 1791, Edward Blanchard Letter Book, Mss 766 1786–1794 B639/110, HBS.

37. Samuel Martin to Mr. Baldwin, May 1766, Martin Family Papers, Add MS 41350/27, BL; Nathaniel Phillips to Hilton & Biscoe, 6 July 1766, Slebech Estate Records, 11485/126, NLW.

38. Daniel Roberdeau to John Thornton, 17 January 1775, Daniel Roberdeau Papers, MMC-3586, LOC, microfilm; "The Humble Petition of Richard Morgan," 5 April 1785, HO 47/2/184–5, TNA.

39. "12 May 1730," Waste Book, Cunyngham Family Papers, CS96/3102/11, NAS.

40. "Quacquo a negro sold by Waterman to Coleman, 22 September 1730," Examined by Mitchel Sewall, Suffolk Files, Docket 30085, MSA.

41. Fitch Hall to Benjamin Hall, 9 August 1797, Hall Family Papers, 267, MED; Fitch Hall to Malcolm Ross, 22 December 1798, Hall Family Papers, 265, MED.

42. Leonard Wray, *The Practical Sugar Planter: A Complete Account and Manufacture of the Sugar-Cane* (London, 1848), 401.

43. William Blathwayt, "Reflections on a paper concerning America," c. 1685, William Blathwayt Papers, BL 416, HL.

44. "Articles of Agreement betwixt the Proprietors of the Easter and Wester Sugar houses of Glasgow and John Nasmith Apothecary in Hamilton," 1711, RH15/120/73, NAS; "Lord Advocate Stewart, on John Nasmith's new invention," 13 March 1712, SP 54/4/90, TNA.

45. "13 May 1752," "7 August 1754," and "16 April 1755," Acts of Barbados, CO 30/1/358, 373, 376, TNA. On contemporaneous patents for rum distillation in Jamaica, see Aaron Graham, "Patents and Invention in Jamaica and the British Atlantic Before 1857," *EHR* 73:4 (Nov. 2020): 940–63.

46. Edmund Burke, *List of Patents for Inventions & Designs, Issued by the United States from 1790–1847* (Washington, DC, 1847), 99–119.

47. Fitch Hall to Benjamin Hall, 9 August 1797, Hall Family Papers, 267, MED; Fitch Hall to Malcolm Ross, 22 December 1798, Hall Family Papers, 265, MED.

48. Michael Krafft, *The American Distiller, or, The Theory and Practice of Distilling* (Philadelphia, 1804), "Advertisement."

49. Hugh Amory and David D. Hall, eds., *A History of the Book in America: Volume I—The Colonial Book in the Atlantic World* (Chapel Hill: University of North Carolina Press for the American Antiquarian Society, 2007), 8.

50. B. Lintot, *The Practical Distiller* (London, 1718); Peter Shaw, *Three Essays in Artificial Philosophy, or Universal Chemistry* (London, 1731); John Richardson, *The Philosophical Principles of the Science of Brewing* (York, 1788).

51. Dovaston, "Agricultura Americana"; Shannon, *Practical Treatise*.

52. Martin, *Essay upon Plantership*, 53–62; Nicholson, "Observations upon Brewing, Fermentation and Distillation," Add MS 39683, BL; Caines, *Letters on the Cultivation*, 108–18.

53. Samuel McHarry, *The Practical Distiller* (Harrisburg, 1809), preface.

54. Cooper, *Complete Distiller*, preface.

55. Shannon, *Practical Treatise*, 2:44–48, 52–63.

56. William Belgrove, *A Letter to the Planters of St. Christopher's*, 16 February 1757, Bodrhyddan MSS, NLW; William Belgrove, *A Treatise upon Husbandry or Planting* (Boston, 1755).

57. Martin, *Essay upon Plantership*, preface.

58. Belgrove, *Treatise upon Husbandry*; Dovaston, "Agricultura Americana"; Kein, *Essay on Pen-Keeping*; Joshua Peterkin, *A Treatise on Planting, from the Origin of Semen to Ebullition*, 2d ed. (Basseterre, St. Christopher's, 1790).

59. McHarry, *Practical Distiller*, preface.

60. Peterkin, *Treatise on Planting*, i–xx.

61. "Different Ways to Set Liquor," *Douglass and Aikman's Almanack and Register for the Island of Jamaica* (Kingston, 1781), 49–56.

62. April G. Shelford, "Pascal in Jamaica; or, The French Enlightenment in Translation," *Proceedings of the Western Society for French History* 36 (2008): 53–74.

63. Thomas Thistlewood, "List of Books," 1777, Thomas Thistlewood Papers, OSB MSS 176/11/76, BRBL.

64. Burnard, *Mastery, Tyranny, and Desire*, 30. Book lists from other planters suggest that Thistlewood's library was uncommonly extensive but that other planters read a variety of British- and Caribbean-published books pertaining to sugarcane agriculture and distillation. Thistlewood's tendency to borrow books from neighbors and acquaintances further suggests that he lived among

other planters with complementary reading patterns. "Books Bought, 1717," Account Book of Robert Cunyngham of St. Christophers, Cunyngham Family Papers, CS 96/3096/17, NAS; "Books Bought, 1721," Account Book of Robert Cunyngham of St. Christophers, Cunyngham Family Papers, CS 96/3097/34, NAS; "Inventory of Stores Utensils etc on Pleasant Hill," 24 May 1784, Slebech Estate Records, 8867, NLW; J. Shand letter, 14 July 1804, "In Chancery; Chambers and others vs. Goldwin & others," C 112/163, TNA; "A Catalogue of Books in the Library of the late Captain Hartman of Golden Spring, St. Anne Jamaica, 1810," MS 207, NLJ.

65. *The Charter, Laws, and Catalogue of Books, of the Library Company of Philadelphia* (Philadelphia, 1770), 9–13.

66. *A Catalogue of the Books Belonging to the Library Company of Philadelphia* (Philadelphia, 1807).

67. Robert Jenkins to Thomas Robison, 11 March 1784, Robison Family Papers, Coll. #5/1/3, MEHS.

68. Martin, *Essay upon Plantership*, vi.

69. Few authors could make a living entirely from book sales in the eighteenth century. Terry Belanger, "Publishers and Writers in Eighteenth-Century England," in *Books and Their Readers in Eighteenth-Century England: New Essays*, ed. Isabel Rivers (Leicester: Leicester University Press, 1982), 20–22.

70. Smith, *From Lived Experience*.

71. Peterkin, *Treatise on Planting*, 18.

72. Martin, *Essay upon Plantership*, 57. See also Kein, *Essay on Pen-keeping*, 78.

73. In 1790 and 1791, six individuals made their mark rather than signing their name for labor performed at the Brown, Benson, and Arnold distillery: Bills Against Distill House, Arnold Family Papers, JCB.

74. Nuala Zahedieh, "Colonies, Copper, and the Market for Inventive Activity in England and Wales, 1680–1730," *EHR* 66:3 (Aug. 2013): 805–25; Zahedieh, "A Copper Still and the Making of Rum in the Eighteenth-Century Atlantic World," *Historical Journal* 65:1 (Feb. 2022): 149–66.

75. "Directions for copper suitable for two large and one small still," c. 1788, Arnold Family Papers, Box 6, JCB.

76. Wm. Thoyts & Son their price of a copper & Still, c. 1773, Forbes Family Papers, A727.1413/40, FA; "9 May 1774," William Forbes Notebooks, A727.1457/1, FA.

77. J. Foster Barham to William Forbes, 15 September 1775, Forbes Family Papers, A727.1471/50, FA.

78. Messr. Maitland Order, 15 August 1789, Forbes Family Papers, A727.1850/34, FA.

79. Orders received from Mr. Richard Horne, 20 December 1773, Forbes Family Papers, A727.1437/44, FA.

80. Krafft, *American Distiller*, 30.

81. *Georgia Gazette*, 19 July 1764. For the general consistency of the hierarchy of prices even as costs fluctuated, see Dailey & Bogert to Moses Brown, 13 August 1798, Moses Brown Papers, 766 1750–1845 B879/1/2, HBS.

82. George Walker Letters, December 1754, E20508, and Edward Ireland to William Fitzherbert, 11 March 1785, E20547, Fitzherbert Papers—Turner's Hall Plantation, DRO, microfilm.

83. Sam Rollstone Letter, 12 July 1756, E20511, Fitzherbert Papers—Turner's Hall Plantation, DRO, microfilm.

84. Samuel Redhead to William Codrington, 18 July 1758, Codrington Papers, ANA, microfilm; Charles Thomson Memorandum Book, 1754–1774, Gratz Case 14/30/3, LCP.

85. Daniel Roberdeau to William Turnbull, 25 November 1766, Roberdeau Family Papers, Am.1295, HSP.

86. Samuel Thomas Smith to Nathaniel Holmes, 26 November 1754, Bourn Papers, MS Am 579/7/32, HOUGH.

87. Simon Horner to Maynard Clarke, 30 September 1759, C 104/248 (II), TNA; John Boylston to P. P. Livingston, 24 September 1773, Boylston Family Papers, Ms. N-4, vol. 68, MHS.

88. Bernadette Bensaude-Vincent, "'The Chemist's Balance for Fluids': Hydrometers and Their Multiple Identities, 1770–1810," in *Instruments and Experimentation in the History of Chemistry*, ed. Frederic L. Holmes and Trevor H. Levere (Cambridge, MA: MIT Press, 2000), 153–84.

89. Leadbetter, *Royal Gauger*.

90. "An Act for better ascertaining the true and exact Gauge and Tare of Cask," 11 September 1736, Acts of Barbados, CO 30/1/303, TNA.

91. J. Beresford, Jam. Agar, Tho. Allan & Rob. Clements to the Lord Lieutenant, 17 July 1773, T 1/501/3, TNA; Eaton and Benson to Joshua Ward, 5 November 1782, Ward Family Papers, MSS 46/14/2, PEM; Journal for Pearl Estates, 1803, Chancery Records, C 110/105/2, TNA.

92. Bensaude-Vincent, "'Chemist's Balance for Fluids,'" 163.

93. *Notice is Hereby Given to All Dealers in Brandy, Rum, Malt, or Melasses-Spirits, Arrack, &c* (London, 1746).

94. Bensaude-Vincent, "'Chemist's Balance for Fluids,'" 164–65. On thermometers in the rum industry, see Instructions to Capt. James Brown, 15 December 1789, Brown Family Business Records, BFBR 101/6, JCB; Samuel Bosworth letter, 9 July 1791, US Custom House Records, MSS 28/SG 2/1, RIHS.

95. For Caribbean planters purchasing "beads" or "bubbles," see 1786 journal, Mesopotamia Estate, Barham Papers, MS. Clar Dep b.33/2/11, BOD; Madeys Estate Plantation Account, 1797–1803, C 110/103/3, TNA.

96. Diary of Nathaniel Phillips, 1788, Slebech Estate Records, 9418, NLW; a Copy of Phillipsfield Boiling and Still House Books, 1790, Slebech Estate Records, 8443, NLW.

97. Samuel Martin to Samuel Martin, July 1758, Martin Family Papers, Add MS 41346/217, BL.

98. Samuel Redhead to William Codrington, 18 July 1758, Codrington Papers, ANA, microfilm.

99. Fitch Hall to Benjamin Hall, 9 August 1797, Hall Family Papers, 267, MED.

100. Mr. Perkin's observation, 1777, Cases Regarding Excise Duty, Messrs James, Perkins and Jewkes and Messrs Langdon Attlee and Moody, 44352/9/3/4/1, BRO.

101. George Benson to Benjamin Bourne, 27 October 1792, Benjamin Bourne Papers, MSS 11/1, RIHS.

CHAPTER 4

1. Clark renders the overseers "technically knowledgeable, paternalistically benevolent, and self-consciously genteel": Tim Barringer et al., "Catalogue: Life and Labor in Jamaica, 1807–34," in *Art and Emancipation in Jamaica: Isaac Mendes Belisario and His Worlds* (New Haven: Yale Center for British Art, 2019), https://www-aaeportal-com.proxy.library.upenn.edu/?id=-18645.

2. Thomas Roughley, *The Jamaica Planters Guide* (London, 1823), 104.

3. Belgrove, *Treatise upon Husbandry*, 18.

4. Thompson, "Drax's Instructions," 590.

5. David Watts, "Origins of Barbadian Cane Hole Agriculture," *JBMHS* 32:3 (1968): 143–51; Nicholas Radburn and Justin Roberts, "Gold Versus Life: Jobbing Gangs and British Caribbean Slavery," *WMQ* 76:2 (Apr. 2019): 229–31.

6. Barnium to Joseph Foster Barham, 22 April 1765, Barham Papers, MS Clar Dep c. 357/1, BOD.

7. David Collins, *Practical Rules for the Management and Medical Treatment of Negro Slaves, in the Sugar Colonies* (London, 1803), 181; Roughley, *Jamaica Planters Guide*, 121–22.

8. Roughley, *Jamaica Planters Guide*, 104–6.

9. Roughley, *Jamaica Planters Guide*, 102; Collins, *Practical Rules*, 180.

10. Roughley, *Jamaica Planters Guide*, 99–100; Collins, *Practical Rules*, 176–77.

11. Collins, *Practical Rules*, 176.

12. It rose to 59 percent by 1802: Richard S. Dunn, *A Tale of Two Plantations: Slave Life and Labor in Virginia and Jamaica* (Cambridge, MA: Harvard University Press, 2014), 144.

13. Jennifer L. Morgan, *Laboring Women: Reproduction and Gender in New World Slavery* (Philadelphia: University of Pennsylvania Press, 2004), 148–49.

14. Morgan, *Laboring Women*, 3.

15. Typically, only infants who were expected to survive were recorded. Dunn, *Tale of Two Plantations*, 159.

16. Planters made certain concessions to nursing mothers by suggesting that they be moved to the second gang and providing limited nursing breaks. However, by employing nurses to watch over children while their mothers worked, enslavers also limited a mother's access to her children during work hours: Roughley, *Jamaica Planters Guide*, 102–3; Sasha Turner, *Contested Bodies: Pregnancy, Childrearing, and Slavery in Jamaica* (Philadelphia: University of Pennsylvania Press, 2017), 68–111. Morgan identifies African-descended women nursing their children for longer than Europeans were accustomed as a means of regulating fertility and one area where women could preserve West African practices in the Americas: Morgan, *Laboring Women*, 66.

17. Historians ascribe these changes to humanitarian impulses, economic self-interest, or as a response to the abolition of the slave trade. Regardless of the motivations, pro-natal policies responded to the Enlightenment ethos of the late eighteenth and early nineteenth centuries: J. R. Ward, *British West Indian Slavery, 1750–1834: The Process of Amelioration* (Oxford: Clarendon, 1988); Christa Dierksheide, *Amelioration and Empire: Progress and Slavery in the Plantation Americas* (Charlottesville: University of Virginia Press, 2014); Turner, *Contested Bodies*.

18. Dovaston, "Agricultura Americana," Codex 60 ENG, 281–82, JCB.

19. Roughley, *Jamaica Planters Guide*, 62, 81, 104; Dovaston, "Agricultura Americana," 245–46.

20. John Alleyne Letter, 15 June 1748, Fitzherbert Papers—Turner's Hall Plantation, E20503, DRO, microfilm.

21. Approximately 80 percent of mixed-race children in Jamaica remained enslaved: Daniel Livesay, *Children of Uncertain Fortune: Mixed-Race Jamaicans in Britain and the Atlantic Family 1733–1833* (Chapel Hill: University of North Carolina Press for the OI, 2018), 25.

22. Roger Hope Elletson letter, 1 February 1771, Roger Hope Elletson Letters, ST 14/2, HL; Colleen A. Vasconcellos, *Slavery, Childhood, and Abolition in Jamaica, 1788–1838* (Athens: University of Georgia Press, 2015), 53–55; Dunn, *Tale of Two Plantations*, 90–91.

23. Morgan, *Laboring Women*, 113–15.

24. Nugent, *Lady Nugent's Journal*, 40. For a theorization of "black femme freedom," albeit in a different colonial context, where women "used every tool at their disposal, even their own bodies, to secure some safety and security for themselves," see Jessica Marie Johnson, *Wicked Flesh: Black Women, Intimacy, and Freedom in the Atlantic World* (Philadelphia: University of Pennsylvania

Press, 2020), 85–101. Marisa Fuentes cautions against overemphasizing sexual relationships of the enslaved as "acts of will, agency, choice, and volunteerism": Fuentes, *Dispossessed Lives*, 49.

25. Littleton, *Groans of the Plantations*, 19. This passage was copied by a Barbadian planter active in the eighteenth and nineteenth centuries: Lucas Manuscript, Lucas MSS Misc. Notes 5/ 476, BPL.

26. Dovaston, "Agricultura Americana," 126.

27. "A list of Negroes on Mesopotamia Estate," 1 January 1763, Barham Papers, MS Clar Dep. B. 37/2, BOD.

28. For a similar argument focused on the antebellum United States, see Daina Ramey Berry, "'In Pressing Need of Cash': Gender, Skill, and Family Persistence in the Domestic Slave Trade," *Journal of African American History* 92:1 (Winter 2007): 22–36.

29. Miles Ward Day Book, Ward Family Papers, MSS 46/42, PEM; "George Dodd's agreement with Brown & Benson," 18 January 1792, Brown Family Business Records, BFBR 370/6, JCB; "Particulars of a Well-arranged Distillery of Messrs. Hodgson and Co. Situate at Battersea, Surrey. Which will be sold by Auction by Wistanley and Sons, at the Mart on Friday, the 10th of October 1817," D72/20, Wandsworth Heritage Service, London.

30. Roughley, *Jamaica Planters Guide*, 87.

31. Turner, *Contested Bodies*, 233–35.

32. Dunn, *Tale of Two Plantations*, 84–94. The two men used different spellings.

33. Roughley, *Jamaica Planters Guide*, 90–91.

34. James Chisholme to William Anderson, 5 December 1803, Nisbet Family Papers, MS 5476/125, NLS.

35. *A Genuine Narrative of the Intended Conspiracy of the Negroes at Antigua* (Dublin, 1737), 14.

36. Ashton Warner, *Negro Slavery Described by a Negro: Being the Narrative of Ashton Warner, a Native of St. Vincent's*, ed. S. Strickland (London, 1831), 31–32.

37. William Cowper, "The Negroe's Complaint," in *The Poetical Works of William Cowper* (London, 1830), 1:242.

38. Randy M. Browne, *Surviving Slavery in the British Caribbean* (Philadelphia: University of Pennsylvania Press, 2017), 3–5.

39. Martin, *Essay upon Plantership*, 51.

40. Taylor, "Multum in Parvo," MS 105 v. 2/520–521, NLJ; "18 July 1734," Waste Book 1731–34, Cunyngham Family Papers, cs96/3104/69, NAS; Jamaica House of Assembly, *Report, &c.*, 8 January 1788.

41. Eight of thirteen had been born in Africa: Dunn, *Tale of Two Plantations*, 329.

42. "A list of my Negros sworn to before John Spooner by John Rhode my overseer," 1729, Cunyngham Family Papers, CS96/3102/3, NAS.

43. Mr. Richard Beckford's Instructions to Thomas Thistlewood, 10 April 1754, Thomas Thistlewood Papers, OSB MSS 176/86/29, BRBL.

44. "A List of Negroes on Mesopotamia Estate 31 December 1764," 1764 Journal, Barham Papers, MS Clar Dep b. 37/1, BOD; "A List of Negroes on Mesopotamia Estate 31 December 1765," 1765 Journal, Barham Papers, MS Clar Dep b. 37/1, BOD; "A List of Negroes and other slaves belonging to Drax Hall Plantation, 1 January 1781, Beckford v. Aylesbury, C 107/143, TNA; "List of Negroes on Mesopotamia Estate," 1 January 1782, Barham Papers, MS Clar Dep. B. 37/2, BOD; Madey's Estate Annual Accounts, 1805, Hurd v. Law, C 110/103, TNA.

45. "A List of the Negroes belonging to the Russel's Rest Whitehall and Windward estates of Lady Frances Stapleton decd. Taken by John Queeley Manager there 28th August 1773," Bodrhyddan MSS, NLW.

46. John Pretor Pinney to James Williams, 13 February 1799, as quoted in Christine Eickelmann, "The Mountravers Plantation Community, 1734–1834," 530–31, https://seis.bristol.ac.uk/~emceee/. William Stapleton's Nevis plantation found itself in this position in 1729, imperiling the rum yield: David Stalker to William Stapleton, 27 June 1729, Ryland Stapleton MSS 4.10., UMSC, transcription.

47. "Appraisement of Negroes, Cattle & Plantation Utensils belong to the Estate called Jolly Hill, taken the 7 June 1783," Francis Russell Hart Collection, Ms. N-189/1/5, MHS.

48. Bernard Moitt, *Women and Slavery in the French Antilles, 1635–1848* (Bloomington: Indiana University Press, 2001), 52–53; Robert Harms, *The Diligent: A Voyage Through the Worlds of the Slave Trade* (New York: Basic, 2008), 345.

49. Père Labat, *Nouveau voyage aux isles de l'Amérique* (Paris, 1724), 3:420.

50. Paul Cheney, *Cul de Sac: Patrimony, Capitalism, and Slavery in French Saint-Domingue* (Chicago: University of Chicago Press, 2017), 63–68.

51. Trevor Burnard and John Garrigus, *The Plantation Machine: Atlantic Capitalism in French Saint-Domingue and British Jamaica* (Philadelphia: University of Pennsylvania Press, 2018), 8.

52. Even on the eve of the Haitian Revolution, when rum production in the French colonies had expanded considerably, Saint Méry counted 793 sugar works and 182 distilleries in Saint-Domingue. Fewer than one in four plantations were making their own rum: Médéric Louis Elie Moreau de Saint Méry, *Description topographique, physique, civile, politique et historique de la partie française de l'isle Saint-Domingue* (Philadelphia, 1797), 100.

53. Burnard and Garrigus, *Plantation Machine*, 16.

54. Spirits comparable to rum were alternatively called tafia, guildive, rhum, and eau-de-vie de la canne. I generally replicate the word used by the observer. Mr. Worsam to Mr. Gordon, 23 August 1720, *CSP Volume 32, 1720–1721*, ed. Cecil Headlam (London, 1933), 211; Frank Wesley Pitman, *The Development of the British West Indies, 1700–1763* (New Haven, 1917), 202–5.

55. Robert Louis Stein, *The French Sugar Business in the Eighteenth Century (Baton Rouge: Louisiana State University Press, 1988)*, 72; Mandelblatt, "Atlantic Consumption," 9–27.

56. British mercantilist policies allowed intercolonial trade but banned refining sugar in the West Indies: Burnard and Garrigus, *Plantation Machine,* 166; Stein, *French Sugar Business*, 66.

57. Estimate from Michel-René Hilliard d'Auberteuil, *Considérations sur l'état présent de la colonie française de Saint-Domingue* (Paris, 1776), 317. On ritual use of rum by the enslaved in Saint-Domingue, see John D. Garrigus, *A Secret Among the Blacks: Slave Resistance Before the Haitian Revolution* (Cambridge, MA: Harvard University Press, 2023), passim.

58. "Edit du Roi, touchant l'etat de la discipline des esclaves négres de l'Amérique Françoise, donné a Versailles, au mois de Mars 1685," in *Code Noir, ou recueil d'edits, déclarations et arrets concernant les esclaves négres de l'Amérique* (Paris, 1743), 12.

59. Carolyn E. Fick, *The Making of Haiti: Saint Domingue's Revolution from Below* (Knoxville: University of Tennessee Press, 1990), 29.

60. M. E. Descourtilz, *Voyages d'un naturaliste, et ses observations faites sur les trois règnes de la nature* (Paris, 1809), 2:375, 3:114–15, 178, 185.

61. Saint Méry, *Description topographique*, 51; Fick, *Making of Haiti*, 42–45. Sara Johnson notes that Saint Méry's "achievements were, at every turn, predicated upon his extraction of labor, physical and intellectual, from enslaved people and people of color": Johnson, *Encyclopédie Noire*, 4.

62. As quoted in Bertie Mandelblatt, "L'alambic dans l'Atlantique: Production, commercialisation, et concurrence de l'eau-de-vie de vin et de l'eau de vie de rhum dans l'Atlantique français au XVIIe et au début du XVIIIe siècle," *Histoire, Économie & Société* 2 (2011): 68. See also Mims, *Colbert's West India Policy*, 220–22; Burnard and Garrigus, *Plantation Machine*, 166. Similar arguments

were made by Dutch planters in Suriname: Karwan Fatah-Black, "Paramaribo as Dutch and Atlantic Nodal Point, 1650–1795," in *Dutch Atlantic Connections, 1680–1800: Linking Empires, Bridging Borders*, ed. Gert Oostindie and Jessica V. Roitman (Leiden: Brill, 2014), 67.

63. Wim Klooster, "Inter-Imperial Smuggling in the Americas, 1600–1800," in *Soundings in Atlantic History: Latent Structures and Intellectual Currents, 1500–1830*, ed. Bernard Bailyn and Patricia L. Denault (Cambridge, MA: Harvard University Press, 2009), 171.

64. James Pritchard, *In Search of Empire: The French in the Americas, 1670–1730* (Cambridge: Cambridge University Press, 2003), 206–7.

65. Col. Dunbar to Mr. Popple, 21 October 1730, *CSP Vol. 37, 1730*, ed. Cecil Headlam and Arthur Percival Newton (London, 1937), 321–31.

66. Robert Morris to William Bingham [transcript], 4 December 1776, Robert Morris Collection, HL; David Geggus, "The French Slave Trade: An Overview," *WMQ* 58:1 (Jan. 2001): 126; Pitman, *Development of the British West Indies*, 222–23; Kenneth J. Banks, "Official Duplicity: The Illicit Slave Trade of Martinique, 1713–1763," in *The Atlantic Economy During the Seventeenth and Eighteenth Centuries: Organization, Operation, Practice, and Personnel*, ed. Peter A. Coclanis (Columbia: University of South Carolina Press, 2005), 229–51.

67. Governor Worsley to the Council of Trade and Plantations, 26 March 1723, *CSP Vol. 33, 1722–3*, ed. Cecil Headlam (London, 1934), 221–38. Ann Pérotin-Dumon suggests that cabotage was so prevalent in Guadeloupe that it decreased the significance of the island's leading ports even as trade grew: Pérotin-Dumon, "Cabotage, Contraband, and Corsairs: The Port Cities of Guadeloupe and Their Inhabitants, 1650–1800," in *Atlantic Port Cities: Economy, Culture, and Society in the Atlantic World, 1650–1850*, ed. Franklin W. Knight and Peggy K. Liss (Knoxville: University of Tennessee Press, 1991), 65–66. Barbados's Governor Worsley's plan to combat coastal smuggling called for a boat that had been seized from smugglers to be "manned by six white men . . . instead of Blacks," because the enslaved could not testify in court.

68. Deposition of Peter Joyce, 3 October 1735, Lucas Manuscript, Lucas Transcripts 17/36, BPL. See also Dawson, *Undercurrents of Power*, 164–90.

69. Governor Worsley to the Council of Trade and Plantations, 26 March 1723, *CSP Vol. 33, 1722–3*, 221–38.

70. For descriptions of foreign ports and neutral islands being used to clear French produce, see Dorothy Goebel, "The 'New England Trade' and the French West Indies, 1763–1774: A Study in Trade Policies," *WMQ* 20:3 (Jul. 1963): 339–40; Pritchard, *In Search of Empire*, 203–7; Kenneth J. Banks, *Chasing Empire Across the Sea: Communications and the State in the French Atlantic, 1713–1763* (Montreal: McGill-Queen's University Press, 2006), 206–7. For French molasses being packaged in foreign barrels, see "6 December 1750," in *Journal of the Commissioners for Trade and Plantations January 1749–1750 to December 1753 Preserved in the Public Record Office* (London, 1932), 129–31; Alan L. Karras, "Transgressive Exchange: Circumventing Eighteenth-Century Atlantic Commercial Restrictions, or the Discount of Monte Christi," in *Seascapes: Maritime Histories, Littoral Cultures, and Transoceanic Exchanges*, ed. Jerry H. Bentley et al. (Honolulu: University of Hawaii Press, 2007), 127–28. For examples of false forced release, see "The Petition of Charles Dupui," 18 September 1752, *Minutes of the Provincial Council of Pennsylvania* (Harrisburg, 1851), 5:580–81; Manuel Covo, "Commerce, empire et révolutions dans le monde atlantique: La colonie française de Saint-Domingue entre métropole et États-Unis (ca. 1778 – ca. 1804)" (PhD diss., École des Hautes Études en Sciences Sociales, 2013), 282. For descriptions of how New York merchants adopted many of these methods, as well as the flag of truce trade, during the Seven Years' War, see Thomas M. Truxes, *Defying Empire: Trading with the Enemy in Colonial New York* (New Haven: Yale University Press, 2008).

71. Even after the free port system emerged, the overseer of a Cul de Sac plantation, Jean-Baptiste Corbier, suggested trade through Le Môle was "impossible to destroy" and bolstered the contraband trade: Corbier père to Ferronnays, 25 November 1776, AN, T 210. Thanks to Paul Cheney for sharing his transcription of topical Corbier letters with me. For a general description of smuggling's enduring presence, see Frances Armytage, *The Free Port System in the British West Indies: A Study in Commercial Policy* (London: Longman Green, 1953), 44–47.

72. Banks, *Chasing Empire*, 178.

73. McCusker, "Rum Trade," 402.

74. Covo, "Commerce, empire et revolutions," 306–20.

75. Corbier fils to Ferronnays, 30 April 1788, AN, T 210.

76. Daniel Roberdeau to Isaac Winn, 22 February 1775, Daniel Roberdeau Papers, MMC-3586, LOC, microfilm. See also Welcome Arnold to Wall, Tardy & Co., 4 June 1785 and 8 December 1786, Arnold Family Papers, Welcome Arnold Copy Book 2, JCB.

77. Stephen Holland to Moses Brown, 13 June 1792, Moses Brown Papers, 766 1750–1845 B879/1/1, HBS.

78. Scott, *Common Wind*, 47–50.

79. Jennifer L. Morgan, *Reckoning with Slavery: Gender, Kinship, and Capitalism in the Early Black Atlantic* (Durham, NC: Duke University Press, 2021), 173.

80. *Boston Evening Post*, 31 July 1749. See also *City Gazette*, 29 March 1796.

81. *New-York Gazette*, 13 September 1758.

82. *Boston Gazette*, 1 July 1771.

83. The narrative that follows is drawn from depositions collected as part of "Quacqo a negro sold by Waterman to Coleman, 22 September 1730," Suffolk Files, Docket 30085, MSA. Thanks to Jared Hardesty for recommending this source.

84. *Boston News-Letter*, 17 July 1729. See also *Boston Gazette*, 13 June 1726; *New-England Weekly Journal*, 12 June 1727 and 3 July 1732; *Boston Gazette*, 30 July 1733.

85. For a count of rum distilleries in Boston in 1730, see Eck, "Spirits of Massachusetts," 76. For a survey of the market for bondspeople described in Boston newspapers, see Robert E. Desrochers Jr., "Slave-for-Sale Advertisements and Slavery in Massachusetts, 1704–1781," *WMQ* 59:3 (Jul. 2002): 623–64. For an interpretation of printers as participants in the trafficking of enslaved people, see Jordan E. Taylor, "Enquire of the Printer: Newspaper Advertising and the Moral Economy of the North American Slave Trade, 1704–1807," *EAS* 18:3 (Summer 2020): 287–323.

86. "Chapter 144. Order Directing the Commissioners of Impost to refund the Duty of Two Deceased Negroes," 21 August 1727, in *The Acts and Resolves, Public and Private, of the Province of the Massachusetts Bay* (Boston, 1903), 11:188.

87. Olaudah Equiano, *The Interesting Narrative of the Life of Olaudah Equiano, or Gustavus Vassa, the African* (London, 1789), 89–91.

88. A prominent early eighteenth-century merchant, John Colman was instrumental in the development of the Long Wharf, had a history of trading with other Boston distillers, and owned a Boston rum distillery by 1726. John Colman to Thomas Amory, 28 August 1716, Liebmann collection of American historical documents relating to spirituous liquors, New York Public Library; John Colman to Benjamin Colman, 4 February 1726, Benjamin Colman Papers, Ms. N-1013/1/3, MHS; Henry Edes, "Note on John Colman," *Publications of the Colonial Society of Massachusetts, Volume VI: Transactions, 1899, 1900* (Boston, 1904), 87–90.

89. The outcome of the lawsuit remains unclear.

90. Walter Johnson, *Soul by Soul: Life Inside the Antebellum Slave Market* (Cambridge, MA: Harvard University Press, 1999), 125. Jared Ross Hardesty's interpretation of this particular event

tends to follow a similar logic, describing Quacqo as "an enslaved 'cooper' who could not make casks": Hardesty, *Unfreedom: Slavery and Dependence in Eighteenth-Century Boston* (New York: New York University Press, 2016), 108.

91. Roughly 19 percent of enslaved people advertised for sale in Massachusetts were tradesmen: Desrochers, "Slave-for-Sale Advertisements," 631, 637.

92. *Boston News-Letter*, 5 June 1704; *Boston Gazette*, 2 January 1738. For evidence of his wealth see John Coney, Monteith, ca. 1705, silver, New Haven, Yale University Art Gallery; "John Colman" and "Judith Hobbie Colman," ca. 1710–1720, oil on canvas, Smith College Museum of Art, Northampton, MA; Jacob Hurd, Salver, c. 1730, silver, Historic Deerfield, Deerfield, MA.

93. Sessional Papers of the Antigua Assembly, 21 August 1739, CO 9/12/205, TNA; Zachary Bayly Edwards to Bryan Edwards, 3 September 1780, Bayly v. Edwards, C 107/68, TNA.

94. The fact that Quacqo could make a fish barrel, even slowly, suggests that he had some experience coopering.

95. Other instances exist where enslaved people possibly feigned ineptitude to improve their circumstances: Desrochers, "Slave-for-Sale Advertisements," 638.

96. Complaints about slave sales in Massachusetts were more likely to revolve around legal status: Desrochers, "Slave-for-Sale Advertisements," 639.

97. Jared Ross Hardesty, "'The Negro at the Gate': Enslaved Labor in Eighteenth-Century Boston," *NEQ* 87:1 (2014): 72–98.

98. Elaine Forman Crane, *A Dependent People: Newport, Rhode Island, in the Revolutionary Era* (New York: Fordham University Press, 1985), 25–29.

99. Inventory of Thomas Child, 9 February 1753, Suffolk County Probate Court Docket Books, 47/431-5, MSA; Inventory of Andrew Johonnot, 4 July 1760, Suffolk County Probate Court Docket Books, 57/70, MSA. For other inventories of Boston distillers that claimed humans as property, see "Thomas Amory's Inventory Suffolk Probate Records Vol 23, page 165," c. 1728, Amory Family Papers, Ms. N-2024/148/25, MHS; Inventory of James Hughes, 15 October 1751, Suffolk County Probate Court Docket Books, 45/423-6, MSA.

100. 10 December 1761, 11 March 1762, 25 March 1762, and 24 February 1763, Chevalier Daybook, Amb.1937, HSP.

101. Richard Derby to Samuel Fisk receipt, 23 June 1763, Derby Family Papers, MSS 37/14/9, PEM; Receipt of Richard Derby to Joseph Grafton, 25 January 1763, Derby Family Papers, MSS 37/15/5, PEM.

102. Cornelius Harnett to William Wilkinson, 19 November 1777 and 20 November 1777, Cornelius Harnett Letters, 311-z, SHC.

103. *Boston Evening-Post*, 25 August 1735; *Boston Gazette*, 30 January 1750.

104. Hardesty, *Unfreedom*, 104–35.

105. Crane, *Dependent People*, 83.

106. "Edward Greene Indian at distill house," Arnold Family Papers, Laborer's Book #4, Commenced Jan 10 1791, p. 86, JCB.

107. On visibility in domestic roles, see Catherine Molineux, "Hogarth's Fashionable Slaves: Moral Corruption in Eighteenth-Century London," *ELH* 72:2 (2005): 497. For a survey of Black Britons—especially domestic laborers—prior to emancipation, see Gretchen Holbrook Gerzina, *Black London: Life Before Emancipation* (New Brunswick, NJ: Rutgers University Press, 1995), esp. 29–67. For a biographical account of one domestic servant, see Christine Eickelmann, "Within the Same Household: Fanny Coker," in *Britain's Black Past*, ed. Gretchen H. Gerzina (Liverpool: Liverpool University Press, 2020), 141–60.

108. Quoted in Kathleen Chater, "Black People in England, 1660–1807," *Parliamentary History* 26 (June 2007): 79; Michael Bundock, *The Fortunes of Francis Barber: The True Story of the Jamaican Slave Who Became Samuel Johnson's Heir* (New Haven: Yale University Press, 2015), 76–77.

109. *Public Ledger*, 10 May 1760.

110. *Daily Advertiser*, 29 March 1775. See also *Daily Courant*, 10 June 1720.

111. Simon P. Newman, "Freedom-Seeking Slaves in England and Scotland, 1700–1780," *English Historical Review* 134:570 (Oct. 2019): 1137.

112. *Daily Advertiser*, 24 March 1738.

113. *Williamson's Liverpool Advertiser*, 16 November 1764. See also *Caledonian Mercury*, 31 August 1756.

114. Stephen Mullen et al., "Black Runaways in Eighteenth-Century Britain," in Gerzina, *Britain's Black Past*, 84.

115. Mullen, "Black Runaways," 88–95.

116. Newman, *New World of Labor*, 148–49; Newman, "Freedom-Seeking Slaves," 1159.

117. *Daily Advertiser*, 20 April 1736.

118. Gerzina, *Black London*, 29–35.

119. *Public Advertiser*, 17 April 1771. See also *F. Farley's Bristol Journal*, 23 January 1762.

120. *Public Advertiser*, 20 December 1759; *Daily Advertiser*, 5 January 1744; *London Evening Post*, 23 July 1728.

121. Hopkins's experiences of distilling would have largely entailed working with grains and perhaps fruits, and his work was not tied up in the same transatlantic currents that defined the invention and production of rum in the two preceding centuries. Nonetheless, his testimony is the most direct statement of how an enslaved distiller thought about and experienced their work that my research has uncovered.

122. Deposition of John Hopkins, John Grayson v. ADMR of John Little, 1879-002/73–77, Montgomery County [VA] Chancery Records.

CHAPTER 5

1. S. Max Edelson, *The New Map of Empire: How Britain Imagined America Before Independence* (Cambridge, MA: Harvard University Press, 2017), 197–248; Murphy, *Creole Archipelago*, 87–89.

2. Richard H. Grove, *Green Imperialism: Colonial Expansion, Tropical Island Edens and the Origins of Environmentalism, 1600–1860* (Cambridge: Cambridge University Press, 1995), 264–308; Anderson, *Mahogany*, 98–103; Katherine Johnston, "Endangered Plantations: Environmental Change and Slavery in the British Caribbean, 1631–1807," *EAS* 18:3 (Summer 2020): 273–78.

3. "26 March 1764," in *Acts of the Privy Council of England, V.4: 1745–66*, ed. James Munro (London, 1911), 582–83; "Whereas by Our Commission," 24 April 1771, Papers of the Greg Family Relating to Estates in the West Indies, MSS. W. Ind. T. 2/29, Rhodes House, Oxford University.

4. "An Act to Appropriate for the Benefit of the Neighbourhood the Hill Called the King's Hill," 2 April 1791, in *Laws of St. Vincent* (London, 1884), 2.

5. "26 March 1764," in *Acts of the Privy Council*, 607; "An Act to lay a Tax on all Woodlands," 2 June 1772, *The Laws of the Colony of Dominica* (Roseau, 1818), XI.

6. Cary Helyar to William Helyar, 4 June 1672, Helyar Papers, DD/WHh/1090/3/22, SOM.

7. James Helyar to William Helyar, Helyar Papers, DD/WHh/1090/7/17, SOM; "A Generall List of Negroes Belonging to Bybrooke Plantation Began the 15 March 1687 [1688]," Helyar Papers, DD/WHh/1090/3/42, SOM; Dunn, *Sugar and Slaves*, 168, 213–23.

8. Ligon, *True & Exact History*, 24.

9. Dunn, *Sugar and Slaves*, 27–28; David Watts, *The West Indies: Patterns of Development, Culture and Environmental Change Since 1492* (Cambridge: Cambridge University Press, 1990), 186; John F. Richards, *The Unending Frontier: An Environmental History of the Early Modern World* (Berkeley: University of California Press, 2003), 421; Pluymers, *No Wood*, 161–80.

10. Watts, *West Indies*, 391; J. R. McNeill, *Mosquito Empires: Ecology and War in the Greater Caribbean, 1620–1914* (Cambridge: Cambridge University Press, 2010), 29.

11. Fatah-Black, "Paramaribo as Dutch and Atlantic Nodal Point," 58–59; Mary Draper, "Timbering and Turtling: The Maritime Hinterlands of Early Modern British Caribbean Cities," *EAS* 15:4 (Fall 2017): 782.

12. Robert Bruce to Ascanius William Senior, 1 May 1771, Nassau Senior Papers, E002, NLW; Robert Bruce to Ascanius William Senior, 24 July 1777, Nassau Senior Papers, E032, NLW.

13. Radburn and Roberts, "Gold Versus Life," 223–56.

14. Dovaston, "Agricultura Americana," Codex 60 ENG, 147, 183–84, JCB; Zachary Bayly Edwards to Bryan Edwards, 3 February 1799, Bayly v. Edwards, C 107/68, TNA.

15. Some also recommended burning coal. Shannon, *Practical Treatise*, 2:46.

16. "Journal of a Plantation from 28 Sept. 1756 to February 1 1757," Walter v. Evans, C 104/8/16, TNA.

17. Humphrey Grant to Roger Hope Elletson, 27 April 1770, Roger Hope Elletson Letters, ST 14/1, HL.

18. Island Estate 1780 Ledger, Barham Papers, MS Clar Dep b. 33/1, BOD.

19. Joseph Foster Barham to John Graham, 9 May 1790, Barham Papers, MS Clar Dep c.376/2, BOD.

20. *The Art of Making Sugar* (London, 1752), 6; William Beckford, *A Descriptive Account of the Island of Jamaica* (London, 1790), 2:20.

21. Ezekiel Dickinson to Dickinson and Salmon, 13 November 1782, Dickinson Family Papers, SOM, microfilm.

22. B. W. Higman, "The Spatial Economy of Jamaican Sugar Plantations: Cartographic Evidence from the Eighteenth and Nineteenth Centuries," *Journal of Historical Geography* 13:1 (Jan. 1987): 31.

23. Lyndsey Bates, "Surveillance and Production on Stewart Castle Estate: A GIS-Based Analysis of Models of Plantation Spatial Organization" (Master's thesis, University of Virginia, 2007); James A. Delle, *The Colonial Caribbean: Landscapes of Power in Jamaica's Plantation System* (Cambridge: Cambridge University Press, 2014), 99–106; Louis P. Nelson, *Architecture and Empire in Jamaica* (New Haven: Yale University Press, 2015), 127.

24. Douglas V. Armstrong, "Cave of Iron and Resistance: A Preliminary Examination," *JBMHS* 61 (2015): 178–99; Michael Sivapragasam, "After the Treaties: A Social, Economic and Demographic History of Maroon Society in Jamaica, 1739–1842," (PhD diss., University of Southampton, 2018), 32–33, 43–44, 116–17.

25. Thomas Trapham, *A Discourse of the State of Health in the Island of Jamaica* (London, 1679), 27–28.

26. John Gardner Kemeys, *Free and Candid Reflections Occasioned by the Late Additional Duties on Sugars and Rum* (London, 1783), 71.

27. John Graham to Joseph Foster Barham, 5 September 1794, Barham Papers, MS Clar Dep c. 357/2, BOD.

28. The letter reflects the prevailing view of the era that drunkenness was a personal failing of nonelite people who the author denigrated rather than a medical disorder: Thomas Barritt to Nathaniel Phillips, 5 January 1796, Slebech Estate Records, 11569, NLW.

29. 9 May 1777, "An Accompt of Negroes Work Done on the Plantation of John Mills esq. Nevis," Mills Papers, Vol. 4, MOL.

30. John Pool to the Dutchess of Chandos, 15 May 1780, Stowe-Brydges Papers, STB Box 26/38, HL; Anne Eliza Brydges to Poole & East, 10 November 1780, Stowe-Brydges Papers, STB Box 25/28, HL.

31. "Trial of Morgan's Newport," 9 November 1736, CO 9/10/55, TNA.

32. "Trial of Tom Hanson's Quashee," 24 November 1736, CO 9/10/66–67, TNA.

33. "Some Reasons Humbly Offer'd for Consideration for Stoping the further Execution of Slaves," 17 January 1737, CO 9/10/93–95, TNA.

34. Minutes of the Antigua Council, 25 May 1742, CO 9/12/14, TNA.

35. The cost of constructing a still house was estimated to be £1600—£200 more than the mill and £600 more than the boiling house: Bryan Edwards, *History, Civil and Commercial, of the British Colonies of the Americas* (London, 1793), 2:253.

36. John Joseph James Vernon to Justinian Casamajor, "Lease of plantation & slaves in Antigua," 26 January 1798, Francis Russell Hart Collection, Ms. N-189 OS 2, MHS.

37. Matthew Mulcahy, *Hurricanes and Society in the British Greater Caribbean, 1624–1783* (Baltimore: Johns Hopkins University Press, 2008), 125–26; Nelson, *Architecture and Empire*, 65–96.

38. Edward East to Duchess of Chandos, 29 September 1780, Stowe-Brydges Papers, STB Box 26/9, HL.

39. *Art of Making Sugar*, 31.

40. Martin, *Essay upon Plantership*, 44.

41. On insect damage see Joseph Herbert to William Stapleton, 24 June 1726, Ryland Stapleton MSS. 4.10., UMSC, transcription. On seasoning see "The Estates of Nathaniel Phillips in the Parish of St. Thomas in the East Jamaica to be Managed in the following manner by his attorneys Thomas Hibbert Thomas Barritt and Robert Logan," 1784, Slebech Estate Records, 8864, NLW.

42. Beckford, *Descriptive Account*, 2:26.

43. "A Fair Estimate of Samuel Martins Plantation in New Division in Antigua, according to the general rule of appraisement," 24 June 1768, Martin Family Papers, Add MS 41353/84, BL.

44. Caines, *Letters on the Cultivation*, 104–5.

45. Bybrook Account, 1696–7, Helyar Papers, DD/WHh/1089/2/23, SOM; "Lease of Three Houses Plantation, St. Philip, 30 March 1650," *JBHMS* 22 (1955):115–18; William Anderson Letter, 13 April 1809, Nisbet Family Papers, MS5466/57, NLS.

46. "Quantitys of the Several following Goods Produce of the said Island Exported as appears by the Custom House Books there," [c. 1748], Dickinson Family Papers, SOM, microfilm.

47. Long and Drake to Joseph Foster Barham, 17 August 1762, Barham Family Papers, MS. Clar Dep. C. 360/1/3, BOD.

48. Caines, *Letters on the Cultivation*, 205–8.

49. I include molasses in this calculation because of its centrality to the transatlantic history of rum. I estimate the size of an average stave at 48 inches long, 4.5 inches wide, and 1 inch thick. This computes to 1.5 board feet per stave. I have not accounted for the considerable waste from cutting and fitting staves together or staves discarded at their source for issues of quality.

50. Nathaniel Phillips to Hibert, Perrier & Horton, 1 January 1779, Slebech Estate Records, 11484/6, NLW.

51. Amory to Thomas Tooke, 22 September 1722, Amory Family Papers, MS. N-2024/137/70, MHS; *The Importance of the Sugar Colonies to Great-Britain Stated* (London, 1731), 9.

52. "Mr. Irving formerly Inspector General of the Imports and Exports of North America and Register of Shipping Called In," [c. 1783], Add MS 38345/136–151, BL.

53. Lemuel Roberts, *Memoirs of Lemuel Roberts, Containing Adventures in Youth, Vicissitudes Experienced as a Continental Soldier, His Sufferings as a Prisoner, and Escapes from Captivity, with Suitable Reflections on the Changes of Life* (Bennington, VT, 1809), 4–10.

54. Benjamin Franklin to Ezra Stiles, 29 May 1763, FO.

55. Stephen Hales, *Vegetable Staticks, or, An Account of Some Statical Experiments on the Sap in Vegetables* (London, 1727), 358.

56. Wood sellers in Philadelphia "lived at a great distance from the town" because wealthier landowners closely managed their timber reserves: Peter Kalm, *Travels into North America*, 2d ed., trans. John Reinhold Forster (London, 1748), 1:72–73.

57. William Cronon, *Changes in the Land: Indians, Colonists and the Ecology of New England* (New York: Hill and Wang, 1983); Strother E. Roberts, *Colonial Ecology, Atlantic Economy: Transforming Nature in Early New England* (Philadelphia: University of Pennsylvania Press, 2019), 97–125.

58. "An Act to Appropriate," in *Laws of St. Vincent*, 2.

59. Ezekiel Dickinson to Dickinson and Salmon, 13 November 1782, Dickinson Family Papers, SOM, microfilm. See also Grove, *Green Imperialism*, 272–73.

60. Letter to Matt and John Mills, 30 April 1752, Mills Papers, vol. 1, MOL. On drought's effect on British Caribbean societies, see Alexander Jorge Berland and Georgina Enfield, "Drought and Disaster in a Revolutionary Age: Colonial Antigua During the American Independence War," *Environment and History* 24:2 (May 2018): 209–35; Matthew Mulcahy, "'Miserably Scorched': Drought in the Plantation Colonies of the British Greater Caribbean," in *Atlantic Environments and the American South*, ed. Thomas Blake Earle and D. Andrew Johnson (Athens: University of Georgia Press, 2020), 65–89.

61. Letter to Edward Forbes, 25 May 1752, Mills Papers, vol. 1, MOL; Samuel Martin to Samuel Martin, 13 June 1775, Martin Family Papers, Add MS 41348/220, BL.

62. John Venn to Elletson, 26 August 1761, Stowe-Brydges Papers, STB Box 25/25, HL.

63. John Pool to the Duchess of Chandos, 15 May 1780, Stowe-Brydges Papers, STB Box 26/ 38, HL.

64. Samuel Martin to Samuel Martin, 16 June 1758, Martin Family Papers, Add MS 41346/210, BL; Samuel Martin to Samuel Martin, 24 February 1775, Martin Family Papers, Add MS 41348/210, BL.

65. Samuel Martin to Rev. Mr. Wharton, 21 June 1774, Martin Family Papers, Add MS 41351/4, BL; Samuel Martin to Samuel Martin, 13 June 1775, Martin Family Papers, Add MS 41348/220, BL.

66. Edward East to the Duchess of Chandos, 29 September 1780, Stowe-Brydges Papers, STB Box 26/9, HL; Nathaniel Phillips to Thomas Barritt & Robert Logan, 24 October 1784, Slebech Estate Records, 11484/71, NLW.

67. Samuel Martin to George Thomas, 1 June 1767, Martin Family Papers, Add MS 41350/47, BL.

68. Samuel Martin to Edward Otto Bayer, 22 August 1758, Martin Family Papers, Add MS 41349/59, BL; Josiah Martin to Barry Anderson, 30 November 1737, Martin Family Papers, Add MS 41352/137, BL.

69. "A Fair Estimate of Samuel Martins Plantation in New Division in Antigua, according to the general rule of appraisement," 24 June 1768, Martin Family Papers, Add MS 41353/84, BL; Edwards, *History, Civil and Commercial*, 2:249.

70. Peterkin, *Treatise on Planting*, 97.

71. Samuel Martin to Samuel Martin, 24 February 1775, Martin Family Papers, Add MS 41348/210, BL.

72. Benjamin Rush, *An Inquiry into the Various Sources of the Usual Forms of Summer and Autumnal Diseases in the United States* (Philadelphia, 1805); Kathleen M. Brown, *Foul Bodies: Cleanliness in Early America* (New Haven: Yale University Press, 2009), 10.

73. Belgrove, *Treatise upon Husbandry*, 15; Samuel Martin to Edward Otto Bayer, 22 August 1758, Martin Family Papers, Add MS 41349/59, BL; Littleton, *Groans of the Plantations*, 18.

74. McNeill, *Mosquito Empires*, 40–41.

75. McNeill, *Mosquito Empires*, 56.

76. Stuart B. Schwartz, *Sea of Storms: A History of Hurricanes in the Greater Caribbean from Columbus to Katrina* (Princeton: Princeton University Press, 2015), 41.

77. Robert Hall to William Helyar, 30 June 1701, Helyar Papers, DD/WHh/1090/3/4, SOM; "Thursday 27 [May 1779]," Journal of Somerset Vale Plantation overseer, Codex Eng 180/20, JCB.

78. James Cragge to James Chisholme, 30 July 1800, Nisbet Family Papers, MS 5465/60, NLS.

79. Hugh James to John Jackson, 28 October 1780, Douglas v. Harrison, C 110/141, TNA.

80. "State of the Buildings," 12 January 1781, Fitzherbert Papers—Turner's Hall Plantation, 20756, DRO, microfilm.

81. Benjamin Rush, *Medical Inquiries and Observations* (Philadelphia, 1789), 85–88; Simon Finger, *The Contagious City: The Politics of Health in Early Philadelphia* (Ithaca: Cornell University Press, 2012), 108.

82. "A Remonstrance and Petition from Divers Inhabitants of the City of Philadelphia," 24 January 1763, in *Votes and Proceedings of the House of Representatives of the Province of Pennsylvania* (Philadelphia, 1775), 5: 238–39.

83. Chevalier Daybook, Amb.1937, HSP; Chevalier Journals, 1770–1781, Am.936, HSP. McCusker estimates a larger average annual output of forty-one thousand gallons per North American distillery: McCusker, "Rum Trade," 434.

84. *Pennsylvania Gazette*, 10 March 1763.

85. *Pennsylvania Gazette*, 27 August 1783.

86. E. C. Wells et al., "Social and Environmental Impacts of British Colonial Rum Production at Betty's Hope Plantation, Antigua," in *Archaeologies of the British in Latin America*, ed. C. E. Orser (New York: Springer, 2019), 235–53.

87. G. J. Sheehan and P. F. Greenfield, "Utilisation, Treatment and Disposal of Distillery Wastewater," *Water Research* 14 (1980): 257–59.

88. "A Remonstrance and Petition from Divers Inhabitants of the City of Philadelphia," 24 January 1763, in *Votes and Proceedings*, 5: 238–39.

89. Mark Reinberger and Elizabeth McLean, *The Philadelphia Country House: Architecture and Landscape in Colonial America* (Baltimore: Johns Hopkins University Press, 2015), 75.

90. *Pennsylvania Gazette*, 28 February 1762 and 31 July 1766.

91. *Pennsylvania Gazette*, 5 November 1788.

92. *Independent Gazetteer*, 28 August 1790; *Pennsylvania Gazette*, 1 September 1790.

93. William Currie, *Memoirs of the Yellow Fever in Philadelphia* (Philadelphia, 1798), 23.

94. Jacquelyn C. Miller, "The Wages of Blackness: African American Workers and the Meanings of Race During Philadelphia's 1793 Yellow Fever Epidemic," *PMHB* 129:2 (Apr. 2005): 163–94.

95. Thomas Condie and Richard Folwell, *History of the Pestilence Commonly Called Yellow Fever* (Philadelphia, 1798), 85.

96. For a description of recently emancipated and indentured Philadelphians continuing to work in the industries in which they had been enslaved along the Philadelphia waterfront, see Gary B. Nash and Jean R. Soderlund, *Freedom by Degrees: Emancipation in Philadelphia and Its Aftermath* (New York: Oxford University Press, 1991), 167–70.

97. Philip R. P. Coelho and Robert A. McGuire, "African and European Bound Labor in the British New World: The Biological Consequences of Economic Choices," *JEH* 57:1 (Mar. 1997): 90.

98. Trevor Burnard, "'The Country Continues Sicklie': White Mortality in Jamaica, 1655–1780," *Social History of Medicine* 12:1 (Apr. 1999): 46; Burnard, *Mastery, Tyranny, and Desire*, 16; Brown, *Reaper's Garden*, 17.

99. Lowell Ragatz, *The Fall of the Planter Class in the British Caribbean, 1763–1833* (New York: Century, 1928), 3; Richard B. Sheridan, *Doctors and Slaves: A Medical and Demographic History of Slavery in the West Indies, 1680–1834* (Cambridge: Cambridge University Press, 1985), 187; B. W. Higman, *Plantation Jamaica, 1750–1850: Capital and Control in a Colonial Economy* (Mona: University Press of the West Indies, 2005), 17. Katherine Johnston has recently argued that "slavery's stakeholders developed and manipulated the climatic defense of slavery despite their experiences, not because of them": Johnston, *Nature of Slavery*, 4.

100. Thomas Tryon, *Friendly Advice to the Gentlemen-Planters of the East and West Indies* (London, 1684), 58–60.

101. Lucas Manuscript, Lucas MSS Misc. Notes 5/ 126, BPL.

102. Bell, *Inquiry into the Causes*, 18–21; "A List of Negroes Along the Drax Hall Estate," 1 January 1780, Beckford v. Aylesbury, C 107/143, TNA.

103. Trevor Burnard, "Passengers Only: The Extent and Significance of Absenteeism in Eighteenth-Century Jamaica," *Atlantic Studies* 1:2 (2006): 182–88.

104. David Hancock, *Citizens of the World: British Merchants and the Integration of the British Atlantic Community, 1735–1785* (Cambridge: Cambridge University Press, 1995), 279–82; S. D. Smith, *Slavery, Family, and Gentry Capitalism in the English Atlantic: The World of the Lascelles, 1648–1834* (Cambridge: Cambridge University Press, 2006), 226–59; Nelson, *Architecture and Empire*, 235–67.

105. John Campbell to John Campbell, 5 August 1793; John Campbell to John Campbell, 14 August 1797, both in Campbell Family Papers, BRBL, microfilm. For a description of Samuel Martin's similar conclusion about Antigua, see Katherine Johnston, "The Constitution of Empire: Place and Bodily Health in the Eighteenth-Century Atlantic," *Atlantic Studies* 10:4 (2013): 454–55.

106. James Robertson, *Gone Is the Ancient Glory: Spanish Town, Jamaica, 1534–2000* (Kingston: Ian Randle, 2005); Jack P. Greene, *Settler Jamaica in the 1750s: A Social Portrait* (Charlottesville: University of Virginia Press, 2016), 139–42.

107. The highest mortality rates for white settlers were in November and December, while the highest rates for the enslaved were October through January: Burnard, "'Country Continues Sicklie,'" 57; Roberts, *Slavery and the Enlightenment*, 175–77.

108. Johnston, "Constitution of Empire," 447.

109. S. D. Smith, "Paying the Levy: Taxable Wealth in Bridgetown, Barbados, 1680–1715," *History of the Family* 12 (2007): 116–29; Murphy, *Creole Archipelago*, 95–102.

110. Lowcountry planters also sought refuge in their town houses during peak disease times: Peter McCandless, *Slavery, Disease, and Suffering in the Southern Lowcountry* (Cambridge: Cambridge University Press, 2011), 261–65.

111. Martin, *Essay upon Plantership*, ix–xvi.

112. Belgrove, *Treatise upon Husbandry*, 56–58.

113. N. A. T. Hall, "Some Aspects of the 'Deficiency' Question in Jamaica in the Eighteenth Century," *Caribbean Studies* 15:1 (Apr. 1975): 5–19; Livesay, *Children of Uncertain Fortune*, 26–28; Murphy, *Creole Archipelago*, 94–95.

114. Samuel Martin to Samuel Martin, 31 January 1774, Martin Family Papers, Add MS 41348/157, BL.

115. J. Shand Letter, 21 March 1802, "In Chancery; Chambers & Others vs. Goldwin & others," C 112/163, TNA.

116. Edwards, *History, Civil and Commercial*, 2:7.

117. Charles Rowe to Joseph Foster Barham, 20 January 1790, Barham Papers, MS Clar Dep c. 357/2, BOD; Henry Plummer to Joseph Foster Barham, 23 September 1799, Barham Papers, MS Clar Dep c. 357/2, BOD. See also William Dickson, *Letters on Slavery* (London, 1789), 42.

118. Edward East to Duchess of Chandos, 10 April 1781, Stowe-Brydges Papers, STB Box 26/11, HL.

119. Burnard, "Passengers Only," 189.

CHAPTER 6

1. Thomas Robison to Robert Ilsley, 20 June 1805, Robison Family Papers, Coll. #5/3/10, MEHS.

2. "Advertisement of sale of lots," c. 1800, Robison Family Papers, Coll. #5/3/7, MEHS; Thomas Robison to Foltz & Lorenz, 1 December 1785, Robison Family Papers, Coll. #5/1/12, MEHS; Description of Robison property, c. 1805, Robison Family Papers, Coll. #5/3/10, MEHS.

3. Thomas Robison to Phyn, Ellices & Inglis, 24 May 1790, Robison Family Papers, Coll. #5/2/5, MEHS.

4. Shipping Receipt for the Eagle, 14 August 1790, Robison Family Papers, Coll. #5/7/5, MEHS; Robison to James Constable, 29 January 1791, Robison Family Papers, Coll. #5/2/6, MEHS.

5. William Willis, *The History of Portland from 1632 to 1864* (Portland, 1865), 636n2.

6. Venture Smith, *A Narrative of the Life and Adventures of Venture, a Native of Africa* (New London, 1798), 13.

7. John J. McCusker and Russell R. Menard, eds., *The Economy of British America, 1607–1789* (Chapel Hill: University of North Carolina Press for the OI, 1985), 291. Here I count "British voyages" as including those organized in current or former colonies: "Trans-Atlantic Slave Trade Database," SlaveVoyages.org, https://www.slavevoyages.org/voyages/soZ1Zn3o.

8. Coughtry, *Notorious Triangle*, 5–8; Randy J. Sparks, *Where the Negroes Are Masters: An African Port in the Era of the Slave Trade* (Cambridge, MA: Harvard University Press, 2014), 163–85; Sean M. Kelley, "American Rum, African Consumers, and the Transatlantic Slave Trade," *African Economic History* 46:2 (2018): 3–4; Kelley, *American Slavers: Merchants, Mariners, and the Transatlantic Commerce in Captives, 1644–1865* (New Haven: Yale University Press, 2023). For an influential argument downplaying the significance of the triangular trade to which these scholars respond, see Gilman M. Ostrander, "The Making of the Triangular Trade Myth," *WMQ* 30:4 (Oct. 1973): 635–44.

9. Benezet, *Mighty Destroyer*, 12.

10. Fernando Ortiz, *Cuban Counterpoint: Tobacco and Sugar*, trans. Harriet de Onís (Durham, NC: Duke University Press, 1995), 25; Williams, *Capitalism and Slavery*, 61. The central conclusions of this chapter nonetheless align with Williams's larger point that British and colonial industry expanded and modernized in order to supply the transatlantic slave trade.

11. John Thornton, *Africa and Africans in the Making of the Atlantic World, 1400–1800*, 2d ed. (Cambridge: Cambridge University Press, 1998), 43–71; David Eltis, *The Rise of African Slavery in the Americas* (Cambridge: Cambridge University Press, 2000), 164–92; Rebecca Shumway, *The Fante and the Transatlantic Slave Trade* (Rochester: University of Rochester Press, 2011), 87; David Northrup, *Africa's Discovery of Europe, 1450–1850*, 3d ed. (Oxford: Oxford University Press, 2014), 55–61, 83–110; Robert S. DuPlessis, *The Material Atlantic: Clothing, Commerce, and Colonization in the Atlantic World, 1650–1800* (Cambridge: Cambridge University Press, 2016), 59–69.

12. McCusker, "Rum Trade," 474–75, 481–82.

13. Coughtry, *Notorious Triangle*, 82–83.

14. George Metcalf, "A Microcosm of Why Africans Sold Slaves: Akan Consumption Patterns in the 1770s," *Journal of African History* 28:3 (1987): 380; Kelley, "American Rum," 10–11, 17.

15. Herbert S. Klein, *The Atlantic Slave Trade* (Cambridge: Cambridge University Press, 1999), 75–80.

16. Eltis, *Rise of African Slavery*, 300–1.

17. "Wilhelm Johann Müller's Description of the Fetu Country, 1662–9," in *German Sources for West African History 1599–1669*, ed. Adam Jones (Wiesbaden: Steiner, 1983), 213.

18. "A Journall going up the river Gambia & return from the 18th March incl. anno 1660, untill the 2nd of June incl. anno 1661," "Royal African Company, Misc. Papers," Stowe Papers, ST 9/16, HL.

19. Edwyn Stede and Stepehn Gascoigne to Royal African Company, 26 March 1683, T 70/16/49, TNA. Some Akan speakers continued to prefer brandy over rum: Lila O'Leary Chambers, "Alcohol Diplomacy, Gender and Power in the Late Seventeenth-Century Gold Coast Slaving Complex," *PP* 264:1 (2024): 17.

20. John Barbot, *A Description of the Coasts of North and South-Guinea, and of Ethiopia Inferior, Vulgarly Angola* (London, 1732), 172.

21. Eltis, *Rise of African Slavery*, 301.

22. Francis Moore, *Travels into the Inland Parts of Africa* (London, 1738), 109; "A Scheme of Trade," 7 March 1707, T 70/22/15, TNA.

23. Jean-Baptiste Gaby, *Relation de la Nigritie* (Paris, 1689), 26.

24. Moore, *Travels*, 126.

25. *Travels in Africa, Performed by Silvester Meinrad Xavier Golberry, in the Western Parts of That Vast Continent*, 2d ed. (London, 1808), 2:215.

26. "Müller's Description of the Fetu Country," 213.

27. Barbot, *Description of the Coasts*, 274.

28. Akyeampong, *Drink, Power, and Cultural Change*, 22, 28–30; Emmanuel Kwaku Akyeampong and Samuel A. Ntewusu, "Rum, Gin and Maize: Deities and Ritual Change in the Gold Coast During the Atlantic Era," *Afrique* 5 (2014).

29. "Voyage of the Hannibal, 1693–1694," in *Documents Illustrative of the History of the Slave Trade to America*, ed. Elizabeth Donnan (New York: Octagon, 1969), 1:392–93.

30. "Observations on the Trade to Africa and Angola by the Reverend Mr. Gordon," [1714], Stowe Papers, ST 9/48–51, HL.

31. "The Royal African Company: Committee Report on the State of the Trade," in Donnan, *Documents Illustrative*, 2:250–53.

32. Barbot, *Description of the Coasts*, 433.

33. William Johnson to Royal African Company, 20 March 1718, T 70/26/63, TNA; "Committee Report on the State of Trade," 23 February 1721, T 70/123/9–14, TNA; Coughtry, *Notorious Triangle*, 109.

34. Ludewig Ferdinand Rømer, *A Reliable Account of the Coast of Guinea*, trans. Selena Axelrod Winsnes (Oxford: Oxford University Press for the British Academy, 2000), 160.

35. "Remonstrance of the Colony of Rhode Island to the Lords Commissioners of Trade and Plantations," 24 January 1764, *Records of the Colony of Rhode Island and Providence Plantations, in New England: 1757–1769*, ed. John Russell Bartlett (Providence, 1861), 6:378–83.

36. Coughtry, *Notorious Triangle*, 110–11.

37. Kelley, *American Slavers*, 86–87.

38. John Cahoone Jr. to Stephen Ayrault, 27 October 1736, in Donnan, *Documents Illustrative*, 3:130–31.

39. Eck, "Spirits of Massachusetts," 47–56.

40. *Boston News-Letter*, 7 August 1704.

41. Archibald Cumings to John Cokburne, 2 March 1717, *CSP Volume 29, 1716–1717*, ed. Cecil Headlam (London, 1930), 267.

42. Between 1720 and 1730, the number of active distillers in Boston grew from twenty-five to forty: Eck, "Spirits of Massachusetts," 76.

43. "Preface," Amory Family Papers, Ms. N-2024/137, MHS.

44. It is unclear whether this "still" was for turpentine or rum: Thomas Amory to Edward Moseley, 18 October 1722, Amory Family Papers, Ms. N-2024/137/71, MHS.

45. Thomas Amory to William Jones, 27 January 1725, Amory Family Papers, Ms. N-2024/137/81, MHS; Thomas Amory to William Jones, 21 September 1727, Amory Family Papers, Ms. N-2024/137/94, MHS.

46. Thomas Amory to William Jones, 27 January 1725, Amory Family Papers, Ms. N-2024/137/81, MHS.

47. Amory to Nicholas Oursell, 16 July 1726, Amory Family Papers, Ms. N-2024/137/87, MHS.

48. Amory to Edward Moseley, 9 April 1722, Amory Family Papers, Ms. N-2024/137/64, MHS; Amory to Mosely, 13 January 1726, Amory Family Papers, Ms. N-2024/137/84, MHS.

49. Amory to Samuel Baker, 17 June 1722, Amory Family Papers, Ms. N-2024/137/72, MHS.

50. Amory to George Bennington, 25 January 1725, Amory Family Papers, Ms. N-2024/137/80, MHS; *Boston News-Letter*, 7 January 1725 and 18 October 1725.

51. Thomas Amory to William Rhett, 8 July 1719, Amory Family Papers, Ms. N-2024/137/34, MHS; Thomas Amory to Joseph Bachelder & co., 12 December 1719, Amory Family Papers, Ms. N-2024/137/37, MHS.

52. Thomas Amory to William Rhett, 8 July 1719, Amory Family Papers, Ms. N-2024/137/34, MHS.

53. Thomas Amory to Edward Moseley, 23 March 1724, Amory Family Papers, Ms. N-2024/137/75, MHS.

54. Amory to Nicholas Oursell, 16 July 1726, Amory Family Papers, Ms. N-2024/137/87, MHS.

55. Deposition of Joseph Knowlton, 27 March 1729, Malbone Family Collection, MSS 549, RIHS. The captain of that first voyage, George Scott, opened his own distillery by 1741: Kenneth Scott, "George Scott, Slave Trader of Newport," *American Neptune* 12 (1952): 225.

56. Godfrey Malbone Sr. Account Book, 1728–1738, Malbone Family Collection, MSS 549, RIHS.

57. Invoice of the Sloop Diamond, 20 April 1738(?), Godfrey Malbone Sr. Account Book, 1728–1738, Malbone Family Collection, MSS 549, RIHS.

58. *New-York Weekly Journal*, 19 June 1738.

59. John Holroyd, *Observations on the Commerce of the American States with Europe and the West Indies* (Philadelphia, 1783), 24.

60. McCusker, "Rum Trade," 474–75, 481–82.

61. "Remonstrance of the Colony of Rhode Island," 24 January 1764, *Records of the Colony of Rhode Island*, 6:378–83.

62. For sales of wood to distilleries, see Nathaniel Holmes to Barth. Gedney, 18 September 1752, Melatiah Bourne Records, 733 1727–1803 B 775/10, HBS; Isaac Osgood Daybook, 1770–1776, Isaac Osgood Account Books, MSS 1285.1, PEM. For hired craftsmen and distillery maintenance, see Joseph Mackintyer Account, Miles Ward Ledger, 1767–1768, Ward Family Papers, MSS 46/50, PEM. For boatbuilding to facilitate the trade of rum in West Africa, see "Voyage for Timothy Fitch by Peter Gwinn," 8 November 1760, Slave Trade Letters, A (5), MED.

63. David Richardson, "West African Consumption Patterns and Their Influence on the Eighteenth-Century English Trade," in *The Uncommon Market: Essays in the Economic History of the Atlantic Slave Trade*, ed. Henry A. Gemery and Jan S. Hogendorn (New York: Academic, 1979), 325–26. The New England advantage was likely smaller than previously calculated: Kelley, "American Rum," 4–6.

64. Kelley, *American Slavers*, 419n5.

65. "Memorial of agent of Massachusetts Bay, Mr. [Joseph] Maudinit, abt. Duties on molasses," 27 February 1764, T 1/430/228–9, TNA.

66. "Remonstrance of the Colony of Rhode Island," 24 January 1764, *Records of the Colony of Rhode Island*, 6:378–83.

67. Edward Ireland to William Fitzherbert, 11 March 1785, Fitzherbert Papers—Turner's Hall Plantation, E20547, DRO, microfilm.

68. *Pennsylvania Gazette*, 2 November 1769.

69. William Fisher to Benjamin Williams, 28 June 1752, William Fisher Letterbook, Am. 06775, HSP; December 1772, Accounts of Sales, 1771–8, Heard Family Business Records, MSS 766 1754–1898/AB-2, HBS; Benjamin Backus receipt, 4 July 1776, Andrew Huntington Papers, MS 77743/2/13, CHS.

70. Ryberg & Co. to Brown Benson & Ives, 9 October 1792, Brown Family Business Records, BFBR 301/4, JCB.

71. Brown Benson & Ives to Ryberg & Co., 27 February 1793, Brown Family Business Records, BFBR 301/4, JCB.

72. Josiah Smith Jr. to John Smith Jr., Josiah Smith Lettercopy book, 3018/141–143, SHC.

73. *Now in the Press, and Next Week Will Be Published, for the Benefit of My Fellow Citizens and Their Posterity* (Philadelphia, 1771).

74. Charles Thomson Memorandum Book, 1754–1774, Gratz Case 14/30/3, LCP; Henry McCulloh Letter, 30 January 1766, Fanning and McCulloh Papers, 252-z, SHC.

75. Cooper, *Complete Distiller*, 104.

76. Robison to George Salmon, 20 January 1789, Robison Family Papers, Coll. #5, Vol. 3, MEHS.

77. Robert Jenkins to Thomas Robison, 8 July 1789, Robison Family Papers, Coll. #5/2/3, MEHS.

78. Thomas Robison to Phyn Ellice & Inglis, 14 July 1790, Thomas Robison Papers, Coll. 928/1/4, MEHS; Thomas Robison to Haffey & Co., 44 June 1791, Robison Family Papers, Coll. #5/2/7, MEHS.

79. Shipping Receipt for the *Eagle*, 14 August 1790, Robison Family Papers, MEHS, Coll. #5/7/5.

80. Robison to James Constable, 29 January 1791, Robison Family Papers, Coll. #5/2/6, MEHS.

81. George Bollard to Thomas Robison, 8 July 1791, Robison Family Papers, Coll. #5/2/7, MEHS.

82. Thomas Hodges, "Copy of Instructions to Capt. Henry Skinner Master of the Ship Eagle," 10 February 1791, Robison Family Papers, Coll. #5/2/7, MEHS.

83. Thomas Reed to Thomas Robison, 24 July 1791, Robison Family Papers, Coll. #5/2/7, MEHS; "Various documents pertaining to sale of slaves in Havana," 1791, Robison Family Papers, Coll. #5/2/7, MEHS.

84. Robison to Edgar, 24 March 1792, Robison Family Papers, Coll. #5/2/8, MEHS.

85. Janet Schaw, *Journal of a Lady of Quality*, ed. Evangeline Walker Andrews (New Haven, 1921), 153; Samuel Graves to Philip Stephens, 22 September 1775, ADM 1/485/357–38, TNA.

86. Samuel Thomas Smith to Nathaniel Holmes, 26 November 1754, Bourne Family Papers, MS Am 579/7/32, HOUGH.

87. John Boylston to P. P. Livingston, 24 September 1773, John Boylston Letterbook, 1768–1789, Boylston Family Papers, Ms. N-4/68, MHS.

88. Daniel Tillinghast to Aaron Lopez, 21 June 1770, in *Commerce of Rhode Island, 1726–1800* (Boston, 1914), 1:334.

89. The rum in question was likely sold on the Isle of Man and quite possibly destined for West Africa. Jeremiah Osborne to Aaron Lopez, 1 April 1768, *Commerce of Rhode Island*, 1:235.

90. Brown & Benson to Hazard & Robinson, 10 September 1790, Brown Family Business Records, BFBR 168/3, JCB. See also Stearns, *American Herbal*, 283.

91. 14 March 1796, 4 May 1796, and 19 May 1796, in Journal of the Slave Ship Mary, GTM-170907, GUSC.

92. *Boston Gazette*, 1 November 1725; Melvil to African Committee, 26 December 1751, T 70/29/9, TNA.

93. "Invoice of the Cargo of the Success, 1749," in Donnan, *Documents Illustrative*, 3:143.

94. Coughtry, *Notorious Triangle*, 85.

95. "Bill of Lading of the *Whydah*, 1762," in Donnan, *Documents Illustrative*, 3:188.

96. Shoolbread letter, 29 September 1778, T 70/1483/80, TNA.

97. Timothy Fitch to William Ellery, 14 January 1759, Slave Trade Letters, A (6), MED.

98. Daniel Tillinghast to Aaron Lopez, 21 June 1770, in *Commerce of Rhode Island*, 1:334.

99. Rømer, *Reliable Account*, 195–235.

100. Mill to African Company Committee, 12 March 1772, T 70/31/419, TNA.

101. Rømer, *Reliable Account*, 56, 58.

102. Rømer, *Reliable Account*, 235. See also Mungo Park, *Travels in the Interior Districts of Africa* (London, 1799), 27.

103. "19 June 1750," in Darold D. Wax, "A Philadelphia Surgeon on a Slaving Voyage to Africa, 1749–1751," *PMHB* 92:4 (Oct. 1968): 483.

104. Willem Bosman, *A New and Accurate Description of the Coast of Guinea, Divided into the Gold, the Slave, and the Ivory Coasts* (London, 1705), 404.

105. John Newton, *Thoughts upon the African Slave Trade* (London, 1788), 10–11.

106. Rømer, *Reliable Account*, 142.

107. Barbot, *Description of the Coasts*, 274.

108. Ashley to Montgomery & Co., 3 June 1793, in *Proceedings of the Massachusetts Historical Society* 44 (1910–1911): 668.

109. Quoted in Coughtry, *Notorious Triangle*, 86.

110. Price to Africa Co. Committee, 16 March 1787, T 70/33/143–51, TNA; Miles to Shoolbread, 10 August 1775, T 70/1482/44, TNA; Skinner to Africa Co. Committee, 28 March 1755, T 70/1523, TNA.

111. Letter from Thomas Rogers, 5 September 1764, NYHS Slavery Collection, nyhs_sc_b-01_f-11_r11.

112. 18 January 1750, in *Journal of the Commissioners for Trade and Plantations from January 1749/50 to December 1753, Preserved in the Public Records Office* (Burlington, Ontario: TannerRitchie, 2010; repr. of 1932), 32; Peleg Clarke to John Fletcher, 6 July 1776, in Donnan, *Documents Illustrative*, 3:319.

113. Reuben Harvey to Christopher Champlin, 18 February 1784, in *Commerce of Rhode Island*, 2:194.

114. "The Memorial of David Barclay & Sons of London on Behalf of Miller & Boulton of the Island of Antigua," 22 April 1765, T 1/451/450, TNA; *Georgia Gazette*, 23 May 1765; Frances Wilkins, *Manx Slave Traders: A Social History of the Isle of Man's Involvement in the Atlantic Slave Trade* (Kidderminster, UK: Wyre Forest, 1999), 41–45.

115. Kelley, "American Rum," 22.

116. "News Items Relating to Slave Trade," in Donnan, *Documents Illustrative*, 3:186–87.

117. John Duncan to Samuel and William Vernon, 21 August 1770, NYHS Slavery Collection, nyhs_sc_b-01_f-04_d15.

118. Samuel Rhodes to Samuel Waldo, 26 August 1737, in Donnan, *Documents Illustrative*, 3:47.

119. Stephanie E. Smallwood, *Saltwater Slavery: A Middle Passage from Africa to American Diaspora* (Cambridge, MA: Harvard University Press, 2007), 33–64.

120. Timothy Fitch to Peter Gwinn, 12 January 1760, Slave Trade Letters, P:11, MED.

121. "12 September 1750," in Wax, "Philadelphia Surgeon," 479.

122. Nicholas Brown to Joseph, John, and Moses Brown, 12 September 1764, in Donnan, *Documents Illustrative*, 3:207.

123. Sarah Deutsch, "Elusive Guineamen: Newport Slavers, 1735–1774," *NEQ* 55 (June 1982): 253.

124. Kelley, "American Rum," 10–18.

125. John Fletcher to Peleg Clarke, 30 April 1774, in Donnan, *Documents Illustrative*, 3:288–89.

126. Timothy Fitch to Peter Gwinn, 27 November 1769, Slave Trade Letters, P:13, MED.

127. John Duncan to Samuel and William Vernon, 28 June 1770, NYHS Slavery Collection, nyhs_sc_b-01_f-04_d17; Metcalf, "Microcosm," 385–86.

128. Peleg Clarke to John Fletcher, 6 July 1776, in Donnan, *Documents Illustrative*, 3:318–19.

129. John Bell to John Fletcher, 15 December 1776, in Donnan, *Documents Illustrative*, 3:324.

130. Quoted in Coughtry, *Notorious Triangle*, 114.

131. Miles to Shoolbread, 21 August 1778, T 70/1483/74, TNA.

132. Phyn & Ellice to Robison, 11 June 1784, Robison Family Papers, Coll. #5/1/4, MEHS.

133. Quoted in Ty M. Reese, "'Eating' Luxury: Fante Middlemen, British Goods, and Changing Dependencies on the Gold Coast, 1750–1821," *WMQ* 66:4 (Oct. 2009): 867; Coughtry, *Notorious Triangle*, 115–18.

134. "Memoirs of the Life of Florence Hall," [c. 1810], Powel Family Papers, 1582/46/9, HSP.

135. Metcalf, "Microcosm," 378–82.

136. Gerard Gore, James Phipps, and Robert Blean to the Royal African Company, 23 March 1715, in Donnan, *Documents Illustrative*, 2:193.

137. Metcalf, "Microcosm," 385–86.

138. William Moore Jr. to Aaron Lopez and Company, 7 November 1774, in Donnan, *Documents Illustrative*, 3:295.

139. *Report of the Lords of the Committee of Council Appointed for the Consideration of All Matters Relating to Trade and Foreign Plantations* (London: House of Lords, 1789).

140. Thomas Taylor to Vernon and Readwoods, 4 September 1756, NYHS Slavery Collection, nyhs_sc_b-01_f-13_t08. See also "25 March 1796," in Journal of the Slave Ship Mary, GTM-170907, GUSC.

141. Deposition of William Raymond, 25 September 1776, Boylston Family Papers, Ms. N-4, box 7, MHS.

142. "4 May 1796," in Journal of the Slave Ship Mary, GTM-170907, GUSC.

143. Equiano, *Interesting Narrative*, 72.

144. William Smith, *A New Voyage to Guinea* (London, 1744), 112.

145. John Atkins, *A Voyage to Guinea, Brasil, and the West-Indies* (London, 1737), 171.

146. For one unsuccessful attempt to reduce dashees that ended with an English governor choosing to "stop their mouths" with rum and tobacco, see Sparks, *Where the Negroes Are Masters*, 65. For an examination of how European traders presented the African use of intoxicants as "disorderly" and uncivil, see Chambers, "Alcohol Diplomacy," 1–37.

147. Nicholas Owen, *Journal of a Slave-Dealer: "A View of Some Remarkable Axcedents in the Life of Nics. Owen on the Coast of Africa and America from the Year 1746 to the Year 1757,"* ed. Eveline Martin (London, 1930), 52.

148. Moore, *Travels*, 254; *Journal of James Watt: Expedition to Timbo, Capital of the Fula Empire in 1794*, ed. Bruce L. Mouser (Madison: University of Wisconsin Press, 1994), 4, 68.

149. "Report of House of Commons Committee regarding trade with African forts," 1753–56, T 70/176/17, TNA.

150. Thomas Melvil to Company of Merchants Trading to Africa, 26 August 1751, CO 388/45/151, TNA.

151. "21 July 1750," in Wax, "Philadelphia Surgeon," 475.

152. Rømer, *Reliable Account*, 56, 58.

153. "Report of House of Commons Committee regarding trade with African forts," 1753–56, T 70/176/15, TNA. See also "Diaries regarding the trade of the Royal African Company in Ghana and Benin," T 70/1466, TNA.

154. "22 February 1777," in *Journal of the Commissioners for Trade and Plantations from January 1776 to May 1782* (London, 1938), 132.

155. Reese, "'Eating' Luxury," 861–62.

156. Kelley, "American Rum," 14.

157. Owen, *Journal of a Slave-Dealer*, 56.

158. Thomas Winterbottom, *An Account of the Native Africans in the Neighbourhood of Sierra Leone* (1803), 103–4.

159. "Voyage of the Hannibal," in Donnan, *Documents Illustrative*, 1:398; Thompson, "Drax's Instructions," 585; James Grainger, *The Sugar Cane: A Poem* (London, 1764), 128; Simon P. Newman et al., "The West African Ethnicity of the Enslaved in Jamaica," *SA* 34:3 (2013): 376–400.

160. James B. Hedges, *The Browns of Providence Plantations: Colonial Years* (Cambridge, MA: Harvard University Press, 1952). On the China trade and US development as a capitalist nation, see Dael Norwood, *Trading Freedom: How Trade with China Defined Early America* (Chicago: University of Chicago Press, 2022). On South American trade, see Rood, *Reinvention of Atlantic Slavery*. On artificial light, see Zallen, *American Lucifers*. On iron, see Robert Martello, *Midnight Ride, Industrial Dawn: Paul Revere and the Growth of American Enterprise* (Baltimore: Johns Hopkins University Press, 2010).

CHAPTER 7

Epigraph: *Songs of the Late Charles Dibdin*, ed. T. Dibdin (London, 1850), 32–34.

1. *Charles Dibdin and Late Georgian Culture*, ed. Oskar Cox Jensen et al. (Oxford: Oxford University Press, 2018).

2. In 1797, £4.58 million of state expenditures totaling £46 million went to the navy's Victualling Board: Roger Morriss, *The Foundations of British Maritime Ascendancy: Resources, Logistics and the State, 1755–1815* (Cambridge: Cambridge University Press, 2011), 102–3.

3. Rum was taxed as a foreign spirit: Patrick K. O'Brien, "The Political Economy of British Taxation, 1660–1815," *EHR* 41:1 (Feb. 1988): 11.

4. Peter Mathias and Patrick O'Brien, "Taxation in Britain and France, 1715–1810: A Comparison of the Social and Economic Incidence of Taxes Collected for the Central Government," *Journal of European Economic History* 5:3 (Winter 1976): 618–19.

5. Christopher Codrington to the Lord President, 12 September 1691, in *CSP Volume 13, 1689–1692*, ed. J. W. Fortescue (London, 1901), 527–42.

6. John Brewer, *The Sinews of Power: War, Money and the English State, 1688–1783* (Cambridge, MA: Harvard University Press, 1988).

7. Siân Williams, "The Royal Navy and Caribbean Colonial Society During the Eighteenth Century," in *The Royal Navy and the British Atlantic World, c. 1750–1820*, ed. John McAleer and Christer Petley (London: Palgrave Macmillan, 2016), 31.

8. Edward Long, *The History of Jamaica* (London, 1774), 2:308.

9. Andrew Jackson O'Shaughnessy, *An Empire Divided: The American Revolution and the British Caribbean* (Philadelphia: University of Pennsylvania Press, 2000), 170.

10. O'Shaughnessy, *Empire Divided*, 49.

11. Morriss, *Foundations of British Maritime Ascendancy*, 37; O'Shaughnessy, *Empire Divided*, 208.

12. Long, *History of Jamaica*, 2:309–10. For another plantation owner's plea for a robust military presence in the Caribbean, see [Samuel Martin], *A Plan for Establishing and Disciplining a National Militia in Great Britain, Ireland, and in All the British Dominions of America* (London, 1745), 77–78.

13. Trevor Burnard and Aaron Graham, "Security, Taxation, and the Imperial System in Jamaica, 1721–1782," *EAS* 18:4 (Fall 2020): 468.

14. James Knight, *The Natural, Moral, and Political History of Jamaica, and the Territories Thereon Depending (1746)*, ed. Jack P. Greene (Charlottesville: University of Virginia Press, 2021), 522–23, 640–41.

15. Jason T. Sharples, *The World That Fear Made: Slave Revolts and Conspiracy Scares in Early America* (Philadelphia: University of Pennsylvania Press, 2020), 91–92.

16. Knight, *Natural, Moral, and Political History*, 340, 420–21; Lord Rodney to Philip Stephens, 24 September 1774, in *The Life and Correspondence of the Late Admiral Lord Rodney*, ed. Godfrey Mundy (London, 1830), 144; Duncan Crewe, *Yellow Jack and the Worm: British Naval Administration in the West Indies, 1739–1748* (Liverpool: Liverpool University Press, 1993), 8, 220.

17. Murphy, *Creole Archipelago*, 159–66.

18. Neville A. T. Hall, "Governors and Generals: The Relationship of Civil and Military Commands in Barbados, 1783–1815," *Caribbean Studies* 10:4 (Jan. 1971): 93–112; S. H. H. Carrington, "West Indian Opposition to British Policy: Barbadian Politics, 1774–82," *Journal of Caribbean History* 17 (Nov. 1982): 26–49.

19. John L. Bullion, *A Great and Necessary Measure: George Grenville and the Genesis of the Stamp Act, 1763–1765* (Columbia: University of Missouri Press, 1982), 76.

20. David Syrett, "The Organization of British Trade Convoys During the American War, 1775–1783," *Mariner's Mirror* 62:2 (1976): 169–81.

21. Vice Admiral Vernon to the Custos of the Parish of Westmorland, Jamaica, 29 May 1742, in *The Vernon Papers*, ed. B. Mcl. Ranft (Navy Records Society, 1958), 430.

22. Syrett, "Organization of British Trade Convoys," 175–76.

23. Horatio Nelson to William Locker, 15 June 1785; "Captain Nelson's Narrative of His Proceedings in Support of the Navigation Act for the Suppression of Illicit Traffic in the West Indies," June 1786; Horatio Nelson to Reverend Nelson, 9 February 1787, all in *The Dispatches and Letters of Vice Admiral Lord Viscount Nelson*, ed. Nicholas Harris Nicolas (London, 1845), 1:113–14, 171–86 (at 173), at 213–14; N. A. M. Rodger, *The Command of the Ocean: A Naval History of Britain, 1649–1815* (New York: Norton, 2004), 360.

24. James Pack, *Nelson's Blood: The Story of Naval Rum* (Annapolis: Naval Institute Press, 1982), 15–21.

25. Sir Charles Wager to Vernon, 10 June 1740; Lord Cathcart to Vernon, 22 June 1740, both in *Vernon Papers*, 109, 111.

26. Crewe, *Yellow Jack and the Worm*, 52.

27. "Order to Captains," 4 August 1740, *Vernon Papers*, 417.

28. "Order to Captains," 21 August 1740, *Vernon Papers*, 417–18. For a contemporary argument that "a dram is more pernicious than punch," see Minutes of the Antigua Assembly, 25 June 1740, CO 9/12/266, TNA.

29. Rodger, *Command of the Ocean*, 291.

30. Coll. Codrington to the Lords Commissioners, 30 July 1702, CO 153/7/507, TNA; Daniel A. Baugh, *British Naval Administration in the Age of Walpole* (Princeton: Princeton University Press, 1965), 428–30.

31. Rodger, *Command of the Ocean*, 161.

32. William Spavens, *The Seaman's Narrative* (Louth, 1796), 19.

33. Baugh, *British Naval Administration*, 398.

34. Crewe, *Yellow Jack and the Worm*, 191–201.

35. Norman Baker, *Government and Contractors: The British Treasury and War Supplies, 1775–1783* (London: Athlone, 1971), 216–30.

36. Baugh, *British Naval Administration*, 454–68; Rodger, *Command of the Ocean*, 369.

37. J. Horne Tooke, *Facts Addressed to the Landholders, Stockholders, Merchants, Farmers, Manufacturers, Tradesmen, Proprietors of Every Description*, 3d ed. (London, 1780), 46; Baker, *Government and Contractors*, 247.

38. Gordon E. Bannerman, *Merchants and the Military in Eighteenth-Century Britain: British Army Contracts and Domestic Supply, 1739–1763* (London: Pickering & Chatto, 2008), 128.

39. Colonel Barré speech, 15 May 1777, in *The Parliamentary Register, Volume 6* (London: John Stockdale, 1802), 210. For rum use by soldiers in the Seven Years' War, see Stephen Brumwell, *The British Soldier and War in the Americas, 1755–1763* (Cambridge: Cambridge University Press, 2002), 128.

40. Baker, *Government and Contractors*, 161–62.

41. Lord North Speech, 21 February 1777, *Parliamentary Register, Volume 5* (Stockdale), 278.

42. Report of Messr. Long, Neave, Glover, and Crichton, on the Reference of Mr. Atkinson's Rum Contract," 16 July 1777, *Parliamentary Register, Volume 7* (Stockdale), 187.

43. Colonel Barré Speech, 30 March 1778, *Parliamentary Register, Volume 8* (Stockdale), 176–77.

44. Richard Atkinson, *Mr. Atkinson's Rum Contract: The Story of a Tangled Inheritance* (London: 4th Estate, 2020), 95–115.

45. Tooke, *Facts Addressed*, 60.

46. O'Shaughnessy, *Empire Divided*, 165.

47. Thomas Shirley to Rodney, 16 January 1781, *Letter-Books and Order-Book of George, Lord Rodney, Admiral of the White Squadron, 1780–1782* (New York, 1932), 152–53. For an example of the financial benefits of this arrangement for colonies, see Alvin Rabushka, *Taxation in Colonial America* (Princeton: Princeton University Press, 2008), 637.

48. Crewe, *Yellow Jack and the Worm*, 188–90.

49. Letter to Nelson, 4 May 1787, *Dispatches and Letters of Nelson*, 1:232–33.

50. "Trial of Monk's Mingo," CO 9/10/58–59, TNA; Roger Norman Buckley, *The British Army in the West Indies: Society and the Military in the Revolutionary Age* (Gainesville: University of Florida Press, 1998), 196; Siân Williams, "The Royal Navy in the Caribbean, 1756–1815," (PhD diss., University of Southampton, 2014), 167–78.

51. Jerome S. Handler, "Joseph Rachell and Rachael Pringle-Polgreen: Petty Entrepreneurs," in *Struggle and Survival in Early America*, ed. David G. Sweet and Gary B. Nash (Berkeley: University of California Press, 1981), 382–88; Marisa J. Fuentes, "Power and Historical Figuring: Rachael Pringle Polgreen's Troubled Archive," *Gender & History* 22:3 (Nov. 2010): 564–84.

52. Minutes of the Antigua Assembly, 25 June 1740, CO 9/12/266, TNA.

53. Bell, *Inquiry into the Causes*, 17–18.

54. *Recollections of James Anthony Gardner*, ed. R. Vesey Hamilton and John Knox Laughton (1906), 48.

55. Rodney Order Book, 19 March 1782, *Letter-Books and Order-Book*, 2:603–4.

56. Nelson to William Locker, 16 March 1785, in *Dispatches and Letters of Nelson*, 127–28; *A Sailor of King George: The Journals of Captain Frederick Hoffman, 1793–1814*, ed. A. Beckford Brown and H. B. Wolryche-Whitmore (London, 1901), 43.

57. Nelson to Reverend Nelson, 29 December 1786, in *Dispatches and Letters of Nelson*, 204.

58. Peter Pellizzari, "A Struggle for Empire: Resistance and Reform in the British Atlantic World, 1760–1778" (PhD diss., Harvard University, 2020), 330.

59. Alexander Boumer to Colin Drummond, 22 April 1775, Jeremiah Wadsworth Papers, MS Wadsworth/1/2, CHS.

60. Daniel Roberdeau to David Jackson, 1 April 1776, Daniel Roberdeau Papers, MMC-3586, LOC, microfilm.

61. Samuel Barrett to Jeremiah Wadsworth, 9 June 1777, Jeremiah Wadsworth Papers, MS Wadsworth/3/1, CHS.

62. "Rules for Regulation of the Navy of the United Colonies," 28 November 1775, in *Journals of the Continental Congress, 1774–1789* (Washington, DC, 1905), 3:383.

63. *Pennsylvania Journal*, 16 May 1781; *Pennsylvania Evening Post*, 10 July 1777.

64. *Pennsylvania Evening Post*, 9 January 1777.

65. Andrew Huntington to Jeremiah Wadsworth, 21 October and 26 October 1776, Jeremiah Wadsworth Papers, MS Wadsworth/2/3, CHS.

66. Andrew Huntington to Joseph Trumbull, 20 November 1776, Andrew Huntington Papers, MS 77743/1/8, CHS.

67. Daniel Roberdeau to Thomas Hollingsworth, 10 July and 17 July 1781, Daniel Roberdeau Papers, MMC-3586, LOC, microfilm.

68. *An Act to Prohibit for a Limited Time the Making of Whiskey and Other Spirits from Wheat, Rye, or Any Other Sort of Grain, or from Any Meal or Flour* (Philadelphia, 1778).

69. "Peter Kalm's Description of How Sugar Is Made from Various Types of Trees in North America" (1751), trans. Esther Louise Larsen, *Agricultural History* 13 (Jul. 1939): 151.

70. *Connecticut Gazette*, 5 June 1778.

71. Jed Huntington to Colonel Wadsworth, 30 August 1778, Wadsworth Family Papers, MS 101921/1, CHS.

72. Janet Macdonald, *The British Navy and Victualling Board, 1793–1815: Management Competence and Incompetence* (Suffolk: Boydell, 2010), 22–23.

73. Robert Cassidy to the lords Commissioners of the Admiralty, 23 June 1853, in *Accounts and Papers of the House of Commons [Navy], Volume 34* (London, 1855), 1–2.

74. O'Brien, "Political Economy of British Taxation," 3–17.

75. Burnard and Graham, "Security, Taxation, and the Imperial System," 472.

76. Rabushka, *Taxation in Colonial America*, 728–29.

77. Burnard and Graham, "Security, Taxation, and the Imperial System," 473.

78. Carrington, "West Indian Opposition," 39–43; Aaron Graham, "The Colonial Sinews of Imperial Power: The Political Economy of Jamaica Taxation, 1768–1838," *Journal of Imperial and Commonwealth History* 45:2 (2017): 188–209.

79. Graham, "Colonial Sinews," 197.

80. David W. Blight, *Yale and Slavery: A History* (New Haven: Yale University Press, 2024), 56.

81. Rabushka, *Taxation in Colonial America*, 502, 688–91.

82. O'Brien, "Political Economy of British Taxation," 11.

83. "Act CXXIV" and "Act VIII," in *The Statutes at Large; Being a Collection of All of the Laws of Virginia*, ed. William Hening (New York, 1823), 2:128, 212.

84. Nicholls, *Politics of Alcohol*, 38–44.

85. *A Letter to a Friend in the Country, In Relation to the New Law Concerning Spirituous Liquors* (London, 1743), 15.

86. Lord North Speech, 15 March 1780, *Parliamentary Register, Volume 16* (Stockdale), 451.

87. Lord Penrhyn Speech, 13 March 1786, *Parliamentary Register, Volume 21* (London: J. Debrett, 1787)417.

88. Albert B. Southwick, "The Molasses Act—Source of Precedents," *WMQ* 8:3 (Jul. 1951): 389; Gilman M. Ostrander, "The Colonial Molasses Trade," *Agricultural History* 30:2 (Apr. 1956): 79.

89. Thomas C. Barrow, "Archibald Cummings' Plan for a Colonial Revenue, 1722," *NEQ* 36:3 (Sept. 1963): 391.

90. Mr. Bladen Speech and Mr. Barnard Speech, 21 February 1733, in *Proceedings and Debates of the British Parliaments Respecting North America*, ed. Leo Stock (Washington, DC, 1937), 4:182.

91. Eck, "Spirits of Massachusetts," 88.

92. Thomas C. Barrow, *Trade and Empire: The British Customs Service in Colonial America, 1660–1775* (Cambridge, MA: Harvard University Press, 1967), 136.

93. Barrow, *Trade and Empire*, 137.

94. Lord North Speech, 15 March 1780, *Parliamentary Register, Volume 16* (Stockdale), 451.

95. Dietz, "Politics of Whisky," 41.

96. Nathaniel Ware to George Grenville, 22 August 1763, in Bullion, *Great and Necessary Measure*, 221–23.

97. Bullion, *Great and Necessary Measure*, 83–94.

98. Brewer, *Sinews of Power*; Ashworth, *Customs and Excise*.

99. *Notice Is Hereby Given to All Dealers in Brandy, Rum, Malt, or Melasses-Spirits, Arrack, &c.* (London, 1746).

100. Peter Mathias, "Agriculture and the Brewing and Distilling Industries in the Eighteenth Century," *EHR* 5:2 (1952): 251. See also Ashworth, *Customs and Excise*, 212–14.

101. Jo. Manesty Letter to Benjamin Wilson, 18 March 1758, Hincks Family Papers, Dhincks/61, Cheshire Record Office.

102. Ten primary distilleries were scattered over the rest of England in 1750: McCusker, "Business of Distilling," 193–97; *Impartial Observations on the Mode of Levying the Distillery Duties* (Edinburgh, 1786), 52.

103. Ashworth, *Customs and Excise*, 212, 226.

104. "An Account of the number of gallons rates of duty and ammounts of revenue arising from home made spirits in the last fifty years distinguishing each year," 9 March 1787, Chatham Papers, PRO 30/8/296/59, TNA.

105. "First Report from the Committee Appointed to Enquire into the Illicit Practices Used in Defrauding the Revenue of this kingdom," 24 December 1783 in *Parliamentary Register, Volume 14* (London: J. Debrett, 1784), 156; Dietz, "Politics of Whisky," 36.

106. *True State of the British Malt-Distillery*, 42; *Impartial Observations*, 53–54.

107. "Observations on the Application of the Rectifying Distillers," c. 1788, Chatham Papers, PRO 30/8/296/213, TNA.

108. "State of the Evils arising to the Revenue of Excise in Scotland, and to the public and fair trader there, from the pernicious practice of using small stills for the distillation of spirituous liquors," 29 October 1772, T 1/490/126, TNA.

109. Richard Ellison, Joseph Atlay, and James Graham to Distillery General, 4 November 1782, Chatham Papers, PRO 30/8/296/114, TNA.

110. Richard Ellison, Joseph Atlay, and James Graham to Distillery General, 4 November 1782, Chatham Papers, PRO 30/8/296/114, TNA.

111. "Present Regulations for the Distillery Business," Chatham Papers, PRO 30/8/296/229, TNA; *First Report from the Committee, Appointed to Enquire into the Illicit Practices Used in Defrauding the Revenue* (London, 1784), 18; The Humble Petition of Richard Morgan, 5 April 1785, HO 47/2/184–5, TNA.

112. Cases Regarding Excise Duty, Messrs James, Perkins and Jewkes and Messrs Langdon Attlee and Moody, 1777, 44352/9/3/4/1, BRO.

113. Order from Melatiah Brown to Ebenezer Frost, 15 March 1763, Bourne Family Papers, MS Am 579/1/149, HOUGH.

114. *Courts of Admiralty in Colonial America: The Maryland Experience, 1634–1776*, ed. David R. Owen and Michael C. Tolley (Durham, NC: Carolina Academic Press, 1995), 329–30, also 325–26.

115. Barrow, *Trade and Empire*, 96, 142–43.

116. "Extract of a Letter from Governor Bernard to the Earl of Hillsborough," 9 July 1768, in *Letters to the Ministry from Governor Bernard, General Gage and Commodore Hood* (Boston, 1769), 51.

117. Ashworth, *Customs and Excise*, 165.

118. "Papers relating to claim by Henry Haskins and James Cross," 1778, 44352/9/3/4/2, BRO.

119. Daniel Roberdeau to Isaac Winn, 15 December 1783, Daniel Roberdeau Papers, MMC-3586, LOC, microfilm.

120. Phyn & Ellies to Robison & Edgar, 5 April 1783, Robison Family Papers, Coll. #5/1/2, MEHS; Bryan Edwards to W. Cadell, 29 January 1784, MS 565, NLJ.

121. Nelson to William Locker, 15 June 1785, in *Dispatches and Letters of Nelson*, 1:113–14.

122. George Shand to Thomas Robison, 10 March 1785, Robison Family Papers, Coll. # 5/1/8, MEHS.

123. Thomas Robison to Captain Jacob Smally, 22 March 1786, Robison Family Papers, Coll. # 5/1/12, MEHS.

124. Mr. Broughton, "Proposal to Check the Smuggling of Brandy & Rum," c. 1763, T 1/424/243A-243B, TNA; David Chan Smith, "Fair Trade and the Political Economy of Brandy Smuggling in Early Eighteenth-Century Britain," *PP* 251:1 (May 2021): 81–82, 97.

125. Petition of Barnaby Neile, 21 December 1749, T 1/335/86, TNA.

126. "Inquiry into the Smugling Trade, carried on from the Isle of Man to this Kingdom," 4 January 1765, T 1/451/64–6, TNA.

127. Mark Gregory, "Relating to the Smuggling of Rum," 9 January 1787, Chatham Papers, PRO 30/8/296/44, TNA.

128. Richard Ellison, Joseph Atlay, and James Graham to Distillery General, 4 November 1782, Chatham Papers, PRO 30/8/296/114, TNA.

129. J. Beresford, Jam. Agar, Tho. Allan & Rob. Clements to the Lord Lieutenant, 17 July 1773, T 1/501/3, TNA.

130. "Mr. Beaufoy Speech," 4 May 1786, *Parliamentary Register, Volume 20* (London: J. Debrett, 1787), 164–65.

131. Murray, "Gauge of Rum," Chatham Papers, PRO 30/8/296/99, TNA.

132. Samuel Martin to William Willock and Co., 23 May 1776, Martin Family Papers, Add MS 41351/86, BL.

133. Shannon, *Practical Treatise*, 1:203.

134. Hibbert, Perrier & co. to Nathaniel Phillips, 6 May 1783, Slebech Estate Records, 8623, NLW.

135. Indenture Between Louis René de Joachim and Peter Francis Venault de Chamilly, 9 March 1804, E/ROU/1/5, LMA. For a discussion of rumors that highly toxic and corrosive lapis infernalis (silver nitrate) was being mixed into spirits, see *True State of the British Malt-Distillery*, 21–22. For contemporaneous counterfeiting of Madeira wine, see Hancock, *Oceans of Wine*, 82–84.

136. George Smith, *A Compleat Body of Distilling, Explaining the Mysteries of That Science*, 3d ed. (London, 1738), 38–39.

137. Cooper, *Complete Distiller*, 75–76.

138. Cooper, *Complete Distiller*, 104–05.

139. William Pitt Speech, 13 March 1787, *Parliamentary Register, Volume 21*, 413.

140. John W. Tyler, *Smugglers and Patriots: Boston Merchants and the Advent of the American Revolution* (Boston: Northeastern University Press, 1986), 5–6, 253–77.

141. Williams, *Capitalism and Slavery*; Robert Paul Thomas, "The Sugar Colonies of the Old Empire: Profit or Loss for Great Britain," *EHR* 21:1 (Apr. 1968): 30–45; R. B. Sheridan, "The Wealth of Jamaica in the Eighteenth Century: A Rejoinder," *EHR* 21:1 (Apr. 1968): 46–61; Philip R. P. Coelho, "The Profitability of Imperialism: The British Experience in the West Indies, 1768–1772," *Explorations in Economic History* 10:3 (Spring 1973): 253–80; David Eltis and Stanley L. Engerman, "The Importance of Slavery and the Slave Trade to Industrializing Britain," *JEH* 54:3 (Mar. 2001): 506–24.

CHAPTER 8

1. Patricia A. Matthew, "Serving Tea for a Cause: The Kitchenware That Helped British Women Fight Against 'Blood Sugar' on the Home Front," *Lapham's Quarterly*, 28 February 2018.

2. When studying this movement, scholars have largely focused on sugar: Andrea Major, *Slavery, Abolitionism and Empire in India, 1772–1843* (Liverpool: Liverpool University Press, 2012), 293–320; Julie L. Holcomb, *Moral Commerce: Quakers and the Transatlantic Boycott of the Slave Labor Economy* (Ithaca: Cornell University Press, 2016).

3. Thompson, "Drax's Instructions," 587–88.

4. Taylor, "Multum in Parvo," MS 105 v.2/524–525, NLJ.

5. Roberts Vaux, *Memoirs of the Lives of Benjamin Lay and Ralph Sandiford* (Philadelphia, 1815), 15–23; Marcus Rediker, *The Fearless Benjamin Lay: The Quaker Dwarf Who Became the First Revolutionary Abolitionist* (Boston: Beacon, 2017). On an earlier Quaker worldview that "fundamentally accepted slavery," see Katharine Gerbner, "Antislavery in Print: The Germantown Protest, the 'Exhortation,' and the Seventeenth-Century Quaker Debate on Slavery," *EAS* 9:3 (Fall 2011): 552–75, at 553.

6. Benjamin Lay, *All Slave-Keepers That Keep the Innocent in Bondage, Apostates* (London, 1737), 34. On widespread Quaker opposition to spirits as a post–Revolutionary War development, see Rorabaugh, *Alcoholic Republic*, 37–38.

7. John Woolman, *The Journal of John Woolman* (Philadelphia, 1774). See also Woolman, *Considerations on Keeping Negroes: Recommended to the Professors of Christianity, of Every Denomination, Part Second* (Philadelphia, 1762); Holcomb, *Moral Commerce*, 27–35.

8. Michael Goode, "Dangerous Spirits: How the Indian Critique of Alcohol Shaped Eighteenth-Century Quaker Revivalism," *EAS* 14:2 (Spring 2016): 258–83.

9. Bronwen Everill, *Not Made by Slaves: Ethical Capitalism in the Age of Abolition* (Cambridge, MA: Harvard University Press, 2020), 48.

10. Christopher Leslie Brown, *Moral Capital: Foundations of British Abolitionism* (Chapel Hill: University of North Carolina Press for the OI, 2006), 461.

11. *Boston Gazette*, 30 January 1750; *Boston Evening-Post*, 13 July 1770; *Connecticut Journal*, 21 November 1787; *Windham Herald*, 31 July 1800.

12. Martin, *Essay upon Plantership*, 61.

13. *Boston Gazette*, 1 July 1771.

14. *Public Advertiser*, 19 November 1763.

15. *Report of the Lords of the Committee of Council Appointed for the Consideration of All Matters Relating to Trade and Foreign Plantations* (London: House of Lords, 1789), Part III, no. 37.

16. William Fox, *An Address to the People of Great Britain, on the Propriety of Abstaining from West India Sugar and Rum*, 16th ed. (Edinburgh, 1791), 4–5.

17. Andrew Burn, *A Second Address to the People of Great Britain: Containing a New, and Most Powerful Argument to Abstain from the Use of West India Sugar* (Rochester, 1792), 10–11; Carl Plasa, *Slaves to Sweetness: British and Caribbean Literatures of Sugar* (Liverpool: Liverpool University Press, 2011), 42; Erin Pearson, "'A Person Perverted into a Thing': Cannibalistic Metaphors and Dehumanizing Physicality in Late Eighteenth-Century British Abolitionism," *ELH* 83:3 (Fall 2016): 741–69.

18. William Cowper, "Pity for Poor Africans," *Poetical Works of William Cowper* (London, 1830), 1: 244.

19. William Stuart to W. A. Senior, 20 February 1786, Nassau Senior Papers, E071, NLW. Vincent Brown notes related actions and purported conspiracies in seventeenth-century Jamaica: Brown, *Tacky's Revolt*, 104, 109. Christopher Leslie Brown attributes increased organized resistance to slavery in the late eighteenth century to a "shifting sense of the possible": Brown, *Moral Capital*, 292.

20. C. L. R James, *The Black Jacobins: Toussaint L'Ouverture and the San Domingo Revolution*, 2d ed. (New York: Vintage, 1963), 361; Fick, *Making of Haiti*, 95–106; Laurent Dubois, *Avengers*

of the New World: The Story of the Haitian Revolution (Cambridge, MA: Belknap, 2004), 94–97; Garrigus, *Secret Among the Blacks*, 158–67.

21. On American newspaper reports from the revolutionary Caribbean that spread fear but also, at times, legitimated enslaved revolutionaries' goals of liberty, see James Alexander Dun, *Dangerous Neighbors: Making the Haitian Revolution in Early America* (Philadelphia: University of Pennsylvania Press, 2016), 63–65; Jordan E. Taylor, *Misinformation Nation: Foreign News and the Politics of Truth in Revolutionary America* (Baltimore: Johns Hopkins University Press, 2022), 180.

22. Francis McMahon, *Narrative of the Insurrection in the Island of Grenada, in the Year 1795* (Grenada, 1822), 48–49.

23. For scholarship highlighting the influence of the French Revolution, see Edward L. Cox, "Fedon's Rebellion 1795–96: Causes and Consequences," *Journal of Negro History* 67:1 (Spring 1982): esp. 12; Michael Duffy, "The French Revolution and British Attitudes to the West Indian Colonies," in *A Turbulent Time: The French Revolution and the Greater Caribbean*, ed. David Barry Gaspar and David Patrick Geggus (Bloomington: University of Indiana Press, 1997), 78-101; Laurent Dubois, *A Colony of Citizens: Revolution and Slave Emancipation in the French Caribbean, 1787–1804* (Chapel Hill: University of North Carolina Press for the OI, 2004), 227–36; Michael Craton, *Testing the Chains: Resistance to Slavery in the British West Indies* (Ithaca: Cornell University Press, 1982), 180–94; Kit Candlin, *The Last Caribbean Frontier, 1795–1815* (New York: Palgrave Macmillan, 2012), 1–23. For an emphasis on the internal dynamics of Grenada, see Tessa Murphy, "A Reassertion of Rights: Fedon's Rebellion, 1795–96," *La Révolution Française* 14 (2018): 1–26. For accounts seeking to better understand enslaved participants in the insurrection, see Caitlin Anderson, "Old Subjects, New Subjects and Non-Subjects: Silences and Subjecthood in Fédon's Rebellion, Grenada, 1795–96," in *War, Empire and Slavery, 1770–1830*, ed. Richard Bessel et al. (New York: Palgrave Macmillan, 2010), 201–17; Kit Candlin, "The Role of the Enslaved in the 'Fedon Rebellion' of 1795," *SA* 39:4 (2018): 685–707.

24. Gordon Turnbull, *A Narrative of the Revolt and Insurrection in the Island of Grenada* (London, 1796), 16; John Hay, *A Narrative of the Insurrection of the Island of Grenada, Which Took Place in 1795* (London, 1823), 33.

25. Victor Hugues, "The Commissioners delegated by the national convention to the Windward Islands, to the committee of public safety," 8 June 1795, in *American Minerva*, 3 November 1795.

26. *A Narrative of the Insurrection and Rebellion in the Island of Grenada* (Barbados, 1798), 41.

27. Samuel Cary to Samuel Cary, 12 May 1795, in "Documents: The Island of Grenada in 1795," ed. Joel Montague et al., *The Americas* 40:4 (Apr. 1984): 535; Hay, *Narrative*, 32.

28. *Daily Advertiser*, 8 June 1795; Turnbull, *Narrative*, 11.

29. Candlin, "Role of the Enslaved," 693.

30. Laurent Dubois, "'The Price of Liberty': Victor Hugues and the Administration of Freedom in Guadeloupe, 1794–1798," *WMQ* 56:2 (1999): 384–85.

31. Hay, *Narrative*, 32.

32. McMahon, *Narrative of the Insurrection*, 14–15.

33. *A Brief Enquiry into the Causes of, and Conduct by, the Colonial Government, for Quelling the Insurrection in Grenada* (London, 1796), 55–56.

34. Hay, *Narrative*, 73.

35. Turnbull, *Narrative*, 64.

36. *Brief Enquiry*, 64.

37. Hay, *Narrative*, 53.

38. Cary to Cary, 12 May 1795, in "The Island of Grenada in 1795," 534–36.

39. Cary to Cary, 12 August 1795, in "The Island of Grenada in 1795," 536–37.

40. *Brief Enquiry*, 122–23.

41. Commissioners of Forfeited Estates claims allowed and paid [1794–1796], EAP295/2/5/2, BL, Endangered Archives Programme, https://eap.bl.uk/archive-file/EAP295-2-5-2.

42. Samuel Cary to Joseph Marryat, 6 May 1795, in "The Island of Grenada in 1795," 533–34. See also "Review: A Brief Enquiry into the Causes of, and Conduct Pursued by, the Colonial Government, for Quelling the Insurrection in Grenada," *Monthly Review* 22 (1797): 325–26.

43. Brown, Benson & Ives to Ryberg & Co., 7 June 1792, Brown Family Business Records, BFBR 301/3, JCB.

44. George Weare Braikenridge to Francis Jerdone, 13 August 1792, Jerdone Family Papers, Mss. 39.1 j47/2/5, WMSC.

45. "Report Relative to the Culture and Produce of Sugar in the East-Indies, 29 Feb. 1792," in *East-India Sugar: Papers Respecting the Culture and Manufacture of Sugar in British India* (London, 1822), appendix 1, 6. See also Seymour Drescher, *Econocide: British Slavery in the Era of Abolition*, 2d ed. (Chapel Hill: University of North Carolina Press, 2010), 52.

46. Richard Huzzey, "The Moral Geography of British Anti-Slavery Responsibilities," *Transactions of the Royal Historical Society* 22 (2012): 116.

47. Thomas Clarkson, *The History of the Rise, Progress, and Accomplishment of the African Slave Trade by the British Parliament* (London, 1808), 1:348. For two examples, see John Valton, *Reasons for Abstaining from West-India Rum & Sugar, Suited to the Understandings of the Common People* (London, 1792); and *No Rum!—No Sugar! Or, The Voice of Blood, Being Half an Hour's Conversation Between a Negro and an English Gentleman* (London, 1792).

48. Braikenridge to Jerdone, 13 August 1792, Jerdone Family Papers, Mss. 39.1 j47/2/5, WMSC.

49. William Bell Crafton, *A Short Sketch of the Evidence Delivered Before a Committee of the House of Commons for the Abolition of the Slave Trade*, 3d ed. (London, 1792), 21.

50. Samuel Bradburn, *An Address to the People Called Methodists Concerning the Criminality of Encouraging Slavery*, 5th ed. (London, 1792), 15.

51. Seymour Drescher, *Capitalism and Antislavery: British Mobilization in Comparative Perspective* (New York: Oxford University Press, 1987), 216–17n47. Trade of both cotton and coffee increased in this era, seemingly undeterred by nonconsumption: Beckert, *Empire of Cotton*; Michelle Craig McDonald, "From Cultivation to Cup" (PhD diss., University of Michigan, 2005).

52. Everill, *Not Made by Slaves*, 65.

53. Clarkson, *History of the Rise*, 3:118–20. Holcomb suggests as many as five hundred thousand people joined the movement: Holcomb, *Moral Commerce*, 61.

54. Charlotte Sussman, *Consuming Anxieties: Consumer Protest, Gender, and British Slavery, 1713–1833* (Palo Alto: Stanford University Press, 2000), 110–29; Holcomb, *Moral Commerce*, 107–22.

55. Crafton, *Short Sketch*, 22.

56. Ragatz, *Fall of the Planter Class*, 264.

57. William Wilberforce to Zachary Macaulay, 23 August 1793, in Robert Wilberforce and Samuel Wilberforce, *The Life of William Wilberforce*, 2d ed. (London, 1839), 2: Appendix, 413.

58. James Madison to Thomas Jefferson, 10 July 1791, FO; *Remarks on the Manufacturing of Maple Sugar with Directions for Its Further Improvement* (New York, 1791); Drescher, *Econocide*, 116–17.

59. E. Colebrooke, From the Collector of Calcutta, 21 October 1792, in *East-India Sugar*, appendix 1, 176.

60. Benjamin Rush, *An Account of the Sugar Maple-Tree of the United States* (Philadelphia, 1792), 10. For Rush's general opposition to rum and other distillates, see Rush, *Medical Inquiries and Observations upon the Diseases of the Mind* (Philadelphia, 1784).

61. *General Advertiser*, 19 August 1791.

62. *Daily Advertiser*, 16 September 1791. See also *Federal Gazette*, 25 January 1792; Robert Southey, *Poems by Robert Southey* (Boston, 1799), 24–25.

63. *General Advertiser*, 5 August 1791.

64. These schemes are usually described in isolation from each other: David W. Maxey, "The Union Farm: Henry Drinker's Experiment in Deriving Profit from Virtue," *PMHB* (Oct. 1983): 607–29; Alan Taylor, *William Cooper's Town: Power and Persuasion on the Frontier of the Early American Republic* (New York: Knopf, 1995); Christopher Fyfe, *A History of Sierra Leone* (Oxford: Oxford University Press, 1962); Ulbe Bosma, *The Sugar Plantation in India and Indonesia: Industrial Production, 1770–2010* (Cambridge: Cambridge University Press, 2013).

65. *General Advertiser*, 6 August 1791; Samuel Hopkins, *Historical Memoirs, Relating to the Housatunnuk Indians* (Boston, 1753), 27.

66. John Lawson, *The History of Carolina, Containing the Exact Description and Natural History of the Country* (London, 1714), 105.

67. "Peter Kalm's Description," 150.

68. "Peter Kalm's Description," 155.

69. *Essex Journal & New Hampshire Packet*, 1 September 1790. See also J. P. Brissot de Warville, *New Travels in the United States of America* (Dublin, 1792), 302; David Macpherson, *Annals of Commerce, Manufactures, Fisheries, and Navigation* (London, 1805), 209–11.

70. *Massachusetts Gazette*, 4 July 1765. See also Robert Livingston to Benjamin Franklin, 5 September 1782, FO.

71. *Federal Gazette and Philadelphia Daily Advertiser*, 11 April 1790; Thomas Jefferson to Benjamin Vaughan, 27 June 1790, FO; Petition of Jonathan Williams Jr. to the Patent Board, 20 November 1792, FO.

72. Joseph Fay to Thomas Jefferson, 29 November 1791, FO. See also Jefferson to Fay, 30 August 1791, FO.

73. Lyman Butterfield, ed., *Letters of Benjamin Rush* (Princeton: Princeton University Press, 1951), 1:579. For accounts attributing the rise of maple sugar production to Quaker influence, see Warville, *New Travels*, 302; *Independent Chronicle and the Universal Advertiser*, 15 November 1792; Maxey, "Union Farm," 607–29; Holcomb, *Moral Commerce*, 66–67.

74. *Poor Richard Improved* (Philadelphia, 1788).

75. Taylor, *William Cooper's Town*, 115–17.

76. Benjamin Rush, "Memorable Facts, Events, Opinions, Thoughts &c.: Recorded by Benjamin Rush in the Years 1789–1791," in *The Autobiography of Benjamin Rush: His 'Travels Through Life' Together with His* Commonplace Book *for 1789–1813*, ed. George Corner (Princeton: Princeton University Press, 1948), 177.

77. Maxey, "Union Farm," 613–18; Taylor, *William Cooper's Town*, 117–19.

78. *Dunlap's American Daily Advertiser*, 12 April 1791.

79. Taylor, *William Cooper's Town*, 119–26.

80. John Licklaen, *Travels in the Years 1791 and 1792 in Pennsylvania, New York and Vermont*, ed. and trans. Helen Lincklaen Fairchild (New York, 1897), 49; *Pennsylvania Mercury*, 10 September 1789.

81. Warville, *New Travels*, 302–3.

82. *Daily Advertiser*, 15 April 1791.

83. Thomas Jefferson to Benjamin Vaughan, 27 June 1790, FO.

84. Maxey, "Union Farm," 610–11.

85. *Poor Richard Improved*; *Independent Gazetteer*, 26 August 1789; *Federal Gazette and Philadelphia Daily Advertiser*, 11 April 1790; *Eastern Herald*, 30 January 1792.

86. Licklaen, *Travels in the Years*, 43.

87. *Cumberland Gazette*, 11 April 1791. See also *Daily Advertiser*, 15 April 1791.

88. Thomas Jefferson to George Washington, 1 May 1791, *PGWDE*.

89. *General Advertiser*, 14 December 1790.

90. Licklaen, *Travels in the Years*, 43, 49; *Pennsylvania Mercury*, 10 September 1789.

91. *New-York Packet*, 13 April 1790; *ClayPoole's Daily Advertiser*, 20 July 1791.

92. Taylor, *William Cooper's Town*, 123.

93. Taylor, *William Cooper's Town*, 133–34.

94. Krafft, *American Distiller*, 91–92.

95. *Gazette of the United States*, 24 June 1800.

96. *Olio*, 27 January 1803.

97. Ohio also distilled 1.2 million gallons of spirits, but it is unclear if any of that volume came from maple: Tench Coxe, *A Statement of the Arts and Manufactures of the United States of America, for the Year 1810* (Philadelphia, 1814), 22, 41.

98. Although most relocated Black Loyalists did not have experience on sugar plantations, some West Indian refugees from London and, eventually, Jamaican Maroons may have had experience making sugar and rum: *An Account of the Colony of Sierra Leone* (London, 1795), 62–63.

99. Wadstrom, *Essay on Colonization*, 258, also 204.

100. "19 May 1791" and "14 July 1791," Minutes of the Sugar Refiners Committee, MS 8189/11, 19, LMA; *A Report of the Proceedings of the Committee of Sugar-Refiners, for the Purpose of the Effecting a Reduction in the High Prices of Sugar, by Lowering the Bounty on Refined Sugar Exported, and Correcting the Evils of the West-India Monopoly* (London, 1792).

101. *Journal of James Watt*, 54.

102. *Account of the Colony of Sierra Leone*, 62–63; Fyfe, *History of Sierra Leone*, 46, 57, 72–73.

103. Wadstrom, *Essay on Colonization*, 262. For recently emancipated slaves' resistance to performing the most arduous tasks of plantation production, see Thomas C. Holt, *The Problem of Freedom: Race, Labor, and Politics in Jamaica and Britain* (Baltimore: Johns Hopkins University Press, 1992), 115–76; Dubois, *Colony of Citizens*, 85–123.

104. "19 May 1791" and "14 July 1791," Minutes of the Sugar Refiners Committee, MS 8189/11, 19, LMA.

105. Individual farmers occasionally attempted to produce small amounts of sugar and rum in the nineteenth century: Fyfe, *History of Sierra Leone*, 354, 422.

106. Martin A. Klein, ed., *Breaking the Chains: Slavery, Bondage, and Emancipation in Modern Africa and Asia* (Madison: University of Wisconsin Press, 1993); Indrani Chatterji and Richard M. Eaton, eds., *Slavery and South Asian History* (Bloomington: Indiana University Press, 2006); Richard B. Allen, "Satisfying the 'Want for Labouring People': European Slave Trading in the Indian Ocean, 1500–1850," *Journal of World History* 21:2 (Mar. 2010): 45–73; Major, *Slavery, Abolitionism and Empire*.

107. Seymour Drescher, *Abolition: A History of Slavery and Antislavery* (Cambridge: Cambridge University Press, 2009), 268–71.

108. Major, *Slavery, Abolitionism and Empire*, 189–232.

109. Richard B. Allen, "European Slave Trading, Abolitionism, and 'New Systems of Slavery' in the Indian Ocean," *PORTAL: Journal of Multidisciplinary International Studies* 9:1 (2010): 45–73.

110. "Extract Fort William Revenue Consultations," 5 June 1776, in *East-India Sugar*, appendix 1, 12–13; John Crawfurd, *History of the Indian Archipelago* (Edinburgh, 1820), 1:475–76; P. J. Marshall, *The Making and Unmaking of Empires: Britain, India, and America, c. 1750–1783* (Oxford: Oxford University Press, 2007), 227–72.

111. "On reading the Petition of Mr. George Graham," 18 December 1776, East India Company Minute Books, IOR B 92/502, BL; P. J. Marshall, "Bengal Commercial Society of 1775: Private British Trade in the Warren Hastings Period," *Historical Research* 42:106 (Nov. 1969): 181–82.

112. Letter from Messrs Rumbold, Charlton, and Raikes, 22 October 1777, East India Company Minute Books, IOR B 93/363, BL; "Resolved that for the reasons therein mentioned," 21 January 1778, East India Company Minute Books, IOR B 93/512–13, BL.

113. "Wanted by J. Levett in Bengal," 24 September 1773, Forbes Family Papers, A727.1455, FA; "The Memorial of Mr. Joseph Hodgson," 8 November 1775, East India Company Minute Books, IOR B 91/284, BL; "On Reading the Request of Mrs. Dorothy Touchett," 22 January 1777, East India Company Minute Books, IOR B 92/562, BL; "On Reading the Request of Mrs. Dorothy Touchett," 4 December 1777, East India Company Minute Books, IOR B 93/435, BL.

114. "23 September 1773," William Forbes Order Book, A727.1442, FA.

115. "The request of Mr. Michael Herries," 28 September 1774, East India Company Minute Books, IOR B 90/211, BL.

116. "On reading the petition of Mr. John Levett," 9 December 1774, East India Company Minute Books, IOR B 90/310, BL; "The Request of Mrs. Dorothy Touchett," 5 January 1780, East India Company Minute Books, IOR B 95/408, BL; "Extract letter from Board of Trade," 8 November 1791, *East-India Sugar*, appendix 1, 42–3.

117. Letter from Court, 5 April 1776, *Fort William–India House Correspondence*, ed. R. P. Patwardhan (Delhi, 1970), 7:149.

118. "Wanted by J. Levett in Bengal," 24 September 1773, Forbes Family Papers, A727.1455, FA.

119. "Resolved that for the reasons therein mentioned," 21 January 1778, East India Company Minute Books, IOR B/93 512–13, BL.

120. Marshall, "Bengal Commercial Society," 182. See also "On Reading the Several Requests," 12 June 1782, East India Company Minute Books, IOR B 98/180, BL.

121. "Fort William Revenue Consultations," 5 June 1776, *East-India Sugar*, appendix 1, 14.

122. *Three Letters Addressed to a Friend in India, by a Proprietor: Principally on the Subject of Importing Bengal Sugars into England* (London, 1793), 31–33; "Report of Committee of Warehouses," 29 February 1792, *East-India Sugar*, appendix 1, 16.

123. *Three Letters Addressed to a Friend*, 31–33; Marshall, "Bengal Commercial Society," 184–85.

124. "Bengal Board of Trade Consultations," 4 September 1792, *East-India Sugar*, appendix 1, 101, 106.

125. William Fitzmaurice, "Bengal Commercial Consultations," 8 February 1793, *East-India Sugar*, appendix 1, 215.

126. Drescher, *Econocide*, 126–27.

127. Macpherson, *Annals of Commerce*, 4:232.

128. Minutes of the Sugar Refiners Committee, MS 8189/11–19, LMA. See also "On reading the memorial of the buyers of sugar," 17 July 1793, East India Company Minute Books, IOR B 117/275, BL.

129. "Committee of Warehouses Report," 17 June 1795, East India Company Minute Books, IOR B 121/286, BL.

130. "Committee of Warehouses Report," 1 November 1797, East India Company Minute Books, IOR B 126/616, BL.

131. A. Lambert to Cornwallis, "Extract Bengal Public Consultations," 8 September 1790, *East-India Sugar*, appendix 1, 19; Fitzmaurice, "Bengal Commercial Consultations," 8 February 1793, *East-India Sugar*, appendix 1, 213; Marshall, "Bengal Commercial Society," 183.

132. "A Report from the Committee of Shipping," 7 December 1791, East India Company Minute Books, IOR B 114/646, BL; Letter from Bengal, 1 March 1800, *East-India Sugar*, appendix 2, 37; "Extracts from the Reports on the External Commerce of Bengal, 1798–1799," *East-India Sugar*, appendix 4, 37–38.

133. "Extracts from the Reports on the External Commerce of Bengal, 1796–1797," *East-India Sugar*, appendix 4, 37.

134. Gilb. Francklyn, *Remarks on a Pamphlet Entitled Bengal Sugar* (London, 1795), 27–28; Jonathan Eacott, *Selling Empire: India in the Making of Britain and America, 1600–1830* (Chapel Hill: University of North Carolina Press for the OI, 2016), 316–20.

135. Letter to Bengal, 28 August 1800, *East-India Sugar*, appendix 2, 13; Letter to Madras, 31 October 1799, *East-India Sugar*, appendix 2, 24; Letter from Bengal, 31 December 1798, *East-India Sugar*, appendix 2, 37; Letter from Bengal, 13 January 1804, *East-India Sugar*, appendix 2, 40; Letter from Bengal, 31 July 1807, *East-India Sugar*, appendix 2, 41–42.

136. "The Committee of Warehouses in a Report," 6 April 1791, East India Company Minute Books, IOR B 111/1042–44, BL.

137. "From the Resident at Soonamooky," 14 February 1793, *East-India Sugar*, appendix 1, 154–56.

138. "The Committee of Warehouses in a Report," 6 April 1791, East India Company Minute Books, IOR B 111/1042–44, BL; Letter to Bengal Government, 6 May 1791, *East-India Sugar*, appendix 2, 4.

139. "The Committee of Warehouses in a Report," 6 April 1791, East India Company Minute Books, IOR B 111/1042–44, BL.

140. Bengal Board of Trade Consultations, 4 September 1792, *East-India Sugar*, appendix 1, 106. For another account of experts relocated from the Caribbean, see "Extract Proceedings of the Board of Revenue at Fort St. George," 9 November 1797, IOR F 4/67/1481, BL.

141. "Bengal Board of Trade Consultations," 4 September 1792, *East-India Sugar*, appendix 1, 106.

142. For an account of a similar and concurrent transformation in indigo production techniques in Bengal, see Prakash Kumar, "Planters and Naturalists: Transnational Naturalists on Colonial Indigo Plantations in South Asia," *Modern Asian Studies* 48:3 (May 2014): 720–53.

143. "Letter from a Gentleman in Bengal to his Friend in England," 5 March 1793, *East-India Sugar*, appendix 3, 49.

144. "Extract Board of Trade Consultations," 7 August 1792, *East-India Sugar*, appendix 1, 53.

145. Fitzmaurice, "Bengal Commercial Consultations," 6 February 1793, *East-India Sugar*, appendix 1, 212.

146. Henry Thomas Colebrooke, *Remarks on the Husbandry and Internal Commerce of Bengal* (London, 1806), 128–31.

147. "Extract Board of Trade Consultations," 7 August 1792, *East-India Sugar*, appendix 1, 53.

148. Fitzmaurice, "Bengal Commercial Consultations," 6 February 1793, *East-India Sugar*, appendix 1, 212. Apologists for slavery alternatively described Indian workers as "exposed to every species of subjection": Francklyn, *Remarks on a Pamphlet*, 23.

149. Fitzmaurice, "Bengal Commercial Consultations," 6 February 1793, *East-India Sugar*, appendix 1, 211–13, at 213.

150. Letter from Bengal, 31 December 1798, *East-India Sugar*, appendix 2, 37; Letter to Bengal, 28 August 1800, *East-India Sugar*, appendix 2, 13.

EPILOGUE

1. Smith, *Slavery, Family, and Gentry Capitalism*, 180, 189.

2. Thomas Henry Strenk, "The Top Rum Trends in 2022," Beverage Dynamics, 28 March 2022, https://beveragedynamics.com/2022/03/28/the-top-rum-trends-in-2022/.

3. James Anderson to George Washington, 22 February 1797, *PGWDE*.

4. George Washington to John Fitzgerald, 12 June 1797, *PGWDE*.

5. John Fitzgerald to George Washington, 12 June 1797, *PGWDE*.

6. McCusker, "Rum Trade," 434; "General State of the Revenue on Stills, and on Spirits Distilled in the United States, from Foreign and Domestic," 1792, *American State Papers: Finance* (Washington, DC: 1832), 1:250–51.

7. In comparison, Rhode Island distilleries sent 5.2 million gallons of rum in the sixty-four years prior to declaring independence. Coughtry, *Notorious Triangle*, 82–83.

8. Thomas Digges Letter, 28 July 1820, Col. John Fitzgerald Papers, GUSC.

9. Douglas A. Irwin, "The Welfare Cost of Autarky: Evidence from the Jeffersonian Trade Embargo, 1807–09," *Review of International Economics* 13:4 (Sep. 2005): 641–42.

10. Coxe, *Statement of the Arts and Manufactures*, 22. Molasses spirits production continued in US ports in the twentieth century, though much of it was used for the manufacture of munitions: Stephen Puleo, *Dark Tide: The Great Boston Molasses Flood of 1919* (Boston: Beacon, 2012), 11.

11. Smith, *Caribbean Rum*, 201–2.

12. T. M. Devine, *Clanship to Crofters' War: The Social Transformation of the Scottish Highlands* (Manchester: Manchester University Press, 1994), 130–34.

13. *Views and Notices of Glasgow in Former Times* (Glasgow, 1848), 99.

14. Pack, *Nelson's Blood*, 56–57.

15. Pack, *Nelson's Blood*, 67; Rodger, *Command of the Ocean*, 495–96.

16. Cassidy to the lords Commissioners of the Admiralty, 23 June 1853, in *Accounts and Papers*, 1–2.

17. Smith, *Caribbean Rum*, 206–7.

18. For references to rum production in Martinique taking off during and after the Seven Years' War, see Antoine de Lavalette, *Lettres sur les opérations du P. De Lavalette, Jésuite, et Supérieur-Général des Missions des Isles-françaises du vent de l'Amérique, nécessaires aux négocians* (1760), 13–14. For accounts of Cuba's sugar boom in the late eighteenth and nineteenth centuries, see Manuel Moreno Fraginals, *The Sugarmill: The Socioeconomic Complex of Sugar in Cuba, 1760–1860*, trans. Cedric Belfrage (Monthly Review Press, 1976); Franklin W. Knight, "Origins of Wealth and the Sugar Revolution in Cuba, 1750–1850," *Hispanic American Historical Review* 57:2 (May 1977): 231–53; Reinaldo Funes Monzote, *From Rainforest to Cane Field in Cuba: An Environmental History Since 1492*, trans. Alex Martin (Chapel Hill: University of North Carolina Press, 2008).

J. R. McNeill suggests that the sugar boom in Cuba began decades earlier: McNeill, *Atlantic Empires of France and Spain: Louisbourg and Havana, 1700–1763* (Chapel Hill: University of North Carolina Press, 1985), 162–66.

19. Smith, *Caribbean Rum*, 212.

20. Charles Mackenzie, *Notes on Haiti, Made During a Residence in That Republic* (London, 1830), 2:169.

21. Tom Gjelten, *Bacardi and the Long Fight for Cuba: The Biography of a Cause* (New York: Viking, 2008), 12–24; Smith, *Caribbean Rum*, 215–17; Pack, *Nelson's Blood*, 94–95.

22. Colin Powell and Joseph Persico, *My American Journey* (New York: Random House, 1995), 14.

23. Tom Bruce-Gardyne, "Appleton Estate: A Brand History," Spirits Business, 24 July 2018, https://www.thespiritsbusiness.com/2018/07/appleton-estate-a-brand-history/.

24. "Sector Capsule: Spirits in India," *Euromonitor International Sector Capsules*, October 2022.

25. Clarissa Wei, "The Silent Epidemic Behind Nicaragua's Rum," Vice, 27 November 2011, https://www.vice.com/en/article/qkxv7v/the-silent-epidemic-behind-nicaraguas-rum.

26. *2022 List of Goods Produced by Child Labor or Forced Labor*, US Department of Labor, https://www.dol.gov/sites/dolgov/files/ILAB/child_labor_reports/tda2021/2022-TVPRA-List-of-Goods-v3.pdf, 24-28.

27. "Key Growth Strategies for Emerging Beverage Alcohol Brands," NIQ, 17 February 2023, https://nielseniq.com/global/en/insights/education/2023/key-growth-strategies-for-emerging-beverage-alcohol-brands/.

28. Bosma, *World of Sugar*, passim; Megha Rajagopalan and Qadri Inzamam, "The Brutality of Sugar: Debt, Child Marriage and Hysterectomies," *New York Times*, 24 March 2024.

29. For a recent reckoning concerning slavery and whiskey production in the US South, see Clay Risen, "Jack Daniel's Embraces a Hidden Ingredient: Help from a Slave," *New York Times*, 25 June 2016. For a call for similar questions to be asked about rum, see Céline Bossart, "Decolonizing the Whitewashed World of Caribbean Rum," Liquor.com, 23 March 2021, https://www.liquor.com/decolonizing-rum-industry-5117059.

INDEX

Locators in italics indicate a figure. Locators in bold indicate a table.

ACKNOWLEDGMENTS

I am elated to thank so many people and organizations that nurtured this project and its author.

As a young student, I benefited from teachers—especially Mrs. Lacey and Mr. Murray—who selflessly provided space for individual exploration. They showed me where research and hard work could take me. My professors and classmates at Carleton College sharpened my ideas through classes that were at once rigorous and supportive. I am especially thankful that Susannah Ottaway and Serena Zabin have remained close friends and mentors.

Georgetown University proved to be the ideal environment for me to turn a passion for the study of history into a profession. Chad Frazier, Oliver Horn, Graham Hough-Cornwell, Thom Loyd, Robynne Mellor, and, especially, Elena Abbott made class—and time outside of it—fun. Elena joined with fellow members of "Team Atlantic"—Mike Hill, Jess Hower, Chelsea Berry, Kate Steir, and Cory James Young—in reading many, many dissertation chapter drafts. I am thankful that Adrienne Kates and Brian Taylor continue to be big parts of my life. Seminars taught by Denver Brunsman, Chandra Manning, and Marcy Norton pushed me to approach familiar topics from new directions. John McNeill and Adam Rothman offered feedback as members of my dissertation committee that I continue to mull over. And Alison Games was exactly what I needed in a dissertation supervisor. She was equal parts encouraging and demanding and deserves as much credit as anybody for the form that this project ultimately took.

I was fortunate to spend my final year of graduate school as a dissertation fellow at the McNeil Center for Early American Studies, an institution that I have in many ways never left. Each of the directors I have known—Dan Richter, Kathy Brown (as interim), and Emma Hart—have helped bring this book to fruition in their own ways. The Friday Seminars regularly exposed me to new and exciting ideas that are sometimes hard to stay engaged with during one's first years teaching full-time. The day after my own seminar in the fall of 2020, the center helped to host a manuscript workshop for me. Dan and Kathy joined

Adrian Finucane, David Hancock, Laura Keenan Spero, Roderick McDonald, Marcy Norton, and Jason Sharples to offer penetrating feedback that structured the reorganization of the manuscript that followed. I hope each participant sees how their intellectual generosity shaped this book.

The Invention of Rum came together during my first six years at Widener University. I thank associate deans Mara Parker and Paul Goldberg, deans David Leaman and Lisa Grimm, the provost's office, and members of the Faculty Grants and Awards Committee for supporting me as a teacher-scholar. My history department colleagues—Rachel Batch, Richard Hopkins, Erika Huckestein, and Yufeng Mao—modeled the highest degree of collegiality. Outside of the department, Scott Van Bramer has been a wise mentor and Christine Woody a frequent and trusted collaborator. Finally, I want to thank students who mulled over new ideas with me that I explore in this study.

The multisited research at the heart of this book was dependent on the generosity of many different organizations. As an undergraduate, I was incredibly fortunate to take part in a summer historic trades internship at Mount Vernon. In graduate school, I continued to work at the distillery, which undoubtedly shaped the direction that my research took. I thank the Purkey family for letting me live in their nursery in the months before their daughter was born and Steve Bashore for welcoming me back to the distillery when my schedule allowed. I am deeply appreciative of the Huntington Library, John Carter Brown Library, Library Company of Philadelphia, Massachusetts Historical Society, and Phillips Library at the Peabody Essex Museum for supporting research in their collections through short-term fellowships. At a formative moment, an SSRC Dissertation Proposal Development Fellowship seminar organized by Judith Carney and Paul Gootenberg helped me clarify what exactly I wanted to do. Additionally, the Cosmos Club Foundation, the Folger Shakespeare Library, Institute of Historical Research, the Mid-Atlantic Conference on British Studies, the New England Regional Fellowship Consortium, and the Omohundro Institute offered financial support for research in other archives. Librarians and archivists at forty-five repositories helped me access the records I sought. Their incredible knowledge of the collections often guided me to additional resources as well. A semester-long NEH postdoctoral fellowship at the Library Company of Philadelphia provided uninterrupted time for research and writing when I needed it most.

In recent years, several organizations have pioneered ways to support early-career faculty balancing their responsibilities as teachers and researchers. I have been fortunate to participate in two of these endeavors. The 2019 Omohundro Institute Scholars Workshop, convened by Cathy Kelly, Paul Mapp, Josh Piker,

Nick Popper, and Nadine Zimmerli helped me begin to think of my dissertation as a first draft of a book manuscript. As a member of the second cohort of the Bright Institute at Knox College, I benefited from Cate Denial's vision for how to support professors at teaching institutions in all that they do. Our seminar leaders—David Chang, Christian Crouch, and Vanessa Holden—directed incredibly stimulating discussions that expanded my thinking in critical ways. I thank David especially for talking with me about how one can responsibly write about the history of alcohol in early America. Of course, my cohorts in both Williamsburg and Galesburg were integral to these wonderful experiences.

Throughout this journey, I have benefited from meeting a group of amazingly generous, fun, and smart people. I thank Scott Cave, Mary Draper, Katie Johnston, Ernesto Mercado-Montero, Tessa Murphy, Hayley Negrin, and Casey Schmitt for joining me in various writing groups. I enjoyed countless evening constitutionals with Mary when our travels aligned and have regularly looked to Katie and Tessa for their sage advice and unflagging friendship. Sarah Barber, Paul Cheney, Allan Greer, Jared Hardesty, Matt Mulcahy, Nick Radburn, Katherine Smoak Radburn, and Suze Zjilstra shared sources with me that advanced my research in tangible ways. Kentz Gustave and Claire Steele offered research assistance. Ben Shaw lent his indexing expertise to this project. And Alexis Broderick, Mikkel Dack, Will Fenton, Susan Pennybacker, Christian Pinnen, and Nora Slonimsky shared their insights from within and beyond the parameters of early American and Atlantic history.

Feedback offered in more formal settings also moved this project forward. Segments of the book manuscript received thoughtful engagement at annual meetings of the the Association of Caribbean Historians, the North American Conference on British Studies, the Omohundro Institute, the Organization of American Historians, and the Society for Historians of the Early American Republic. I am also thankful for invitations to present my work at the American Philosophical Society Museum; Georgetown's Early Modern Global History seminar; the Johns Hopkins University Atlantic Seminar; the Museum of Fine Arts, Houston; the Yale Early American History seminar; and classes at Syracuse University and the University of Southern California. Focused workshops hosted by the Commodities of Empire Research Project, the German Historical Institute, the McNeil Center for Early American Studies, the Summer Academy of Atlantic History, and the University of Utah supported especially generative exchanges.

Part of the first chapter was previously presented at the Workshop on the Fiftieth Anniversary of Richard S. Dunn's *Sugar and Slaves* and published in the Fall 2022 special issue of *Early American Studies*. I am thankful to Trevor

Burnard and Alison Games for pushing me to refine and sharpen my argument. An earlier version of parts of Chapter 8 originated in a workshop convened by Felix Brahm and Eve Rosenhaft at the German Historical Institute, London, and appeared in *Global Commerce and Economic Conscience in Europe, 1700–1900: Distance and Entanglement*, published by Oxford University Press. I thank both publishers for their permission to reuse this work.

In early 2019, I applied for the SHEAR Dissertation Prize, figuring that it would save me the awkwardness of sending a cold-call email to Bob Lockhart. I was genuinely shocked to receive the award. That summer, Bob, Joanne Pope-Melish, and Dan Richter met with me to begin discussing how the dissertation could grow into a book. In the five years since, Bob has been an incredible champion of this project, whether that entailed organizing a manuscript workshop, offering feedback on each chapter, or exercising considerable patience. Dan Livesay, an anonymous reviewer for the press, and series editor Kathy Brown offered model reader reports that helped me cross the finish line.

And then there are the (mostly) nonhistorians. I thank friends who supported me in Mechanicsburg, Northfield, Philadelphia, and Washington, DC. Lou Ann Thorsness and Jim and Julie Huckestein have been generous and understanding in-laws throughout. My siblings—Holly, Tim, and Maddie—would probably tell you that it makes sense that I became a professor given how much time I spent lecturing them growing up. I thank my mother, Martha Stigelman, for teaching me to think creatively, and my father, Ted Smith, for helping me appreciate the power of the written word. Zora came along in 2021 and has enriched everything that I do. Her sense of humor, kindness toward others, and boundless curiosity inspire me to constantly do my best. And her mother and my wife, Erika, has given so much to us both. Erika has supported me through the ups and downs accompanying a thirteen-year project, and I cannot begin to express what she means to me as a partner and, as our daughter says, "best friend for always." With love, I dedicate this book to Erika and Zora.